Tourism Strategies and Local Responses in Southern Africa

TOURISM STRATEGIES AND LOCAL RESPONSES IN SOUTHERN AFRICA

Edited by

Petri Hottola

University of Oulu
Finland

www.cabi.org

CABI is a trading name of CAB International

CABI Head Office
Nosworthy Way
Wallingford
Oxon OX10 8DE
UK

Tel: +44 (0)1491 832111
Fax: +44 (0)1491 833508
E-mail: cabi@cabi.org
Website: www.cabi.org

CABI North American Office
875 Massachusetts Avenue
7th Floor
Cambridge, MA 02139
USA

Tel: +1 617 395 4056
Fax: +1 617 354 6875
E-mail: cabi-nao@cabi.org

A catalogue record for this book is available from the British Library, London, UK.

Library of Congress Cataloging-in-Publication Data

Tourism strategies and local responses in Southern Africa / edited by Petri Hottola.
p. cm.
Includes bibliographical references and index.
ISBN 978-1-84593-508-5 (alk. paper)
1. Tourism--South Africa. I. Hottola, Petri. II. Title.
G155.S57T687 2009
916.80068'4--dc22

2009006848

ISBN: 978 1 84593 508 5

Typeset by Columns Design, Reading, UK.
Printed and bound in the UK by MPG Books Group.

The paper used for the text pages in this book is FSC certified. The FSC (Forest Stewardship Council) is an international network to promote responsible management of the world's forests.

Contents

Contributors

Dr Chris Boonzaaier, *Associate Professor, Department of Anthropology & Archaeology, University of Pretoria, Lynnwood Road, Pretoria 0002, South Africa. E-mail: chris.boonzaaier@up.ac.za*

Lauren Dyll MA, *Lecturer, Department of Culture, Communication and Media Studies, Faculty of Humanities, Development and Social Sciences, Howard College, MTB Building level 2, University of KwaZulu-Natal, Durban 4041, South Africa. E-mail: dyll@ukzn.ac.za*

Dr Petri Hottola, *Professor, Department of Geography, University of Oulu, PO Box 3000, 90014 University of Oulu, Finland. E-mail: petri.hottola@oulu.fi*

Dr Øystein Jensen, *Associate Professor, Faculty of Social Science – Norwegian School of Hotel Management, University of Stavanger, 4036 Stavanger, Norway. E-mail: oystein.jensen@uis.no*

Julia Jänis MSc, *Researcher, Finnish University Network for Tourism Studies and Department of Development Studies, University of Helsinki, PO Box 59, 00014 University of Helsinki, Finland. E-mail: julia.janis@helsinki.fi*

Dr Kenneth Kamwi Matengu, *Senior Research Fellow, Multidisciplinary Research Centre, Social Sciences Division, University of Namibia, P/Bag 13301, Windhoek, Namibia. E-mail: kmatengu@unam.na*

Dr Joseph E. Mbaiwa, *Senior Research Fellow (Tourism Studies), Harry Oppenheimer Okavango Research Centre, University of Botswana, Private Bag 285, Maun, Botswana. E-mail: Jmbaiwa@orc.ub.bw*

Maaria Niskala MSc, *Researcher, Department of Geography, University of Oulu, PO Box 3000, 90014 University of Oulu, Finland. E-mail: maaria.niskala@gmail.com*

Dr Steven Robins, *Associate Professor, Department of Sociology & Social Anthropology, Stellenbosch University, Private Bag XI, 7602 Matieland, South Africa. E-mail: slr@sun.ac.za*

Dr Christian M. Rogerson, *Professor, School of Geography, Archaeology & Environmental Studies, University of Witwatersrand, Private Bag, PO Wits 2050, Johannesburg, South Africa. E-mail: Christian.Rogerson@wits.ac.za*

Dr Jarkko Saarinen, *Professor, Department of Geography, University of Oulu, PO Box 3000, 90014 University of Oulu, Finland, and Department of Management, University of Botswana, UB 00701, Gaborone, Botswana. E-mail: jarkko.saarinen@oulu.fi*

Dr Harri Siiskonen, *Professor, Department of History, University of Joensuu, PO Box 111, 80101 Joensuu, Finland. E-mail: harri.siiskonen@joensuu.fi*

Dr Marja Spierenburg, *Associate Professor, Department of Culture, Organisation and Management, VU University Amsterdam, De Boelelaan 1081, 1081 HV Amsterdam, The Netherlands. E-mail: mj.spierenburg@fsw.vu.nl*

Dr Kees van der Waal, *Professor, Department of Sociology & Social Anthropology, Stellenbosch University, Private Bag XI, 7602 Matieland, South Africa. E-mail: csvdw@sun.ac.za*

Dr Harry Wels, *Associate Professor, Department of Culture, Organisation and Management, VU University Amsterdam, De Boelelaan 1081, 1081 HV Amsterdam, The Netherlands. E-mail: h.wels@fsw.vu.nl*

Foreword

Southern Africa is currently one of the world's most significant 'laboratories' for observing the role of tourism in economic and social development. Countries in the region have become a focal point for understanding the adoption of ecotourism, pro-poor tourism, cultural tourism and even food tourism strategies as public policy approaches in the developing world. However, regardless of the type of strategy that is adopted, the key issue remains: exactly how can tourism provide greater net benefits for the destination communities than can other forms of development? The concern is not only what the most appropriate form of tourism development is but also why tourism should receive support as opposed to other forms of economic development. Therefore, the fundamental question of 'why tourism?' remains central to appreciating the trajectory of economic and social development in the region.

Tourism has long been recognized by researchers as having both advantages and disadvantages for development, depending on the characteristics of the location in which it is occurring. Tourism, like other forms of cultural mobility, is a major contributor to both modernization processes and the development of new postcolonial forms of identity and knowledge. Such processes are only expanded through the adoption of information and communication technology (ICT) by the tourism industry, and also by other industry and community stakeholders. Yet the adoption of ICT, along with the development of new transport and travel connections, become vital to overcoming the peripherality of the region relative to major international markets. Furthermore, such adoption leads to a two-way flow of people and knowledge. For example, as this foreword is being written, people in New Zealand are potentially almost as aware of the political, economic and health crisis in Zimbabwe and its effects on the surrounding countries as are the people in those countries.

The increased connectivity that tourism-related transport and communication helps bring to the regions of Southern Africa clearly represents the 'two-edged sword' provided by tourism. Accessibility is fundamental to tourism. Transport connections provide new means of conducting international business, including tourism, but they provide opportunities for people to leave as well as to attract. Similarly, ICT allows regions and destinations to promote themselves to the world and make them more accessible in the tourism consumer's mental map of destinations to visit and activities in which to engage. However, at the same time, such communications accessibility can also allow images of political, economic, social and environmental events and occurrences to be conveyed to the outside world, some of which governments may regard as undesirable from the perspective of policy and national image. Tourism, therefore, is not so much a passport to development but a conduit between tourism-generating regions and destinations that provides for the flow of economic, natural, cultural and social capital.

The chapters in this book provide a valuable addition to our knowledge of the way in which tourism connectivity and development are contributing to postcolonial and modernization processes in Southern Africa. They also demonstrate the significant role that tourism can play in encouraging sustainable economic development at the local and community levels. Just as importantly they indicate that, in order to understand the effects of tourism and development, research needs to be conducted over various scales of analysis in space and time in order effectively to inform tourism policy. It is, therefore, hoped that the research contained in this book will constitute not just a welcome addition to academic research on tourism in Southern Africa that will inform students of tourism both in the North and South, but also that such research may contribute to genuine improvement in the contribution of tourism to development in the region.

C. Michael Hall
Richmond, Christchurch
New Zealand

Acknowledgements

The idea for this book was born within the Finnish University Network for Tourism Studies (FUNTS) research project *Tourism and the Regional Modernization of Namibia*, funded by the Academy of Finland for 2006–2008. Some of the results of project were to be published in the form of a project publication. Funding being available, a decision to invite other writers with similar interests to participate in compilation of the book was made in late 2007. Later on, the idea was presented to CABI, and a partnership was established for a book, *Tourism Strategies and Local Responses in Southern Africa*, now available for worldwide distribution.

One network connecting several of the authors was ATLAS (Association for Tourism Leisure Education) and its international conferences and research groups, which brought us together in Viana do Castelo in Portugal, Kampala in Uganda and Shimla in India. Another one was created by IGU (International Geographical Union) and its commission of Geography of Tourism, Leisure and Global Change. The editing work was initiated at the University of Joensuu and finished at the University of Oulu, both members of FUNTS.

At this moment, it is my pleasure to acknowledge and thank all the people and institutions involved in the work. First, I would to express my gratitude to the Academy of Finland for the funding, without which this volume and other publications would never have surfaced. Secondly, there is FUNTS, which facilitated the research initiative and its execution in an amicable working environment. In FUNTS, its former director Arvo Peltonen, coordinator Ulla Ritola-Pesonen and project secretaries Anne Loikkanen and Arja Lappalainen deserve a special mention. Katja Pasanen helped with collecting the reference materials.

Sisko Porter, the foremost English language expert in Finnish geography, did a mammoth task in checking and correcting our English. 'It may be a living language', but a degree of consistency is required in an edited book.

At the University of Joensuu Press, Mika Saarelainen prepared the maps and figures of the publication. Within the CABI books editorial team Sarah Hulbert coordinated the process, with plenty of patience and helpful advice. Lesley King prepared our individual copyright contracts.

In the field in Namibia, several organizations worked with us. From the partner University of Namibia (UNAM), Fritz Becker and Susanne Scholz earn a special mention. Wilka Ashipala collected several of the local references for us. Numerous others, too many to be mentioned individually, supported the research team's work in a variety of locations, from the coastal deserts to the tropical Caprivi Strip. C. Michael Hall, a trusted friend of FUNTS and the driving force of the IGU commission of Tourism, Leisure and Global Change (together with its chair Jarkko Saarinen), provided a foreword in a spirit of cooperation.

Thank you once again for your contributions in the publication process!

Petri Hottola
University of Oulu, Finland
One degree below the Polar Circle

1 Introduction: Development Through Tourism?

PETRI HOTTOLA

Introduction

Development policies appear to be among the most underrated official papers in Southern Africa. When prospecting for authors for this book, I met academics who would not touch the issue of tourism development strategies, even with complete freedom to criticize them. Meanwhile, the Government of Namibia ordered another draft tourism development strategy from a European Union consultant, without any explicit goals for development. According to a common view, governmental and non-governmental organizations create these 'pamphlets of wishful thinking on a grandiose scale', print them, make a few speeches and hold press conferences, then bury the strategies deep in the dustbin. As the cynics say, the policy papers are thought to have zero effect on the reality of tourism and the people involved, being mainly published in an attempt to attract development donors. Therefore, one should not waste time on this 'complete nonsense', as one of the African academics, a seasoned figure, commented.

There is a certain truth in the critical evaluations. At its worst, a tourism development policy may become a strategic way of appearing decisive, while making a firm decision *not* to make a decision. Moreover, they are frequently riddled with unrealistic expectations. As an example, tourism may be seen as having enormous potential for economic and social development in any location of a nation, however central or peripheral, or whatever the situational context happens to be. Potential there may be, but it is not that easy to harness in a sustainable way. Tourism is not the last-resort magic potion for socio-economic remedies but a demanding field of economic activity that needs to be addressed in a systematic, professional way. Caution is necessary, too – tourism also has a well-documented ability to bring negative consequences.

When genuinely attended, the strategic goals of tourism development are, however, anything but nonsense. They incorporate long-term, goal-oriented thinking with explicit end results. Sound development goals are not based on unrealistic expectations but could be realized with the available resources. They are in line with positive development aspirations, working towards the common good, and supported by a wide range of political actors. Three sets of such tourism development strategies have a specific role in this volume:

1. The draft tourism white paper of the Government of Namibia, Ministry of Tourism and Environment (MET 2005a).
2. The Strategic Framework for Sustainable Tourism Development in South Africa of the Department of Environmental Affairs and Tourism (DEAT 2005).
3. The tourism policy of Botswana (Government of Botswana 1990).

In these papers, the idea of sustainable development through tourism (see Beeton 2006) is addressed by the following definitions of strategic goals:

1. Namibia. Tourism that promotes:

- economic growth;
- employment creation;
- poverty reduction;
- black economic empowerment;
- environmental and ecological sustainability; and
- reduction of regional inequalities.

2. South Africa:

- Tourism with dignity, encouraging mutual respect for all cultures and eliminating all forms of discrimination on the basis of language, religion, culture, race, gender, age, wealth and ability.
- Tourism that involves education, training, awareness and capacity-building programmes, especially aimed at previously neglected groups.
- Tourism that works as a catalyst for human development, focusing on gender equality, career development and the implementation of national labour standards.
- Tourism that empowers community structures through, for example, involvement in the marketing of cultural experiences and practices to tourists.
- Tourism that encourages community participation in the planning, development, implementation and management of tourism projects.

3. Botswana:

- Tourism that shifts the mix of tourists away from casual campers towards those who occupy permanent accommodation.
- Substantially increasing the financial returns from tourism for the people of Botswana, especially those living in the local communities where wildlife abides, while simultaneously ensuring that tourist activities are carried out in an ecologically sustainable way.

The mission of this volume is to bring together up-to-date case studies that reflect the realities of everyday tourism operations and the strategic tourism development goals. It is, after all, the experiences and perceptions of the people in the field that count. They are the very persons who are supposed to concretize the projected development through tourism in postcolonial Southern Africa. Four out of the eleven case studies focus on Namibia, two of the cases occur in South Africa, one in Botswana and one in Madagascar. Two texts are based on cross-border situations, between South Africa, Botswana and Mozambique, and one has a wider Southern African scope. The stages of the tourism development policy cycle as defined by Howlett and Ramesh (1995, 11) – agenda setting, policy formulation, decision making, policy implementation and policy evalution – have not yet been completed in Southern Africa. Some nations are at the first stage, others are about to enter the third and none has yet carried out a comprehensive policy evaluation. It is hoped that this book will become a thought-provoking contribution towards the fourth stage.

In the following chapters, the terms 'policy' and 'strategy' have synonymic features, both referring to goal-setting action plans as defined by government offices in an attempt to bring about change by guiding people to making the best choices available. The official strategies evaluated are socially and politically constructed, reflecting the stakeholder preferences among the regionally and temporally specific development aspirations. At the grassroots level, the actors may well have their own agendas, born from the everyday of tourism development and its struggles for power and sustainability. *Tourism Strategies and Local Responses in Southern Africa* aims to be a debate between the policies and their actors in the field and a polemic among academic observers with a variety of views on the developments, through which lessons may be learned for the improvement of development through tourism and for the implementation of future research programmes.

The Structure of the Book

In the south-western corner of the continent of Africa lies the 19 years young nation of Namibia, with a history of German and, more recently, South African colonial rule. Julia Jänis starts the book by exploring the opportunities and challenges of implementing a national tourism policy in Namibia, as perceived by tourism entrepreneurs. How do the people running the businesses see the relevancy and realism of the state development goals in tourism? What are the contradictions involved? Have the ideas of black economic empowerment, environmental sustainability or poverty eradication been understood and supported by the tourism sector? The answers have been collected in three fields of tourism typical of Namibia – private game farms, private lodges and community-based tourism enterprises (CBTEs). Geographically, the field studies range from the Damara-dominated rural Erongo to the neighbourhood of Windhoek, the capital region in the hills of Khomas, and the remote eastern Caprivi, where conservancies and lodges work side by side on a stretch of land surrounded by the mighty Kavango and Zambezi rivers. No such evaluation had been conducted in Namibia before Jänis's work.

South Africa – a former 'Star of Africa' among the British colonies, later a regime of white supremacy and today a 'Rainbow Nation' – has a leading role in regional tourism in Southern Africa. In Chapter 3, Christian M. Rogerson presents the South African experiences for local economic development (LED) in rural route tourism, also a potentially strategic tool for development through tourism in the rest of Southern Africa. Tourism development projects such as the Midlands Meander route of KwaZulu-Natal would be a source of great pride anywhere in the world. The route's rural tourism based on arts, crafts, agricultural produce and scenic environment has expanded in an exceptional way during its 15 years of existence. The concept has created thousands of jobs and a vibrant economic scene in mostly domestic tourism. A partnership between local governments, NGOs, community-based groups and the private sector has proved to be successful, also in terms of development strategies, and may provide a guiding model for similar ventures. However, in order fully to succeed, the process requires a leadership with not only clear vision but also understanding of development needs in order to guarantee that all policy issues will actually be attended. For a number of reasons, the role of regional administration is underlined in this chapter.

In Chapter 4, Lauren Dyll discusses the modernization approach to tourism development, both in theory and practice. She provides a necessary critique of one of the core ideologies hidden between the lines in the region's development strategies, and also in the present book. This auto-ethnographic work focuses on seldom-approached corners of Southern Africa, the Northern Cape of South Africa and Ngwatle in southern Botswana, listening to the voices of people recently introduced to tourism, arguably against their will. According to Dyll the modernization model, even though widely adopted, does not necessarily work for ethnic minorities such as the ≠Khomani and !Xoo, who are left in a marginalized position in the one-sided process which could be called 'modernization's monologue'. The situation of ethnic minorities is a particularly problematic issue in tourism and development.

Continuing with the minority debate, Jarkko Saarinen and Maaria Niskala focus on the Ovahimba of Kaokoland in north-western Namibia on the border with Angola. The Ovahimba, or Himba – and particularly their attractive, traditionally dressed women – have become the predominant cultural branding tool of Namibia as a tourism destination. Chapter 5 discusses their commoditization in the Namibian tourism promotion, thereby defining their symbolic role in Namibian tourism development policies. According to Saarinen and Niskala, commodified cultural identity has become a cultural constraint in terms of community-based tourism development and the empowerment of the Ovahimba through tourism. Simultaneously uplifted and marginalized by tourism, the Ovahimba form an illuminating case of the situation of a sizeable, culturally distinctive minority within Southern Africa. They have gained power in the business of tourism with their distinctive culture, but developments also involve a number of challenges.

Community-based catering services are not something one would necessarily expect to find in rural Africa. The Hananwa of Blouberg in Limpopo Province (formerly Transvaal) of South Africa are, however, in the process of establishing them. In his contribution, Chris Boonzaaier addresses the applicability of a government tourism policy to the catering service and to a visitor *motse* constructed on top of Blouberg Mountain. The tourism homestead development attempts to provide services for visitors on the African Ivory Route, a tourism route aimed at empowering and benefitting disadvantaged rural people in the spirit of the DEAT principles. Chapter 6 also discusses the aspect of gender equality. The status and role of Hananwa women are expected to improve with their involvement with tourism. There are a number of issues to be solved before this community-based venture will prosper: will the Hananwa be able to succeed in the new business, and will it actually deliver the social 'goods' the DEAT policy attempts to promote?

Botswana, the wealthiest Southern African nation in terms of GDP per capita and with its history as the British Bechuanaland Protectorate before independency in 1966, lies in the centre of the region. In Chapter 7, Joseph E. Mbaiwa takes us on a field trip to the flood-lands of the Okavango Delta (cf. the book cover), the main location of his research commitments. He starts by introducing the Botswana approach to strategic tourism development, as stated by its tourism policy and executed in a number of locations nationwide, including the delta. The more specific aim of this work is to analyse the effectiveness of tourism development in the simultaneous achievement of successful nature conservation and better means of subsistence in the Okavango Delta. Contrary to many critical voices, community-based tourism enterprises may succeed in a partnership with government conservation bodies and private businesses if guided by strict but fair resource management practices. The Botswana partnership model for hunting and wildlife tourism is another approach that could also be adopted by neighbouring nations, with their yet unsolved problems in similar situations.

Between Sandwich Harbour and the Skeleton Coast, the Central Coastal Region of Namibia has world-class resources for wildlife tourism, particularly bird tourism. It has the largest concentration of migratory birds in sub-Saharan Africa, the Walvis Bay Lagoon being the best-known wetland in the region. Moreover, the coast has fine infrastructure and tourism services. One would therefore expect to see a vibrant bird tourism sector with a number of interlinked operations. Nevertheless, not much is happening, even though a closely related form of wildlife tourism, coastal 'dolphin cruises', has already gained exceptional volume with its annual 100,000 customers. In Chapter 8, Petri Hottola critically analyses the resources and restraints of coastal bird tourism in Namibia. The reasons for the current inertia are both local and national, including several structural weaknesses in the young postcolonial state. Tourism development has become subordinated to other, conflicting policies which block not only bird tourism but economic development in general. The strategic goals of development through tourism are not easy to realize, even in the more developed and well-resourced parts of Southern Africa such as the coast of Namibia.

Today, one-third of new HIV infections are contracted in Southern Africa, which also has the highest prevalence of AIDS in the world. Not surprisingly, the HIV/AIDS pandemic is a factor that is repeatedly brought out in the case studies of this book. Just like any other feature of social life in Southern Africa, the business of tourism is far from immune to its consequences. On the contrary, mobility being linked with the spread of the disease, a sector with seasonal employment and travelling customers has more than average risks to contend with. In practice, the development of tourism has become a victim of health policies which have been undermined by traditional beliefs and resistance to change. Nevertheless, the industry has started to work to minimize the damage by strategic choices in line with development through tourism. In Chapter 9, Harri Siiskonen, a historian with a record of studies in the region, particularly in Namibia, explores the awareness and responses of the Southern African tourism sector to control HIV/AIDS, and the perceptions on the effects of the disease on its operational environment. Apparently, no such regional analysis has been attempted before, even though a small number of HIV/AIDS surveys have been conducted in selected Southern African tourism destinations.

On the eastern edge of Southern Africa lies the unique island of Madagascar, with its French colonial past and Malagasy present, and another version of the African wildlife tourism product supplemented by cultural attractions. Øystein Jensen, a Norwegian researcher, has studied the interplay between local service suppliers and incoming tour operators in order to define a working model for respective situations in other destinations. This work focuses on the operational centre of Antananarivo, the island's capital, and two regions, Fianarantsoa and Vakinakaratra, with local tourism attractions. In the context of international tourism, the most lucrative market for many developing nations, the modes of interaction between the local and foreign stakeholders have a major effect on the outcomes of tourism, also from the 'development first' point of view. An incoming tour operator may develop products out of local resources by itself, or in cooperation with local actors, thereby providing knowledge, employment and income. The process of mutual learning is, however, a complicated one and has a number of critical points, as described by Jensen in Chapter 10.

In Chapter 11, Kenneth Matengu elaborates on the applicability of information and communication technology (ICT) for school-based tourism marketing in Namibia, based on experiences and studies in his former home region, the eastern Caprivi Strip. The polemic for and against the idea of schools as future marketing hubs for community-based tourism, in a region where no other options are available, will raise more questions than answers, reflecting both the complexity of the issue and the prevalent confusion in this field. According to the European view, ICT is a medium of vast potential and ready to be used for numerous purposes that are supposed to be immediately beneficial for development. Locally in Southern Africa, the capacity to use the ICT instrument is not yet there, and the issue becomes less than straightforward, to say the least. The new technological innovations meet a society not ready for them, and without a consensus on the contents that the technology is supposed to distribute.

The Great Limpopo Transfrontier Park is one of the highest-profile nature conservation efforts in the world. It comprises three national parks in South Africa, Zimbabwe and Mozambique, protecting an invaluable part of African natural heritage. From the viewpoint of tourism, transfrontier projects have considerable potential in attracting investments and economic activity, partly due to their large scale and visibility in the media. The existence of communal lands in Southern Africa does, however, create a specific setting for the management of the parks, as in the Great Limpopo Transfrontier Park. In Chapter 12, Marja Spierenburg, Harry Wels, Kees van der Waal and Steven Robins discuss the possibilities for communities in or close to the park to benefit from its existence, focusing on the partnerships between the Makuleke community, the park's management and the private sector, and on a comparative situation on the Mozambican side in the former Coutada Sixteen National Park. The results of cooperation have been a double-edged blessing, or less, for the local communities. The chapter also serves as an important critique of such partnerships, recommended by some other authors in this volume.

At the end of the book, some of the lessons learned from the Southern African case studies are brought together to outline the current issues of strategic tourism development, in terms of both academic research and applied work in the tourism sector. There is also some editorial debate with the contributors on selected controversial issues. The chapters have a connecting theme in the discourse on tourism development strategies, and particularly on the applicability of various partnership models in Southern Africa, with its unique location-specific features. Should community-based tourism be autonomous, or should the developments be led by the state, with its national responsibilities, together with the private sector, with its business skills? How should tourism resources be used in the best possible way, to benefit all cooperating partners?

2 Tourism Development Strategies in Namibia: Private and Community Perceptions on the National Policy

JULIA JÄNIS

Introduction

Following increasing globalization, tourism policies and strategies in Southern Africa tend to reflect a neoliberal development agenda that emphasizes the role of the private sector and global competitiveness, as measured by efficiency and foreign investments. Simultaneously, the principles of environmental sustainability have been incorporated into tourism planning and there is supposed to be more room for community participation. On the other hand, finding a balance between the pressures for economic growth, topicality of environmental concerns and diverse social needs of local communities has remained a challenge.

Due to external pressure and political preference, the competitiveness of the tourism sector appears to be highly prioritized. In Namibia, the conflict between the aims of increasing the participation of Namibians – particularly those from previously disadvantaged groups – and developing tourism through encouraging foreign investment has been discussed in a governmental tourism policy (MET 2005a, 24). Similar challenges reflecting the conflicting priority between the tourism industry per se and the local population's development needs have been documented in South Africa (Rogerson and Visser 2004a), Zambia (Matenga 2005; Giampiccoli 2006), Lesotho (Mashinini 2003) and Botswana (Leechor and Fabricius 2005).

Despite liberalization and global integration, national governments have a major role in formulating tourism policies and strategies and in regulating the tourism industry (Hall 2008). In addition, it has become obvious that tourism planning and strategies in Southern Africa must be set within the broader development processes taking place in those countries (Telfer and Sharpley 2008). However, as Kerr (2003, 31) points out, it is often ignored that a tourism policy may be subordinate to wider economic development policies. In a similar vein, Sofield (2003, 24) notes that a government's role in tourism may differ according to a range of variables, of which one major determinant will be a set of values governing policy approaches.

The purpose of this chapter is to discuss what opportunities and challenges there are for implementing a national tourism policy in Namibia and, therefore, to analyse the role of tourism in Namibia's post-apartheid transformation process. This will be done by reviewing the perceptions of private- and community-based tourism entrepreneurs of the major development objectives of the Namibian tourism policy. These are: (i) economic growth; (ii) employment creation; (iii) poverty reduction; (iv) black economic empowerment; (v) environmental and ecological sustainability; and (vi) reduction of regional development inequities (MET 2005a). These objectives have appeared in national development plans and therefore they have been widely endorsed. The focus is at the local level of individual tourism entrepreneurs whose knowledge, understanding and attitude towards the policy objectives are essential for the implementation process. The significance of 'local knowledge' in assessing public policies has been highlighted by Yanow (2003, 236).

Particularly, this chapter asks: How are the tourism policy objectives understood and supported by the entrepreneurs at the local level and what practical constraints can be demonstrated for achieving them? Furthermore, it is questioned how relevant and realistic the policy objectives are for the local stakeholders and how their understanding of the objectives might affect policy implementation. First, the chapter outlines the tourism policies and strategies in Namibia, followed by a brief description of research methods and stakeholders. The various tourism entrepreneurs' perceptions on the six tourism policy objectives are discussed in more detail and major differences are presented. Finally, an overall conclusion is provided.

Tourism Policies and Strategies in Namibia

Immediately after independence in 1991, the Namibian Government declared tourism a priority sector that was expected to diversify the economy. The Namibia Tourism Development Plan (NTDP) was completed with the assistance of The European Commission in 1993 and it was succeeded by the Development Phase from 2000 to 2005 (Novelli and Gebhardt 2007, 444). The major aim of the NTDP was to increase employment and income through tourism, promote protection of wildlife and natural resources as well as spread tourism over large areas (MET 1995a). Sustainable tourism development was identified as the main objective of the programme.

The first major government document, White Paper on Tourism, was approved in 1994 and it stated the major objectives of tourism development in Namibia, such as aiming at high-yielding quality tourism through spatial tourism development and high standards of service while generating income and employment for Namibian society (Government of Namibia 1994). A Policy on the Promotion of Community-based Tourism was approved by the Namibian Government in 1995 and it resulted in the establishment of communal 'conservancies', which are provided with concessionary rights for tourism development (MET 1995b). Conservancies are part of the 'community-based natural resource management' (CBNRM), which was enabled by legislation in Namibia in 1996. Currently, there are more than 50 conservancies covering over 118,000 km^2, which represents 14.4% of Namibia's total land area (NACSO 2007, 10).

The actual tourism policy has been in process since 1995. The first comprehensive draft was circulated for stakeholders in 2005 and the most recent draft was completed in 2007. Both drafts state that the policy aims to provide a framework for the mobilization of tourism resources to realize the long-term national development objectives identified in Namibia's Second National Development Plan (2001/2–2005/6) and the subsequent Third National Development Plan (2007/8–2011/12). However, the earlier draft from 2005 is more explicit about how tourism can contribute to the development objectives, and therefore any reference to 'tourism policy' in the following sections refers to the 2005 version. Interestingly, the 2007 draft is more focused on tourism as a viable and competitive economic sector and has less emphasis on the role of tourism in national development priorities. The 2007 draft was prepared by an external consultant provided by the EU, and therefore it can be questioned whether this change in emphasis reflects the views of the Namibian Government or the consultant.

Similarly, an interesting shift took place between the two drafts in terms of discussing a future tourism strategy. The 2005 draft highlights the importance of preparing a national tourism strategy and action plan to articulate the practical implementation of the policy (MET 2005a, 11). However, the 2007 draft proposes a national tourism growth strategy that implies a clear emphasis on a growth-focused approach common in neoliberalism and adopted by the Namibian Government (Jauch 2001; MET 2007; Schilcher 2008). Furthermore, the 2005 draft discusses the challenges and opportunities of community-based tourism (CBT) as a means of distributing the benefits of tourism, whereas the 2007 draft omits CBT and mentions only the need for partnerships between the private sector and local communities in order to distribute the benefits.

Research Methods and Stakeholders

The research draws from three interdisciplinary fields, i.e. development studies, tourism studies and public policy research. As a qualitative and interpretive inquiry, the aim is to understand the tourism policy from the perspective of policy-relevant actors and the meanings they attach to phenomena within their social realities (Ritchie and Lewis 2003, 3; Yanow 2006, 13). An interpretive policy analysis has provided guidelines for studying a tourism policy from a non-conventional perspective. According to Yanow (2000, 9), 'Interpretive policy analysis explores the contrasts between policy meanings as intended by policymakers and the possibly variant and even incommensurable meanings made of them by other policy-relevant groups'.

The field research was carried out from December 2006 to February 2007 and from June to August 2008. Semi-structured interviews and field observation were carried out in three private trophy hunting farms, four private tourist lodges and four community-based tourism enterprises. The six tourism policy objectives were discussed with a total of 30 interviewees, and informal discussions were carried out with a further 52 individuals. An interview guide was used in the interviews in order to ensure that relevant issues were covered systematically and with some uniformity, while still giving emphasis to the interviewees' own interpretation of, and meaning attached to, the topics (Patton 2002).

Trophy hunting is an important niche tourism in Southern Africa, embodying abundant wildlife resources. According to the Namibia Professional Hunters Association, some 7000 international hunters were expected during the 2008 hunting season (New Era 2008c). Of all tourism in Namibia, trophy hunting has a substantial economic value as it is estimated to contribute 14% to the whole tourism industry and generate NAD500 million per year (Novelli and Humavindu 2005, 175; New Era 2008b). Three trophy hunting farms were studied in the central Khomas region, which hosts important tourist facilities and represents typical freehold land in Namibia characterized by privately owned commercial farms (see Fig. 2.1). The farm owners are white Namibians of either German or South African origin, continuing farming activities in the second or third generation.

Private lodges provide accommodation throughout Namibia, and their share of all tourism accommodation provision in Namibia is estimated to be at 17% (WTTC 2006). Four lodges in the Caprivi region are part of the research. Caprivi is a narrow strip bordering four other countries in north-eastern Namibia. A rich migrating wildlife population and wetlands make it a particular tourist destination in mostly semi-arid Namibia but, due to past political instability and slow economic development, the region's tourism potential is not yet fully recognized. Three of the lodges are situated in an urban location while one lodge is in a rural area under a partnership agreement with the surrounding conservancy.

Community-based tourism enterprises (CBTEs) operate predominantly in rural Namibia and are characterized as being locally planned, owned and managed tourism entities (e.g. Timothy 2002; Beeton 2006). Five CBTEs are part of this research, four of them in the Caprivi region and one in the Erongo region (see Fig. 2.1), which has significant coastal tourism facilities and rich mineral deposits. Two enterprises provide simple accommodation and four of them sell locally produced crafts for tourists. Even though the term 'enterprise' is not the most applicable in describing their activities and organization, it is used here for the purpose of comparison.

The following section introduces the six tourism policy objectives and illustrates the differences among private and community-based tourism enterprises regarding the understanding and local significance of each objective. Furthermore, the empirical material reflects the cultural, structural and political challenges inherent in Namibian society and affecting the applicability of tourism as a national and local development strategy.

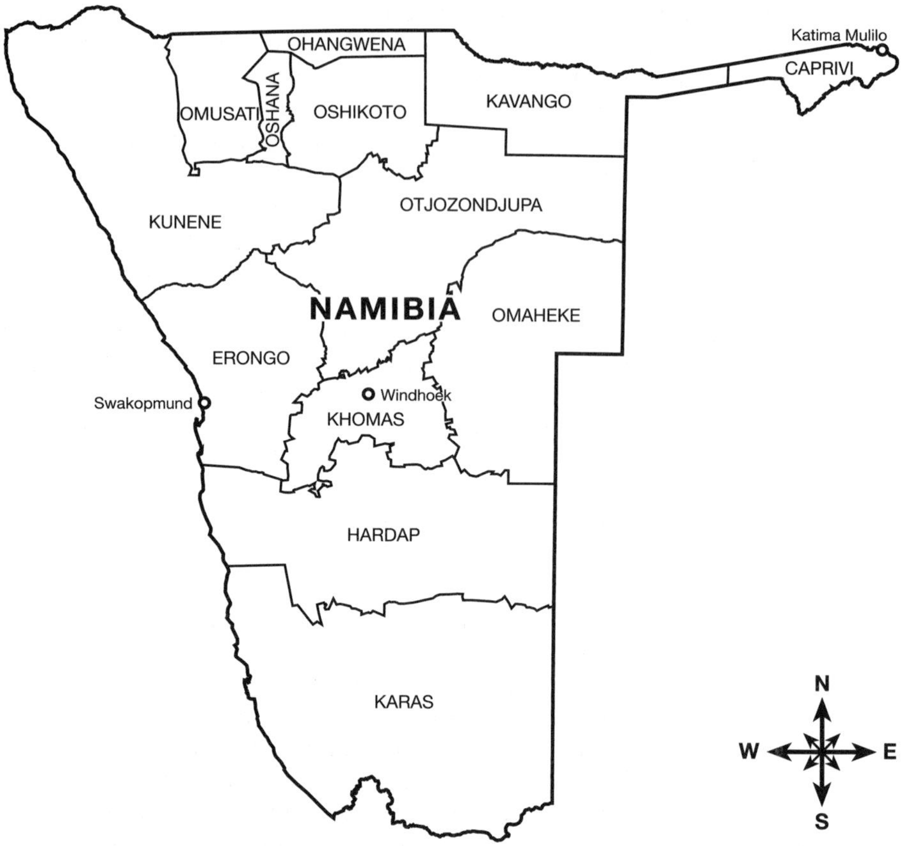

Fig. 2.1. The regional structure of Namibia, with urban centres mentioned in the text.

Perceptions on Economic Growth

The Namibian economy is based mainly on export-oriented primary sector activities such as mining, fisheries and agriculture and a fast-growing service sector (Hansohm 2000). Ever since independence, Namibia has faced the challenge of declining productivity, limited structural change and a dualistic labour market with high unemployment (Hansohm 2000, 22–23). Economic growth has not been able to keep pace with the rapid population increase (Dubresson and Graefe 2001, 54). Furthermore, the Namibian economy is highly characterized by the hegemony of transnational capital and the excessive dependence on South Africa, both of which have caused substantial leakage of tourism revenue (Jauch 2001, 56; Tapscott 2001, 316).

The tourism satellite account carried out in 2006 shows that tourism, directly and indirectly, accounts for 14.2% of Namibia's GDP and 18.7% of all employment opportunities (Namibia Tourism Board 2008). According to the tourism policy, foreign exchange and tax receipts from tourism are the primary drivers of economic growth in Namibia. Increasing tourism, on the other hand, is expected to increase the demand for various services, which stimulates employment and increases the circulation of money at the national and local levels (MET 2005a, 37).

Community-based tourism does not contribute to the national economy in terms of foreign exchange but it does have local economic significance. This was expressed by the informants either as financial contribution of the enterprise for various charity purposes within the community or as accumulation of income for an individual who could attain a better financial position and support an extended family. In some cases, crafts producers in Caprivi had managed to invest their income in tangible assets such as cattle or agricultural tools, but most of the income was described as going toward daily costs related to food, education and health. A representative of an art centre describes the significance of crafts income: 'If I look at the early artists we started with, I can say that some of their children today they are in big posts and if I look at the source of income they helped their children with, it came from the art centre. So I'm proud to say yes, it has done a lot, more than our imagination.'

Some CBTEs had experienced difficulties in attracting customers, and the informants regarded the poor accessibility and limited scale of operations as reasons for their unpopularity. The issue of scale was important even to the more established CBTEs that were planning to expand and diversify their activities. In general, there seemed to be optimism that, as long as there was increasing supply, the demand would similarly increase. On the other hand, through informal discussions and observation, it appeared that a need for marketing of the CBTEs and their tourism products was hardly understood. For this reason, many organizations in Namibia advocate partnerships between private enterprises and CBTEs (Roe *et al.* 2001; Asheeke and Katjiuongua 2007). Two of the case-study CBTEs and one lodge were engaged in a partnership. Despite the obvious benefits of such arrangements they also had various difficulties, which have been documented by Jänis (2008, 15).

A multiplier effect, commonly understood as economic activities spurred by a tourism enterprise, was not described by any of the informants but, through informal discussions and observation, it was manifested in various ways. Similarly, the aspects of profit making and accumulation were not mentioned by any of the informants. Some enterprises had put excess income in their bank accounts but lacked clear plans as to how to invest it. The lack of entrepreneurial skills in community-based tourism has been acknowledged by Halstead (2003), Mbaiwa (2003, 2005a) and Murphy and Roe (2004).

In contrast to the CBTEs, the representatives of private enterprises were openly proud of their significant contribution to the national economy through taxes, levies and other transactions. The farms in the Khomas region were also aware of their multiplier effect through marketing, other required services such as taxidermists and purchase of various items such as food and beverages. However, the food supplies to the farms and partly for the lodges in the Caprivi region were bought in the capital city of Windhoek. Only two lodges in Caprivi claimed to be making use of local suppliers. Whatever the circumstances, the majority of retail supplies in Namibia are imported from South Africa (Dubresson and Graefe 2001, 61).

Farm owners asserted that hunters contributed financially to the larger tourism industry since many of them and their families undertook tours and shopping in Namibia after hunting. One farm owner expressed it as his honour to contribute to the economy through attracting hunters to spend more: 'It's not a matter of getting people to spend all their money at your place and then go back. This country has so much to offer, we don't just market ourselves, we market the country.' Farmers also remarked that they contributed significantly more to the economy compared with the days when they had only cattle. As hunting farms, they also employ more people and consequently more is contributed through salaries.

Specific concern was expressed about foreign ownership of trophy hunting farms, which leads to leakage of tourism revenue: 'These outfitters use the peace and stability of the country and the resources and they contribute nothing back to the country'. Foreign ownership is similarly widespread in other tourism enterprises, and the Namibian Foreign Investment Act grants liberal conditions to potential foreign investors (Jauch 2001, 39). This reflects the dilemma of opening the economy for highly needed foreign tourism investments on the one hand and trying to minimize leakage and retain the profits within Namibia on the other. As the fastest growing sector in Namibia, tourism is extremely attractive for potential foreign investors (Jauch 2001, 54).

In the Caprivi region the lodge informants felt that, despite their substantial contribution to the national economy, they have been neglected with regard to the tourism development in the region: 'This Caprivi has been neglected for many years by the government. Although they collect the levies and make the stipulations and rules and laws their contribution to tourism in Caprivi is nearly zero.' The government was alleged to have put limited effort into marketing and promoting the region. The informants also emphasized that tourism facilities needed to be upgraded and infrastructure had to be improved in Katima Mulilo, the region's provincial capital.

Employment Creation

Unemployment, currently standing at 36.7%, has been one of the prevailing challenges in Namibia since independence, even though the problem derives from colonial times (Government of Namibia 2007, 36). Therefore, job creation is one of the major objectives of the government. Unemployment is worst among the youth and women, with 64.6% of youths aged 15–19 being unemployed (Government of Namibia 2007, 180). The declining output of the agricultural sector, the limited size of the domestic market, a relatively small manufacturing sector and lack of required skills are the major causes for this persisting unemployment (Bank of Namibia 2004, 9).

Tourism is expected to create significant employment opportunities for Namibians. In 2006, the number of tourism-related jobs was 20,588 (Namibia

Tourism Board 2008). The tourism policy asserts that tourism is a labour-intensive industry requiring a broad range of workers at all levels. Employment can take place in direct tourism services where there is also a possibility to progress from junior to senior level. Tourism is also claimed to have a considerable multiplier effect in terms of ancillary services and products required by the industry. In order to create more employment, the policy proposes an increase in the volume of tourism and delivering the benefits throughout the country.

All the informants in the CBTEs complained about the lack of formal job opportunities, apart from the tourism activity in which they were involved. On the other hand, work in tourism was only supplementary to their main sources of livelihood, such as agriculture, as the salaries are rather low in tourism employment and it has a seasonal nature. While community-based tourism can generate a variety of benefits such as communal income and community development projects, employment at the individual level was still preferred. Salaries provide individuals with secure income which helps to fulfil the responsibilities over extended families and purchase locally valued assets such as cattle.

The most significant constraint in the CBTEs in terms of employment creation was attributed to the lack of funds and limited scale of the enterprises. Therefore, in order to increase employment opportunities, expansion was considered necessary. Through informal discussions and observation, it became obvious that insufficient or misappropriated funds, difficulties in accessing donor funding and lack of skills in enterprise development make expansion slow and difficult. The local awareness of these problems was, however, limited. Similar challenges have been documented in community-based tourism throughout Southern Africa (e.g. Scheyvens 2002; Mbaiwa 2004; Manyara 2007).

Crafts production may not be classified as employment in the real sense of the concept but it was nevertheless regarded as self-employment or a source of additional income, with specific importance for women (see Fig. 2.2). In Caprivi, due to low educational levels, crafts production has provided a substantial income for many young school leavers with few chances of further education. In addition, the informants said that a significant number of women in the study areas belonged to single-headed households. Murphy and Roe (2004, 127) also draw attention to the fact that the majority of crafts producers in Caprivi come from households that do not own cattle, although they are considered an important asset and a source of income. Furthermore, the advantage of crafts production is that it can be carried out when people are less occupied with agricultural production.

Unlike the CBTE informants, private entrepreneurs looked at the entire issue of employment creation from an employer's perspective. They were aware of their substantial significance in providing employment but, due to the lack of formal tourism training in Namibia, they are largely responsible for training their employees. All of the private entrepreneurs interviewed had employed non-skilled workers whom they had trained on the job. While such entry-level positions had provided new opportunities for people without

Fig. 2.2. Crafts production and sales provide valuable income for women in rural Namibia.

prior education or training in the field, it also left workers less informed about their rights and lacking documentation concerning the acquired skills.

In the Caprivi region, where an estimated 39% of the population suffers from HIV/AIDS, the lodges had the problem of their employees becoming sick and attending funerals (UNAIDS 2006, 18). Furthermore, this loss of employees created the additional burden of training new people for positions. Similar problems have been documented throughout Namibia, and therefore some private enterprises have started to train two people for the same function in order to ensure continuity (Asheeke and Katjiuongua 2007, 80).

Most of the informants in the private enterprises emphasized the importance of providing employment for women. Many of the duties in the tourism sector are suitable for female workers, but women were also favoured because of their perceived reliability: 'The women are more reliable. That goes back to culture; they are responsible for the children, not the man. Just that mere fact makes them more reliable. Men are prone to drink and things like that....' Some informants explained that, apart from tourism, there are few formal employment opportunities for women, especially in rural Namibia. According to the tourism policy, tourism employs a disproportionately large number of women compared with other industries, which may be due to the lower wages and the nature of service industries (MET 2005a, 40).

Trophy hunting farms, as other private farms in Namibia, are specific social spaces with distinct power hierarchies that derive from colonial times (Werner 2002). Entire families usually stay on the farms and, apart from salaries, they are provided with accommodation and free food rations. However, families are also separated when one family member works on a farm and another takes care of their cattle outside the farm. Employment opportunities on trophy hunting farms were perceived to be rewarding by the farm owners, but disciplinary hearings about work ethic were mentioned as being common, and excessive use of alcohol had caused disputes in each of the three farms: 'I always say to the guys there's one reason why I will fire you immediately. That is if I find out or see that you are unthankful for anything. If you drink and you don't respect the fact that you have a job, then you are unthankful and I don't want you.'

Some private entrepreneurs expressed concern about the differences in working cultures between white employers and black employees. There was a perception that it requires some effort for the black employees to catch up with the efficiency, speed and service culture required in a tourism enterprise. A lodge owner expressed his concern over the matter: 'For a black man to understand white culture ... what he wants in the morning, how his eggs should be turned over and all that is alien to a black culture'. On the other hand, the enterprises had specifically employed local people whose educational level and exposure to tourism were limited. The lack of tourism training in practical skills has been acknowledged as a major constraint in Namibia, including the tourism policy which states that: 'Current training programmes do not reflect the needs of tourism industry' (MET 2005a, 27). According to Asheeke and Katjiuongua (2007, 60), in 2003 the number of people who had attended formal tourism courses in the previous 11 years represented about 1% of the total number of workers in the sector.

Poverty Reduction

Poverty in Namibia is related to complex historical and geographical factors, but socio-cultural and political aspects are equally important. In terms of GDP, Namibia belongs to lower middle income countries, but income and wealth distribution have remained highly unequal since colonial times (Schade 2000). The dualistic pattern of the agricultural sector, low soil fertility and general aridity of the Namibian climate contribute to a large extent to rural poverty. Gender inequality and HIV/AIDS are regarded as current challenges related to poverty throughout the country (Schade 2000; Government of Namibia 2007, 236). According to Mbai and Sherbourne (2004, 13), the 15 government budgets since independence show that spending on defence, security and intelligence has risen, whereas the amounts allocated to health, education, housing and agriculture have been declining since the mid-1990s.

According to the tourism policy, tourism is expected to reduce poverty through increasing government revenue that can be distributed to address poverty reduction measures. Poverty can also be addressed through creating jobs and business opportunities around the country that benefit local communities directly. This refers to direct tourism expenditure by tourists and tour operators, which the policy regards as having a considerable multiplier effect at the local level.

The provision of income and employment at an individual level was regarded as the most important mechanism for reducing poverty through the CBTEs. However, the informants acknowledged that poverty is also caused by a lack of basic services and high HIV/AIDS prevalence. Even though the government was considered responsible for solving such problems, the SWAPO-led government was alleged by some informants in both the Caprivi and Erongo regions to be concentrating its development efforts more in the northern Ovambo regions, where the majority of the leading supporters of the SWAPO party live.

In Caprivi, where 43.5% of households are classified as poor, the women engaged in crafts production emphasized the significance of additional income needed to educate the children and to pay increasing health-related costs resulting from HIV/AIDS (Government of Namibia 2007, 273). The disease had even affected their crafts production, as illuminated by one representative of a craft centre: 'What we have realised is that in most of the cases the women don't produce as much as we want the crafts. Like in the peak season when we have a lot of tourists coming in, the women will say "because I'm looking after five orphans, because their parents died out of HIV/AIDS and other diseases" ... so you find that their income goes down.'

In the Erongo region, it was seen as a responsibility of the CBTE to help less wealthy individuals in the village in various emergencies such as funerals. This was usually facilitated through small financial assistance or loans. Interestingly, one informant was convinced that there was no poverty in the area. Other informants of the same enterprise regarded high youth unemployment and overconsumption of alcohol as dimensions of poverty. In general, it was manifested in the interviews that the whole concept of poverty is relative, multidimensional and context specific, an aspect which has not received adequate attention in the debate on 'pro-poor tourism' (e.g. Goodwin 2007; Hall 2007; Harrison 2008).

Most informants in the private enterprises emphasized that their role in poverty reduction took place through employing Namibians who support their extended families with their salaries. In addition, some farm owners regarded it as their responsibility to educate their employees about issues they related to poverty, such as birth control, alcohol abuse and the importance of primary education. The farms and some lodges also participated in activities that could be defined as 'corporate social responsibility', which is becoming increasingly common in the tourism sector worldwide (e.g. Meyer 2007). The farms participate in a Namibia Hunting Association's school fund that supports the education of the farm workers' children. One lodge was supporting a local orphanage and another had opened a public telephone accessible to villagers.

The private entrepreneurs' understanding of the reasons for and scope of poverty in Namibia reflected their personal experiences within their own social settings: 'If people are willing to work, there shouldn't be poverty in the country. That's my personal view. If you are willing to work for a few dollars per hour then there's always work. And there are always things that need to be done. But one can't always afford to pay people what they expect.' One informant regarded ethnic background as a contributing factor: 'To reduce poverty through tourism? I don't think so. But it depends then also on the tribe. As I said before, in Okavango they are trying to make something out of wood, a chair or a table or crafts. That I accept, but the rest ... no ways.' Despite the official policy of reconciliation and 'de-ethnicitation' of a public sphere, such prejudices prevail, as highlighted by Diener (2001, 255), who states that 'the hidden side of public life is rife with inter-ethnic suspicion'.

In general, most informants in the private sector agreed that their contribution to poverty reduction in Namibia was limited. Some were openly pessimistic about the role tourism could play in alleviating poverty. This is interesting when compared with the emphasis placed on the private sector by the tourism policy and the Namibian Government. However, the significance of women's employment was emphasized and it was regarded as playing an essential role in poverty reduction.

Black Economic Empowerment

Namibia, like its former ruler South Africa, has a history of institutionalized segregation through the apartheid policy. Both countries have introduced 'broad-based black economic empowerment' (BBEE) as a government intervention to engage the black majority in the mainstream economy. The entire concept originates in South Africa, where it has been systematically practised in the field of tourism (Rogerson 2004a; Cornelissen 2005, 70). Officially, BBEE consists of increasing the ownership, management and control of productive assets by black Namibians through the promotion of small and medium-sized enterprises, human resource and skills development as well as through employment equity and preferential procurement (Gaomab 2005). In practice there is still an ongoing debate about what BBEE is really about and how it should be carried out (Institute for Public Policy Research 2007).

The tourism policy considers BBEE one of the important goals of tourism. In fact, the tourism sector was the first one in Namibia to adopt its own charter on BBEE and to discuss openly the draft before its adoption in 2004 (Namibia Economist 2004). However, the charter is a voluntary guideline that does not legally bind any actors. Moreover, it is stated in the tourism policy that, unlike other countries in a similar situation, Namibia does not provide any financial instruments to support BBEE activities (MET 2005a, 23).

Most of the informants in the CBTEs were unaware of the BBEE concept even though, as 'previously disadvantaged Namibians', they represent the target of the BBEE policy. There may be various reasons for this, such as the political nature of the concept, accessibility of information and media to people as well as the educational level of individuals. Those that were familiar with the concept were at the managerial level and expressed their concern over the widely acknowledged misuse of BBEE for the benefit of a few individuals within government circles: 'That one to me is not existing. I always read it in the newspapers and when I try to follow it, it is the black rich people who are benefiting. So I would say it doesn't exist. It is for rich people, not for us.'

It was acknowledged that political leaders representing the ruling SWAPO party have used BBEE to enhance their careers and to provide economic opportunities, especially for the Ovambo people who constitute the major supporters of the party. One informant expressed his understanding of such preference: 'If I'm a president I would make sure my group receives more because that is where the support lies. I can consider that if I develop this, this much can come in. That's how the government political situation is within our country.' Until recently, the SWAPO party has enjoyed support throughout Namibia due to its central role in the liberation struggle against South African occupation (e.g. Melber 2003).

As the different aspects of BBEE were explained, there was agreement about the need for training, skills development and external support. Naturally, such statements reflected more the structural problems that the CBTEs faced than the implementation of BBEE. Many informants were aware that government support for their activities might be minimal, whereas possibilities for donor funding were viewed more optimistically. All the CBTEs had already received some donor funding, particularly for training purposes. However, the whole relationship between donor organizations and CBTEs in Namibia is multifaceted, and avoiding donor dependency remains a challenge (Palm and Pye 2001; Vorflauer 2007).

In the private sector, BBEE was mainly regarded as an apparent and unpreventable process that took place in the form of training non-skilled workers from entry to upper levels. Two lodges belonging to larger chains had specific BBEE policies. Similar criticism was given by the CBTEs concerning the manner in which BBEE had been wrongly implemented purely for the political purposes of the elite, which was claimed to have enriched the rich instead of targeting the poor.

The majority of the informants emphasized specific problems and challenges related to implementing BBEE in the tourism sector. While it was agreed that black Namibians need to be employed in different tourism enterprises, many claimed that to have black people at a managerial level encompassed limitations. The farm owners expressed doubt about whether black hunting farms could be successful, for the simple reason that the overseas hunters would not feel safe and comfortable with them. Moreover, socializing was considered an important part of a hunting holiday but it was perceived that the black hunters would not be able to socialize with the white guests. However, there are an increasing number of black 'professional hunters', and the Namibia Professional Hunting Association has made a specific effort to encourage black Namibians to engage in the trophy hunting sector (NAPHA 2008).

Some lodge owners were similarly doubtful about black Namibians' abilities to cope with the tourism industry at a managerial level, due to their inexperience and lack of skills in the service attitude required in tourism. In addition, doubts were expressed about possible black tourism entrepreneurs' abilities to cope with the bureaucracy within the industry. An alternative was, however, suggested: 'So what the government should be doing, they should be saying "let's find ways where African culture and African traditions are beneficial to tourism" and build on that. There are lots of people in this country, black people, who could do very well at tourism if they had [been] or were allowed to do it the way they wanted.'

There was discontent with the Namibian Government, which was claimed to be enforcing BBEE as purely a matter of skin colour. Many emphasized that the government should put more effort into the provision of sufficient training and skills, since eventually it is qualifications that matter most to the tourism employer. None of the informants admitted it openly, but it could be interpreted from some of the answers that there is also an apparent fear of competition within the tourism industry if more black Namibians start to acquire shares and higher positions in the enterprises. Currently only 0.1% of tourism enterprises are owned by black Namibians (Karamata and Gwari 2007, 42).

Environmental and Ecological Sustainability

The major single factor characterizing Namibia's natural environment is its aridity, since some 23% of the country is arid and the rest is mainly semi-arid (Seely 2001, 39). The aridity is due to low and highly variable rainfall with high rates of evaporation. High population and livestock densities, especially in the northern areas, have led to overgrazing and a scramble for land, which were further exacerbated by the colonial government's resettlement policies (Fabricius 2004). Following massive hunting expeditions by Europeans which drove many game species to the edge of extinction during the late 19th century, a number of game parks were established (Ranta 2004; Botha 2005). Conservation measures slowly led to the regeneration of various game species even though they, in some cases, implied eviction of indigenous people from the areas (Botha 2005).

According to the tourism policy, the vast Namibian landscapes and wildlife are major tourism attractions and therefore visitor revenue needs to be directed to environmental maintenance. In terms of ecological sustainability, hunting offers revenue whereas culling might otherwise constitute a cost to the state (MET 2005a, 39). This refers to auctioning excessive game animals from the state game parks to private hunting farms (Botha 2005, 183). The need to preserve the endemic wildlife is expressed explicitly, but the policy does not mention a need for environmental responsibility among individual tourism enterprises. This is highlighted also by Seely (2001, 50), who states that 'environment' in Namibia is still often perceived as being synonymous with 'preserving wildlife', and few of the tourist establishments promote conservation of natural resources such as water or energy.

All the CBTEs were directly or indirectly involved with the community-based natural resource management (CBNRM), which was highlighted in the interviews. The members of the CBTEs lived in communal conservancies and were therefore engaged in the management of the natural resources within their areas. Even though the conservancy concept was supported at a general level, a number of challenges were also indicated. The understanding of the meaning and significance of a conservancy appeared to vary between the conservancy members and managers. A manager of one CBTE in a newly established conservancy expressed his concern: 'At the moment people are thinking that there is not really a meaning in the conservancy issue although it is a very important aspect in job creation and conserving it for sustainable development'. The lack of knowledge and awareness among conservancy members is common in some Namibian conservancies and it has been documented by Bandyopadhyay *et al.* (2004).

Poaching was indicated as a continuous challenge for the conservancies. Besides being practised by some residents, concern was expressed for individuals who deliberately came to the conservancies in order to poach. Such people were said to include persons from the economic and political elite at the local and national levels. The resources to tackle poaching were regarded as being inadequate and the game guards who were responsible for reporting the cases were criticized as being too few. In the Caprivi region human–wildlife conflicts were reported to be common, and the compensation procedures were not clear and standardized. Some informants agreed that this tends to reduce residents' support for the conservation. The same has been concluded by Vorflauer (2007) and the WWF (2008b).

In the Erongo region conservation and tourism have to provide room for mining activities, as explained by a local informant: 'Ministry of Mines can give a permit to a miner to mine within our area but I don't have a right to stop it. Also Ministry of Environment and Tourism does not have a right to stop it if they have been given that particular permission.' In a neoliberal growth environment, such conflicts are likely to favour the activities that provide the most economic benefits to the government, even if they occur at a cost for the local environment and communities.

The consumption levels of the CBTEs are rather low and only one of them had recently accessed electricity. Therefore, their major concern was rather the lack of resources than overconsumption. Instead, some informants expressed concern about the tourists who were observed to litter and have little respect for the local environment. In the conservancies specific effort has been placed on environmental education, and the crafts producers said that they had received training on how to harvest wood and palm in a sustainable manner.

Similar to communal conservancies, private farms in Namibia have established freehold conservancies, of which the trophy hunting farms in the Khomas region were members. Freehold conservancies aim at better wildlife management and increased biodiversity. In fact, the number of game species hunted in freehold conservancies has grown significantly. For example, the number of kudu antelopes, one of the most desired trophy animals, has grown by 334% since 1992 (Metzger 2008). It was stressed that hunting activity on the farms was carried out on a sustainable basis; some 30% of annual culling was necessary to keep the total number of game animals small enough in relation to the available space and forage. The farm owners also emphasized that keeping game was more ecologically sustainable than keeping cattle: 'The game use half of the amount of water than cattle would use. In that instance for us having a game farm we save water. Now I will never over-utilize the boreholes.'

Environmental responsibility referring to sustainable use of water and grazing areas was regarded as a necessity for the farm owners' own livelihoods. 'If I'm not environmental, I'll end up jobless in ten years and a lot of other people as well. So it will be stupid for me to overgraze it and destroy it in ten years time. In a country like this with low rainfall it's going to get you. You have to take of the environment, you have to run it and farm it according to the rainfall, there's no doubt about it.' However, farm owners were concerned about poaching, which they regarded as being difficult to tackle due to lack of resources. On the other hand, the rural lodge in Caprivi had a partnership agreement with the surrounding communal conservancy and the lodge had joined forces with the conservancy game guards in an effort to combat the poaching problem.

Nature and conservation areas were regarded as the primary assets for tourism in the Caprivi region, but the lodge informants expressed concern over the impact of increasing tourism on the environment: 'It's very fragile; it will have to be selective tourism and a careful study just how far tourism can be taken'. The lodges in Katima Mulilo were unhappy with the poor infrastructure and insufficient urban facilities: 'We have to improve the concept of the town itself, because how can you look after nature if you can't even look after your municipality?' The town council was perceived by some of the lodges as being uninterested in tourism and unwilling to cooperate with tourism enterprises.

Interestingly, the private enterprises did not express much concern regarding other aspects of ecological sustainability, such as consumption of energy and recycling of waste. Nevertheless, in a study by Asheeke and Katjiuongua (2007), the response from the private sector was positive towards a proposed Namibian eco-awards programme that would be applied as a certification mechanism to ensure more environmentally friendly and sustainable tourism products.

Reduction of Regional Development Inequities

Historically, regional development inequities derive from the colonial practices of land allocation and administration, especially the proposal of the Odendaal Commission in 1964 to create ten ethnic homelands. Establishment of these homelands enforced the territorial, symbolic and structural spatial divide important to the apartheid regime (du Pisani 2000). There are sharp regional variations in human development, as well as in wealth and income distribution (Government of Namibia 2006). In addition to historical reasons, regional disparities stem from political and environmental factors. In terms of the regions studied, the Khomas and Erongo regions are important tourism destinations with high levels of human development, whereas the Caprivi region is a less marketed and visited tourism destination, with one of the lowest levels of human development (Government of Namibia 2006).

According to the tourism policy, tourism can reduce regional development inequities through spreading tourists and the benefits of tourism more equally across the country. This could be achieved by marketing less developed areas with tourism potential and supporting tourism facilities in areas that are en route to an established tourism destination, as well as by promoting domestic tourism.

The regional development inequities were not regarded as disturbing in most of the CBTEs. Many informants had been staying some time outside their home region, especially in larger towns such as Windhoek and Swakopmund. However, despite the deficiencies, they preferred to stay in their home areas where they felt culturally bonded, spoke a shared language and where they had traditional social networks. The informants also emphasized the significance of low living costs and brought up the importance of providing people with opportunities to remain in their home areas instead of migrating to urban centres. Some regarded the CBTEs as having had such an effect, especially on youth, many of whom happily leave for large urban centres in search of job opportunities.

The Erongo region was asserted to be rich in minerals and tourism, but this wealth has not been equally divided within the region. Therefore, it was the intraregional inequity that was their concern rather than the inequity between the different regions in Namibia. The politics of the country and the SWAPO party were considered by one informant to play a central role in this issue: 'But political-wise, you can be within the region and if you are SWAPO then you will think of the SWAPO, not the Damara. If I come to Erongo, former Damaraland, if I apply to whichever position in Erongo regional office then I will give to my SWAPO friend.' This informant was of the opinion that most of the residents of Damara origin vote for alternative parties. In the Caprivi region, the informants claimed that the government has little interest in the region and in improving basic services. This may be due to the recent political history of the region and to some of the prevailing political disputes.

Similar to the CBTEs, the lodge informants in Caprivi expressed concern for the government's indifference to the region's tourism development, which they regarded as having vast unexploited and unexplored potential. The urban lodge owners were also discontented about the state of Katima Mulilo, which they regarded as untidy and disorganized and therefore not enticing for tourists. However, some were optimistic about the future: 'I think Caprivi's day is coming and if the government do what they've promised, it's only a question of spending money. If the government put money available for development, then the spin-off would also go to the private sector who would employ more people and more people would get trained ... so all the government needs to do is to spend money, not to talk about it.'

Interestingly, the government had donated NAD128 million to a water-front project that is expected to erect a three-star hotel, aquarium, a floating restaurant, a hippo and crocodile park and various other amenities in Katima Mulilo at the shore of the River Zambezi, which experiences annual floods. According to private enterprises, the entire project is far from realistic and huge sums of money had already been spent on several feasibility studies and planning. However, there is the competition aspect between the project and existing private tourism enterprises. On the other hand, the CBTEs were rather enthusiastic about the project, which is expected to be completed by the end of 2009 (New Era 2008a).

Farm owners' awareness of regional development inequities seemed to be limited, even though they were aware that their own Khomas region was highly developed. However, all of them believed that tourism can contribute to some extent, especially in the northern parts of Namibia: 'Now if you look in the north, there are so many [of] these concessions and conservancies and the people living there are going to earn the money from the animals hunted and the meat and whatever happens through that. From five years ago until today, I think, it improved about thousand times so that must be a very big impact on those people's lives. I think they are actually better off than the people squatting in Windhoek.'

Conclusions

As the empirical material demonstrates, the effort to promote tourism policy objectives in Namibia becomes complex when reviewed from the perspective of tourism enterprises at the local level. The various enterprises give weight to the aspects that support their immediate interests. For private enterprises, profit and competitiveness weigh naturally more and cannot be sacrificed for the sake of poverty reduction or empowerment, whereas CBTEs operate in largely rural communities and their members are more concerned with ensuring daily income than how to run a successful business enterprise. Furthermore, the policy objectives are somewhat vague and the tourism policy does not propose any mechanism as to how to measure their implementation. In fact, there is even ambiguity within the government itself concerning, for example, the highly contested BBEE (e.g. Jauch 2007a).

The findings indicate that there are many challenges for policy implementation, which is already an inherently complicated process (Dredge and Jenkins 2008, 171). The apartheid legacy is still tangible in Namibian society in terms of the unequal distribution of assets and provides a challenging situation for the tourism industry. For example, private hunting farms represent the highly unequal land distribution which has been the focus of the land reform process in Namibia since independence (Zondi 2003). Furthermore, informants from all the enterprises indicated disenchantment with the present government regarding its development efforts within the country. The private sector is expected to carry out much of the tourism and hospitality training and to play an active role in many duties that belong to the government. However, leaving everything to market forces tends to widen already existing inequalities (Jauch 2001, 104).

CBT is considered an important tool for rural development in Namibia and it generates income in areas with few alternative sources of income and employment (Katjiuongua 2008). However, as this research and many previous studies indicate, the challenges in CBT are many and multifaceted. Even though the CBTEs are expected to perform as business entities, the people running them in the rural areas are often semi-illiterate and come from a farming background, which is reflected in the way they understand, or do not understand, the policy objectives (Symonds 2008). The significance of a few scattered craft centres may not be substantial for the national economy but, in the local context, hundreds of crafts producers may have an impact on the poverty situation and therefore CBT has an established pro-poor focus. However, even within the enterprises studied, misappropriation of funds by influential individuals had taken place and remains a challenge in the entire CBT sector.

Even though much of the tourism development in Namibia rests on the private sector and NGOs, the government has an important role in approving the tourism policy and ensuring that it is implemented. However, it becomes clear from this research that there is also a need for regional tourism planning and strategies where regional and local contexts and characteristics can be taken into consideration. The same has been emphasized by Sofield (2003, 104): 'Despite the attention that may be paid to tourism policy, planning and development by a national government, the practicality, application and implementation of those policies, plans and developments must often be placed in the context of the local levels of authority and their communities'.

3 Local Economic Development and Tourism Planning in Africa: Evidence from Route Tourism in South Africa

CHRISTIAN M. ROGERSON

Introduction

Local economic development (LED) is defined as increases in a 'local economy's capacity to create wealth for local residents' (Bartik 2003, 1). Since the 1970s, under pressure from globalization and the development of new forms of post-Fordist production, national governments have become less able to direct or protect economic investment (Harvey 1989; Glasmeier 2000). Accordingly, localities and communities have been 'thrown onto themselves to take responsibility for their own development' (Helmsing 2001a, 11) and noted for energizing 'place prosperity' (Helmsing 2001b, 7). The rise of a more decentralized bottom-up approach to economic development is geared to strengthen the building blocks of growth, including productive investment, skills and innovative technology, through developing the inherent strengths of each locality (Turok 2005, 348). As Nel (2007, 462) observes, 'LED enjoys not insignificant international appeal as a local development response in an era of globalization and reduced state control and decentralization'. Concern for implementation of LED was apparent initially in developed countries of Western Europe and North America (Harvey 1989; Clarke and Gaile 1998), and subsequently spread to countries of the South (Glasmeier 2000; Rodriguez-Pose and Gill 2003).

Since the mid-1990s, LED activities have been growing in significance across much of the developing world (Rogerson 1995, 1997; Helmsing 2001c; Rodriguez-Pose and Arbix 2001; Wandschneider 2004; Egziabher and Helmsing 2005; Ma 2005; Nel and Rogerson 2005a; Park 2005; Chien 2007; Nel 2007). Decentralization – the deliberate and planned transfer of resources away from central state institutions – represents a key underpinning for the expansion of LED planning in the developing world (Rodriguez-Pose and Tijmstra 2007). For Helmsing and Egziabher (2005, 1), in the developing world, LED becomes 'a process in which partnerships between local governments,

NGOs, community-based groups and the private sector are established to manage existing resources, to create jobs and stimulate the economy of a well-defined territory'. As a general observation, LED planning is more pronounced in the countries of Asia and Latin America than in Africa. Nevertheless, there is a range of LED planning initiatives taking place in several different African countries (Helmsing 2001c; McCormick 2001; Beyer *et al.* 2003; Helmsing and Egziabher 2005; Hill *et al.* 2007; Rylance 2008).

As observed by Thomas and Thomas (2006, 100), 'The potential contribution of tourism to local economic development has become an established subject of academic enquiry'. In many peripheral regions of developed countries, the promotion of rural tourism has been used as a vehicle for catalysing economic growth, job creation and enterprise development (Shaw and Williams 1990; Jones and Munday 2001; Andriotis 2002; Shaw 2004). Within many Western European and North American cities which experienced the impacts of de-industrialization, tourism has functioned as a lead sector for economic regeneration (Law 1992, 1993, 1996; Swarbrooke 2000; Connelly 2007). It was asserted that, if appropriately planned, 'tourism can be the catalyst of radical changes in the economy, morale and appearance of a city in transition' (Owen 1990, 194). Although tourism was not viewed simplistically as an LED elixir, it was considered an industry that could 'breathe new life' into declining or laggard economies, whether in urban or rural areas (Law 1996, 11). Localities externally perceived to be important and interesting visitor destinations 'tend to be significantly better placed to attract new businesses and industries as well as an appropriate workforce' (Karski 1990, 15). Accordingly, tourism is considered a 'prominent' part of LED policy in developed countries and 'the drive for tourism precipitates new team partnerships, spins off into other realms of the local economy, and boosts the local policy machine in various ways that enhance the status and the strength of the local economy' (Stobart and Ball 1998, 236).

In the developing world, the role of tourism as a driver for LED is of no less significance. Goodwin (1998) points out that there is a strong case for intervention at the local level in tourism destinations in order to maximize the benefits of tourism projects, not just for national revenue generation or increase in tourism arrivals but for their LED contribution. The promotion of urban tourism as a vehicle for local economic regeneration and diversification in South Africa parallels the experience of tourism-led LED in many cities of the developed North (Rogerson 2002b, 2004c, 2006a; Rogerson and Visser 2007). In the South, a distinctive element in scholarship on tourism-led LED is to maximize the impacts of tourism for poverty alleviation by fostering strong linkages with local economies, as a part of national development strategies (International Tourism Partnership 2004; Roe *et al.* 2004; Ashley 2006; Meyer 2006; Rogerson 2006b). As argued by Goodwin (1998, 4), 'Local development requires the benefits of tourism be distributed beyond the local or national elites and those who find employment in their hotels and agencies'. Strengthening linkages with local economies, including through the development of local arts, crafts, cultural products and tourism services, offers opportunities for deepening local economies through tourism-led development (Meyer *et al.* 2004; Ashley *et al.* 2005, 2006). In maximizing the local development impacts of tourism, a central role is identified for local government which is 'well placed to bring together private sector tour operators, accommodation providers, local attractions, civil society and economically poor producers' (Goodwin 2006, 4).

Against this backcloth of the emergence of tourism as a lead sector for LED both in developed and developing countries, the aim in this chapter is to investigate the experience of local planning for route tourism in South Africa. Within scholarship and policy development around LED, South Africa offers a striking case study. Since the country's democratic transition in 1994, LED has expanded and consolidated as a critical aspect of planning for post-apartheid reconstruction (Rogerson 2000, 2008a). It is significant that the South African experience of LED planning is closely scrutinized as offering potential 'good practice' for other countries in Africa. LED in South Africa is more advanced, varied and mature than in the rest of sub-Saharan Africa (Rogerson 1997, 2000, 2006c, 2008a; Nel 2001; Nel and Rogerson 2005a,b; Abrahams 2007; Xuza 2007).

Since the 1994 democratic transition, tourism has emerged as a critical sector for promoting national economic growth in South Africa (Rogerson and Visser 2004b). Correspondingly, in terms of planning for LED, tourism has been isolated as a lead sector by various localities (Binns and Nel 2002, 2003; Nel and Binns 2002; Rogerson 2002c, 2006d; Nel and Rogerson 2005a, 2007; Ferreira 2007; Ferreira and Visser 2007; Rogerson and Visser 2007). In 2006, South Africa's national Department of Trade and Industry identified route tourism as one of a group of niche forms of tourism that might be strengthened (ECIAfrica 2006a,b,c). Several studies demonstrate the synergies between route tourism and local economic development planning both in South Africa and the wider region of Southern Africa (Mathfield 2000; Rogerson 2002c, 2004b, 2007a; Ndlovu and Rogerson 2003; Kiambo 2005; ECIAfrica 2006a,b; Donaldson 2007; Lourens 2007a,b; Viljoen 2007; Stoddart 2008; Stoddart and Rogerson 2009). The central objective in this chapter is to provide a synthesis of the experience of planning route tourism as a vehicle for LED in South Africa. This analysis is located within the wider context of international debates and planning surrounding route tourism.

Route Tourism: International Debates and Experience

Tourism routes are 'more than a geographic formula for tourist travel' (HSRC 2006, 37). The concept 'tourism route' refers to an initiative designed to bring together an array of activities and attractions under a unified theme and thereby to stimulate entrepreneurial opportunities in the form of ancillary products and services (Greffe 1994; Meyer-Cech 2003; Meyer *et al.* 2004; Clarke 2005). In the recent history of route development, organizations such as UNESCO and the Council of Europe have applied them for educational, social and cultural aims by sponsoring a range of cultural and heritage route initiatives in Western Europe (Goodey 1997; Moulin and Boniface 2001; Lourens 2007a).

Route promotion has progressively assumed an economic or developmental goal such that it can be observed that the development of themed routes as tourism attractions 'has gained prominence in recent years' (Meyer *et al.* 2004, 1). In several parts of the world the concept of rural trails or heritage routes has been used, particularly in the context of promoting rural tourism (Meyer-Cech 2003, 2005; Olsen 2003). Greffe (1994) suggests that routes provide a unique opportunity for rural operators to achieve 'economies of scale' by establishing networks of different service providers organized in a way that maximizes opportunities and offers a wide array of products and activities. In Western Europe, Moulin and Boniface (2001) focus on the useful role that routes can play in heritage conservation and cultural preservation as well as tourism expansion. Meyer (2004) stresses that routes seem to be a particularly good opportunity for the development of less mature tourism areas with high cultural resources that appeal to special-interest tourists, who often not only stay longer but also spend more to pursue their particular interest. Routes appeal to a great variety of users such as international overnight visitors that visit the route as part of a special-interest holiday, staying visitors that frequent the route (or part of it) on day excursions or urban domestic day visitors.

As stated by Moulin and Boniface (2001, 238), the 'essence of a route is that it is a selected journey or progression among a series of elements'. Route tourism involves the joining together of the tourism resources of a number of smaller centres and collectively marketing them as a single tourism destination region (Briedenhann and Wickens 2004a; Meyer 2004). One of the key benefits of routes is that 'they can tie up several attractions that would independently not have the potential to entice visitors to spend time and money. Using a synergy effect promises to have greater pulling power' (Meyer *et al.* 2004, 1). The planning of tourism routes is a direct parallel of cluster cooperation and involves the development of cooperative planning arrangements and relationships between different localities in order for them to collectively compete as tourism spaces (Michael 2007).

There is considerable variation of routes in terms of length, scale, characteristics and visitor numbers. Among the most successful examples of rural tourism routes are the wine or food circuits, which have been documented in Europe, North America and Australasia (Telfer 2001a,b; Hall *et al.* 2003; Telfer and Hashimoto 2003; Correia *et al.* 2004; Meyer-Cech 2005). In addition to routes based upon wine and food, there are prominent European examples of route-based cultural tourism, the most notable being the *Camino de Santiago* in Spain and France (Murray and Graham 1997; Gonzalez and Medina 2003). France is considered a pioneer of route development linked to heritage, with the innovation of many routes designed to channel visitors to churches or rural chapels (Moulin and Boniface 2001, 244). Beyond France, there are examples of heritage trail or route development in other parts of Europe, including Bulgaria, Portugal, Slovenia and the Baltic states (Goodey 1997; Moulin and Boniface 2001; Lourens 2007b).

The establishment of tourism routes is considered an effective method of tourism distribution, especially for tourists travelling by road (driving, hiking or cycling) within a given geographical area (Meyer-Cech 2003; Meyer 2004; Shih 2006). Tourism products are packaged into 'inclusive and coherent routes through the use of themes and stories (such as folklore, working lives, food and drink routes, religious routes) which help to move the tourist around geographically dispersed attractions' (Clarke 2005, 92). The tourism route brings together a network of actors – municipalities, associations and the local private sector – to work together and cooperate effectively in order to market a local destination (Michael 2003, 2007). The development of such local networks or partnerships is increasingly seen as a necessary element for the growth of small and medium-sized tourism enterprises (Plummer *et al.* 2005, 2006; Michael 2007).

The international experience confirms that well-designed and imaginative tourism routes can generate several positive advantages for destinations (Goodey 1997; Murray and Graham 1997; Telfer 2001a; Meyer-Cech 2003, 2005; Lourens 2007a). As a result of their essential structure and form, routes offer communities the opportunity of direct self-help and 'allow each participating community along a route to benefit from being linked to the experiences, and the knowledge gained, of other participants' (Moulin and Boniface 2001, 243). For Viljoen (2007, 38), routes have a predominantly marketing focus. According to Meyer (2004), there are three important advantages of route development:

- The economic benefit that accrues from spreading tourism more widely by developing tourist facilities, activities and services along tour routes in a manner that might facilitate tourist spending at stopover points.
- The provision of additional employment and income, both directly and indirectly, through local facilities and services required to operate tour programmes.
- Well-designed tourism routes can contribute to expansion of the tourist markets and extend the average length of stay of tourists, through the provision of a variety of attractions and activities.

As has been observed, a route can enhance the overall attractiveness of a product 'by presenting "new" features to its visitors, thus providing a platform for revised marketing programmes with the aim of increasing length of stay and total spending' (Meyer *et al.* 2004, 1). Finally, one must reiterate that one critical advantage of routes is to act as stimulus for small enterprise development within the local economy (Goodwin 2006; Meyer 2006).

The establishment of tourism routes is not, however, a guarantee of success (HSRC 2006, 37). Tourism routes represent a supply-side initiative for destination development and must either respond to or successfully create tourist demand for the attractions on offer. From a review of the record of tourism routes in both developed and developing countries, there are several necessary key preconditions for the establishment of successful routes (Meyer 2004; ECIAfrica 2006a; Lourens 2007a,b). There is a need to evolve cooperative partnerships and a good framework of collaboration between key stakeholders, most importantly between local government, private enterprise, associations and the local tourism economy (Plummer *et al.* 2006). Routes require organization and funding in order to be effective (HSRC 2006, 37). As argued by Meyer (2004, 19), 'leadership in developing routes is essential' and 'if this is not forthcoming from the public sector, all too often the private sector fills this space'. Adequate infrastructure, information provision and marketing promotion of any route initiative are also crucial for long-term success (ECIAfrica 2006a,b).

The participation of local communities and the creation of local opportunities for small and emerging entrepreneurs are considered a vital underpinning for the success of tourism routes, particularly in the context of the developing world (Meyer 2004; Rogerson 2007a). In turn, this requires local governments to be proactive and assume an enabling role in support of both local tourism development and the upgrading of local enterprises, especially in rural areas (Briedenhann and Wickens 2004b; Briedenhann 2007). A pro-poor focus on route development is a further critical consideration for tourism planning in the developing world (Meyer 2004; Lourens 2007a,b). The dispersal of tourists to route-linked attractions in marginalized communities can offer multiple opportunities for economic development and poverty reduction, including the upgrading of local enterprises and increasing the demand of goods and services of the poor (Meyer *et al.* 2004). Nevertheless, a key lesson from international experience is that 'not every route will succeed in attracting tourists, and where a tourist route is formed and driven by established local businesses, it may also fail to include and assist poor and start-up enterprises' (HSRC 2006, 37).

Route Tourism Development in Africa: Evidence from South Africa

Although the benefits of planning for route tourism have long been appreciated in developed countries, it is only recently that the concept of route development has gained recognition in Africa (Viljoen 2007, 3). Route development in Africa can 'play an important part in fostering community participation in the tourism industry and contribute towards conservation of the natural environment' (Viljoen 2007, 126). Across various parts of Africa there is growing interest in the potential for developing tourism routes as vehicles for encouraging sustainable tourism development and for LED (Kiambo 2005; Nel and Rogerson 2007; Rogerson 2007a). The tourism route, it is observed, represents a 'development tool that is increasingly employed for developing tourism and local economies in Africa' (Viljoen 2007, 126). Among recent projects initiated to establish such routes in Africa are the Ksour Route in Algeria, the Slave Route cultural programme between Senegal, Gambia and Guinea, the Ghana National Slave Route Project, the Cape to Namibia Route, the Caprivi Wetlands Paradise Route in Namibia and the Lubombo Route crossing between South Africa, Swaziland and Mozambique (Swaziland National Trust Commission 2007; Viljoen 2007).

The region of Southern Africa is the hub of route tourism development in Africa. Many different tourism routes are in the process of being established or planned, particularly across South Africa and extending into surrounding countries, including Lesotho, Mozambique, Namibia and Swaziland (Kiambo 2005; ECIAfrica 2006a; Viljoen 2007). One illustration is provided by the recently launched Maloti Route, which straddles Lesotho and South Africa and combines the attractions of mountain scenery, rock art, skiing, horse trails and fly fishing (Maloti Route 2007). Viljoen (2007) draws attention to the emergence and planning of tourism routes targeted for economic and social development objectives in the proposed Kavango–Zambezi Transfrontier Conservation Area that encompasses the south-western part of Zambia and the Caprivi region of northern Namibia. Similarly, in planning for the wider spatial distribution of tourism development within Mozambique through the opening up of new niches for tourism, Kiambo (2005, 147) notes that 'national planning draws upon the concepts of "tourism routes" and "tourism circuits" in order to link together a variety of different products'. It is significant that the planning of these tourism circuits in Mozambique is targeted at both domestic and regional (mainly South African) visitors and that a number of cross-border tourism routes are under consideration to link with South Africa, Swaziland, Malawi, Tanzania and Zimbabwe.

Currently, South Africa evidences the highest concentration of route tourism initiatives on the African continent (Rogerson 2002b,c, 2004c, 2007a; Donaldson 2007; Lourens 2007a,b; Stoddart 2008). Figure 3.1 shows the location of the most significant tourism routes. The first tourism routes of the country go back to the 1970s with the establishment of wine routes in the Cape Winelands (Nowers *et al.* 2002). Wine tourism is part of a growth in special-interest tourism and constitutes one of the best-known international expressions of route tourism (Telfer 2001a; Hall *et al.* 2003; Correia *et al.* 2004; Wargenau and Che 2006). The wine route, argues Bruwer (2003, 424), represents the roadway to 'the core attractions of wine tourism – the wines and the winery'. Nowers *et al.* (2002, 195) draw attention to the wine route phenomenon as combining the three goals of tourism, wine sales and brand promotion.

In addition to the Western Cape wine routes, several other themed route tourism initiatives can be observed in contemporary South Africa, the most mature among these being the arts and crafts cluster of the Midlands Meander in the province of KwaZulu-Natal (Mathfield 2000; Rogerson 2002b; Lourens 2007a,b). Among recent applications of route tourism planning in South Africa is the establishment of tourism circuits as part of some ambitious planning for Dinokeng, which is situated in the north-east of Gauteng province. The creation of Dinokeng as a tourism destination offers both domestic and international tourists an 'Africa in a day' circuit designed to provide visitors with a 'window' on Africa's range of natural and cultural experiences (Singh 2008).

The most ambitious route tourism initiative with the highest profile in Africa at present is the African Dream Project, which is organized by Open Africa, a non-governmental organization based in South Africa. This initiative seeks to bring together the tourism splendours of Africa into a continuous network of tourism routes extending from the Cape to Cairo (Briedenhann and Wickens 2004b; Visser 2004b). This organization makes use of 'a

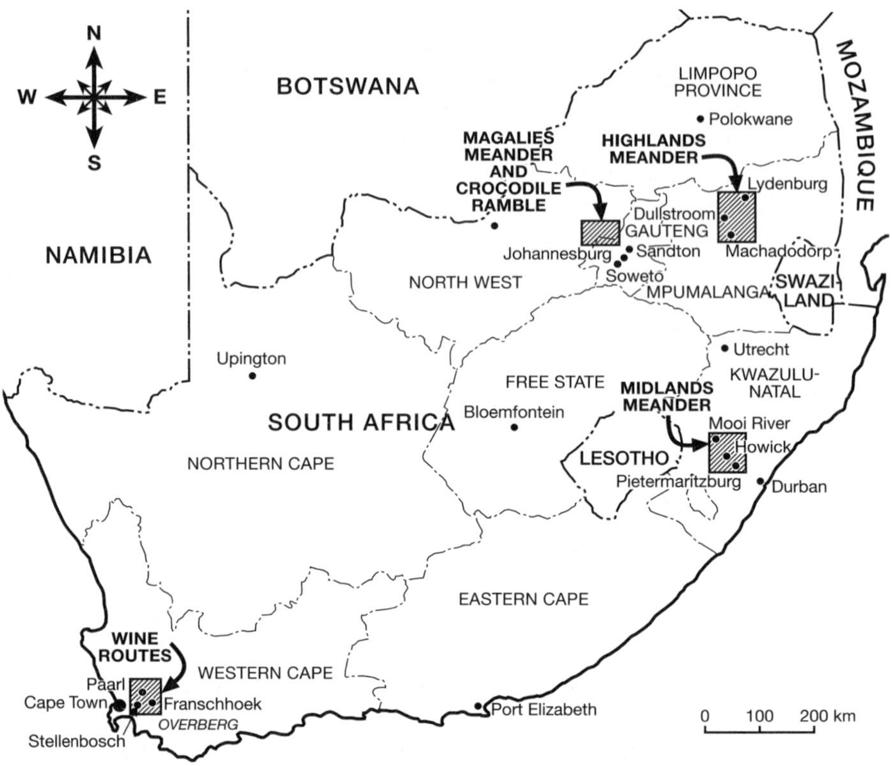

Fig. 3.1. The most significant tourism routes in South Africa.

participatory approach to developing tourism in predominantly rural areas in Africa through tourism, job creation and conservation in a mutually sustainable way' (Viljoen 2007, 4). The themes of the routes are varied and encompass arts and crafts, heritage, townships, fossils, shipwrecks and old mission stations (HSRC 2006). Open Africa has six core activities:

- to respond to community requests regarding the formation of routes by facilitating the route development process;
- to assist in raising the funds necessary to cover the costs of establishing routes;
- to develop and act as custodian of the web site on which the routes are loaded;
- to market the Open Africa brand for the network;
- to facilitate the management and dissemination of the hands-on knowledge that builds up within the network; and
- to act as a support base for the established routes and to deliver proof to them of the value of being part of the network (Open Africa 2006, 1).

By 2007, according to Viljoen (2007, 5), Open Africa 'had developed over 40 community-driven routes', mainly in South Africa but extending also into surrounding countries. Briedenhann and Wickens (2004b, 200) suggest that 'possibly the most important facet of the project is the fact that the marketing of the routes is electronically facilitated by the project coordinators'. The Open Africa approach uses a system devised through interactively linking together geographical information systems technology with the Internet. This has produced what is claimed to be a 'fully inclusive and community-participative workshop method for developing tourism routes' (Viljoen 2007, 4).

The South African experience of route tourism planning has so far been mixed, with only a few successful initiatives (Rogerson 2004b; Lourens 2007a). The highest-profile initiative, Open Africa, which is a strong advocate for route tourism development in the region, has been much criticized (ECIAfrica 2006b; HSRC 2006; Lourens 2007b). With only eight functioning routes out of over 40 projects described as 'flourishing', the Open Africa experience has, at best, been uneven. HSRC (2006) is highly critical of the Open Africa 'model' for route development and argues that, while the organization has established routes, its marketing is not functioning to bring in tourists. One of its errors has been to develop 'too many routes over a short period of time' (Lourens 2007b, 88). The short period of intervention in the establishment of Open Africa routes is 'not meaningful enough to ensure lasting effects' (Lourens 2007b). The Open Africa programme has led to an oversupply of tourism themed routes with little demand and produced weak management and support structures, causing many routes to collapse. In many respects, the failures of Open Africa are mirrored by the experience of parallel supply-led route initiatives in South Africa that have often been initiated by foreign donors (Ndlovu and Rogerson 2003). Overall, it is argued that Open Africa has not only failed to galvanize sustainable benefits for poor communities but, in many cases, has caused distrust and substantial barriers to achieving meaningful participation in poor communities across Southern Africa (HSRC 2006).

Despite the negative commentaries concerning Open Africa, research by Briedenhann and Wickens (2004a), ECIAfrica (2006a) and HSRC (2006) demonstrate the potential for *appropriately planned* and *appropriately supported* tourism routes to act as a stimulus for community-based LED in poorer communities and remote rural areas of South Africa. Route tourism planning is allied closely to the promotion of the development of small-sized enterprises as a means of sharing the growth of tourism expansion in post-apartheid South Africa (Rogerson 2008b). For rural tourism development in South Africa, it is suggested that the route concept 'can be a very strong tool in unifying attractions and products under one marketing umbrella' (ECIAfrica 2006b, 15). In terms of attractions, Briedenhann and Wickens (2004b, 196) point to the fact that probably 'the most fundamental change that has taken place in rural tourism has been the recognition that African culture and history are valid and sought-after components of South African tourism offerings'.

In examining the potential for community-based route tourism in South Africa, ECIAfrica (2006a,c) identifies the category of a 'marginalized community-based tourism enterprise' (MCBTE), which is the one that does not fall within the mainstream economy and is run by the poorest of the poor

(ECIAfrica 2006c). It is contended that 'improving the conditions of MCBTEs can be viewed as a development challenge' for South African tourism planners (ECIAfrica 2006c, 6). The advancement of community-based tourism is viewed as a means to create opportunities for historically disadvantaged enterprises in South Africa wishing to enter the tourism economy. More particularly, the approach of community-based tourism is considered to offer opportunities to MCBTEs as well as bringing development to peripheral regions and marginalized localities that otherwise offer limited economic prospects (ECIAfrica 2006a,c). For the development of successful community-based routes, marginal enterprises require direct funding support from the national government for enhanced product development and route promotion (ECIAfrica 2006b; Rogerson 2008b).

The best examples of successful route tourism initiatives linked to local economic development in South Africa are initiatives driven by the private sector. Among the most successful examples are the Western Cape Wine Routes (Nowers *et al.* 2002), the Crocodile Ramble (Stoddart 2008), the Magalies Meander (Rogerson 2007a) and the Highlands Meander (Rogerson 2002a). Through the organization and launch of these routes, a positive growth of local tourism has been recorded by clustering and packaging products into themed routes. Criticism, however, is directed at the lack of a pro-poor focus, limited involvement and linkages of successful businesses with disadvantaged black communities. In the Highlands Meander, the weak asset base of local communities precludes their involvement in the tourism economy beyond that of tourism employee (Rogerson 2004b). It has been demonstrated that the distribution of benefits accruing from tourism development in these LED initiatives has resulted in an unequal pattern of beneficiaries. In many cases, successful tourism expansion has occurred but *without* any spreading of development into surrounding poor communities. The prime beneficiaries of the route tourism initiatives have been groups of existing white South African tourism entrepreneurs, an outcome that perpetuates the marginalization of black South Africans from the tourism economy.

Rogerson (2004b, 2007a) argues that, in evolving planning around route tourism development in South Africa, the pro-poor rhetoric of national tourism policymakers must be translated into implementing a set of *pro-poor interventions* designed to empower and support the economic development of those communities that historically have not been beneficiaries of tourism growth in the country. Local governments, through their economic development facilitation activities, have a key role to play in tilting the balance of route development towards a more pro-poor focus (Briedenhann 2007). One recent example of such a shift in route tourism planning is the case of the Crocodile Ramble (Stoddart 2008). In unfolding the planning for this tourism route, local administration has tried to intervene in order to change planning for the Crocodile Ramble from its former exclusive pro-growth (as a private-sector-led initiative) focus to incorporate new planning considerations for promoting pro-poor tourism by supporting a complementary set of attractions in the area's township tourism (Stoddart and Rogerson 2009).

The Midlands Meander: South Africa's Showcase for Route Tourism

In the annals of South African tourism planning, the Midlands Meander is the showcase of private-sector-driven route tourism initiatives (Lourens 2007a). It is the oldest African example of using routes as the basis for tourism-led LED. The Midlands Meander is a route tourism destination geographically situated in the province of KwaZulu-Natal and strategically located along the N3 national highway that links Gauteng, South Africa's economic heartland, to the coastal city of Durban. The core product offering of the Midlands Meander is the area's arts and crafts, agricultural produce and scenic rural environment. Mathfield (2000, 54) first recognized that the Midlands Meander represented an example of a successful, locality-bound route that 'has expanded exponentially'. The positive impacts and experience of this route tourism initiative have functioned as inspiration and stimulus for the launch of similar private-sector-led initiatives in other parts of South Africa (Stoddart 2008).

The Midlands Meander was founded as an unplanned local economic initiative during 1985 by five visionary arts and crafters, with the objective of encouraging rural tourism growth and of expanding market access for the area's small arts and crafts enterprises (Mathfield 2000). By 1988, the Meander had evolved into a local tourism association with 57 members, mainly suppliers of arts and crafts or hospitality products. By 1994, the association was consolidated to the point where it had a formal constitution and issued its first colour brochure dedicated to marketing the route products. From these humble beginnings, by 2006 the Midlands Meander Association had metamorphosed into a vibrant network of 229 members, estimated as covering 80% of the tourist establishments in the region. The association annually prints 250,000 brochures, which are distributed both locally and internationally to promote this tourism destination (Lourens 2007a).

The enterprises on the Meander provide employment opportunities to an estimated 2500 people directly, with additional support for 36,000 people through indirect multiplier impacts. The value of the Midlands Meander tourism industry was estimated for 2006 as approximately R200 million per annum (Lourens 2007b, 83). Tourism demand is predominantly from domestic, self-drive, independent travellers drawn mostly from KwaZulu-Natal province, followed by Gauteng. Consumer surveys disclose that primary motivations for travelling around the Midlands Meander are 'to get away from the city', to be 'surrounded by beautiful scenery' and 'to experience something different' (Lourens 2007b, 76). Satisfaction levels of visitors are high, with the Meander's information services, restaurants, friendliness of staff and attractions recording top performance (Lourens 2007b, 78).

The Meander has diversified its product base beyond the original focus on arts and crafts (Mathfield 2000). As visitor numbers expanded, the Meander emerged as an attractive investment proposition for accommodation providers. Many new entrepreneurs – a mixture of both lifestyle and opportunistic entrepreneurs – have converted old farmhouses or outbuildings to cater for a spectrum of market needs, from luxury to low-budget backpackers. Indeed, in 1999–2006, rapid growth was reflected in the doubling of the supply of rooms in the area. By 2006, the Meander boasted a number of top-class hospitality establishments as well as a range of guest houses and small bed and breakfast establishments (Lourens 2007b, 81). In addition, the product mix encompassed a number of newer product offerings such as health spas, golf courses, adventure activities, cultural experiences (offered by local black communities), fine dining, hiking trails and creative tourism experiences such as cooking courses. Further, the Association has actively promoted a number of special events, particularly in the low tourism season, such as a Midlands Meander Marathon, local dam swim (Midmar Mile), 'slow food' festival and creative festival (Lourens 2007b).

The Midlands Meander is the flagship South African case of how the private sector conceptualized and developed tourism as a once marginal economic sector and transformed it into the lead sector for LED. The leadership for development of this route tourism initiative has been provided by the Midlands Meander Association, which has evolved into a competent destination management organization. As the area has changed from an emerging tourism destination to a more mature one, the association shifted focus from simply marketing the attractions of the area to placing considerable emphasis upon product quality assurance, including environmental responsibility. For example, the association developed specific joining criteria for new products in the area in order to ensure that visitor expectations were continually met and thus building a good reputation for the destination (Lourens 2007a,b). Since 2000, the management of the Meander has actively pursued opportunities to assist emerging (black) artists and the development of tourism products in local communities. A new category of association membership was established as part of the Meander's outreach initiative and commitment to supporting and promoting local artists in the community.

The successes of the Meander are based upon a combination of factors. Lourens (2007b, 84) stresses the significance of having a 'clearly identified unique selling point' to establish the route, namely 'cottage industries in the country'. The area has evolved a wide range of complementary products that add value to the generic product. The build-up of management capacity has been critically important in the private sector route association. The Midlands Meander Association successfully overcame fragmentation, developed capacity and mobilized a range of diverse stakeholders, including local government, to collaborate for the development of the local economy (Lourens 2007a). The local council played a useful facilitative role in support of the Midlands Meander in terms of forging linkages between various spheres of government relating to particular tourism development issues, such as questions of road signage (Rogerson 2004b). Overall, in identifying success factors, the 'special role of local government and private sector stakeholders during the implementation and management of routes cannot be overemphasized' (Lourens 2007b, 91).

It is evident that many emerging South African routes have a shortage of tourism management, marketing skills and funding (ECIAfrica 2006a). The marketing of a route to a variety of market niches requires skilled management that understands the various tourism channels as well as the need for adequate financing. In the case of the Midlands Meander, core funding was secured through membership fees paid by private sector enterprises. It is acknowledged, however, that in poorer areas or peripheral regions of South Africa the prospect of a successful route initiative is militated against by 'the inability of individual enterprises to contribute towards membership fees: the basic building block of a meaningful initiative' (Lourens 2007b, 90).

Conclusions

It is argued in this chapter that the South African experience of developing tourism routes may offer certain lessons for the introduction of route tourism initiatives in other parts of Africa. The organization and support for route tourism in South Africa represent a critical local planning response for promoting an acceleration of tourism arrivals and, in certain cases, for achieving the broader objective of local 'shared growth', which is an important issue for tourism-led LED across Africa (Rogerson 2007b). In terms of strategic tourism development, the 'shared growth' is not only economic growth but also poverty reduction, employment creation, empowerment of disadvantaged groups, reduction of regional inequities within nations and ecological sustainability.

From the extensive record of route tourism initiatives in South Africa, the important work of Lourens (2007b) signals several key steps for the establishment and positioning of new routes. In establishing a tourism route, committed leadership is required to see potential and to develop a vision for a region. The conceptualization of a route must be based upon solid market research that identifies key target markets. In addition, an audit of products in the area must be conducted. A subsequent step is to scrutinize the area's tourism assets and isolate the unique selling features or experiences of an area and its products. Once the unique selling features are known, a macro-level strategic plan must be prepared to combine market requirements and the area's tourism assets. For a route driven by a private sector, the next step would be to determine the potential size of an association's membership base. Tourism product owners with 'the ability to complement the unique features and main themes of the route must be lobbied to join the organization from the early stages' (Lourens 2007b, 93). In completing the phase of route establishment, the recommended subsequent steps are the development of a clear brand identity, operational plan and financial management plan.

The South African record of route tourism successes and failures points to the vital initial role of the provision of necessary infrastructure in the form of adequate roads, telecommunications and signage as an essential starting point for route development in emerging destinations. In addition, it points to critical roles for the public sector, particularly concerning adequate macro-planning and ensuring a wider distribution of benefits by incorporating a pro-poor focus. Above all, the South African planning of route tourism underscores the importance of securing adequate financial resources for the establishment and support of sustainable route management organizations that are able to run the routes in a successful way.

Acknowledgements

Thanks are due to Marlien Lourens for critical inputs into this chapter, to Mrs Wendy Job for the preparation of the accompanying figure and to the National Research Foundation, Pretoria, for research funding support.

4 Community Development Strategies in the Kalahari: an Expression of Modernization's Monologue?

LAUREN DYLL

Introduction

This chapter examines aspects of South African and Botswanan national tourism agendas and approaches with regard to development among indigenous peoples. The comparative case study focuses on two communities – the ≠Khomani of Witdraai, in the Northern Cape of South Africa, and the !Xoo in Ngwatle, southern Botswana (see Fig. 4.1). Empirical research within the communities provides 'the specific' contextual illustrations that speak to and/or contradict 'the general'. Development 'for' the communities is primarily based on land reform and tourism and frequently reflects what can be termed as 'modernization's monologue'. Development and tourism strategies tend to implement a unidirectional flow of policies from governments and non-governmental organizations (NGOs), prescribing Western sociopolitical and technological values without engaging in a conversation with the supposedly beneficiary communities. Modernization, when applied to Third World nations, is thus often criticized as a 'veiled synonym for Westernization' (Servaes 1995, 41).

Despite South Africa's adoption of the key phrases 'participatory development,' 'grassroots communication' and the provision of 'human benefits' (de Villiers 2008), empirical examples reveal that modernization remains the preferred strategy. Modernization is not, however, an automatically workable model. Nevertheless, the World Bank, IMF and national development agencies continue to plan in terms of modernization approaches (cf. Bond 2004; Hirsch 2005).

My methodology incorporates auto-ethnography read through field experiences (2001–2008), interviews and observations from the field and draws on research undertaken since 1995 (cf. Tomaselli 1999; Holman Jones 2005; Tomaselli *et al.* 2008). Such experience, and being sensitive to the 'messiness' of development in practice, is important in understanding popular

Fig. 4.1. The location of research sites in South Africa and Botswana.

resistance to what Belinda Kruiper calls 'Western-type development stuff' (cf. McLennan-Dodd 2002). Kruiper, a Khoi descendent who married into the ≠Khomani, previously worked for the South African San Institute (SASI) (cf. Bregin and Kruiper 2004). An organic intellectual representing ≠Khomani perspectives (Tomaselli 2005), she is centrally involved in a variety of development, art and educational projects.

A Methodology Creating Dialogue

Purposive, opportunistic and snowball sampling were used to identify suitable informants in both communities. Informants speak Afrikaans in the Northern Cape. At Ngwatle, a few speak Afrikaans or English and Sesarwa, a mixture of Afrikaans, Setswana and !Kung. Key informants who speak Afrikaans or English were employed as translators. Our interactions were also assisted by two research affiliates fluent in the early Afrikaans dialect that typifies the expression of both groups. Our informants requested that their names be included in the write-up of interviews as they want to be written into history (cf. Tomaselli *et al.* 2008). Methods of documentation included audiotape recordings that were later transcribed, as well as written ethnography/field notes.

The research involves topics on representation and identity, cultural tourism and development. The new South African tourism offers 'enormous potential as a catalyst for economic and social development across the whole country' (DEAT 2005, 6). Early studies featured mostly the economic prospects of tourism. This economism led to a wave of studies that focused on the sociocultural, which placed tourism under critical scrutiny (Visser 2004a). There is therefore a need for cultural tourism-as-development to be investigated from a cultural studies perspective. My research aims to fill in the gap in the literature of the implementation of tourism-as-development that details the 'nitty-gritty' that arises out of the cultural context.

'Central to participatory research is the maintenance of an ongoing relationship between social researchers and community representatives, in the interests of assisting the planning and implementation of transformation aimed at meeting community needs, alleviating problems and facilitating community development' (Kelly and van der Riet 2001, 159). Researchers have visited the Northern Cape and Ngwatle every year since 1995, returning to the communities to provide feedback with written papers, photographs or videos produced from previous field trips.

Participatory research links with auto-ethnography (cf. Ellis and Bochner 2000; Holman Jones 2005; Tomaselli *et al.* 2008), where researchers problematize their positions within researcher–community relations. Personal experiences, interviews and observations from the field are included so that the research operates 'along a chain of more or less elaborated dialogues between a researcher and an ever-increasingly abstracted hierarchy of partners in the dialogue' (Tomaselli and Shepperson 2005, 11). Auto-ethnography 'permits readers to feel the moral dilemmas confronting researchers, to think *with* our narratives, instead of simply about them, and to join actively in the decision points which define the method' (Ellis and Bochner 2000, 735).

Auto-ethnography was complemented by a livelihoods survey, which generated data relating to how people at Ngwatle make a living (Njagi 2005). This involves crafts production and sale supported by Ghanzi-Craft and the local Nqwaa Khobee Xeya Trust (NKXT). Informal activities include hunting (legal and illegal), translating and operating *shebeens* (small alcohol-vending establishments). Formal employment is rare, but is occasionally available through the Trust, Safari Botswana Bound (SBB), local farms and public works programmes (Njagi 2005, 60–62). About 40% of the survey's respondents are recipients of regular government 'destitute rations'.

≠Khomani enterprise is measured via SASI's Cultural Resource Audit (CRA), which manages cultural resources as the primary means of development and leverages national and international donorship (Crawhall 2001). CRA creates an inventory of the community's cultural resources to produce tangible results that represent, explain and manage what is otherwise invisible (Crawhall 2001). Robins (2001, 834) questions whether the presentation of the ≠Khomani as a cohesive community with untapped traditional knowledge was a strategic fiction fashioned by the Bushmen and their NGO allies during the land claim. The optimistic images and narratives were replaced by reports of conflict, homicide, suicide, alcohol abuse, AIDS and social fragmentation (Robins 2001). Donors and NGOs provide aid according to specific agendas. These 'donor double visions' of Bushmen as both First Peoples and modern citizens-in-the-making, along with the CRA, are crucial in 'proving' the ≠Khomani's traditional knowledge, perhaps opening the door for donorship for them as a First People (Robins 2001, 833).

Despite their poverty, the !Xoo evidence a socially cohesive community and contented lifestyle (cf. Simões 2001; Dyll 2004). However, the traditional ≠Khomani, as recipients of huge amounts of state and donor aid, complain incessantly about being 'poor' and exploited. This contradiction is explained below.

South Africa: The ≠Khomani

The ≠Khomani lodged a land claim in 1991 in and around the then Kalahari Gemsbok National Park, from which they had been forcibly removed in 1972. Approximately 200 adults, for the first time, gathered as a community and, though lacking a cohesive identity (Robins 2001), named themselves the ≠Khomani (large group) to further the purposes of the land claim (cf. White 1995; Tomaselli 2005). After years of negotiation and verification, the claim was finally settled on 21 March 1999 (Grossman and Holden 2002).

Different ≠Khomani constituencies diverged on how to use their new land rights. The group nicknamed the *westerse mense* (Western people) became pastoralists. The remaining 80 or so who constitute the Kruiper clan identify themselves as traditionalists. Dawid Kruiper, the leader, and most of his patrilineal kin have, since 1991, earned their income through cultural tourism. They migrate between Andriesvale in the Northern Cape and, between 1991 and 2003, the Kagga Kamma Nature Reserve, among other sites in North West Province. The Kruipers adopted the identity of the romanticized image of pre-modern Bushmen popularized in *The Gods Must Be Crazy* (1980, 1989, 1991, 1993, 1996) films. Despite having been recipients of millions in aid since 1999, they remain poverty-stricken and socially dysfunctional. Apart from acting for television companies, they sell crafts on the roadside. In 2000, the ≠Khomani Sîsen Crafts Project was established with the help of SASI; it sells crafts in the area and retails them via curio stores in Cape Town.

The land restitution offered opportunities for two modes of development: agriculture and cultural tourism. SASI embarked upon cultural tourism as the primary strategy. Cultural tourism on a larger scale is embodied in !Xaus Lodge publicity, as 'the focal centre for experiencing the scenic unspoiled splendour of this vast arid land; to be drawn into the fascinating rituals, traditions and historical culture of … the first people of Southern Africa' (!Xaus Lodge 2008).

!Xaus Lodge is co-owned by the ≠Khomani and Mier communities, developed on ≠Khomani and Mier heritage lands. The Mier, classified as a 'coloured' community, also benefited from the claim. The third principal party is South African National Parks (SANParks). The agreement was signed by the government in the 'national interest, to finally settle the land claims of the communities and to establish a positive, cooperative relationship between the community and SANParks' (!Ae!Hai Kalahari Heritage Park Agreement 2002, 167).

During the 1990s and into the new millennium:

> Tourism has begun to find much wider recognition as an economic sector with the potential to make a contribution towards 'development' in destination areas ... Several question marks have been raised concerning the efficacy of tourism-led economic development, especially when tourism is the 'last resort' for development planning ... Given the often-limited opportunities for the participation of local people in the benefits of and decision-making about tourism, the oft-quoted arguments about tourism as a positive 'vehicle' for development' have consequently been questioned.
>
> (Rogerson and Visser 2004b, 2–3)

Although cultural tourism is often criticized as exploitative (cf. Bester and Buntman 1999), the reality is that it is often one of the few forms of self-employment for indigenous people (Tomaselli 1999).

The strategic framework for sustainable tourism development of the Department of Environmental Affairs and Tourism (DEAT) 2006 embraces the discourse of participatory development and the protection and promotion of indigenous rights. Objectives relevant for discussion in the present chapter are to:

- develop tourism with dignity – encouraging mutual respect for all cultures and eliminating all forms of discrimination on the basis of language, religion, culture, race, gender, age, wealth and ability;
- provide tourism education, training, awareness and capacity-building programmes, especially aimed at previously neglected groups;
- use tourism as a catalyst for human development, focusing on gender equality, career development and the implementation of national labour standards;
- empower community structures through, for example, involvement in the marketing of cultural experiences and practices to tourists; and
- encourage community participation in the planning, development, implementation and management of tourism projects.

While these aims are a positive reinforcement of a move towards participatory development, life at the grassroots level at times contradicts these good intentions.

Botswana: The !Xoo

The ≠Khomani's case is an investment success story in comparison with their northern neighbours in Botswana. The South African Government recognizes the rights of indigenous people and the symbolic importance of the return of heritage land. Botswana, in contrast, does not recognize the Bushmen (or Basarwa, the official Botswanan term) as indigenous. They are, instead, viewed as the 'poor and marginal beneficiaries of a government development programme' (Saugestad 2001, 26). Since independence in 1966, Botswana has earned a reputation as a 'shining example of democracy', has a good human rights record and no discrimination in any formal laws or regulations exists. However, a closer examination of Botswana's policies suggests otherwise (Good 2003). One of Botswana's main projects has been to create:

> a unified nation-state out of the diversified Bechuanaland Protectorate, trying to apply an old Western concept of nationalism to the context of new African states with mostly arbitrary boundaries. In this process, 'ethnicity' has been linked to 'tribalism' and has been seen as an anathema to unified national development...Botswana has chosen to elevate the culture and language of the numerically dominant Tswana people to a new national, neutral standard. In effect, this 'Tswanadom' has become the dominant symbol for the whole Botswana nation, and has been presented as the image of a non-racial, culturally homogenous state.
>
> (Saugestad 2001, 28)

Botswana avoids the term 'indigenous' as 'recognizing a group as indigenous implies a commitment to let the views, values and aspirations of the group in question guide their own development' (Saugestad 2001, 31). Denying the Bushmen the status of indigenous therefore disqualifies them from claiming specific rights or exemption from modernization (cf. Mikalsen in press).

Ngwatle is situated in Kgalagadi District 1 (KD1), a controlled hunting area (CHA). The CHA is designated for community use and management by rural area dweller (RAD) communities. RADs provide one strategy for the government to avoid ethnic categories. It is a conventional, low-intensity rural development programme that includes groups other than Bushmen (cf. Hitchcock 1998; Saugestad 2001).

KD1 hosts three settlements within its boundaries. Ukhwi is the largest, with about 450 people, while around 180 reside in Ngwatle and 170 in Ncaang. The major ethnic groups in the area are the !Xoo and the Bakgalagadi. Historically, Bushmen worked for and were dependent on the Bakgalagadi and were perceived as inferior (cf. Flyman 2000). The Nqwaa Khobee Xeya Trust (NKXT), a community-based organization, manages land use. Despite the direct involvement of the government in planning projects, the Trust asserts the importance of community participation. The KD1 concession is managed by Safari Botswana Bound (SBB), which caters to international tourists and hunters. Unlike RADs, Ngwatle is not provided with a clinic and formal school, and is poverty-stricken and dependent on government for water and provisions. Its income is generated via selling crafts through Ghanzi-Craft and the Trust, informal activities such as hunting, translating and operating *shebeens* as well as formal employment from SBB (Hitchcock 1998; Njagi 2005; Tomaselli 2007).

Features of the four main development paradigms (modernization, dependency, development support communication and participatory development) exist alongside one another in both communities studied. This makes development in practice much more complex than how it is portrayed in theory.

Call for Modernization

The United Nations (UN) was formed in October 1945. The UN's multilateral agencies, the World Bank and their most influential member, the USA, aimed to rebuild Europe after World War II. The US-implemented Marshall Plan included humanitarian assistance and aid in resisting communism and reconstituting European markets for US goods. Having achieved success in Europe, President Truman proposed development of the Third World. Truman (1949) noted that this world was primitive and stagnant. Poverty was seen as a threat both to them and to more prosperous areas and, for the first time in history, humanity possessed the knowledge and skill to relieve the suffering of these people (cf. Melkote and Steeves 2001). The relief was to be delivered via modernization and investment in much the same way as had occurred in Europe. In the 1960s, the notion of development included investment in technology, especially in agricultural production and techniques, industrial machinery and communication infrastructure. Development was equated with industrialization.

Macro Theories

The modernization paradigm emerged from both macroeconomic and social evolutionary theory. The macro model was concerned with rapid growth as measured by gross national product (GNP). The two main factors were the productive resources available to a society and the economic institutions to guide the use of the resources (Weaver and Jameson 1978). Investment produces goods and machinery, generating sufficient capital for industrialization and redistribution of income and resources. The trickle-down of benefits to the broader population, for example through the creation of jobs, is an important component in this model (Rostow 1960). The unilinear process of development and associated communication strategies constitutes what I refer to as the 'monologue' nature of modernization.

Monologues suggest single and narrow strategies and explanations, removing empirical complexity from analysis, and may offer solutions that ignore community needs and concerns. For example Kruiper observed that, during the ≠Khomani land claim, SASI had been 'too focused on the political side of the issue. We've been too focused on empowering the Committee and the CPA (Communal Property Association)' (Kruiper 2000). However, 'little real progress was made and the situation deteriorated, with known mismanagement of funds and assets, devaluation of such assets, growing social problems, lack of real support from government and deep and bitter division between members of the families who had lived in the park'

(Grossman and Holden 2002, 1). Eventually, the South African Human Rights Commission (SAHRC) intervened. Its report addressed urgent issues such as the land claim, human rights, government delivery of services, education and policing matters (SAHRC 2004).

The World Bank supported the Enlightenment principle of *laissez-faire* – complete independence from the government and other authorities. This development model was grounded in a neoclassical Western approach. However, this system was frequently insensitive to the needs of minority groups, and resulted in environmental degradation (cf. Melkote and Steeves 2001; Njagi 2005). All countries were assumed to follow a unilinear course of development from traditionalism to modernization as a result of the above-mentioned principles.

The modernization model remains dominant, adapting to the shifting political, economic and technological status of nations. Few formally accepted business or management plans were implemented to manage the funds or to administer land returned to the ≠Khomani (Grossman and Holden 2002, 4). The Northern Cape provincial government agreed to appoint a land manager only in January 2007 to arrest the decline and to institute land management (Grossman 2007). It is of vital importance that national development strategies and development workers advising these communities understand how the ≠Khomani encounter their world, and what their needs are in setting up sustainable prospects. 'There's development being spoken about, San cultural villages being developed ... but amidst all this the people at ground level are floundering, despair is creeping in again, there is a loss of dignity' (Kruiper 2000).

The Department of Environmental Affairs and Tourism (DEAT) allocated R6.5 million to build !Xaus Lodge. However, its construction exemplifies many of the development mistakes made in strategies that lack sufficient knowledge of the local context, in cultural, environmental and market interest terms. Numerous challenges have resulted from the location and poor construction. The Lodge operator lists these as:

- Location far off the tourist route.
- The noisy, expensive fuel-intensive generator is the only electricity supply.
- Salty water.
- Roofing and walkways were poorly designed and had to be rebuilt, delaying the opening of the Lodge.
- Atrocious service roads.
- The Mier and ≠Khomani owners had largely written off the project, which had been neglected for 5 years.
- The funders and state had lost interest.

DEAT (2005) therefore disregarded one of its own objectives to 'encourage community participation in the planning, development, implementation and management of tourism projects'. The appointment of a commercial Lodge operator, Transfrontier Parks Destinations, in 2006 witnessed a dramatic paradigm shift from a modernization top-down approach to a more participatory bottom-up communication in its operational phase (cf. Finlay in press).

One of Botswana's long-term objectives, from The Bushmen Development Programme (1974–1977) to RAD (from 1991), is integration with wider society:

> Most commonly, integration was taken to mean that point of assimilation of the Bushmen into the predominant Tswana agro-pastoral society entirely on the terms of the latter. Total integration was taken to mean that point of assimilation at which Bushmen were no longer identifiable in the society. The perspective was much influenced by evolutionary ideas, with the Bushmen seen as representing an obsolete adaptation which the Tswana had left long ago.
>
> (Saugestad 2001, 121)

The focus on integrating or assimilating Bushmen into modern Botswana society places them within the confines of a colonial dispensation. This is reflected in the words of Gadi, a captivating story teller: 'We left our tradition behind because we could no longer live good lives…The suffering of the Bushman nowadays … The government took away the tradition of the Bushmen and gave his own tradition to them' (Gadi 2003).

The 'civilizing mission' of colonialism is still apparent in the education system in Botswana. Although education can be a positive agent of meaningful development, it can still serve to tutor poor communities against the 'obstacles to modernization' such as tradition, superstition and fatalism. The building of schools and employment of teachers are clearly defined development outputs. However, Saugestad (2001, 161) explains that factors such as quality of teaching, its cultural appropriateness and social surroundings determine to what extent education contributes to a child's development. So far, there has been no change in curricula or teaching material to accommodate the Bushmen's cultural background. Where Bushmen are mentioned in text books they are assigned the role of the quintessential 'other' of the less civilized past. They have cultural and material problems in adapting to mainstream education and they need to be supported throughout their school careers. The children are burdened with expectations from both teachers and educators, but find themselves without the support needed to answer the expectations (cf. also Biesele 1995, 2000).

There is a duality in the status of First People. With strong traditions that are often frowned upon by the modern world, they are expected to take part in it while also *wanting* to be involved in aspects of it. This is expressed in ≠Khomani Lys Kruiper's thoughts about her son's education:

> … our children … today … still live the way we did in the past but they also go to school. So now they don't want forever to live the life we used to live. If my child tells me today, no mother I don't want to live like that anymore, I will talk to him. What I am saying is if the day comes when I'm not around anymore, my child must know what I left him with. And he will know how to make his own life without having to say that traditions cannot work in a Western life. He will know how to do that.
>
> (Kruiper 2007)

SAHRC addressed some of these challenges to education for ≠Khomani children in the 2004 inquiry into human rights violations within the community. Concerns were raised about the failure of the Andriesvale–Askham schools to manage the integration of children with traditional ways of living – both socially and within the school curriculum. The opinion was expressed that the schools should equip children with a broader education and combine learning needs related to the immediate environment and unique cultural composition of the ≠Khomani with those of the formal curricula and the realities of the wider South African and global contexts (SAHRC 2004, 25). The lure of income generation from cultural tourism and selling 'traditional' Bushman artefacts at roadside stalls also hinders education among ≠Khomani children. They experience difficulty in functioning in a confined environment when they are used to being free to move about the land. The focus on cultural tourism therefore plays its part in obstructing development, as the report summated that 'tourism and education are clashing' (SAHRC 2004).

Other findings in the report support my argument that modernization's monologue still functions in eradicating tradition as an obstacle to development. The Department of Social Affairs tends to neglect the basic needs of the ≠Khomani children, citing community division and the children's 'foreign cultural background' as obstacles (SAHRC 2004, 29). However, SAHRC (2004, 30) made recommendations to counteract this attitude towards education and tradition such as:

- Management components of the schools attended by ≠Khomani San children need to develop new and innovative ways to address the education-related problems experienced by the ≠Khomani San community.
- Priority should be given by the Department of Education to further the language project, aimed at encouraging the use of indigenous language among ≠Khomani San children.

If the recommendations are put into action, education may serve as an agent for development for the community and no longer further the stigma of 'being Bushman'.

In Botswana, the objective of 'integration' is the RAD settlement strategy. RADs require that people abandon their nomadism for nucleated villages. Communities are urged to relocate due to costs of providing services such as water, schools and clinics. For standard infrastructural investments, there must be a minimum size of user population (Saugestad 2001; Hitchcock 2002). This occurred in Ngwatle, as residents informed us that 'Ngwatle is no longer a recognized settlement'. They are 'encouraged' to relocate to neighbouring villages with RAD status in order to access better clinics and schools. They suspect that this is why the government's water service to Ngwatle is slow and neglectful (Miriam 2003). On arrival in Ngwatle in 2003, the first thing I noticed was that one of the two water tanks which had been broken and was lying on its side in 2002 had still not been fixed. Even more devastating was the allegation that an elderly lady had died of thirst. The community members were to attend her funeral that night.

Rostow's (1960) unilinear evolutionary model proposes that every society would pass through five stages, starting from traditional society and leading to the last phase of high mass consumption where the majority of people could afford consumption of luxury goods. He argues that traditional economies were hampered by limited production facilities, based on pre-Newtonian notions of science and technology, and constrained by rigid social structure and 'irrational psychological attitudes'.

The Molopo Lodge, located next to Witdraai where the traditional ≠Khomani live, operates a liquor store at its entrance. Some ≠Khomani craft sellers sit at the roadside opposite the store. They price their crafts in terms of the cost of a bottle of brandy or cheap wine. The Lodge managers complain that alcohol abuse causes fighting and frustration in the community. When Rostow speaks about the linear path along which developing communities should pass, through the purchasing of basic necessities to that of luxury goods, it is evident that there is a clash between what is proposed at the macro level and what occurs on the ground. Some ≠Khomani sacrifice the purchasing of 'necessities' in order to purchase what in Western terms is seen as a 'luxury' item. This behaviour would be considered 'irrational' by modernization theorists. In July 2007 I purchased a painted ostrich egg from artist Silikat van Wyk. When asked by a new researcher to the group on what he would spend the R200, his answer was a new pair of shoes and call time to phone his daughter. However, 3 hours later we saw Silikat again, this time intoxicated and still wearing his old soleless shoes.

Micro Theory

The concept of *empathy* is central to value changes among traditional individuals as a pre-requisite for modernity. Empathy is 'the capacity to see oneself in another fellow's situation ... which is an indispensable skill for people moving out of traditional settings' (Lerner 1958). Empathetic people are assumed to evidence a higher degree of capacity for change. It was believed that mobility stimulated urbanization, which increases literacy and consequently economic and political participation. Lerner also placed his trust in the mass media to stimulate mobility and economic development, since they are the 'motivators' and 'movers' for change and development. Although Lerner's theories were clear and optimistic, these values do not fit neatly into the Kalahari development context.

Silikat exemplifies Lerner's concept of empathy. Silikat wants to be an accountant (Kruiper 2000). He therefore has the 'capacity to see [himself] in another fellow's situation'. However, SASI is not aiming at the development of individuals, except within specific projects. Silikat is a talented artist with exceptional business skills (cf. McLennan-Dodd 2003; Dyll 2007). He 'told the committees before, is there no way of helping? You know like a workshop where [he] can also maybe train the people. Like [his] Bushmen people' (van Wyk and Kruiper 2001). This would give Silikat the opportunity to develop respect not only for himself but for those he trains, as knowledge would be coming from a community member and not from government programmes or NGOs.

Important questions surround the notion of community development: 'How can you develop a community? When we talk about developing a community we're looking at structures, municipal offices, toilets, towns, roads', following the guidelines of the modernization development paradigm (cf. Shepperson and Tomaselli 2002). 'Where does the community then come in? Who's going to feed them? Who's going to create jobs?' (Kruiper 2001b). Another hindrance to Silikat's ability to develop himself, and an example of how 'messy' development can be, is the 'tyranny of the community' (cf. Dyll 2007). The fact that his art appeals to passing tourists has caused problems for him in his clan. They are jealous that his art sells and not theirs. He used to conduct tracking tours for tourists; however, the community would not allow this as he was earning more than they were (Carter 2001). This again points to the disjuncture between the theoretical concept of empathy and what occurs in reality in a country or community with different beliefs, values and lifestyles from developed nations. Silikat's empathy does not assist in his personal development, and his innovative ideas will not be seen and used because, in an African context, the community shapes the individual (cf. Blankenberg 1999). It is therefore important that national development strategies take the differences and local ontologies into account when implementing development strategies.

Development Communication and the Role of the Media

Lasswell (1948) conceptualized mass media effects as 'WHO says WHAT in which CHANNEL to WHOM and with what EFFECT?'. Based on this concept, a framework called the hypodermic needle (Berlo 1960), or bullet theory of communication effects (Schramm 1964), emerged. The early models of communication effects became popular with communication for development professionals after World War II. They assumed a linear process that occurs when someone sends a message via a channel to a receiver and gets a response called feedback. When the initiative and ability of the message lie overwhelmingly with the senders, who are the creators of national development agendas or local community development agencies, the result is an impersonal one-way flow of messages to the 'subjects' of development. This model reinforces my argument of modernization communication models as being of the same nature as a monologue, since they highlight omnipotent sources and passive receivers.

Poor communication and lack of opportunity for feedback have delayed the creation of good relationships, essential for sustainable community development, among government, NGOs and local communities. In the Northern Cape, communication is hampered not only by the lack of infrastructure but also by the absence of efforts to address prejudices, misconceptions and misunderstandings (SAHRC 2004). The members of the broader community claim that they receive no feedback on developments from the CPA. In addition, members of the CPA allege that continuous attempts to communicate with the Minister and Director General of the Department of Land Affairs and the Minister and Director General of DEAT have failed. They claim that this amounts to an infringement of their right to be heard by civil servants, to observe administrative action and to benefit generally from cooperative governance (SAHRC 2004). If this is the case, then DEAT's (2006) objective to 'empower community structures through, for example, involvement in the marketing of cultural experiences and practices to tourists' is not being met.

Research after World War II suggested that mass media were agents more of reinforcement than of direct change. Despite the shift in emphasis, the role of communication in the Third World was still interpreted as a transmission of information and persuasion, especially in agriculture, health and education. Researchers discovered that 'individuals were more influenced in their political decisions by members of their primary and peer groups than the combined mass media' and that overall exposure to mass media was low (Melkote and Steeves 2001, 109). This two-step flow accounts for the indirect effect of mass media: the first step of influence is from the mass media to opinion leaders, while the second step is from the leaders to others in the community (Katz and Lazarsfeld 1955). However, the two-step flow of communication does not always occur on the ground. Kort Jan, an elder in the !Xoo community, explained that the Trust board, as the 'opinion leaders' in Ngwatle, 'talk amongst themselves but never tell anybody' (Kort Jan 2002), illustrating the lack of feedback inherent in the top-down communication mode.

In postwar development, the mass media served as agents and indices of modernization. Media 'had the potential to blow the winds of modernization into isolated traditional communities and replace the structures of life, values, and behaviors there with ones seen in modern Western societies' (Melkote and Steeves 2001, 144). Media provided the ideal vehicle for preparing individuals in developing nations for social change by establishing a climate of modernization. Schramm (1964) extends Lerner's arguments in favour of modernization through mass media, which he terms 'the magic multipliers' of development benefits. He argues that mass media could accomplish the transition to new customs, practices and social relationships. Schramm, unlike Lerner, takes cultural linkages into account, acknowledging resistance to change and urging understanding and participation, although he still maintains a strong correlation between high media exposure and development.

The developmentalist approach assumed that progressive change would come from the centre and trickle out to the periphery. The connection between those perceived as 'haves' and 'have-nots' would eradicate the latter's parochial practices and sentiments that constituted a supposed 'barrier' to development. Mass media and technology are imperative for functioning in modern society – but the case is not that one should not introduce technology to marginalized communities but that, rather, one cannot assume that the messages communicated via media are accessed or transparently understood by these communities. The notion of the media as an agent of change is a correct one (cf. Tomaselli and Dunn 2001), but the role of the media operates differently in Africa as overall exposure to media, other than radio, is low.

To compound the problem, disadvantaged communities, or the 'subjects in modernization', do not have the necessary infrastructural resources to transform 'communicated' ideas (via the mass media such as radio, television and the Internet – agents of modernization) into actions. In addition, many poor areas do not have electricity. Television became a symbol of elitism in Africa, a representation of modernity and therefore an *agent for* and *symbol of* modernity.

Within the diffusion of innovations paradigm, the assumed route for change from a traditional to a modern person was the communication and acceptance of new ideas from sources external to the social system. Rogers (1962) defines an innovation as an idea, practice or object perceived as new by an individual, and then uses technology as a synonym for an innovation. The emphasis of this approach was again on communication effects as it supported the ability of media messages and opinion leaders to persuade target audiences to adopt exogenously conceived innovations (Melkote and Steeves 2001, 145).

This approach was evident on a micro level in the Sîsen Craft project, when the manager or 'opinion leader' allegedly imposed a method of mass craft production foreign to the ≠Khomani. Kruiper (2001a) claims the project initially encouraged:

> one person drilling holes, the next person forming the beads, one burning the image ... She's working with people learning craft in order to survive. And she comes as the person to teach them. But we have natural artists. There's Silikat, he's a natural teacher, he's inspired so many young people who are brilliant artists today ... Why should he not be then one of the first identified who could have ... set up the project?

Rogers (1962) sets out five stages in the process of acceptance, namely: awareness, interest, evaluation, trial and adoption. This highlights another unilinear model within modernization's monologue. Diffusion studies differentiated groups of people in terms of personality, media behaviour, social status and how these categories affected their rate of adoption. For example, early adopters were usually younger, had higher financial and social status and were equipped with better mental ability than later adopters, called laggards. Diffusion of innovations therefore emphasized the nature and role of communication in facilitating dissemination within local communities.

!Xaus Lodge owners include the Mier, a coloured community accustomed to modern life and all that comes with it (tertiary education and training; new media such as cell phones and the Internet). The ≠Khomani, many of whom live at the margins of the modern world, lack formal education and depend primarily on cultural tourism as a means of survival. If one were to situate the two communities in terms of Rogers' definition of early adopters and laggards, one could argue that the Mier operate as the early adopters and the ≠Khomani as the laggards, based on their media behaviour and social status. Deon, a guide and craft maker at the Lodge, resigned as he felt he was not being taken seriously and, displaying a desire for change and personal development, or empathy, explained that he did not have access to opportunities to 'network', such as being granted permission to use the single Internet portal, and vehicles, as they were simply to focus on the cultural tourism.

Deon's attitude towards 'work' further complicates the situation and highlights the complexity of community development. Deon complained that they were asked to perform other tasks at the Lodge, such as making beds, but refused as 'there is no earning'. For him, work means 'being himself', doing what he usually does, sitting around the fire making crafts, creating his own space and time and, only after that, would he be able to assist elsewhere. This is indicative of how research and media attention have positioned the traditional ≠Khomani in relation to entertainment and intellectual production (Tomaselli 2005, 2007). To be a 'Bushman' in the tourism sector holds currency, particularly if you are ≠Khomani and even more so if you are a Kruiper. During the same trip, I was walking along the road when two Kruiper brothers presented themselves to us in an almost James Bond fashion: '*Die naam is Kruiper, Pien Kruiper*' (The name's Kruiper, Pien Kruiper). Unlike Bond, however, these men stretched out their arms, not in handshakes but as hands expecting handouts. I have dubbed this the 'Kruiper currency' – organized begging replaces formal job descriptions.

Extension Agents and External Constraints

UNESCO and the World Bank attempted to counter perceived backwardness by sending extension agents to the Third World. The extension system was to 'decide what innovations were best for its clients, followed by campaigns to convince them of their choice' (Melkote and Steeves 2001, 56). The opportunity for the innovations to assist communities depends on whether development workers take into account local people's ontologies. In a conversation with Belinda Kruiper, she advised that for problematizing and establishing solutions to development issues, and perhaps assisting in the implementation of innovations, 'NGOs should let the Bushmen draw in the sand to explain how they feel and what they want. They are not stupid or illiterate, they have different ways and one is drawing in the sand' (B. Kruiper 2002). This made sense to me as in a previous conversation with Toppies Kruiper he described the traditionalists' relationship with SASI, the Sîsen Craft Project and the *westerse mense*.

He also explained the idea behind the cultural village that had been built a couple of years before. Unfortunately, the village was not successful. In all his explanations, Toppies drew pictures in the sand to reaffirm what he was saying or perhaps to explain more clearly. In encouraging mainly top-down methods of communication, development workers cast doubt on the validity of local methods and knowledge, and gain only a superficial understanding of the people's development needs. Disregard for local knowledge became a problem for SANParks and the construction of !Xaus Lodge. During a visit to the lodge before it was completed in July 2007, the ≠Khomani advised the builders that they were using the incorrect thatch for the chalet roofs. Their warning was ignored and the wind wreaked havoc on the initial roofing.

Only in the 1970s did US communication scholars realize there was an alternative, that of external constraints on adoption. They turned their attention to communication constraints such as the lack of access to media and illiteracy in the Third World. While perhaps not negating the possibility of 'internal psychological factors' working against adoption, a positive turn was that they began to focus on searching for factors that could make projects more relevant to the needs of disadvantaged groups, by prioritizing basic needs, including food, shelter, education and employment (Melkote and Steeves 2001).

An area with external constraints to development is Ngwatle. Access to water is restricted and they have only one water tank, which is filled approximately every 2 weeks by the local government. RAD villages are provided with salt water for their livestock, unlike in Ngwatle. In a conversation with Jon Jon, the importance of the role of water in development was made clear. He explained that the small pre-school was for *die klein kinders* (the small children), but that they often cannot attend because when there is no water the children cannot concentrate (Jon Jon 2002). The school therefore lies vacant on occasion and, in this context, education is unable to operate as an agent of development.

The ≠Khomani are also negatively affected by external constraints. Blade Witbooi and Dawid Gooi are roadside craft sellers. Blade and Dawid completed a tracking course and armed guard training in order to work at !Xaus, as SANParks requires two armed guards with the tracker in a group of ten. Blade and Dawid, however, decided not to work there. When we spoke to Blade he explained his decision: 'At the Lodge we would have taken the visitors for walks. But I just felt ... see I don't have a certificate yet. I still have not been empowered. And that is a big job. A responsible job ... Look I also need the acknowledgement through my certificate. Then I am legal. Then I will be empowered' (Witbooi 2007).

In order to pass the armed guard course and receive certificates, an examination needs to be written in English. This highlights the insensitivity of the programme to the specifics of the Northern Cape and disputes DEAT's (2006) objective to 'develop tourism with dignity … [and] eliminate all forms of discrimination on the basis of language, religion, culture, race, gender, age, wealth and ability'. The *lingua franca* spoken in the area is Afrikaans, and therefore examining in English excludes the majority of people, particularly Bushmen, from formal employment. Bureaucracy serves as an external constraint, alienating Blade and Dawid from employment at the Lodge that is co-owned by the ≠Khomani. This also suggests that the pro-literacy bias associated with the modernization paradigm still harmfully impacts members of marginalized communities.

Criticisms

The modernization paradigm has been criticized for the abstractness, ahistoricity and inappropriateness of many of its models in relation to Third World development. The criticism stems from Rostow who had 'taken the pre-requisites of economic growth from the historical experience of the West and applied them as pre-conditions for growth in non-Western nations in the future' (Melkote and Steeves 2001, 175). However, the local context of developing countries made it difficult for them to recreate the development path of the West.

The dependency/disassociation theory grew from within developing countries in the 1970s in reaction to the modernization paradigm. The original version of dependency theory was outlined by Baran (1957) and Gunder Frank (1967). They argue that the prevailing conditions in developing nations are not a stage in the evolution towards development but rather a result of international structures imposed from the West. Baran (1957) contends that the capitalist countries had become 'developed' by exploiting their colonies for centuries. Gunder Frank (1967) elaborated the theory with his concept of 'metropolis–satellite' or 'centre–periphery' to characterize the nature of imperialist economic relations.

Dependency creates a vicious cycle. The government and even NGOs have been accused of depending on and exploiting the idea of the 'authentic pre-modern Bushman' to turn the Northern Cape into an attractive tourism area. Due to the desire for tourism, '[SASI] still want the Bushmen community in skins and [they] want to use the platform to develop them to bring funding in but hold them there as an attraction' (Kruiper 2001b). This notion is supported by Robins' (2001) discussion of 'donor double vision' and how the global discourses on indigeneity are brokered by NGOs in order to attract funding. This image of pristine First People is then reappropriated at the grassroots by the Bushmen. The South African Government, NGOs, donors and the ≠Khomani themselves are therefore dependent on the image of the 'traditional Bushman' in order to attract funding. This discourse appears to be pigeonholing the ≠Khomani as being able to engage only in cultural tourism as development, negating opportunities to develop themselves in other ways. It is evident that some ≠Khomani welcome a change from cultural tourism and wish to start other development projects. As the previous manager of the *Tentepark* in Witdraai, where the majority of cultural tourism took place, Abraham Meintjies (2002) told us: 'All my previous plans came to nothing. I'm now starting with a new idea for the whole of next year to see if that will be successful … the project of a vegetable garden for the Lodges around here … Fresh vegetables and so on to supply them with. That is the first development idea that I can put forward.'

However, during the most recent research trip in July 2008, there was still no vegetable garden. Without assisting these initiatives, the economy of 'organized begging' (Ellis 2001) will continue. There is dependency on NGOs, both for handouts and as scapegoats, to lay the blame for the lack of progress.

For communities removed from the centre, developmentalism has eroded their control over their lifestyles, natural resources and local narratives, and their cultural meanings and social arrangements have been devalued (Melkote and Steeves 2001, 156). Belonging to a marginalized indigenous minority usually goes hand-in-hand with poverty. 'Welfare programmes directed towards indigenous minorities often increase dependency, instead of reducing it, since aid is directed to symptoms rather than to the underlying causes of poverty' (Saugestad 2001, 31). In Botswana, the Trust signed an agreement that gave SBB exclusive rights to conduct hunting and photographic safaris in KD1 and sold 25% of its wildlife quota to it. Individuals are therefore able only to act as guides for tourists who hunt, and they are dependent on a portion of meat from the hunt and some payment.

The criticism of insensitivity stems from the consequences of mega-development projects such as hydroelectric dams, tourism, highways and mines. In most cases, these developments have displaced people from their land, livelihoods and communities. The Botswana Government claimed to be relocating Bushmen from the Central Kalahari Game Reserve (CKGR) in the name of development. A Minister of Local Government, Margaret Nasha (2002), stated that 'The issue of the Basarwa here is a human-rights issue. Can you allow a section of the population to continue living in the manner they are doing, and not accessing information, education for their children and health facilities?' She then contradicted herself by equating the Bushman's forced removal to that of culling elephants – ignoring the *human* in Botswana's claimed concern for human rights. 'Sometimes I equate it to the elephants. We once had the same problem when we wanted to cull the elephants and people said no' (Nasha 2002).

The issue here is that the Bushmen wanted to stay in CKGR, and to continue living as they had. The idea that most development strategies based within the dominant paradigm benefit the already wealthy is reiterated here. Much speculation has occurred as to why the government is insistent on moving the Bushmen, ranging from mining diamonds to tourism (cf. Good 2003; Mikalsen in press). Ngwatle resident Gadi (2003) questions: 'We ask [the government] why we have to move. They say ... this place of ours, there are diamonds, there is gold. But they haven't yet taken any diamonds or gold. They say that is why we have to move, it is because of that.'

Conclusions

In order for community development to assist the poor, it can no longer be as highly prescriptive as it is with modernization's monologue, which privileges mass communication and neglects informal communication channels that are more salient to poorer sectors in society, especially those in rural areas. Participatory communication opens up horizontal communication, therefore deconstructing modernization's monologue through *dialogue* that enables participants to identify and explore issues that have meaning for them.

Modernization in general is optimistic. However, its practitioners lack self-criticism. Although there are points of positive reference within modernization, it is necessary to examine the power relations within development schemes to ensure that they are participatory and not prescriptive. We have to ask ourselves: development for whom and under what circumstances?

This may be easier said than done, however. The terms 'empowerment', 'participatory' and 'sustainability' are quite often glibly adopted by national agendas. They can be seductive traps for well-meaning community development donors, while they are notoriously difficult to achieve in practice (cf. Chennells 2005). Participatory development needs certain parameters:

- a cohesive community;
- full participation and open communication between donors;
- NGOs/Trusts and the broader community where community members do not feel alienated from the 'development discourse'; and
- access to resources and basic services, suitable basic skills training in hospitality, tracking as well as in banking and bookkeeping – basically, how to cope with modernity, skills which appear to be missing from the Northern Cape and Ngwatle communities.

Development is particularly difficult due to the 'donor double vision' of Bushmen as both First People and modern citizens-in-the-making (Robins 2001, 833). The contradictions embedded within these discourses on tradition and civic citizenship deter development. Possible consequences include:

- further intra-community division between the 'traditional' ≠Khomani and *westerse* Bushmen;
- concentration on cultural tourism as the sole means of development for the 'traditional' group; and
- dependency on donors, film companies and researchers based on their image as 'traditional pre-modern Bushmen'.

This dual mandate speaks to the problematic colonial legacy of the dichotomy between modernity and tradition. However, the everyday experiences of the ≠Khomani negate the neat dichotomy of 'modern' and 'traditional' as: 'The hybridized conditions of everyday life in the Kalahari include "local" knowledge, practices and identities as well as [Bushman] access to "exogenous" cyber-technologies, fax machines, cellular phones and international indigenous peoples' conferences in Europe and North America' (Robins 2001, 835).

Extreme marginalization is possibly the consequence of this double vision for the !Xoo. Botswana's national agenda of integration-as-development, its desire for Bushmen to be assimilated as modern citizens and the !Xoo's refusal to move to larger settlements with RAD status have resulted in their village being denied basic services.

'Modernity continues to be associated with progress, development, "the West", science and technology, high standards of living, rationality and order, while tradition is associated with stasis, stagnation, underdevelopment, poverty and superstition' (Robins 2001, 835).

Botswana's development agenda urges Bushmen to be 'citizens-in-the-making' and views tradition as inimical to development, therefore embodying the ideology of modernization. In contrast, South Africa's development agenda valorizes Bushmen as First People and, as a result, many development agendas for indigenous people involve cultural tourism. Respect for Bushmen in South Africa is therefore a far cry from Botswana's attitude.

The point of departure for community development should be less of a focus on externally introduced ideas, technology and innovations, which at times undermine the indigenous communities' capacity for development. Rather than blaming the failure of development and economic growth on cultural barriers or tradition, we should investigate the propensity of indigenous communities to create their own innovations.

Acknowledgements

The financial assistance of the KwaZulu-Natal University and the National Research Foundation, Social Sciences and Humanities, toward this research is hereby acknowledged. Opinions expressed and conclusions arrived at are those of the author and not necessarily attributed to the Foundation. I am indebted to Prof. Keyan Tomaselli for his insightful comments and assistance in completing this chapter.

5 Selling Places and Constructing Local Cultures in Tourism: the Role of the Ovahimba in Namibian Tourism Promotion

Jarkko Saarinen and Maaria Niskala

Introduction

> Romanticized by tourists, Namibia's Himba struggle to maintain control of their life and lands.
>
> (Lange 2008, 1)

In Southern Africa, the tourism industry is a growing and important element in the regional economies. Many Southern African countries presently see the promotion of tourism as a good strategy that can be used to attract foreign capital and investors through 'showing' local indigenous cultures (Binns and Nel 2002; Saarinen 2007a). As a result, many rural and peripheral places and communities in the region are currently tied to wider economies and cultural and social networks through the development of the tourism industry, which is ever more global in scale (see Rogerson 1997, 2007b; Visser and Rogerson 2004).

Tourism is also increasingly used as a medium for many societal and economic goals in Namibia (see Government of Namibia 1994). In general, tourism is considered to have major potential for employment and income generation in the country, and the role of community-based tourism and community-based natural resource management with tourism development elements in particular are highlighted by government policy (MET 2005a, 2007; see Massyn 2007). However, as generally acknowledged, tourism is a highly polarized activity with impacts on space and time not evenly distributed (Hall and Page 1999, 1; Milne and Ateljevic 2001). Therefore, the developmental role and potential of tourism in different places and communities may vary greatly. The benefits and control over the resources and practices in development can also be problematic from a local community perspective.

These challenges in the local–global nexus in tourism development highlight the need for discussion of the nature of tourism and community relations and the role of local communities in tourism development. There exists a wide area of research on tourism planning, development and community participation (see Selin 1999; Hall 2000; Tosun 2000; Scheyvens 2002) that correctly address the problems of, e.g. communication, involvement, empowerment and uneven power relations. In addition to these crucial issues, the symbolic roles in which people are placed in tourism products may have a great effect on their possibilities in participating in tourism, its planning and development, and on having control as a resource of tourism (Mowforth and Munt 1998). In this respect, one of the key issues is how communities and people are depicted and used in tourism products, practices and promotion.

This chapter discusses the role of local people in tourism promotion and development. The purpose is not to evaluate the factual practices, involvements or levels of participation but to analyse the roles in which local people are placed in the commoditization of indigenous cultures in tourism marketing. The specific aim of the case study is to examine the representations of the local people, namely the Ovahimba, in tourism development by analysing the Namibian tourism promotion. By analysing the representations, the chapter aims also to discuss the possible effects of the role of the Ovahimba in terms of development driven by tourism. Namibia is internationally known by its desert landscapes and nature-based or ecotourism-driven images and products in tourism. However, indigenous groups, such as the Ovahimba and the San, have also played a role in Namibian tourism images (see Kanguma 2000; Rothfuss 2000; Bollig and Heinemann 2002; Bruner 2002). It can be assumed that, in the future, the role of indigenous cultures will grow more significant as a consequence of premeditated segment diversification among international tourist arrivals in Namibia.

It is clear that Western discourses and images of the Ovahimba are not based on the present growth of international tourism and tourism promotion alone – they go back more than a century (Bollig and Heinemann 2002). However, the discussion and analysis here are limited to the present-day depictions and their content analysis. The research material is based on contemporary tourism brochures. Brochures can play a fundamental role in the formation of destination images (Echtner and Prasad 2003; Molina and Esteban 2006) and they can be seen as texts and sites of cultural production; instrumental elements in creating discourses of place, people and their identities (Jenkins 2003; Pritchard and Morgan 2003; Hottola 2006a).

First, we discuss the developmental role of tourism within regional and local contexts, which is followed by an introduction to the idea of community-based tourism and its role in the Namibian tourism policy. After that, the role of the Ovahimba in Namibian tourism promotion is examined, with a discussion on the meaning of its representations in tourism. The final, concluding, discussion aims to make connections between the representations of the Ovahimba constructed in place promotion and the possible outcomes of these images to community-based tourism and participatory approaches in tourism development and planning in the future.

Tourism, Local Communities and Regional Development

As widely noted in literature, tourism development can have a favourable developmental impact at both local and national levels, introducing new, external sources of income and employment into the tourism economy and its operational cycles (Archer 1982; Roehl 1998). On the other hand, tourism may also entail undesirable forms of change and costs as far as other local sources of livelihood or societal issues, for example, are concerned (Kariel 1989; Butler 1999). Burns (1999) refers to this duality of perspectives by the terms 'tourism first' and 'development first'. In the 'tourism first' perspective, the development and needs of the industry are in the main focus of evaluation; the emphasis is on the maintenance of tourism activities. This may lead, as Mitchell and Reid (2001, 114) state, to a situation where 'local people and their communities have become the objects of development but not the subjects'. In that case, tourism is not used as a vehicle but rather as an end in itself, without any active integration towards regional or local development goals (Saarinen 2006, 2007b).

In the 'development first' perspective, the evaluation of tourism and its impacts is placed in the wider spatial context of local and/or regional development needs. It aims to 'decentralize' tourism and place the local and regional needs in the centre; the role of tourism can be seen as a potential tool, but not as a goal, for regional and local development. From the 'development first' perspective, there should also be elements aiming to integrate tourism with the goals of local communities, traditional economies, land use patterns and planning procedures, etc. 'Development first' represents an alternative approach grounded on the involvement of local communities, participatory planning procedures and local needs over the control of resources (see Selin 1999; Walpole and Goodwin 2000, 572; Scheyvens 2002). These goals are integrated with the idea of community-based tourism in research literature and development policies.

Community-based tourism is often labelled as being an alternative form of tourism (Telfer and Sharpley 2008, 124). According to Krippendorf (1982), alternative tourism aims to ensure that tourism policies should no longer concentrate on economic and industrial necessities alone. Thus, there is a strong emphasis on the needs of local people and their physical and societal environment and wider needs in community-based resource management processes and policies (see Cater and Lowman 1994; Mowforth and Munt 1998). In general, community-based tourism aims to ensure that members of local communities have a high degree of control or even ownership in tourism activities, its limits and resources used (Scheyvens 2002; Saarinen 2006). Local people should receive a significant share of the economic benefits of tourism in the form of direct revenues and employment, upgraded infrastructures, environment and housing standards, etc. (Stronza 2007). According to Telfer and Sharpley (2008), there are two major goals in community-based tourism. First, it should be socially sustainable, which refers to the role of local control and participation in tourism operations and the shared socio-economic benefits. Secondly, and more crucially, community-based tourism means respect for local cultures, identities, traditions and heritage. Therefore, local people and communities are involved with and depicted in ways that are ethically sustainable and acceptable.

The need for community-based tourism is widely recognized in Namibian tourism development policies (MET 2005a, 2007). The Ministry of Environment and Tourism (MET 2005b) has initiated the Community-based Tourism (CBT) Policy, which aims at exploring ways in which communities can benefit from the tourism industry and that promote social and economic development and conservation in communal areas. Underpinning this policy lies the growing role of tourism within the nation and concerns over the local-level benefits of the increasingly global industry; tourism is seen as a vital industry but it must benefit the local residents of the places that tourists actually visit. With this emphasis, the government sees tourism as a process that will lead to higher living standards by encouraging people to conserve the environment.

The key issues in the CBT Policy – and community-based tourism in general – are the questions of participation and empowerment: how to integrate local communities into tourism planning and how to ensure a sufficient level of power and control in decision-making processes over the use of natural and cultural resources in tourism development. Tourism and community-based resource management literature includes different participation channels in planning and development processes (see Swarbrooke 1999; Hall 2000; Scheyvens 2002; Jones and Murphree 2004). The Namibian Ministry of Environment and Tourism (2005b) CBT Policy also underlines the role of participation and empowerment: the main principles of the policy are that local people must be consulted and their ideas should be included in tourism planning and legislation. In addition, legislation should assist and support tourism development, the informal tourism sector should be organized and recognized as representing community interests, and large businesses operating on communal land should involve and benefit local residents.

These goals are essential but relatively difficult to achieve in practice. Some of the main practical problems in community-based tourism are related to the idea of community and participation. The former issue refers to the non-homogenous nature of local communities and their inner hierarchies, power structures and changes in time and place. The basic question is: Who represents the local communities and are there conflicting arguments about how are they integrated into the planning and development processes? The latter focuses on problems in participation processes. In this respect, Tosun (2000) identifies three major challenges in community participation, which are operational, structural and cultural by nature. Operational limits of participation refer to problems in communication and information sharing and lack of coordination between different policy levels and actors involved. Structural limits include power issues and organizational barriers, while cultural limits of participation indicate cultural and knowledge differences between tourism development actors and local people. Cultural differences construct an obstacle between the tourism industry and local people in terms of participation, planning and development.

In the case of indigenous cultures and their role in tourism, the cultural limits of participation are often evident (see Hintch and Butler 1996). These cultural limits are based, e.g. on the differences in norms, values or educational levels, but they can also be constructed or highlighted in tourism development processes, such as product design and marketing. Next, the constructions of local cultures and identities are examined by analysing Namibian tourism promotion and the roles and representations that the promotion creates concerning the local people, namely the Ovahimba, in tourism.

Constructing Cultures and Identities in Tourism: the Ovahimba in Namibia

Modern tourism has become a major element in constructing and constituting the way in which we see other places and cultures. In order to develop, tourism must produce and construct representations of destinations for marketing purposes (Echtner and Prasad 2003; Jenkins 2003). Thus, the question of representations and their production can be seen as crucial for tourism (Squire 1994; Crang 1997; Pritchard and Morgan 2003). As a concept, representation can be understood as a form of presenting an object not by copying it but by representing it in either a new form and/or a new textual environment; it is not simply a presentation of objects and issues. Representations integrate meanings to cultural structures by simultaneously referring to the 'real' and 'imaginary' worlds of objects and phenomena (Hall 1997, 15–17; see also Edensor 1998; Hottola 1999).

Alongside tourist destinations, tourism brochures can be seen as the sites of representations that are part and parcel of the discourses of tourism development and specific tourist attractions (see Hall 1992, 291; Dann 1996). The discourses are constructed in social practices, such as place promotion, and at the same time they construct and transform social reality and the physical environment by virtue of the practices and policies attached to them. Thus, power issues are always involved in discourses and representations (Saarinen 1999; Cheong and Miller 2000). According to Kotler *et al.* (1993), one of the major practices that manifest power in tourism is the production of representations for the purposes of place promotion. Place promotion spatializes meanings, representations and history for non-local people's consumption. Moreover, it aims to promote the cultural features of a destination by packaging real and/or imagined representations into a marketable product. However, while this process makes the cultural features of the destination known, it also stereotypes and modifies the signs and symbols involved (see Edwards 1996; Meethan 2001).

From the local perspective, one possible result of this process can be the marginalization of local communities and lifestyles, in which local traditions, livelihoods and other such cultural elements are depicted in images as 'other', primitive, pre-modern, economically lower and non-profitable as compared with tourism development and tourist cultures (see Favero 2007). Finally, such rhetoric may be concretized in land-use planning, regional politics and economic investments favouring non-locally oriented developments.

The Ovahimba (Himba) form an ethnic minority in north-western Namibia and south-western Angola. Most of the Ovahimba live in the northern part of the Kunene region (former Kaokoland home region) in north-western Namibia. There are different estimations of the size of the population, ranging from 25,000 to 35,000 (Bollig and Heinemann 2002; see also Crandall 2000; Lange 2004). Traditionally, they are regarded as pastoralists, nomadic people whose main livelihood is based on livestock (cattle and goats) and seasonal, small-scale subsistence farming. Recently, some Ovahimba communities have also turned towards tourism-related activities. The role of tourism has increased due to the growing numbers of tourists in the region. Recent drier years have also forced some people to find additional sources of income. In addition, the transformation towards tourism has happened indirectly through the establishment of nature conservancies in the mid-1990s and communal land reform in 2002, both of which have provided improved possibilities for control over resources and land use (see Massyn 2007).

The history of tourism is relatively short in the northern Kunene region. Although the region has attracted individual travellers for over a century, the northern parts of South-west Africa (see Warmelo 1951; Bollig and Heinemann 2002) – now the Republic of Namibia – opened to international tourism due to the nation's independence in 1990 (Henrichsen 2000). Prior to that, the region was so-called Bantustan, a homeland under South African rule with restricted access and limited opportunities for trade. Nowadays, the region receives increasing international flows of visitors but, as the statistics of regional tourism in Namibia are based on estimations, it is difficult to make accurate judgements concerning the actual growth rate (see Rothfuss 2000).

In a wider global tourism perspective, the northern Kunene region represents a periphery of a periphery (Weaver and Elliott 1996). Although the supporting infrastructure of tourism in the region has increased since the 1990s, it is still relatively underdeveloped compared with the Windhoek and Swakopmund areas, for example. Despite this underdeveloped character, tourism in the region is said to be socially exclusive. This is perhaps based on the poor accessibility, making travelling expensive (Rothfuss 2000). In addition, the shortage of direct connections from international airports (and South Africa) and the long distances do not encourage short visits. In recent years, 'fly-in-safari' products have been developed, and they refer to small-scale, aircraft-based short visits from touristic core areas such as Swakopmund situated in coastal Namibia. Still, with the relatively high travel costs to Namibia, they form a rather expensive combination when compared with international tourism to South Africa and visits to its peripheries.

The natural and cultural features of the Kunene region are widely used in Namibian tourism promotion. The role of the Ovahimba is especially well recognized in literature (Bollig and Heinemann 2002). They dominate the images of Kunene but they are also used in wider Namibian and even in

Southern African tourism promotion. The Ovahimba are often represented in a primitive, exotic or erotic sense, with references to colonial eras and the nostalgic, wild and heroic past of early discoveries of Africa (see Bruner 2002; van Eeden 2006). Nowadays, Western tourists visit the Ovahimba villages based on these images and their related expectations (see Henrichsen 2000; Kanguma 2000). According to observations by the former author during fieldwork periods from 2005 to 2007, tourist visits are operated mainly via non-local travel agencies and guides (based in Windhoek or international settings), but there are also some local tourism businesses. In addition, individual tourism is in evidence but small in scale. Local communities receive direct benefits, such as food and other supplies and also money, from the visiting tourists or through a contract with the tourism business. Selling crafts and souvenirs is also part of the village visit experience and interaction between hosts and guests. The main interaction between the host and guest, however, seems to be conducted through the lenses of a camera guided by the historically constructed modes of a tourist gaze.

The Ovahimba in Tourism Brochures

The empirical research question asks: Do local people – and especially the Ovahimba – have a role and, if so, what type of role do they have in Namibian tourism promotion? The first part of the question emphasizes the quantity of depictions, while the second part aims to find out what actually is (quality) represented and what the meanings of the depictions are. The research material consists of 32 brochures (with 1154 photo images) that the authors collected from the Namibia Tourism Board (NTB) offices in Windhoek, Namibia, and Cape Town, South Africa, from 2005 to 2006. The approach is grounded in a content analysis in which the coding of images is based on theoretically driven and empirically formed categories (see Dann 1996; Rose 2001). The preliminary analysis is done by simple frequency counts, and further interpretation of the main themes and representations by using previous studies on the Ovahimba and indigenous cultures in tourism promotion contexts.

In general, most of the images in tourism promotion have been related to the natural environment, especially the arid desert landscapes without human elements. The depictions of Namibian nature covered almost 50% of the research material (see Table 5.1). A combination of nature with people and images of tourism facilities was also relatively popular. Depictions of local people covered 12% of the research material, which was lower than the role of tourists in the promotion material: tourists in natural and touristic settings represented 16% of the images shown.

Based on general frequencies, it is fair to say that the representations of Namibia in tourism promotion are dominated by natural environments, with the characterization of a place achieved through tourism facilities such as hotels and pools and tourist activities in nature and resort settings. In contrast to that, the role of local people (non-tourists) is relatively marginal. Who are

Table 5.1. Thematical categories and their subcategories in Namibian tourism promotion material.

Categories and subcategories	Images	
	n	%
Nature	533	46
Nature and people	178	15
Tourists	162	14
Locals	8	1
Tourists and locals	8	1
Collage (mixed elements)	4	0
Local people	139	12
In rural setting	45	4
In urban setting	5	0
Portrayed (no context)	89	8
Tourism facilities	177	15
With tourists	20	2
No people (tourists or locals)	157	14
Heritage and archaeological sites	80	7
Urban scenes	23	2
Other	20	2
Total	1154	100

the locals? Among the images depicting local people, almost half of the pictures actually represented Ovahimbas. Although the Ovahimba are mainly located outside the main tourism zones of Namibia (see Weaver and Elliott 1996; Henrichsen 2000) and represent around 1% of the nation's total population, they seem to dominate the cultural dimension of Namibia in tourism.

In the light of the existing literature (see Henrichsen 2000; Bollig and Heinemann 2002; van Eeden 2006; Novelli and Gebhardt 2007), this minimal role of local people in Namibian tourism promotion was not fully expected. On the other hand, the domination of Ovahimbas among the images of local people was not surprising. However, their placing in the promotion material was out of any recognizable context; most of the pictures (57%) representing Ovahimbas were portrayals depicting people without a geographical or societal background reference. Even when the context – natural landscape (14%) or rural village environment (29%) – was shown, Ovahimbas were represented as standing or sitting passive objects; 87% of the pictures represented Ovahimbas as figures posing for the tourist gaze and cameras. In natural settings, all the people depicted were passively posing, while in the village contexts 43% of the images actually represented Ovahimbas as being there not just because of the camera and tourists, i.e. in the village settings, people were also making crafts, cooking or herding cattle, etc.

The majority of the images depicted 'half-dressed' (as some of the brochure texts formulated the matter) Ovahimba women or women with children (see Table 5.2). However, it should be noted that this wording and evaluation of a dressing code is based purely on Western tourism and its

Table 5.2. The Ovahimba as depicted in different settings in Namibian tourism promotion material, by number; percentages shown in parentheses.

Category	In nature	In village	Portrayed/ collage	Total
Women	4	7	23	34 (44)
Men	2	1	0	3 (4)
Women and men	0	1	0	1 (1)
Children	3	5	11	19 (24)
Women and children	2	9	9	20 (25)
Ovahimba (women) with a tourist	0	0	1	1 (1)
Total	11 (14)	23 (29)	44 (56)	78 (100)

marketing perspective. From the local point of view, the traditionally dressed Ovahimba women are fully and adequately dressed. In contrast to women, Ovahimba men were rarely included in the tourism promotion material – even in the family-oriented pictures that included women and children, men were not present. The female-dominated dimension of place promotion has been noted also by van Eeden (2006, 345), who argues that 'the Himba women symbolize the colonized subject' who are represented for the Western male gaze as passive, static and unchanged figures, elements that were also noted by Kanguma (2000).

Although the focus of this chapter does not include other ethnic and cultural groups in the detailed analysis, it is worth noting that, compared with the Ovahimba, over 40% of the San people depicted in the research material were active, i.e. doing something other than just posing for the camera (e.g. hunting, preparing food, making cultural artefacts or dancing). In addition, 'full family units' were shown. What was also notable compared with the Ovahimba and in the context of this chapter was that most of the San depicted were men (87%). Thus, it seems that the activity or passivity in cultural depictions in tourism may not be so much an issue of ethnicity or indigenousness but of gender.

Discussion and Conclusions

Tourism and related marketing are important elements in constructing and constituting the way in which we see other places, people and cultures. Based on the case study material, Namibia is characterized through natural landscapes and tourist activities and facilities in tourism promotion. Namibian people do not characterize the region and its touristic landscapes. Still, the Ovahimba as a cultural group are relatively important and highly visible (49% of locals, 8% of total research material) in the representations of cultural landscapes of Namibia in tourism. The representations of Ovahimbas are dominated by pictures of women portrayed as primitive, exotic and erotic targets of the Western (heterosexual male) tourist gaze; simply, their role is to pose as passive objects for tourists to gaze at – to be the 'good natives' (see Neumann 2000). In this respect, the Ovahimba are trapped in playing the role of static culture in order to satisfy the needs and expectations of non-local visitors.

The ethnic and gendered landscapes of northern Kunene for tourists to consume are supported by product titles and subtexts such as 'Oryx and Himba Safaris' and 'Himba encounters', placing the Ovahimba at the same level and position as local flora and fauna. This 'primitivization and zooification' have both been typical features in historical Western travel literature when depicting indigenous cultures (see Mowforth and Munt 1998; Neumann 1998; Saarinen 1999; Waitt 1999; Wels 2004). At the same time, the Ovahimba are represented without context, as being out of time, as a part of a landscape where time has stopped. This otherness and image of static and unchanged culture are supported by representations of 'timeless' desert landscapes.

There are many curious and also unethical aspects in the depictions of the Ovahimba, demanding further and deeper analysis. In addition to the unethical dimension of place promotion and cultural representations, the passive and exotic roles of the Ovahimba become problematic when thinking back to the basic premises of community-based tourism, which are highly emphasized in the Namibian tourism policy. Many Ovahimba communities in northern Kunene are becoming more and more influenced by and dependent on tourism. In a positive situation, tourism can support local livelihoods and communities and maintain and develop services and basic infrastructure in the region. In addition, it can be assumed that local communities receive benefits from the tourism industry but, as Telfer and Sharpley (2008) emphasize, community-based tourism should also include shared benefits, with elements of participation and some level of control over the tourism development processes.

According to Edwards (1996), the construction of the 'exotic other' makes indigenous people an integral part of the natural environment but does not suggest their power over it. Edwards also points out that the 'exotization' and lack of power are supported by representing local people without a context. Indeed, it is rather clear that the role and images of the Ovahimba in place promotion do not support and fully empower them to participate actively in tourism production, planning and development processes. Telfer and Sharpley (2008) also highlight the need to respect local cultures, identities and traditions in community-based tourism. Based on the analysis, it is evident that the Ovahimba are not always depicted in ways that are ethically sustainable, indicating the lack of respect for them by the industry. For example, one of the brochures by a Windhoek-based travel agency marketed and sold visits to an 'other kind of Africa' (Die andere Art Afrika) by placing a 'half-dressed' Ovahimba woman on the hood of a Land Rover.

The placement of an Ovahimba woman on the hood of a masculine 4×4 car stereotypically combines the past and present or the primitive and modern, but there are other possible dimensions involved. The brochure image has many similarities with the advertisement analysed by van Eeden (2006). She examined the so-called Land Rover 'Himba' advertisement from

2000 that upset the South African public. According to van Eeden, the advertisement – also using an Ovahimba woman in the context of a powerful 4×4 car (which 'whirlpooled' her breasts when passing by) – was regarded as both racist and sexist, and she concluded that these representations of the Ovahimba were grounded on colonialism and on the images and meanings of discoveries on the African continent by the Western male. Representations such as these construct the Ovahimba as the Other, a process that is based on uneven power relations between the represented and the representer and on different perspectives (us/them, white/black, man/woman, active/passive, First World/Third World, etc.). It also emphasizes the hierarchical positions between different interest groups and scales in the tourism industry.

In Namibia, the tourism industry operates as a link and medium between local, regional, national and larger spatial scales. However, the values, needs and preferences of the industry are often grounded in national or international scales and views representing the core. In tourism planning and development, this type of situation with uneven power relations can lead to the creation and construction of local cultures and identities in tourism images that cannot be judged as sustainable and which may not support the empowerment and participation of local people in tourism development in practice. Thus, the politics associated with the representations of local cultures and the critical evaluation of the basis of such images and related discourses may be regarded as crucial issues for the development of community-based tourism and the long-term sustainability of the industry. The roles the local people have at the symbolic discourse level may affect the very practices that guide the progress of their everyday lives. In the case of the Ovahimba, the static and passive roles may continue to strengthen those economic and social structures that keep them mainly as objects and separate them from the decision-making processes in tourism.

However, the Ovahimba were able to freeze – with support from international pressure groups – the construction of a large hydroelectric power plant planned in the River Kunene basin (see Lange 2008). As Kanguma (2000, 130) states, '... if the Himba were so "primitive", I doubt whether they would know their right to say No to development ...'. The contemporary primitive character of the Ovahimba, and of many other indigenous cultures (e.g. Masai and Zulu) in Africa and worldwide, is largely based on tourism images and related place promotion (see Hottola 2006a). It is evident that, in the case of the hydroelectric power plant, the Ovahimba were able to step out the myth of unchanged and passive culture and use the social capital invested in the networks of families, communities and international groups. Interestingly, tourism development and related practices in the natural resource management processes have not resulted in similar contestation processes by local communities. This may be due to slower and smaller-scale development steps and perceived impacts of the tourism industry in the region, but it can also be related to the beneficial but passive role that the Ovahimba are given in tourism promotion and products.

Concerning the interplay between the tourism industry and the Ovahimba communities, the questions that should be addressed in the future are related to the practical issues of participation and control and the benefits and costs of tourism in local communities. Evidently, tourism in the region has been beneficial with respect to the initial goals of the National Tourism Policy for Namibia (MET 2005a). These goals include the reduction of regional inequities and poverty, and economic growth. The expansion and evolution of tourism activities have also contributed indirectly to nature conservation and ecological sustainability in the region (see Novelli and Gebhardt 2007).

In addition to these important issues, the ideological background and present modes of tourism promotion and products should be studied further. In this respect, the key issues are related to the questions of who are depicting, producing and defining local communities and whose past/present/future possibilities are actually represented and commodified. Local and regional development are always context-dependent (Pike *et al.* 2006, 37), and the analysis of place promotion with the processes influencing and defining communities and their roles and daily lives would also provide tools for a deeper and culturally sensitive evaluation of the outcomes of Namibian tourism policy and, especially, the success of community-based tourism initiatives from a community perspective. Based on both the literature (see Massyn 2007; Novelli and Gebhardt 2007) and the initial analysis here, it seems that tourism development has not contributed sufficiently to broad-based black economic empowerment, which is also named as a strategic goal in the National Tourism Policy plan (MET 2007).

There is a further need to consider the role of communities and local cultures in tourism development and the role of tourism in local and regional development in order to reduce the potential – and often evident – process of uneven social and economic development, which is currently producing identities and marginalized roles for local people, delimiting their already limited possibilities of being included in development and planning processes. Although local and regional developments are increasingly seen as global issues and tourism often represents globalization processes on a local scale, it is worth noting that globalization is not only a top-down process but it also builds interaction between places. What this means is that the local outcomes of globalization are also somewhat dependent on the goals set in different development programmes and policies on the local scale (see Teo 2002). Here the future question is: Are the values, goals, control mechanisms and practices in development actions reflecting more the needs of local communities or the needs of the (mainly non-local) tourism industry? In the northern Kunene region, both perspectives have potential for regional development and will continue to produce culturally defined landscapes of tourism.

6 The Applicability of Government Policy to Community-based Catering Services: the Hananwa of Blouberg, Limpopo Province

CHRIS BOONZAAIER

Introduction

Blouberg (S23°05′ and E29°00′) is the westernmost extension of the Soutpansberg in Limpopo Province. The Hananwa, under the hereditary leadership of the Lebôhô lineage, have occupied the mountain and the nearby surrounding area since at least the 1820s. The Hananwa came there as a group of refugees after they had broken away from the Hurutshe of Botswana. After they had arrived, the Hananwa divided into two groups. One fell under Lebôhô, who settled in the western parts, and the other under Kibi, who settled in the eastern parts of the Blouberg (Roberts 1916; Lestrade 1928; Krige 1937; Breutz 1953, 20; van Schalkwyk 1995, 68–75; Boonzaaier and Philip 2007, 26).

One of the most momentous events in the Hananwa's history after they had settled at Blouberg was the siege in 1894 of traditional leader *Kgoši* Kgalushi (Ratshaatshaa) Lebôhô's stronghold on top of the mountain by Piet Joubert, a general in the Zuid-Afrikaansche Republiek (ZAR) (Sonntag undated, XV). From the beginning of May 1894 until the end of July of the same year, the forces under General Joubert besieged the Hananwa until *Kgoši* Lebôhô surrendered to General Joubert. The *Kgoši* and his councillors were removed to Pretoria and imprisoned. A military tribunal found *Kgoši* Lebôhô guilty of not paying taxes to the government and of not observing the laws of the land, but he was never sentenced. *Kgoši* Lebôhô stayed in prison for 6 years until the British occupied Pretoria in 1900, when he was released. He went home to Blouberg to reign over his people, dying in 1939. After the Hananwa–Boer war, the Hananwa women and children had to work for local farmers for 5 years without any compensation, other than food and clothing, but most of them eventually found their way back to Blouberg (van Schalkwyk and Moifatswane 1991; Joubert and van Schalkwyk 1999; Boonzaaier and Philip 2007, 27; Sonntag undated, 118,119,127,128,147,148).

The Hananwa who live on top of Blouberg today still live in relatively isolated circumstances. There are no roads, but a few footpaths wind their way up the steep slopes through thick forest from the foot of the mountain for several kilometres, and they provide the only access to the mountain. Due to this isolated setting, the community on top of the mountain is still very traditional in its cultural practices. Homesteads (*metse*, singular *motse*) of the traditional Hananwa hut type are spread along the top of the mountain in a traditional fashion. The homesteads are self-sufficient to a large extent: the inhabitants cultivate their own food and tend their own livestock. The people also gather edible plants from their natural environment. The few people who can afford to do so buy items such as soap, personal toiletries, oil and the odd packet of sugar from the *spaza* shop at the bottom of the mountain (Boonzaaier and Philip 2007, 27).

According to Boonzaaier and Philip (2007, 27), most members of the community living on top of the mountain are either very young or relatively old – children under the age of 12 and adults over the age of 45. Women outnumber men five to one. Most economically active men under 45 are working outside the area. Most of the households have some external income, which mostly comes either from an old-age pension, a disability pension or a government child support grant paid to one or more members of the household. Locally, there are virtually no job prospects. This has meant that these people have had to become largely self-sufficient for their daily dietary needs. Whatever they do not cultivate, they collect from nature, particularly in summer when there is an abundance of various edible foodstuffs available in their environment. The variety is much more limited in winter.

Government Policy and Tourism on Blouberg

In 2003, the Limpopo Provincial Government built a visitor homestead (*motse*) on Blouberg on the farm The Grange for use as tourist accommodation (see Figs 6.1 and 6.2). This farm is owned by the Hananwa. The visitor *motse* was designed in terms of the ideal principles of how a *motse* should be laid out according to the Hananwa living on top of the mountain. The visitor *motse* on top of Blouberg is linked to a second visitor *motse* at the bottom of the mountain. Both *metse* form part of the African Ivory Route concept, which is an initiative by the Limpopo Province Directorate Tourism intended to empower and benefit disadvantaged rural communities in the province through tourism. The bottom visitor *motse* is managed by the Directorate Tourism, but the top visitor *motse* was established with the aim of empowering the members of the community on top of the mountain to manage the visitor *motse* by themselves. Hence, the objectives related to the top visitor *motse* satisfy the objectives of the African Ivory Route even better than those related to the bottom visitor *motse*, in that the *motse* and its running are meant to empower the local people to take responsibility for tourism in their own community. The project is intended to promote community-based tourism (CBT) by developing the

Fig. 6.1. Visitor *motse* at the top of Blouberg.

Fig. 6.2. The *motse* kitchen hut (*sethaka*), which is supplied with a refrigerator and a gas stove.

necessary knowledge and skills in the community to run the visitor *motse* (Directorate Tourism 2002; Boonzaaier and Philip 2007, 27).

In principle, the objectives of the Blouberg project are largely in line with those formulated for the South African tourism industry at large, namely:

- to develop tourism with dignity – encouraging mutual respect for all cultures and eliminating all forms of discrimination on the basis of language, religion, culture, race, gender, age, wealth and ability;
- to provide tourism education, training, awareness and capacity-building programmes, especially aimed at previously disadvantaged and neglected groups;
- to encourage participation by all South Africans in tourism planning and policy formulation;
- to promote pride in South Africa's cultural resources;
- to use tourism as a catalyst for human development, focusing on gender equality, career development and the implementation of national labour standards;
- to promote nation-building and peace among the people of South Africa, as well as internationally, and to promote greater respect for human life through tourism;
- to encourage the active participation of all South Africans in tourism development, particularly at local level;
- to empower community structures, for example, by means of involvement in the marketing of cultural experiences and practices to tourists;
- to ensure that all South Africans have equitable access to travel opportunities and tourism attractions;
- to encourage community participation in the planning, development, implementation and management of tourism projects; and
- to monitor and minimize the potentially adverse social impacts of tourism (DEAT 1996, 2005).

Aims and Objectives of the Study

The main aim of this chapter is to evaluate the applicability of the strategic objectives and government policy in regard to community-based catering services among the Hananwa.

The study in this chapter follows on from and refers back to an earlier study by the author, assisted in part by an associate, which set out to determine the community's attitude towards tourism and tourists (Boonzaaier and Philip 2007). The first objective is to obtain a clear indication of the feasibility of catering services to the visitor *motse* on top of Blouberg and the alignment of such a project with wider policy. Any attempt to provide such catering services without a positive attitude and involvement by the community would be a futile initiative from the outset.

A second objective is to determine whether the community can be empowered to benefit financially from the visitor *motse* on top of the mountain;

and if so, in what way. The visitor *motse* belongs to the community. If it is properly managed, the running of the *motse* could provide income in an area where job prospects are otherwise virtually non-existent. Unfortunately, from the time when it was completed at the end of 2003 to the middle of 2004, when the survey for the Boonzaaier and Philip (2007) study was done, the visitor *motse* was largely underutilized in terms of its potential advantages for the Hananwa and the cultural experience that staying there could offer tourists. (It must be stressed that the study was conducted a mere 7 months after the visitor *motse* had been completed, and that only three bookings had been received by the time the survey was done.)

Hence, a feasibility study was done, focusing on the possible role that local food could play in making this incentive work better, both in summer, when crops and wild plant foods are more plentiful, and in winter, when the supply of crop plants is more limited. Because the visitor *motse* is situated on the eastern periphery of The Grange, it is logistically more viable for the people in this area to provide the visitor *motse* with food supplies and services such as the preparation of the food. However, a possible contribution from households from the western side is not excluded. Four factors were considered (Boonzaaier and Philip 2007, 27–28):

- the community's attitude towards tourism in general and the people's expectations with regard to the project in particular;
- the conservation and presentation of the Hananwa cultural heritage, with particular reference to the Hananwa dietary pattern;
- the availability and variety of crop plants during winter and the way the Hananwa normally prepare these foods; and
- the role that the ordinary logistical services such as the provision and preparation of food can play in making the project successful.

To narrow the research area to a more manageable scope, the survey focused mainly on The Grange, on the eastern side of the mountain. There are only 11 *metse* on The Grange, but it was assumed that these would display the same living conditions as those found on the western side of the mountain (generally referred to as Malebôhô by the residents), which consists of 52 *metse*. The western side of the mountain is separated from The Grange by an uninhabited stretch of land, about 4 km long (a rocky outcrop separates the eastern side of the mountain from the western side). Due to the fact that members of the Hananwa community inhabit both The Grange and the Malebôhô area and that the topography and climatic conditions are the same, it was assumed that the chances that conditions at The Grange would be representative of those of the whole community were very high. However, in order to verify this assumption, two households on the western (Malebôhô) side of the mountain were randomly chosen and interviewed (Boonzaaier and Philip 2007, 27).

The study to determine the Hananwa's winter diet was conducted from 28 June to 11 July 2004. The author originally visited the area in summer, but winter was chosen as the focus of the 2004 survey, because it was assumed that what was possible in winter was the minimum potential supply, and that in summer this offering could be larger and more varied. A basic qualitative research strategy was followed. This implies that qualitative research techniques were used in an explorative, descriptive and explanatory study to explore the four factors listed above (Boonzaaier and Philip 2007, 27–28). Selected techniques from the participatory action research (PAR) model were used, as these techniques were appropriate tools for investigating the factors listed. Not only do these techniques complement and reinforce one another but they also aid in triangulation. Each technique enabled the researcher to obtain different perspectives on the topic, as suggested by Pelto and Pelto (1993, 77–81), Strauss and Corbin (1998, 11) and Babbie and Mouton (2001, 275).

For the purposes of the survey, access to the community was gained via the local Blouberg Community Tourism Association, which consists of members of the Hananwa community, and the royal family of Lebôhô. The guides and interpreters came from the study area and they were knowledgeable regarding the language, customs and practices of the Hananwa. This was important, because it is invaluable to follow the correct etiquette when being introduced to the participants in order to establish a trust relationship from the outset.

The person usually responsible for cooking and related chores in every household was the person selected for each interview, because the study focused on food as a topic. The task is usually performed by the youngest or most junior female member in a family. However, the older women were very interested in the questions that were asked, and all of them offered additional answers, most of which confirmed the responses of the participants. Hence, the actual interviews can best be described as focus group discussions (Boonzaaier and Philip 2007).

The PAR approach was followed during the data-gathering process. This approach focuses on the involvement and participation of all the role players in a particular research project in order to achieve solutions for problems or jointly to set objectives. It relies heavily on local knowledge, as well as on the perspectives of the participants regarding their own situation and environment. Local knowledge and perspectives are experience-based, so they represent unique knowledge and insight into the participants' culture and problems. As it is a joint endeavour between the researcher and the community, such a study can best be described as collective generation of knowledge rather than mere collection of data. The research is meant to result in action, with the ultimate goal of improving the quality of life of the communities concerned (Coetzee *et al.* 2001, 545; Strydom 2005b, 408–412). A variety of data-generation techniques can be used in the PAR approach, including surveys, participant observation, qualitative in-depth interviews, focus groups, storytelling and drama (cultural theatre) (Strydom 2005b, 419). The techniques selected for the survey were participant observation and focus group discussions, characterized by in-depth interviews and storytelling (Boonzaaier and Philip 2007).

The strong emphasis on community involvement implies that a deliberate attempt was made to involve the residents of the homesteads that were visited in the course of the research, not only in the collection of data on their winter diet but also in determining their opinions about tourists, the provision of food to the visitor *motse* and the possible contribution of the visitor *motse* towards satisfying particular needs among the local population. The PAR approach enabled the researcher to explore the unique local knowledge and insights of the Hananwa on these aspects within the context of their own particular cultural and natural environment (cf. Collins 1999, 102; Babbie and Mouton 2001, 320).

The interviews were conducted in the context of focus group discussions. In fact, the presence of a number of women in the *metse* that were visited encouraged the involvement of the participants and provided opportunities to investigate the winter diet of the Hananwa in greater depth (Boonzaaier and Philip 2007). The interviews were conducted by means of open conversations (in-depth interviews structured only by a schedule of guideline questions), as described by Greeff (2005, 292), with the specific aim of gaining insight into the dietary patterns of the homesteads that were visited on top of the mountain, in particular into the variety and preparation of foodstuffs. Each participant had opportunities to ask questions, to make comments and to respond to the comments the other participants in the conversation had made. The fact that people were interviewed in a group context undoubtedly contributed to the spontaneity with which the participants contributed to the discussions, as participants are often reluctant to reveal information when interviewed individually. Actually, the participants expressed their preference to be interviewed in a group context.

The technique of obtaining and generating data by means of group discussions in accordance with the PAR method has been reported to be effective, not only among people in rural and semi-urbanized areas, where a high premium is generally placed on group participation (cf. Trollip 1991, 77; Viljoen *et al.* 2005), but also among adults with low literacy skills (Keim *et al.* 1999). Given the size of the groups (small groups of people with a similar background and common interests) and the characteristics of the actual interviews (spontaneous focused discussion of the topic by the participants) among the Hananwa *metse* that were visited, the interviews can best be described as focus group discussions, as delineated by Agar and MacDonald (1995), Schurink *et al.* (1998, 313–320) and Greeff (2005, 298–300).

While the actual interviews were being conducted, the other members of the household went about their normal tasks and allowed the interviewer to observe them in their quotidian tasks, such as fetching water and collecting firewood, herding animals, collecting grass for brooms and preparing various dishes. The researcher found that he had to be highly observant in respect of what food was in the storage hut and the cooking hut/kitchen at each *motse*, because he could not rely solely on the inhabitants' comments on the composition of their diet. Hence, the researcher noted as many of the food types cultivated by the individual *metse* as possible. In this regard, Strydom (2005a, 277) remarks that 'to be able to listen, to see, to inquire, to observe and to write up the notes is of special significance in participation'.

The interviews in the survey did not focus only on the dietary habits of the Hananwa, they also investigated the participants' attitudes towards tourism and tourists in the area (Boonzaaier and Philip 2007, 30). This information provides an indication of how viable and feasible it is to expect the local Hananwa to provide the visitor *motse* with food. In order to obtain as full a picture as possible in this regard, interviews were conducted with inhabitants in each of the *metse* that the researcher visited. Care was taken to include both young and older people in the interviews, which consisted of pre-determined questions. The approach was to give the participants a topic and each was 'allowed maximum opportunity to tell his [or her] story', as suggested by Greeff (2005, 296). When necessary, follow-up questions were then asked to clarify issues (Boonzaaier and Philip 2007, 30).

Most of the people living on top of Blouberg do not understand English or Afrikaans and they mainly speak Sehananwa, a north Sotho dialect (van Wyk 1966, 37). To overcome this difficulty, an interpreter was involved in the survey. Since the researcher speaks Sepedi, a central Sotho dialect (van Wyk 1966), he was able to verify the data, in the sense that he could check that the true meanings of words and sentences were not obscured. Questions about tourism in particular posed problems, as there are no north Sotho equivalents for English terms such as 'tourism' and 'tourist'. The interpreter first had to explain the meaning of the terms before any meaningful interviews could take place. Questions on food and its preparation posed no problems, as indigenous terms exist for all the foodstuffs cultivated by the Hananwa.

Community-based Tourism Development

It is often thought that only a few individuals would benefit from providing services in the form of cleaning, cooking, providing food supplies, etc., to the visitor *motse*. However, on Blouberg, visitors will also be guided along a cultural route. A route has already been developed on both the eastern and western parts of the mountain. As they visit various *metse* on the cultural route, visitors have an opportunity to observe and even participate in authentic cultural practices and activities. This can in turn generate money for the community, as a fixed tariff has been determined for each *motse* that is visited (Boonzaaier and Philip 2007, 28). This means that the places of attraction (the local *metse*) and the people who live there will form part of all three levels of the total product, based on the model developed by Swarbrooke (1995, 45).

This model is based on three products, namely the core, tangible and augmented products. The core product is what really attracts tourists. According to Swarbrooke (1995, 44), the core products are often intangible and highly subjective, such as atmosphere, experience, relaxation or convenience. Tourists seek these intangibles as a solution for their problems or needs (cf. Wang 1999). In order to ensure that tourists have access to the product, the community must work with marketers to turn the core product into a tangible product – an entity which customers can purchase to satisfy their needs. This tangible product can have different characteristics – Swarbrooke (1995, 45) suggests that these may include a brand name, quality (of services), safety, a range of attractions and packaging. The augmented product is aimed at ensuring that tourists are comfortable and satisfied, by the provision of additional services (Swarbrooke 1995, 45). If the Blouberg project is run in a responsible way, in accordance with the principles outlined by Swarbrooke (1995), this will promote tourism in the area as a whole.

The establishment of a visitor *motse* on top of Blouberg, which belongs to the community in the sense that the community is solely responsible for its entire management and can also benefit from it financially by delivering services such as the provision of indigenous food, cooking and cleaning, is based on the principles of CBT development. Such development entails the empowerment of a local community to ensure that the community members participate in their own planning and management and that they also exercise greater control over decision making and the effects that tourism development may have on their culture and environment (Telfer 2002, 47; Grobler 2005, 1). As Timothy (2002, 150) suggests, CBT development 'is about grassroots empowerment as it seeks to develop the industry in harmony with the needs and aspirations of host communities in a way that is acceptable to them, sustains their economies, rather than the economies of others, and is not detrimental to their culture, traditions or ... day-to-day convenience'. Drumm (1998, 212) expresses a similar view.

Two important aspects emerge in the process of CBT development: first, participation by the community in decision making and, secondly, resident involvement in the benefits of tourism. If community members participate in decision making, community members determine their own development goals and have a meaningful voice in the organization and management of tourism in their area (Timothy 2002, 152–153). According to Gunn (1994, 111), when there is community participation, it improves the attitudes of destination communities towards tourism, resulting in a more successful industry. Successful tourism depends, after all, largely on the goodwill and cooperation of the host communities. Furthermore, local attitudes towards tourism are significantly enhanced when residents feel that they have at least some ownership and are involved in the operation of the facilities in their community.

The visitor *motse* on Blouberg provides ample opportunities for residents to become involved in small-scale, family-driven services to the *motse*. The cultural *motse* was designed to accommodate only ten visitors. This policy decision was made to keep the impact on the local people and their environment as low as possible and also to create conditions that allowed tourists to have an authentic cultural experience. Such an approach is supported by Dahles (1997, 23–24, cf. Murphy 1985, 153), who says:

> New forms of tourism are required that consist of smaller-scale, dispersed, and low-density tourism developments located in and organized by communities where it is hoped that they will foster more meaningful interaction between tourists and local residents ... Small-scale tourism developments are much less likely to produce [the] negative socio-cultural effects associated with foreign ownership. Local tolerance to tourism activities is significantly enhanced if opportunities exist for active resident involvement in the ownership and operation of facilities.

Residents receive the benefits of tourism when they gain personally from tourism, particularly from small-scale, locally owned businesses. Locally owned enterprises have the additional advantage in that they can increase multiplier effects in the host community, cut down on foreign exchange leakages and reduce the need for local residents to be absent from their homesteads for prolonged periods while they go in search of jobs (Dahles 1997, 23–24; Telfer 2002, 59). This principle is applied in the case of the Blouberg project: the opportunities that have been created for community members to provide food and associated services to the visitor *motse* on Blouberg could play a significant part in achieving the principles and objectives set by a CBT development approach as envisaged by the South African tourism industry.

Tourism Policies and Community Perceptions

When development projects are initiated from without, the risk of failure is higher than with development projects initiated by members of a community. This is especially true in rural communities, which have apparently come to accept poverty as a given and, as a result, regard any attempts from outside to change their circumstances to improve productivity as 'unrealistic'. In such communities, creativity, voluntary activities and acceptance of responsibility and leadership are not typical (Wassermann and Kriel 1997, 69–70). In the light of this principle, it was necessary to determine the community's perception of and attitude towards tourists and tourism, as the potential for improving the living conditions of the Hananwa people on top of the mountain by giving them an opportunity to share in the provision of food to the visitor *motse* was not identified by the community itself but was identified from without (Boonzaaier and Philip 2007, 31).

Berno (1999, 657) cautions that, when the term 'tourist' is used cross-culturally, it is important to define from an emic stance the native people's understanding of both their own form of travel and of Western tourism. In this case, the Hananwa language has no equivalent term for the terms 'tourism' or 'tourist'. The Hananwa's understanding of tourism is to visit a place other than home, and the participants in the survey were unanimous in their opinion that a tourist is a 'visitor' or 'guest' (Boonzaaier and Philip 2007, 31). They argue that people can 'visit' for various reasons, including seeing family or friends, going to a festival, attending a funeral, etc. However, their definition of 'visiting' implies that the CBT concept was completely new to them. Once the researcher had explained the CBT concept to the participants, they indicated that they supported the idea of community ownership because they think that it will allow them to improve their living conditions, with some outside assistance.

The participants were divided on whether cultural tourism would strengthen their cultural heritage, as opposed to the view that cultural tourism would cause their traditions to change. There was a clear division between the opinions of young adults and adults who are pensioners regarding this issue. The older people in general were initially slightly more suspicious of the project. One old woman was very distrustful and did not want any tourism, saying: 'It is meant to change our lives'. However, once the researcher had explained that they would not be required to change their ways in any way, the older people were more positive. They thought that it was strange that people from the outside would be interested in their culture in general, and in their food and eating habits in particular. They asked why people from outside would be interested in visiting poor people. They fear change and the unknown, but they also have a strong desire to improve their living conditions. They expressed concern that tourists would take their land or make them give up their culture (Boonzaaier and Philip 2007, 31–32). By contrast, the young adults did not share the fears and scepticism that the older generation expressed – they were all very positive about the idea. They felt that tourism could provide a financial injection for the community.

Everyone agreed that tourism would be good in that it would provide job opportunities. One young man revealed considerable insight into the whole concept of CBT when he said:

> Tourism will be very good because then we can teach other people [tourists] about our culture and at the same time learn about other people's culture. Young people of my age miss the opportunities presented by tourism. If people [tourists] would visit us [the people on the mountain], it will provide people like me with the opportunity to stay and work on the mountain.
>
> (Boonzaaier and Philip 2007, 32)

This type of insight suggests that there is a good chance that the implementation of policy will be successful in terms of the people's buy-in to the project. This finding suggests that the project is in line with the South African tourism industry's objectives of providing a catalyst for human development, empowering community structures and encouraging community participation in the planning, development, implementation and management of tourism projects (DEAT 1996, 2005).

Marijuana (*Cannabis sativa*) is found in abundance on Blouberg mountain. In the course of the survey (Boonzaaier and Philip 2007, 32), it became clear that selling marijuana (illegally) was an important source of income for many homesteads. If selling marijuana is more lucrative than providing the visitor *motse* with food, the project will probably fail. Hence, the participants' views regarding the importance of selling marijuana were probed. The participants were divided in their opinions: some would prefer to supply the visitor *motse* with food as an additional source of income and continue to sell marijuana, while others would rather replace selling marijuana by supplying the visitor *motse* with food as a source of income, because they would prefer not to run the risk of being prosecuted by the police for selling marijuana (Boonzaaier and Philip 2007, 32).

Eventually, with one exception, all the participants on top of the mountain, including both those who regarded the provision of food to the cultural *motse* as an additional source of income to marijuana and members of the older generation, expressed a very positive attitude towards tourism and said that they would welcome tourists in their area. However, there was one important proviso: the majority of the participants thought that visitors should be accompanied by a local guide and that they should respect Hananwa etiquette and culture. These findings correspond to a large extent with those of Grobler (2005, 36–53) among the Venda in the Tshivhase area in the Soutpansberg. If the participants' requirements in this regard can be satisfied, it will also meet the South African tourism industry's objectives of developing tourism with dignity, providing tourism education, promoting pride in the cultural resources of the country and monitoring and minimizing the potentially adverse impacts of tourism (DEAT 1996, 2005).

As has been mentioned above, one industry objective is human development, and a particular focus is gender equality and career development. Among the Hananwa, the traditional subordinate position of women among most African communities (Schapera 1959, 188) also prevails. Originally, all income generated by a woman had to be given to her husband (Boonzaaier 1990, 271–277). The survey revealed that the selling of marijuana by Hananwa women has led to a degree of emancipation among the women, because the women are allowed to keep part of the income on condition that it will be used to support their families (Boonzaaier and Philip 2007, 32). This finding suggests that any income derived from the provision of food to the visitor *motse* should not cause any tension between husbands and wives, provided that part of the income is given to the husband (cf. Boonzaaier 1990, 532, 571). The provision and preparation of traditional food for the visitor *motse* provides an excellent opportunity for women and their families. It should be noted that some of the women are already members of the Blouberg Community Tourism Association. Their involvement in the Association is likely to contribute to their emancipation, as their function is to assist with the identification and development of cultural activities that might be attractive to tourists, in line with the industry objective of encouraging the active participation of all South Africans in tourism development, particularly at the local level.

Supplying Traditional Hananwa Foods to the Visitor *Motse*

As already explained above, for the purposes of the survey by Boonzaaier and Philip (2007), it was decided to assess the Hananwa's winter diet and the availability of locally grown foodstuffs in winter (rather than in summer) to gauge the community's ability to provide the *motse* with food. The reason for this decision was that Blouberg is situated in a summer rainfall area and crop production is less extensive in winter. It was assumed that, if the community could supply food during winter, there would be no problem in supplying food in summer, when supplies are more plentiful. The implications of such food provision to the visitor *motse* are also considered here.

The survey (Boonzaaier and Philip 2007, 33–36) showed that the Hananwa staple winter diet includes maize (*Zea mays*), grain sorghum (*Sorghum bicolor*), *marôgô* (*Amaranthus thunbergii*), a variety of pumpkin types (including

Cucurbita pepo and *Lagenaria siceraria*), watermelons (*Citrillus vulgaris*) and beans, especially jugo beans (*Vigna subterranea*). This is similar to the winter diet of the majority of other indigenous groups living in rural areas with a similar climate. All of these foods are grown and harvested during the rainy season (spring to autumn); and maize, *marôgô*, grain sorghum and beans are stored for the winter months. Most of the foods discussed below can be used or adapted for use at the visitor *motse*.

As among other cultural groups, maize (*lefala*) forms the most important part of the daily diet. It is eaten twice a day – on its own for breakfast and served with a side dish such as *marôgô* or pumpkin (*mopotse*) (and sometimes meat) for the main meal (Boonzaaier and Philip 2007, 33). Unlike most Westerners, the Hananwa people eat only two meals a day: one in the late morning and one in the early evening. Food is mostly cooked outside, on an open fire, but the cooking hut is used on rainy days. Traditional beer is customarily made inside. Sorghum can be used as a porridge (also known in South Africa as malted *mabêlê* or *maltebêlê*) but, among the Hananwa, it is more often used for making traditional beer (cf. van Wyk and Gericke 2000, 14; Boonzaaier and Philip 2007, 33).

Marôgô is a major part of the staple winter diet of the Hananwa. The Hananwa often call it *theepe*. The plant has a good nutrient content (Quin 1959, 61; Steenkamp and Schönfeldt 2005, 25), which is of particular significance in an area such as Blouberg, where few animal products are consumed. The leaves are laid out to dry after harvesting and are cooked like spinach and also taste much like spinach. *Theepe* is mostly eaten on its own, but can also be mixed with watermelon or maize meal (Boonzaaier and Philip 2007, 34). The Hananwa usually eat pumpkin as a dish on its own – boiled in water with salt and a dash of sugar. Both watermelon and pumpkin pips are wind dried and then fried in a hot pan with salt (no oil is used), a tasty snack. Watermelon (*morôtsê*) is eaten raw (*mogodu*), dried or cooked (*lerotse*) or in a dish called *thopi* (for which the sliced, seeded and boiled watermelon is mashed and mixed with cooked maize meal), a dish with a slightly sweet taste that goes well with meat.

The community cultivates beans (*dinawa*), often intercropped with maize and pumpkin. There are various traditional recipes for preparing dishes from the cooked, crushed beans, such as *mmoto*, or a dish of beans mixed with samp (*lewa*) (Boonzaaier and Philip 2007, 33–34). In the winter months, few wild resources are used. The people do gather firewood and the leaves of some plants for traditional tea (*mohlwahlwaila*). The tea has a very refreshing taste, not unlike many other commercially available herbal or green teas.

Animal protein sources include chicken, beef, goat meat and mutton. Chicken is eaten most often (boiling the meat at a high temperature until all the water has evaporated and only the oily juices are left and then frying the meat in the juices at the same high temperature until the meat has browned). Chicken feet, head and intestines are favourites and they are available from the local shops at affordable prices. The intestines are washed, cleaned out and then fried in oil. They look and taste similar to calamari (Boonzaaier and Philip 2007, 34). According to Coetzee (1982, 168), no chickens or other domesticated birds were raised in traditional society, but wild birds were often hunted, and were cooked by trussing them, stewing them slowly till soft, and served with gravy. Beef, goat meat and mutton are seldom eaten, except at festivities.

Among the Hananwa, it is taboo for women to eat the 'pope's nose' (*kgôthô ya kgogo*, the rump of a chicken), because it is reserved for the head of the *motse* and it is believed that if a pregnant woman dared to eat this part of a chicken, this would lead to spontaneous abortion (Boonzaaier and Philip 2007, 34–35). In many cultures, pregnant women do not eat eggs, as it is believed that the fetus will grow so huge that she will not be able to give birth, causing her death and that of the child, and it will make her lascivious (Schapera 1959, 133). This belief could not be confirmed among the Hananwa, possibly because one of the researchers and one of the interpreters conducting the survey were men, and women in rural societies will not answer questions of this nature in the presence of a man (Boonzaaier and Philip 2007, 35).

The results of Boonzaaier and Philip's (2007) survey suggest that one of the most basic ways this community can benefit from tourism is by providing the raw food supplies as well as a catering service, which would introduce tourists to the local cuisine. This can be combined with introducing the tourists to the local customs and beliefs concerning food and the preparation and consumption of traditional food. This would be in line with the South African tourism industry policy (DEAT 1996, 2005) of developing tourism with dignity by encouraging mutual respect for all cultures and by alleviating poverty and, for the education of the local people, by developing capacity. It also allows for some education of visitors with regard to the Hananwa culture.

Tourists used to a more varied Western diet might find the local Hananwa winter diet somewhat monotonous, but it is unlikely that they will stay for such extended periods that this would be a problem. Moreover, several traditional dishes could be successfully combined with Western food to provide the best culinary experiences of both worlds to tourists. For the sake of completeness, the dishes listed in the article by Boonzaaier and Philip (2007, 35–36) are repeated here. Some of them were inspired by the traditional recipes described by Coetzee (1982, 119–177):

- *Mabêlê* (sorghum porridge) could be served with Western bacon and eggs and toast for a hearty breakfast.
- *Malana* (head, feet and intestines of chicken) could be served on a bed of rice as a light lunch with a side serving of fresh green salad. (This dish could be called 'Bushveld calamari', and it is suggested that the head and feet be omitted from the dish.)
- *Mmoto* (mashed beans – similar in taste to Mexican refried beans) could be served with chicken cooked in the traditional way with a serving of *marôgô/theepe* for some colour and added nutrition for a fully traditional dinner.
- *Thopi* (a mixture of watermelon and maize meal) could be used as an accompaniment to barbecued meat or chicken with a side serving of *marôgô/theepe* and pumpkin.

- Pan-fried watermelon and pumpkin pips could be served with sun-dried strips of watermelon (another local use for watermelon) as a snack with sundowners or, as Coetzee (1982, 156) suggests, roasted pumpkin pips could be served as an accompaniment to sorghum porridge.

Traditional beverages could be served. They are an acquired taste to most Westerners, but tourists should at least be afforded the opportunity to taste them. Tourists should most definitely be shown how beer in particular is made, in line with the objective of educating tourists. Sorghum beer is prepared in great quantities by the Hananwa both on top and at the bottom of the mountain. Marula beer, which is usually acceptable to most (including Western) tastes, is produced only at the bottom of the mountain, as there are no marula (*Sclerocarya caffra*) trees on top of the mountain. 'Over a period of a few years during which the mountain was also visited during marula time – that is in February – no marula beer was ever found on top of the mountain' (Boonzaaier and Philip 2007, 36). Traditional tea could become a favourite among the health conscious and could be served for mid-morning tea and/ or in the late afternoon.

Apart from the traditional dishes, the local people could prepare a variety of dishes from the ingredients they can supply. All the food products mentioned and produced by the local people should be used in preference to any shop-bought items, which would in any case create additional costs as porters would have to transport the food to the top of the mountain. The service provision and the supply of local goods (in this case foodstuffs) would create capacity and generate income in the area.

Evaluation

Blouberg and its inhabitants provide ample tourism opportunities to satisfy the objectives of the South African tourism industry. The Blouberg visitor *motse* provides feasible opportunities for the local Hananwa to participate as managers, operators and owners of resources and providers of products that are sought after in the tourism industry to benefit the community through the establishment of community-based projects. The variety of food available makes it possible for homesteads to become involved in their own tourism development on a family-owned, small business-scale basis. This accords with both the principles of CBT development and the objectives formulated for the South African tourism industry, as it will enable community members to take ownership of their own enterprises, which results in benefits to the local economy (cf. DEAT 1996, 2005; Dahles 1997, 23).

The visitor *motse* was designed to accommodate only ten people, which suggests that it was the intention (at least from the Provincial Government's side) to promote responsible tourism on top of the mountain. This will undoubtedly help to limit the impact of tourism on the natural, cultural, archaeological and historical assets on the mountain. The limited accommodation capacity of the visitor *motse* could play a large role in ensuring the continued positive attitude of residents towards tourists and tourism in the area. In this way, it is ensured that the 'potential adverse social impacts of tourism' on top of Blouberg are minimized (cf. DEAT 1996, 2005).

This survey (Boonzaaier and Philip 2007) has clearly shown that the cultivation, provision and preparation of food for the visitor *motse* will be the responsibility of the women on the mountain. This finding brings a new dimension to tourism development on Blouberg, as the involvement of women in the visitor *motse* could open the door for women to acquire a greater share in decision making and planning in tourism development. It will also enhance the objectives and principles of CBT as it implies the involvement of all community members, irrespective of gender. In this respect, Timothy (2002, 155) says that:

> The political rights of women and ethnically diverse residents and their entitlement to participate in tourism planning and decision making are ill-defined in tourism policy and practice … Women and racial minorities must be given a louder voice in policy making if the goals of sustainability are to be realised, for these people are an important part of the community who are affected directly and indirectly by tourism.

In the long term, the involvement of women at different levels of tourism development could make a considerable contribution to the recognition of gender equality in the community (cf. DEAT 1996, 2005). The provision of catering services to the visitor *motse* provides higher status and lucrative income opportunities to women. This is in sharp contrast to the subservient, low-paid and lower-skilled positions generally associated with their domestic roles (cf. Scheyvens 2002, 124–125). It is expected that their involvement in tourism will contribute to women's emancipation.

The survey on the Hananwa's perceptions of and attitudes towards tourists and tourism gave a clear indication of the feasibility of tourism on top of Blouberg. It must be emphasized that respecting the cultural values and norms of the Hananwa and a restriction of tourist numbers must be regarded as a prerequisite for sustainable tourism on top of the mountain. This study itself has made a substantial contribution in respect of the aspects required of any strategic tourism development plan, namely by interpreting the findings of a survey of the food-related situation regarding supply and services on Blouberg. Fourie (2006, 95) suggests exploring existing attractions, activities, accommodation, food services, transportation, accessibility, infrastructure and facilities, but such a broad investigation fell beyond the scope of the survey.

However, a strategic tourism development plan also requires that people be empowered to take responsibility for tourism in their own communities. In practice, it requires continuous training programmes to empower the community on top of the mountain to become entrepreneurs and participants in and beneficiaries of the tourism industry. In the developing world (which includes Blouberg), residents usually have little first-hand knowledge or experience of tourism and of being tourists. These are strange concepts to them, as Boonzaaier and Philip's (2007) survey and Grobler's (2005) research have shown (cf. Timothy 2002, 158).

Although great strides have been made in terms of the establishment of community structures (e.g. the Blouberg Community Tourism Association) and training in managing the visitor *motse* and catering services, the following areas of knowledge still have to be addressed in order to develop the Blouberg community's working knowledge of eco-cultural tourism and community development, and to meet the South African tourism industry's objectives more fully:

- tourism, leisure and recreation;
- culture;
- the ecosystem;
- project management;
- the drafting of business plans;
- bookkeeping;
- appreciative participatory planning and action;
- the identification of assets for community-based tourism;
- the impact of tourism;
- destination marketing; and
- leadership development.

In conclusion, the Hananwa of Blouberg already have the ideal combination of factors to turn their cultural heritage into a form of sustainable income, while at the same time preserving their heritage in a way they can, themselves, control. This study of the potential for the provision of catering services and cultural attractions has shown that the strategic goals of DEAT (2005) can be realized, on condition that the positive attitudes of the residents are maintained by providing the necessary training.

7 Tourism Development, Rural Livelihoods and Biodiversity Conservation in the Okavango Delta, Botswana

Joseph E. Mbaiwa

Introduction

Tourism is believed by some to be the most rapidly growing industry in the world (Campbell 1999; WTO 2003). Growth began in the late 1940s (Edwards 2004). From that period, the industry has increased considerably to become one of the main sources of income in many countries. In Botswana, tourism was almost non-existent at the independence of the country from British rule in 1966. However, by 2005 tourism had grown to become the second largest economic sector, contributing 9.5% to the gross domestic product (GDP) of the country (WTTC 2007). Much of the tourism industry in Botswana is nature-based and carried out in national parks, game reserves and other protected areas that contain world-renowned wildlife, biological diversity and natural attributes, as well as unique and spectacular scenery and cultural attractions.

The Okavango Delta, located in north-western Botswana, is one of the main tourist attractions in the country. Like many wetlands in the world, it attracts tourists and many other land users because of the rich natural resources it possesses, particularly the permanent water supply, wildlife, fish and forest resources. As a result, since the 1990s, the Okavango Delta has become one of the most popular international wildlife-based tourism destinations in Africa (Kgathi *et al.* 2004; Magole and Gojamang 2005). The Delta has become a source of income derived from the utilization of flora and fauna through tourism development. Tourism in the Okavango Delta grew rapidly after the adoption of the Tourism Policy of 1990. This policy is the main document used by the government to guide tourism development not only in the Okavango Delta but also in the whole of Botswana (Government of Botswana 1990; DoT 2000). Through this tourism policy, the government aims at diversifying the economy from reliance on diamond mining through tourism development (Government of Botswana 1990).

Botswana's Tourism Policy is driven by three main strategic goals:

- to shift the mix of tourists away from those who are casual campers towards those who occupy permanent accommodation;
- to increase substantially the financial returns from tourism for the people of Botswana, especially those living in the local communities where wildlife abides; and
- to ensure that tourist activities are carried out in an ecologically sustainable way.

These strategic goals guide all tourism development in the country and they have also shaped other policies and strategies such as the Botswana National Tourism Strategy of 2000, the National Ecotourism Strategy of 2002, the Community-Based Natural Resource Management Programme Policy of 2007, and the 7-year National Development Plans and District Development Plans.

While tourism is on the increase in the Okavango Delta, resource competition, land use conflicts and poverty are also increasing and therefore causing resource degradation (Darkoh and Mbaiwa 2005; Arntzen 2006). Various studies (e.g. Fidzani *et al.* 1999; NWDC 2003; Kgathi *et al.* 2004) have found that most people in the Okavango Delta live in poverty. Consequently, it has created conditions for over-harvesting of natural resources by the local people. Resource degradation can be ameliorated partly through the achievement of household livelihood security (Arntzen *et al.* 2003; Kgathi *et al.* 2004; Thakadu 2005). Livelihoods determine the use of natural resources, and therefore changes in livelihoods may affect resource use also in the Okavango Delta. However, the effectiveness of tourism development as a tool for achieving conservation and improved livelihoods has not been adequately evaluated in tourism studies.

Governments of developing countries view tourism investment as a tool for economic development (Hall 1995). The Botswanan government describes tourism development as 'the engine of economic growth' that should diversify the economy of the country from being mineral driven (Government of Botswana 1990). Tourism is viewed as a tool for national and regional development, bringing employment, foreign exchange earnings, balance of payments advantages and important infrastructural developments benefiting both host populations and visitors (Glasson *et al.* 1995). Economists seem to hold that view because they generally see tourism as a route to macro-economic growth through the generation of foreign exchange (Ashley 2000).

For the private sector, tourism is a commercial activity whose main concerns are product development, competitiveness and commercial returns (Ashley 2000). Weibing and Xingqun (2006) argue that tourism is advanced by businesses and governments alike as a development mechanism that can lead people out of poverty and make them equal partners in society. For rural people and the non-governmental organizations that support them, tourism is one component of rural development (Ashley 2000). However, the role of tourism development in promoting sustainable livelihoods and biodiversity conservation has not been adequately studied. This chapter, therefore, analyses the effectiveness of tourism development in achieving better means of subsistence and conservation in the Okavango Delta (see Fig. 7.1). The text is largely based on qualitative research material collected between June and December 2007 at Sankoyo, Khwai and Mababe in the Delta.

Community-based Natural Resource Management

There is a strong debate among conservation scholars (e.g. Brandon 1998; Oates 1999; Terborgh 1999; Duffy 2000) on whether tourism development can be a useful tool with which to achieve improved livelihoods and biodiversity conservation in developing countries. The debate is triggered by the fact that natural resource degradation is seen to be occurring in developing countries, and the communities living in rich biodiversity areas are blamed for being

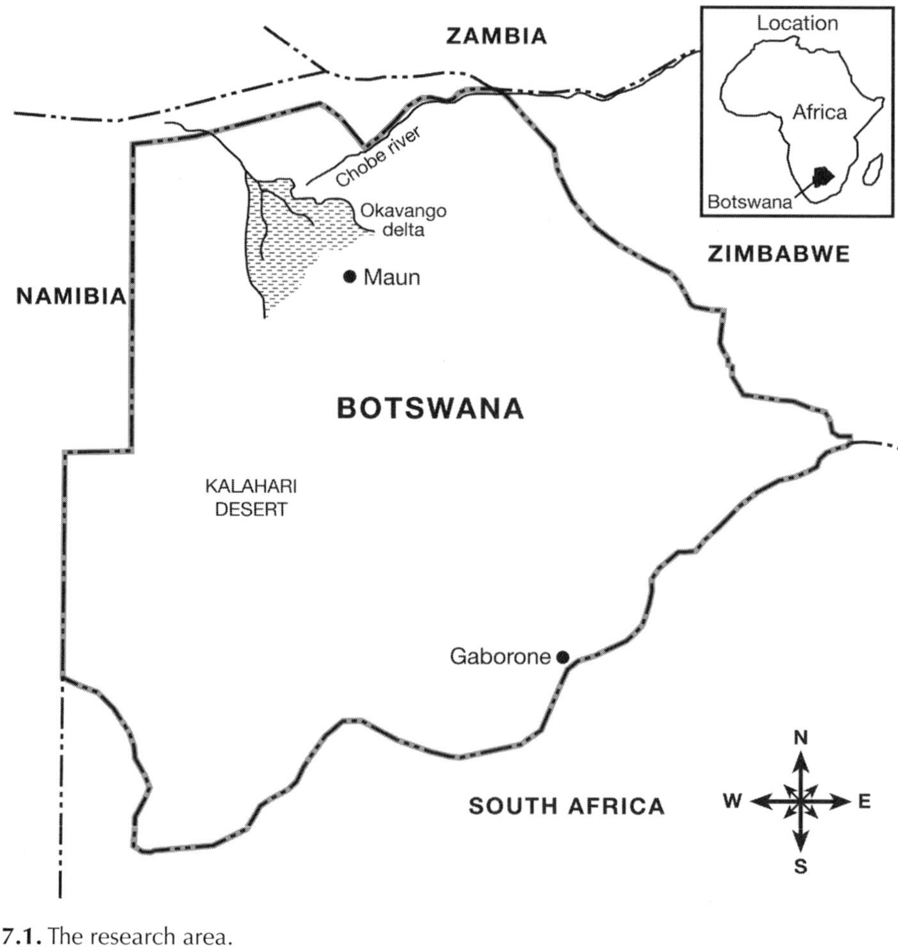

Fig. 7.1. The research area.

one of the main causes of this degradation. Local communities are accused of causing the degradation mainly because they rely on natural resources in their local environments to sustain their livelihoods. Conservation scholars, in particular, have pointed out the over-harvesting of resources, especially wildlife. While the debate is escalating, the Community-Based Natural Resource Management (CBNRM) programme is viewed as a useful tool for achieving biodiversity conservation and improved livelihoods in developing countries (Tsing *et al.* 1999; Twyman 2000).

The CBNRM programme began in Eastern and Southern Africa in the late 1980s. The programmes are described by different names in different African countries. Mbaiwa (2005b) notes that the programme is called the Communal Area Management Programme for Indigenous Resources (CAMPFIRE) in Zimbabwe, the Luangwa Integrated Rural Development Project (LIRDP) and Administrative Design for Game Management Areas (ADMADE) in Zambia, the Living in a Finite Environment (LIFE) programme in Namibia, Tchuma Tchato or 'Our Wealth' in Mozambique, the Conservation of Biodiversity Resource Areas (COBRA) programme in Kenya, Ujirani Mwena or 'Good Neighbourliness' in Tanzania and the CBNRM programme in Botswana. In order to facilitate CBNRM in the Okavango Delta, the Botswanan Government demarcated the entire area into small land units known as Controlled Hunting Areas (CHAs), codenamed NGs and numbered from one upwards (see Fig. 7.2). Local communities willing to participate in CBNRM are therefore allocated CHAs for use as tourism purposes. The main

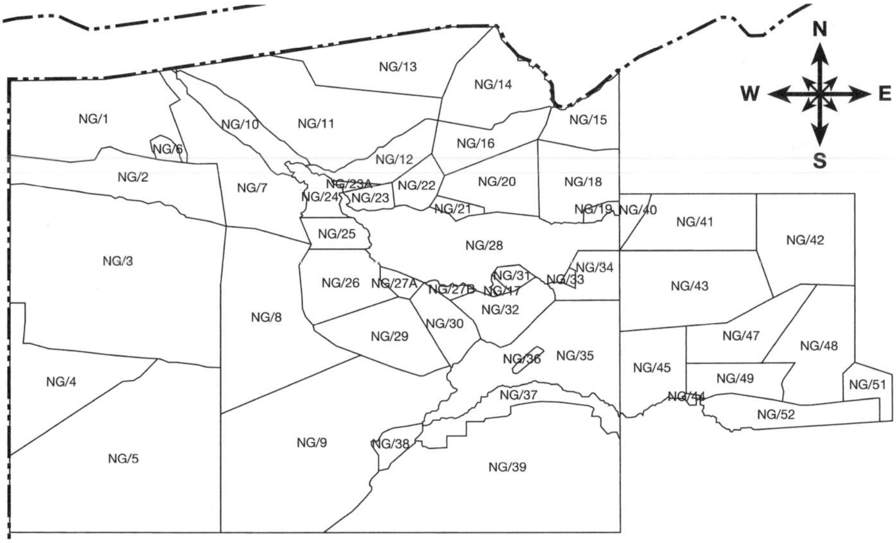

Fig. 7.2. The distribution of Controlled Hunting Areas (CHAs) in the Okavango Delta.

forms of tourism in the Okavango Delta include consumptive (e.g. hunting safaris) and non-consumptive (e.g. photographic) activities.

Tourism development through the CBNRM programme in the Okavango Delta is assumed to alleviate poverty and advance conservation by strengthening the rural economy and empowering communities to manage resources for their long-term social, economic and ecological benefits. The CBNRM programme in general is based on the premise that local populations have a greater interest in the sustainable use of natural resources around them than the centralized or distant government or private management institutions (Tsing *et al.* 1999; Twyman 2000). It means that CBNRM credits the local people with having a greater understanding of, as well as a vested interest in, their local environment, hence they are seen as more able to manage effectively natural resources through local or traditional practices (Leach *et al.* 1999; Tsing *et al.* 1999; Twyman 2000). CBNRM assumes that, once rural communities participate in natural resource utilization and derive economic benefits, it will cultivate a spirit of ownership, and the development of positive attitudes towards resource use will ultimately lead them to use natural resources in a sustainable way (Mbaiwa 2004). However, the effectiveness of CBNRM or tourism development in achieving improved livelihoods and conservation has not been adequately studied. This chapter aims at addressing that research gap.

Tourism Development as a Tool for Improved Livelihoods

Tourism development in the Okavango Delta has so far resulted in improved livelihoods in communities participating in CBNRM. The benefits that have resulted in improved livelihoods include:

- employment opportunities;
- financial benefits from tourism development;
- provision of game meat;
- provision of social services; and
- intangible benefits.

In this study, employment was found to be one of the main benefits that have improved livelihoods at Sankoyo, Khwai and Mababe villages. Employment is provided by not only the safari companies that sublease community areas but also by trusts in the villages. As shown in Table 7.1, at Sankoyo the number of people employed by the Sankoyo Tswaragano Management Trust (STMT) and its Joint Venture Partnership (JVP) partner increased from 51 in 1997, when the Trust began operations, to 108 in 2007. At Khwai, the number increased from five people in 2000 to 76 in 2007. At Mababe, the number increased from 52 in 2000 to 66 in 2007.

The results show that at Sankoyo the percentage of people employed is 28, at Khwai 21 and at Mababe 22.8. These percentages are very high, considering that large proportions of the populations of 372 at Sankoyo, 290 at Khwai and 300 at Mababe are comprised of school-aged children and the

Table 7.1. Employment at Sankoyo, Khwai and Mababe, 1997–2007 (from DWNP 2006; Mbaiwa 2008).

	Sankoyo			Khwai			Mababe		
Year	Trust	JVP	Total	Trust	JVP	Total	Trust	JVP	Total
1997	10	41	51	N/A	N/A	N/A	N/A	N/A	N/A
1998	11	51	62	N/A	N/A	N/A	N/A	N/A	N/A
1999	11	51	62	N/A	N/A	N/A	N/A	N/A	N/A
2000	11	51	62	5	N/A	5	15	37	52
2001	13	9	22	5	N/A	5	15	64	79
2002	35	56	91	8	N/A	8	16	64	80
2003	42	56	98	10	N/A	10	18	64	82
2004	48	56	104	15	40	55	41	18	59
2005	45	56	101	15	50	65	41	25	66
2006	46	56	102	19	55	74	41	25	66
2007	52	56	108	19	57	76	41	25	66

elderly. CBNRM is the most important economic activity that provides employment opportunities in the three villages. The people employed by the trusts and JVP in Botswana are semi-skilled and have jobs such as cooks, cleaners, storekeepers and escort guides. Most CBNRM communities in the Okavango Delta provide training for their members in tourism entrepreneurial skills and business management.

The creation of jobs by community-based organizations (CBOs) and their joint venture partners is a very important strategy of poverty alleviation, as it brings social security into the lives of people who are predominantly poor. Every economy aims at full employment of its labour force, and this is also the case for the rural economies of Sankoyo, Khwai and Mababe. Those employed by CBNRM and other tourism enterprises financially support their families and thereby raise the standard of living in their households. In terms of the utilization of wages and salaries from tourism, the workers of CBOs and safari operators use the money for various household needs. The main uses of the income from tourism are the purchase of food, toiletries and clothes, building of houses, supporting parents and helping meet expenses associated with the schooling of children. Some save the income they derive from tourism in the bank in Maun for future uses, such as paying dowry, sponsoring themselves to school and being prepared for household emergences. Income to pay for such expenses was not available before CBNRM was introduced in the Okavango Delta.

The fair distribution of employment benefits is critical in the sustainability of CBNRM programmes, as well as for biodiversity conservation in the Okavango Delta. A fair distribution of employment benefits by the communities is achieved by community dialogue at the *kgotla* (village square where everyone is allowed to air their viewpoints on the subject under discussion). For example, at the villages of Sankoyo, Khwai and Mababe in 2007, a survey revealed that whenever there are job vacancies at the trust or safari company, there is a *kgotla* meeting held in the village. The villagers determine how many people are already employed in each household and, if two or more people are, they move on to the next household until they find one where there is nobody or just one person working for the tourism enterprises, and then the members of that household are considered for the job. This is carried out in order to ensure that all households in the village should have at least one person employed either by the trust or the safari operator. This fair distribution of employment benefits helps to avoid internal conflicts and promotes both harmony in the communities and success of CBNRM development. Finally, it is important to recognize that the Okavango Delta does not have industrial or manufacturing plants to provide employment. As a result, employment opportunities provided by CBNRM are a significant contribution to the livelihoods of many households.

Income is one of the measures of livelihood in a household and at the community level in the Okavango Delta. Income and other financial gains are some of the major economic benefits that villages derive from tourism development in the delta. Tourism revenue that accrues to communities and households comes largely from the following activities: subleasing of hunting areas, sale of wildlife quota (i.e. wildlife quota fees for game animals hunted), meat sales, tourism enterprises (e.g. lodges and campsites) and camping fees and vehicle hires. A survey carried out at the three villages in 2007 indicates that income from tourism development through the CBNRM programme accrues to individuals, households and the community at large when it is finally distributed; Table 7.2 shows the financial benefits that accrued in 1997–2007.

The data in Table 7.2 show that land rentals and quotas at Sankoyo, Khwai and Mababe have been on the increase since the projects were started in the villages. Game quota fees seem to be the largest source of revenue, accounting for almost half of the revenue generated by each CBNRM activity. Arntzen *et al.* (2007, 44) argue that: 'If one recalls the commercial revenues of the entire Botswana CBNRM program, it becomes clear that STMT is one of the big earners and employers, accounting for well more than 10 percent of the total revenues and employment creation'. Therefore, CBNRM projects, such as that of Sankoyo, can be described as achieving their objectives of rural development, particularly in the sphere of improvement of livelihoods.

Income generation from tourism is important because it is one means by which communities can sustain their livelihoods. Income from tourism subsequently ends up in the households in the form of dividends. For example, between 1996 and 2001, each household at Sankoyo village was paid BWP200 (€20), the sum increased to 250 (€25) in 2002, 300 (€30) in 2003 and to 500 (€50) between 2004 and 2007. The distribution of income to the various households is an important aspect in improvement of rural livelihoods. The 2007 survey found that people at all three villages no longer relied on traditional livelihood activities such as subsistence hunting, the collection of veld products or agriculture. Instead, they have moved to a cash economy where income from CBNRM has become the main source of livelihood in the communities. Tourism development, therefore, has transformed the traditional economies of the villages into a tourism-led or cash economy. As

Table 7.2. Revenue generated by Sankoyo, Khwai and Mababe in 1997–2007, in Botswana pula (BWP) (from DWNP 1995–2007; Mbaiwa 2008).

Year	Land rental	Quota	Other[a]	Total
Sankoyo Tswaragano Management Trust				
1997	285,750	0	12,665	298,415
1998	116,666	60,928	38,826	216,420
1999	151,667	33,470	76,151	261,288
2000	166,833	49,090	148,940	364,863
2001	57,047	55,600	114,801	227,448
2002	492,000	872,550	131,844	1,496,394
2003	466,509	965,772	370,352	1,802,633
2004	562,655	1,096,377	75,634	1,734,666
2005	455,000	1,060,400	612,012	2,127,412
2006	483,250	1,198,700	639,116	2,321,066
2007	613,360	1,272,600	621,537	2,507,497
Khwai Development Trust				
2000	1,057,247	0	72,536	1,129,783
2001	585,220	0	248,305	833,525
2002	1,211,533	0	36,738	1,248,271
2003	348,778	0	97,480	446,258
2004	110,000	857,085	283,482	1,250,567
2005	115,500	1,043,707	405,247	1,564,454
2006	121,275	1,248,500	1,248,500	2,618,275
2007	127,339	1,217,187	1,082,146	2,426,672
Mababe Zokotsama Trust				
2000	60,000	550,000	77,000	687,000
2001	69,000	632,500	127,233	828,733
2002	79,350	702,606	85,961	867,917
2003	91,205	807,996	98,854	998,055
2004	104,940	929,196	149,159	1,183,295
2005	120,681	1,068,575	130,739	1,319,995
2006	120,000	1,202,183	13,500	1,335,683
2007	130,000	1,202,183	29,950	1,362,133

[a]Revenue from net profit from Kazikini and Santawani, meat sales, camping and vehicle hire donations and community development (for Sankoyo Tswarangano Management Trust); rental fees for Letswee camp, camping fees and community development fund (for Khwai Development Trust); community development only (for Mababe Zokotsama Trust).

a result, it is necessary that sustainability in income generation is established through CBNRM to achieve sustainable livelihoods in the Okavango Delta.

For households at Sankoyo, Khwai and Mababe, game meat is one of the benefits they derive from tourism development. Joint venture agreements with safari operators are such that the international clients of the companies take with them only the animal heads and skins (called trophies) and fillets. The animal carcasses are then taken to the villages where they are either sold or distributed to the communities depending on the type of the animal killed.

For instance elephant, warthog and zebra, which are not normally eaten by most residents, are distributed free, whereas meat such as that of impala, kudu and buffalo, which are eaten by most people, is sold by the trust at a minimal price and the money becomes part of the overall trust revenue. Hence, the villagers benefit directly from wildlife resources in their local environments. The method of meat distribution also has the potential to reduce illegal hunting which, before the adoption of CBNRM in the Okavango Delta, was described as a problem.

Revenue generated from CBNRM projects at Sankoyo, Khwai and Mababe is used to fund social services and related community development projects in the villages. The list below shows the amounts (in BWP) used to fund some of the services and community development projects in the three villages (Arntzen *et al.* 2003; Mbaiwa 2004; Schuster 2007; data from reports from Sankoyo, Khwai and Mababe villages):

- assistance with funeral expenses (200–3000 per household);
- support for local sport activities (5000–50,000 per village);
- scholarships (7000–35,000 per village);
- services and houses for the elderly (150–300 per month per person);
- assistance for orphans (40,000 per trust);
- assistance for disabled people (15,000 per village);
- provision of communication tools such as radios;
- transport services, particularly the use of vehicles; and
- installation of water standpipes in households.

Most villages pay for the funeral expenses of community members to the tune of BWP3000 (€300) if an adult dies and BWP1000 (€100) if a minor dies. Vehicles owned by the community are used to collect firewood needed for preparation of meals for the mourners and transport for them to and from Maun, the regional capital, which is also used to transport the dead persons. In addition, the community vehicles are utilized for transporting community members from one village to another and they can also be hired for carrying goods. Sankoyo, Khwai and Mababe are located in remote areas where accessibility in terms of public transportation is very difficult. The availability of transportation through trust vehicles has, therefore, increased the accessibility of these once remote areas, connecting them to regional centres in other parts of the country.

Most villages around the Okavango Delta have been relocated from the inner parts of the wetland, where there are streams of fresh water (Bolaane 2004; Mbaiwa 2005b). As a result, water reticulation in the villages is a problem. In addressing the problem, the CBNRM project at Sankoyo in 2007 funded water provision for 56 households out of the 76 in the village. Mababe funded water for 30 households out of the 54. At the time of the study, Khwai was still digging a trench from the River Khwai to provide water for the village. Another remarkable social service funded by CBNRM in the three villages in 2007 was the construction of houses for the poor or elderly: seven houses at Sankoyo, 18 at Khwai and 10 at Mababe. In each of the three villages, CBNRM paid a monthly allowance of BWP200 (€20) to orphans and BWP500 (€50) to the elderly twice a year.

By 2007, Sankoyo had sponsored 14 students, Khwai 30 students and Mababe 20 students to study for catering and professional guiding, with a total sponsorship of BWP250,000 (€25,000). CBNRM has taken social responsibility for the community members of the three villages and provided them with the necessary livelihood needs. CBNRM has, therefore, transformed the rural communities of Sankoyo, Khwai and Mababe from being beggars living on handouts from the Botswanan Government and donor agencies from Europe and America into productive communities moving towards achieving sustainable livelihoods.

Tourism development through the CBNRM programme in the Okavango Delta has several intangible benefits. At Sankoyo, Khwai and Mababe, the benefits were found to include the following:

- establishment of representative village institutions such as CBOs (trusts), which have become powerful rural development and conservation institutions in the Okavango Delta;
- retainment of the young in rural areas;
- development of tourism entrepreneurship skills;
- exposure to private sector and business thinking; and
- improved working relations with the government and conservation and development organizations.

Tourism development has not only created employment opportunities and generated income for rural communities in the Okavango Delta but it has also developed tourism skills, especially in young people. The fact that young people now have skills in tourism development places them in a competitive position within the tourism industry, not only in the Okavango Delta but also in other parts of the country, indicating that tourism development through the CBNRM programme has a part to play in promoting rural livelihoods in the Okavango Delta and in Botswana as a whole.

Tourism Development as a Tool for Conservation

Community policing and enforcement of conservation practices are among the main achievements of the CBNRM programme in the Okavango Delta. At Sankoyo, Khwai and Mababe, community policing of resources was found to be the responsibility of the residents but controlled by Community Escort Guides (CEGs). CEGs are employed by the communities to enforce the rules of conservation in their CHAs on behalf of their community members. CEGs are trained by the Department of Wildlife and National Parks (DWNP) to escort hunting safaris and ensure that all activities in the community CHA are conducted within the laws of Botswana. CEGs record all kills or wounded animals, monitor illegal wildlife offtake and report any illegal hunting to the Botswana Police Force and DWNP. In photo tourism areas, CEGs ensure that safaris are conducted within the correct zone of the CHA and that photographic activities do not harm the pristine nature of the Okavango Delta either through waste disposal, off-road driving or any other environmentally harmful activities. CEGs conduct routine patrols and anti-poaching and wildlife resource monitoring patrols in their CHAs.

The residents at Sankoyo, Khwai and Mababe reported that CEGs were effective in making their communities observe conservation regulations agreed upon by all members of the community. Failure to observe the law empowers a CEG to arrest the culprit and turn him over to the Botswana Police Service. In addition, those who fail to observe community rules on conservation are suspended from deriving benefits from the CBNRM project in their village until such a time as an assessment can be made and they are found to have redeemed themselves. The community punishment of the offenders through the suspension of CBNRM benefits also indicates that local community institutions of conservation are effective and have the potential to restrain the few individuals that fail to observe agreed-upon community decisions. These measures contribute to lowering of the levels of illegal hunting activities at Sankoyo, Khwai and Mababe as compared with the time before commencement of CBNRM.

Illegal hunting rates have been found to be lower in CBNRM areas than in non-CBNRM areas (see Table 7.3). Informal interviews with DWNP officials in Maun indicate that poaching in CBNRM areas has decreased when compared with the pre-CBNRM time within the same areas. The low levels of illegal hunting in CBNRM areas are critical for effective wildlife conservation. Household interviews at Sankoyo, Khwai and Mababe also confirmed that illegal hunting is at a low level in their villages when compared with the period before CBNRM started operating. Households now recognize the economic value of wildlife through tourism development, a scenario that did not exist before CBNRM was adopted in their villages.

Even though CBNRM has not completely stopped illegal hunting activities in the Okavango Delta, the reduction in illegal wildlife offtake in CBNRM areas shows that when the local communities began to derive economic benefits from tourism development in their CHAs, they put a higher economic value on natural resources around them and began to conserve them. Therefore, CBNRM has the potential to promote conservation of declining species in the long term. However, it will depend on the continued improvement of their livelihoods by tourism development.

The wildlife quota system is one of the pillars underpinning the success of CBNRM activities in the Okavango Delta. DWNP allocates an annual wildlife quota to the communities for tourism purposes. Wildlife quotas are decided after the annual aerial surveys of wildlife populations are carried out. As a result, the number allocated for hunting purposes is determined by

Table 7.3. Reported cases of illegal hunting in the Okavango Delta, 1998–2006 (from Arntzen *et al.* 2003; DWNP 2006).

Area	1998	1999	2001	2002	2003	2004	2005	2006
CBNRM	4	0	0	0	1	2	2	1
Non-CBNRM	23	9	12	13	12	12	10	5
Total	27	9	12	13	13	14	12	6

the number of species counted in a particular CHA. In 2007, the communities involved in safari hunting through the CBNRM programme were allocated 15 elephants each. However, declining species such as the giraffe and sable antelope are not hunted because their numbers are considered to be small. Household interviews at Sankoyo, Khwai and Mababe indicated that the suspension in hunting giraffe and sable antelope had been accepted. This is yet another indicator of the willingness of the communities involved in CBNRM to support conservation.

The contribution to conservation by residents in the Okavango Delta can further be illustrated by the acceptance of the communities to suspend the Special Game Licence (SGL) in favour of the wildlife quota system under the CBNRM programme. Until the late 1980s, the SGL was issued to citizens of Botswana, such as those at Sankoyo, Khwai and Mababe, who depended principally on hunting and gathering of veld products to sustain their livelihoods. The licence was free and intended for subsistence hunting only. The SGL included a species list that the licence holders were suppose to tick as hunted in order to provide feedback to DWNP.

However, CSO (2005) reports that some of the licence holders did not tick the list after killing an animal, in order to use the licence again before reaching the number specified for hunting, thus killing more animals than their licences allowed. Such practices resulted in resource decline, and the SGL system was suspended to usher in the wildlife quota under the CBNRM programme. Therefore, it is an important community contribution to biodiversity conservation by the communities to recognize that SGL was detrimental to wildlife resources in their areas and to accept the wildlife quota system, which promotes regulated, seasonal and selective hunting. Controlled hunting through the quota system is thus not a destructive method, as some of the anti-hunting organizations seem to claim: it promotes both conservation and livelihoods in the remote parts of the Okavango Delta.

Thatching grass is one of the main natural resources harvested by communities in the Okavango Delta. This grass is harvested for thatching huts and for selling to tourism lodges in the Okavango Delta. At Sankoyo, Khwai and Mababe, the communities through their CBNRM project have adopted harvesting practices that promote the conservation of the grass in their areas or CHAs. These practices include:

- harvesting the grass when it is dry;
- harvesting the grass during the right season after the chief has declared it at the *kgotla*;
- allowing non-community members to harvest grass with a permit and leaving some for the village; and
- harvesting only that which is enough for use by individual households.

Several actions are taken against those who harvest thatching grass in their areas without permission of the Board of Trustees, including confiscation of the grass from the individual by CEGs who, in turn, hand the culprit over to the chief for prosecution. Depending on the seriousness of the case, the chief has powers to sentence the individual to a jail term or make him pay a certain amount of money. The various communities have developed conservation ethics and are able to implement the regulations in their CHAs, and thus they positively contribute to the conservation of resources in the Okavango Delta.

CBNRM villages are charged with the responsibility and custodianship of resources and encouraged towards conservation activities in their CHAs. As a result, the government expects them to monitor wildlife populations and the availability of other resources in their CHAs. A monitoring programme known as the Management Oriented Monitoring System (MOMS) has been implemented in the villages starting in 2007, and CEGs perform this work. MOMS is a monitoring approach that deviates from the convention of external scientists or biologists being responsible for monitoring and collecting data, but allows communities to monitor resources on their own in their CHAs. The DWNP technical support team facilitates workshops for the general community members, and the Board of Trustees and CEGs in the villages orient the people on the guiding principles of MOMS. In the workshops, some key issues or areas that local communities feel should be monitored are identified. While MOMS is only a recent innovation and it is too early to analyse its effectiveness, its long-term implications on determining wildlife quotas in the CHAs are an important aspect of conservation.

Conclusions

Since the 1990s, Botswana's tourism development has been driven by strategic goals that aim at substantially increasing the financial returns from tourism for the people of Botswana, especially for those living in the local communities where wildlife abides, and at ensuring that tourist activities are carried out in an ecologically sustainable way. These strategic goals shape the development of community-based tourism development in Botswana, particularly in rich wildlife areas such as the Okavango Delta.

The goal to increase financial returns, especially to those communities living in wildlife areas, is being achieved in the Okavango Delta. This is illustrated by tourism development through CBNRM having improved rural livelihoods at Sankoyo, Khwai and Mababe villages. It is particularly true when considering the socio-economic benefits of employment opportunities, generation of income and provision of social services such as water reticulation, availability of game meat, scholarship of students in hospitability courses, acquisition of skills in the tourism business, establishment of facilities such as recreation halls, and sponsorship of local sporting activities.

Arntzen *et al.* (2007) argue that livelihood options at Sankoyo were very poor before the introduction of the CBNRM project in the village. Local employment opportunities did not exist before CBNRM and people migrated to Maun or into safari camps in the Okavango Delta for employment opportunities. The CBNRM project at Sankoyo has widened and augmented local livelihood options through the CBNRM programme. Arntzen *et al.* (2007) further argue that, given the small population size, the changes have been significant as most households have benefited from employment and tourism development. The impact of CBNRM in improving livelihoods is thus significant when compared with the time before the programme was operational in the Okavango Delta.

The strategic goal to ensure that tourist activities are carried out in an ecologically sustainable way is being achieved in the Okavango Delta through the practices adopted for CBNRM development in rural villages. For example, selective hunting carried out in the winter season alone is now preferred as opposed to unrestricted hunting that used to be carried out year round before CBNRM was introduced. Because of the economic benefits the communities derive from tourism development, the attitudes of the residents were found to be positive towards biodiversity conservation, indicating that direct benefits (e.g. income and employment) resulting from CBNRM are important tools for achieving conservation.

Community policing and monitoring of resources through CEGs in their areas indicate the commitment by the communities to conserve their resources. They are now able to link natural resources and tourism and thus feel obliged to conserve the available resources. They view tourism development or CBNRM as an effective livelihood option that relies on the availability of natural resources. The same is also confirmed in studies in Zimbabwe by Mwenya *et al.* (1991), who argue that successful wildlife conservation is an issue of 'who owns wildlife' and 'who should manage it'. If people view wildlife resources as 'theirs' because they realize the benefits of 'owning' wildlife resources, and understand that wildlife management needs to be a partnership between them and the government, there is a higher potential for them to conserve wildlife species in their areas. In this regard, CBNRM serves as a tool for achieving both conservation and improved livelihoods in the Okavango Delta.

Since CBNRM positively contributes to improving livelihoods and conservation in the Okavango Delta, it is appropriate to state that arguments by the critics of community conservation and development programmes (e.g. Brandon 1998; Oates 1999; Terborgh 1999; Duffy 2000; Diamond 2003) are rather simplistic and misplaced. They claim that community conservation and development programmes are failing to achieve their objectives of rural development and conservation. As a result, they call for the return to authoritarian and centralized forms of resource management. However, the case of CBNRM in the Okavango Delta, specifically at Sankoyo, Khwai and Mababe villages, contradicts the claims as it has been shown that CBNRM is successfully achieving its goals of improving livelihoods and conservation.

The case of CBNRM in the Okavango Delta further illustrates that it is erroneous to generalize and conclude that community conservation and development projects are failing to achieve their objectives, as critics of the programmes seem to claim. Wilshusen *et al.* (2002) state that arguments in favour of government-led authoritarian practices of resource management are being made in isolation of the political, social and economic factors of the particular areas. The case of CBNRM in the Okavango Delta, especially at Sankoyo, Khwai and Mababe, demonstrates that generalizations made without the socio-economic and political considerations are misleading. Consequently, in this chapter, tourism development is viewed as a tool that the remote communities living in rich biodiversity areas such as the Okavango Delta can use to make a positive contribution to biodiversity conservation and sustainability in their livelihoods.

8 Coastal Bird Tourism in Namibia: Postcolonial Resources and Restraints

Petri Hottola

Introduction

Namibia is an African nation in the periphery number four of world tourism, according to Prosser's (1994) classification in which periphery number one is the core. It has ample wildlife resources and has therefore become a special-interest ecotourism destination, with emphasis on safari-style 'big five' tourism, desert landscapes, hunting and fishing. A typical Namibia tour includes the sights of Windhoek, game viewing at the Etosha National Park, perhaps a stopover at Swakopmund, or a visit to Sossusvlei in the heart of the Namib Desert, with its high, red sand dunes. The diversification trend of the African wildlife product into more specialized areas such as birdwatching, already well under way in East Africa (e.g. Okello *et al.* 2005, 163; Manyara *et al.* 2006), is not yet significant in Namibia. There are, however, many neglected resources and business opportunities which would potentially allow this expansion.

Political stability, tourism infrastructure, information and level of development are among the main determinants of tourist arrivals in Africa (Naudé and Saayman 2005). Among the growing millions of birdwatchers (e.g. Curtin and Wilkes 2005) and other nature lovers of Europe, North America and neighbouring South Africa, Namibia has a reputation for being a relatively safe and reliable destination, especially since the end of the Angolan civil war (1975–2002). It has also recently gained an additional edge as a result of East African instability. For example, Kenya struggles with safety issues and infrastructure management, despite its well-established position in the field (Okello *et al.* 2005; Linehan 2008). The volatile political situation in Zimbabwe does, however, constitute a similar image risk for any nation in the Southern African region, including Namibia.

The coast of Namibia is particularly well blessed with birdlife, a plenitude of tourism services, a refreshingly cool climate and detailed travel information in the form of guidebooks and Internet home pages. There are hundreds of thousands of Palaearctic and intra-African migratory birds wintering on coastal lagoons, in addition to resident avifauna. With this favourable setting, Namibia has become especially attractive for independent birding travellers, with whom most of the growth in the sector has recently occurred. Consequently, one would expect to see a thriving bird tourism business with diverse local involvement on the coast. In the field, the opposite was, however, discovered to be true. There are birdwatching visitors, but not as many as one would expect. Only a few international package bird tour operators have included Namibia in their product range.

Additionally, coastal municipalities appear to have little commitment to developing tourism based on wildlife, even though it already plays a key role in the existing business. As is often the case, worldwide, neither the economic importance of wildlife tourism nor its full development potential has been recognized. In Walvis Bay, with its hundreds of thousands of wildlife tourists, the dominant perception is, in the words of a local administrator: 'Tourism has no real importance in Walvis Bay. Swakopmund is the tourist town.' With its commercial harbour, fishing industry and salt works, Walvis Bay is perceived to be the industrial hub of the coast, whereas the neighbouring Swakopmund is known as the town of German colonial heritage and tourism. In reality, tourism is a major economic activity in both towns, and there are industries also in Swakopmund.

The coastal communities have nevertheless been plagued by high unemployment, the consequent social security investment draining their potential for progress. Eager to create an instant transformation to overcome the stagnation of old economies, daydreaming of novel, 'fast money' solutions has gained ground. Most recently, a visit by Angelina Jolie and Brad Pitt to give birth to their firstborn in Langstrand, a gated community-style second home development between Walvis Bay and Swakopmund, initiated another grand vision of US celebrities arriving on the Namibian coast and providing momentum for the desired developments by their generous donations. At the same time, the existing forms of resource-based tourism appear to be neglected and contradictory activities, guided by mainly foreign investors, are introduced in the increasingly congested coastal zone. There seems to be no clear vision of the long-term target of regional developments.

The following field notes bring together some aspects indicative of a bird tourism destination with ample resources but half-hearted commitment to their development:

> On 17 February 2007, I was driving along the coast of Namibia by the Walvis Bay Lagoon, a world renowned bird sanctuary. A lone man with a pair of binoculars and a telescope was walking by the dusty salt road. I stopped, and inquired if he would welcome a lift and some local advice. Gratefully, he accepted, having already walked more than ten kilometres in a largely vain search for services. A participant of an overland tour from Nairobi to Cape Town, the Irishman had decided to do a birding trip during a two-day stop in Swakopmund. The region was, after all, one of the premier birdwatching sites of Africa. First, he had visited the tourist information centre of Swakopmund to

> hire a bird guide, only to hear that there were no professional guides on the coast, and none of the local birdwatchers, who occasionally help tourists on a volunteer basis, was available. Instead, he received some information on Walvis Bay and local birdwatching sites, notably the Swakop River Estuary, and a recommendation to stay in a near-by cottage on stilts, from where it might be possible to observe the estuary. Not much could, however, be seen from the cottages, and there was no access to the wetland. By asking around, he eventually found his way to a seaside observation point and could spend a few moments admiring the birds before sunset.
>
> Early next morning, the man took a shared taxi to Walvis Bay, a twenty-minute ride. After walking through the centre, searching for a tourist information office which today exists only on maps, he relied on the outdated information of brochures and guidebooks, and continued to a nearby wetland, only to find the pools dry and 'birdless'. Not aware of another wetland created in a secret spot beyond high dunes, three kilometres away, he soon gave up, anxious to score before the heat of the noon. From the pitiful remains of what once was a 'Bird Paradise', he walked to the Walvis Bay Lagoon by the Esplanade, hoping to see Red Knots and Bar-tailed Godwits, two bird species of special interest for him. He failed there also, as the introduction of kite-boarding had scared the species away from their traditional stronghold. Already tired of walking, he nevertheless discovered many other shorebirds and flamingos farther along the Esplanade, continuing towards Walvis Bay Salt Works, in the middle of heavy salt truck traffic. Observing endangered Damara Terns had been the highlight of the Lagoon. Nevertheless, without my help he would never have reached the 'birdy' sections of the salt pans, which were too far away to be visited without transportation.

The situation is intriguing and in need of analysis, which was attempted under the wings of a research project *Tourism and the Regional Modernization of Namibia* financed by the Academy of Finland. Eventually, the work became an autopsy of a young postcolonial state, bound by its history and with a shortage of commitment in policy implementation. In this chapter, the focus is on selected situations illustrative of the inertia of bird tourism on the coast and their implications on the strategic goals of tourism development, as stated by the Government of Namibia (MET 2005a):

- economic growth;
- employment creation;
- poverty reduction;
- black economic empowerment;
- environmental and ecological sustainability; and
- reduction of regional inequalities.

This chapter begins with a short introduction to birdwatching as a leisure and tourism activity in the main tourism-originating regions of the West, and conversely in Namibia. In the next section, the resource base of the Central Coastal Region is described and discussed, with some attention paid to the present scale of wildlife tourism in Walvis Bay. This is followed by an analysis of a number of restraints of bird tourism development on the coast (shortage of bird guide services, conflicting land uses and erosion of the resource base) and an overview of recent actions to correct the situation. Finally, conclusions are presented. Seasons refer to the southern hemisphere. Bird taxonomy follows the latest edition of the *Sasol Field Guide for Southern Africa* (Sinclair *et al.* 2002). NAD indicates Namibian dollars, the equivalent of South African rand (ZAR).

Research Methods

The fieldwork was carried out between December 2006 and February 2007 and between June and July 2008, with other visits to the region in November 1998, June 2004 and July 2007. The field materials were measured against 30-years' experience with bird tourism, both as a customer and a tour leader, and journeys to over 1000 bird tourism destinations in 75 countries, including 14 nations in Africa. The work consisted of two parts: (i) evaluation of resources, especially from the viewpoint of a birdwatching visitor; and (ii) identification of the main problem issues, followed by analysis.

The study area included a long coastal stretch of 450 km, from Namibia's southern Skeleton Coast (Torra Bay, Cape Cross) to Walvis Bay and Sandwich Harbour, the coastal part of the Erongo province also known as the Central Coastal Region of Namibia (see Fig. 8.1), and access corridor zones up to 150 km inland, along the main highways to the coast. Erongo is one of the economic growth nodes of Namibia (Government of Namibia 2006; *Namibia Economist* 2008). By Namibian standards, it is a distinctively white region, with sizeable German, Afrikaner and Anglo populations, mixed with mostly Ovambo and Damara immigrants and resident Topnaars, the racial segregation of living quarters being clearly visible in the urban structure, including 'black' and 'coloured' townships, even after the Namibian independency in 1990.

The evaluation and analysis of problem situations were carried out by participatory observation, test runs, document study and stakeholder interviews, particularly in Walvis Bay, the municipality with greatest potential but also with most apparent problems. The interviews were sampled by snowballing, with focus on birdwatchers, tourists, private entrepreneurs, non-governmental organizations (NGOs) and relevant administrators. Additionally, field tours were made to Madagascar in January 2007 and to Uganda in December 2007, the latter in connection with an ATLAS Africa tourism conference at Makerere University, to collect comparative material on entrepreneurial activities in bird tourism. The practical results and recommendations of the project have been published as an evaluation report (Hottola 2008).

Birdwatching as a Form of Leisure and Tourism

For half a century, birdwatching has been one of the mainstream leisure activities in Western societies. Most European and North American nations have significant birdwatching communities and bird observation is

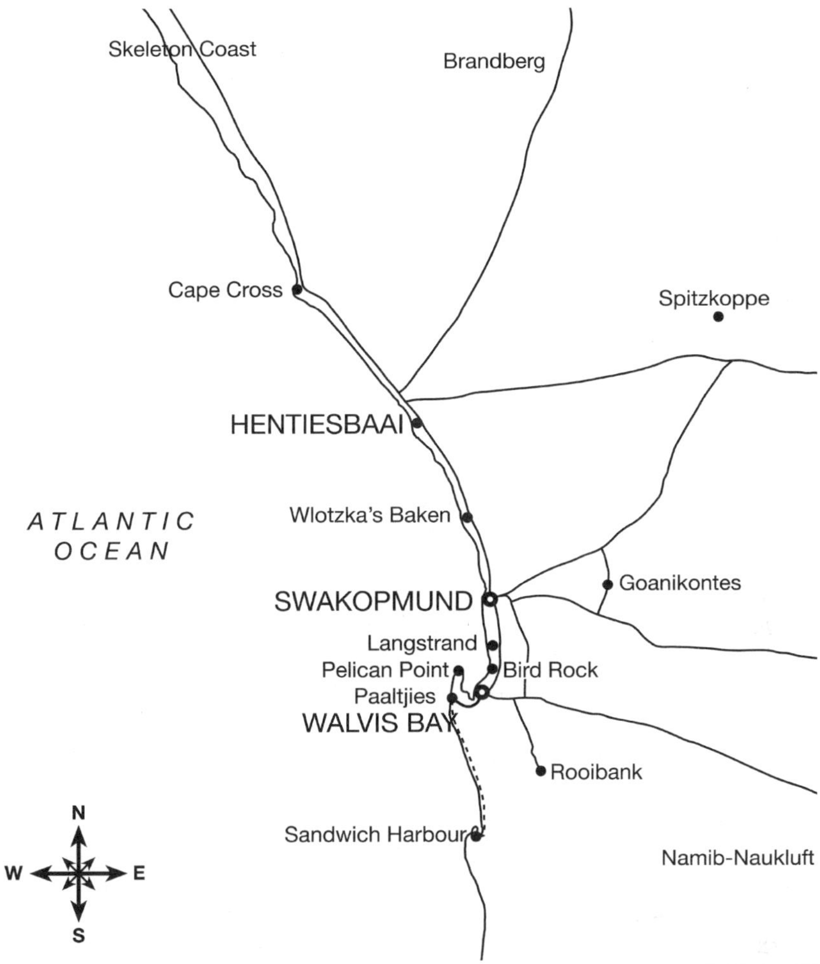

Fig. 8.1. The research area.

increasingly popular also in Australia, India, Japan, China (Jianyang 2006), Taiwan (Tao *et al.* 2004) and Ecuador, to name a few examples. Only in the lowest income per capita Third World, especially in Africa, can birdwatching be seen as an exceptional activity reserved for the well-educated and affluent.

Initially, the growth of memberships in European and North American birdwatching organizations was phenomenal in the 1970s. For example, the Royal Society for the Protection of Birds (RSPB) in the UK gained almost 300,000 new members between 1968 and 1980 (Sheard 1999, 198). In 1997, its membership rate passed the one million mark (Sheard 1999, 193) and has been growing ever since. In the USA, the number of people who call themselves birdwatchers has increased by 27% since 1995 and by 225% since 1982 (Scott and Thigpen 2003, 200). At the beginning of the 21st century, one-third (69 million) of the adult population in the USA viewed, identified or photographed birds. These are impressive figures, and also an indication of a remarkable shift in leisure.

It can be concluded that there are major numbers of potential bird tourism customers in all main tourism-originating regions of the world. In fact, there has been a 'boom' in wildlife tourism in general, and bird tourism in particular, during the past three decades (e.g. Sheard 1999; Mackoy and Osland 2004; Curtin and Wilkes 2005). In the USA, general surveys have revealed that non-residential birdwatching (trips over one mile (0.6 km) from homestead) involved 28.8 million people by the 1980s, with sex, age and race data approximately the same as for the general population but with above-average education and income levels (Shaw and Mangun 1984, in Applegate and Clark 1987, 130; Boxall and McFarlane 1993; Butler *et al.* 1994, 255; Curtin and Wilkes 2005).

In the USA, the first organized bird tours took place in the late 1930s when the National Audubon Society arranged trips to Florida (Peterson 1991, in Hvenegaard 1994, 25). The first transatlantic package tours to Europe occurred in 1961. Since then, there has been a steady but slow growth in the number of operators. In the UK, there are more than 20 travel agencies specializing in birdwatching tours, the majority with global coverage (Holden 1996; Curtin and Wilkes 2005), and some smaller enterprises. Additionally, many wildlife tourism operators include birdwatching in their programmes and also arrange tours tailor-made for bird lovers. Their overseas operations are, however, relatively small.

International bird tourism is, nevertheless, already playing a major role in a number of peripheral locations. Many of the new operators come from the destination countries in the Third World. For example, looking through the Oriental Bird Club (OBC) publications between 2002 and 2007, there is a fourfold increase in the number of operators with advertisements in its bulletins and journals, many of them domestic in the Oriental region. According to Sekercioglu (2002), Costa Rica has generated US$410 million per annum from birdwatching alone, even before the recent expansion. In some Latin American nations, such as Ecuador and the Dominican Republic, bird tourism has been declared a national priority, with consequent tourism development and conservation effort, often with community and donor involvement. In the former, the achievements of the Jocotoco Foundation have been outstanding, with a new nationwide chain of private reserves and guesthouses for bird tourists.

Birdwatchers are not a homogeneous group but divisible into a number of subcategories, with a variety of developments. The primary division is made between casual and committed birdwatchers (birders). In this text, the focus is on birders rather than casual birdwatchers, as peripheral locations such as Namibia favour the committed specialists who are not much affected by distance, perceived safety risks and costs, and may travel independently. This does not mean that there is no market for package bird tourism in Namibia. After the arrival of the Internet and its extensive information resources on bird identification and distribution, accommodation, budget flights and car rentals, choosing independent travel has become a rather attractive option. Many tourists have discovered that they need no middlemen. On the Internet, they can arrange journeys according to their individual needs without leaving their office or home.

The Namibian Birdwatching Community

A working bird tourism sector relies on the support of birdwatching communities, both locally and internationally. Birders provide the information on birdlife, work for the sector and conduct peer-review marketing through a variety of information channels. In Namibia, there are only 200 committed birdwatchers, in comparison with over 10,000 in Finland, 1.5 million in the UK (Sheard 1999, 193) and tens of millions in the USA (Scott and Thigpen 2003, 200). Local groups and organizations, even though reasonably resourceful, tend to be isolated, self-absorbed and driven by one or a few strong individuals (Shäffer 2005). There is no umbrella organization – Namibia has remained the 'back yard' of the neighbouring BirdLife South Africa. Birdwatching equipment – binoculars and telescopes – arrive via South Africa, with prices often twice as high as in the West, being therefore not affordable to most Namibians. There are hardly any academic ornithologists in the country, and the meagre research structure of Namibia is unlikely to employ more in the near future (Brown 2007).

In the Central Coastal Region, there are only around ten committed birders, even though there are many casual birdwatchers. They are quite active and some of them are among the top birders in the nation. The local birdwatchers tend to be middle-aged, with a background in white middle class, and are much occupied with a variety of tasks, with interests specific to their age group. There is limited initiative to incorporate youth into the hobby. For example, competitive activities such as bird races, with high promotional value and popularity among the younger generations, have not been arranged. In a bird race, teams travelling by car try to find more bird species than their competitors in a given area, within a time limit.

Throughout the whole of Southern Africa, birdwatching is predominantly a white leisure activity (see also Shäffer 2005). It is definitely not common among the black majority. In fact, as the internationally known bird guide Brian Finch (2007) commented in an interview in Antananarivo, Madagascar, there are hardly any black birders in the USA. Only in East Africa, recent self-empowering efforts have created a significant change, a new generation of skilful black birders and professional bird guides: people such as the ones who run Avian Watch Uganda (AWU 2008), the first indigenous bird tourism company in Uganda. Cooperation between pioneering individuals, tour companies and governmental organizations has produced dozens of self-employed professionals in bird tourism operations.

The customers of the African bird tourism sector, on the other hand, come predominantly from white African, European, North American and Australian populations, with a few East Asians. The bird tourists met during the fieldwork in Namibia were either domestic or had arrived from South Africa,

Botswana, Zimbabwe, Sweden, Finland, Denmark, Belgium, the Netherlands, Germany, the UK, Ireland, the USA or Australia.

The ethnic segregation in birdwatching as a leisure activity in Namibia has deep roots in history, partly in the colonial apartheid era, and continues to exist, even though people were supposed to look for a new multicultural Namibian identity, with less emphasis on communalism. The political structure of Namibia revolves, after all, around ethnic communities rather than political ideologies or national assimilation. The pioneer in the birdwatching field, the Namibian Bird Club of Windhoek, has until recently had a reputation for being an elite German club, with little interest in reaching across ethnic borderlines. On the other hand, many Namibian birders are English-speaking Anglos. Not many Afrikaners are birdwatchers, unless the watching of birds is done through rifle sights. Among them and the black majority, a utilitarian attitude toward animals remains strong.

According to interviews, this scant black involvement in birdwatching is often seen also as a consequence of lack of education and wealth and not as a result of racial segregation or prejudice, at least not directly. During the fieldwork, two families of black Namibian and Zimbabwean birdwatchers were encountered on the coast. There are black youth in Walvis Bay with a prolonged interest in birding, but with a variety of difficulties in pursuing their interests. As an example, the segregative aspects of Namibian society appear to discourage 'other culture' activities in the communities involved. In Kuisebmond, the black township of Walvis Bay, birdwatching is a more or less alien activity for the majority, even though many whites do it on the other side of the town, and glossy South African birding magazines are sold in supermarkets in the centre. On television, life is about partying and spending money, and little else. For the penniless unemployed, leisure has become a burden, not something to be enjoyed as a respite from work.

Ample Resources

The coast of Namibia has a number of exceptional strengths for bird tourism development:

1. There are millions of wintering and resident birds, notably major populations of shorebirds, terns and flamingos – the largest concentrations of migratory birds in sub-Saharan Africa. Shorebirds are limited globally to only a few suitable wintering habitats, in which birds from very large areas in the northern hemisphere congregate (e.g. Burger 1986). The largest concentrations of birds can be found in the Central Coastal Region, at Sandwich Harbour, Walvis Bay Lagoon (Fig. 8.2) and Salt Works, Swakopmund Salt Works, the Swakop River Estuary, between Langstrand and the Bird Rock guano platform and at the artificial wetlands of Swakopmund and Walvis Bay wastewater treatment plants.

There are several species otherwise difficult to see in Southern Africa (e.g. Redshank, Red-necked Phalarope), regularly present Nearctic vagrants (e.g.

Fig. 8.2. Birdwatchers at the biannual Walvis Bay Lagoon bird count in 2008.

American Golden Plover, Pectoral Sandpiper), Namibian endemics or near-endemics (e.g. Damara Tern, Dune Lark, Herero Chat) and a good variety of seabirds (e.g. albatrosses, petrels, shearwaters and storm petrels). Namibia in general hosts close to 660 bird species, one third of the species on the African continent (Sinclair *et al.* 2002).

2. The operational environment has, albeit decreasingly, beautiful desert sceneries, interesting mammal species (e.g. Heaviside's Dolphin, Cape Fur Seal, Brown Hyena), insects (e.g. White Beetle) and plants (e.g. *Welvitchia*) to search for. The coastal municipalities have the advantage of close proximity of major wildlife reserves such as Namib-Naukluft National Park, the Walvis Bay Lagoon Ramsar (Ramsar Convention on Wetlands) site, the Skeleton Coast Park, Brandberg and Spitzkoppe. Other wildlife tourism resources include the fish stocks of the coast, attractive to anglers (Barnes and Novelli 2008) and the unique desert scenery, with high dunes right by the sea. For conventional beach tourism the coast remains inhospitable, despite its endless beaches. The waters of the Benguela Current are too cold for swimming and sunbathing.

3. The coast is already well known for its birdlife in the main tourism-originating regions of Europe, North America, East Asia and Australia due to media coverage and the role birds have had in regional tourism marketing. Namibia in general has a reputation for being one of the safe travel destinations of Africa, the coast being at the top of the safety ranking.

4. There are a good number and variety of attractive and, in most cases, accessible birdwatching sites close to a plenitude of accommodation, restaurants, supermarkets, petrol stations and other basic tourism services, all connected by a fine road network. In this sense, the Central Coastal Region is the best served in Namibia. Finding a base for birdwatching trips is not a problem for the visitor, even though the accommodations are not specifically designed to meet the needs of birders (cf. Mackoy and Osland 2004, 21–22).

5. Up-to-date bird identification and site guidebooks are available, and additional information can be found on the Internet. In general, bird tourists have the edge by their access to more guidebooks, organizations and Internet information than any other group of wildlife tourists, Namibia being located in an especially well-covered corner of the world. The South African guidebooks (e.g. Sinclair *et al.* 2002) are of exceptional quality and easily available for a competitive price.

6. The weather on the coast is very reliable, with sunny days, practically no chance of rain (Mendelsohn *et al.* 2003, 76–85) and, in summer, the cool temperatures offer a welcome break for people who have travelled in the hot interior. Conversely, potable water is a scarce resource and will have to be either imported or created from sea water by desalination treatment, if the human population on the coast is allowed to increase (see also Barkin and Bouchez 2002).

The fact that the coastal birdwatching scene of Namibia is dominated by shorebirds places some special demands on tourism development. The effect of human disturbance on shorebirds has been well studied in a variety of international locations (e.g. Burger 1981, 1986; Cornelius *et al.* 2001; Finney *et al.* 2005). Human presence is a potential risk for the well-being of birds, particularly in the case of shorebirds. The rapidity of movement and distance to birdwatching locations both correlate strongly to the level of disturbance. Aerial disturbance has a worse than average effect on all birds, but especially on shorebirds. These birds need space for breeding, foraging and resting. For some birds, roosting is also required to maintain body temperature after diving in cold waters (Grémillet *et al.* 1998).

All in all, there is a clear difference in bird numbers between places open for human access and places protected for birds (e.g. Cornelius *et al.* 2001, 1402). In a study at Jamaica Bay reserve in New York, birds were present 42% of the time when people were present, but they were present 72% of the time when people were absent (Burger 1981, 235–240). Slow-walking birdwatchers, horseback riders and clammers did not usually cause birds to flush. Activities involving rapid movement, on the other hand, caused birds to leave the site (Burger 1981, 1986, 128). Gulls and terns were not much affected, but shorebirds were especially vulnerable to human disturbance, leaving for a considerable distance instead of returning to their original place. As a consequence, migratory shorebird roosting areas are normally strictly protected from close and fast-moving human activities (Burger 1986; Cornelius *et al.* 2001; Rodgers and Schwikert 2002; Finney *et al.* 2005, 60–61).

In bird/human contact situations, the concept of critical approach distance has been created to define the correct management of bird reserves (Newsome *et al.* 2002, 201–203). Ideally, any humans should be within the approach (head-on approach without disturbance) and tolerance (tangential approach without disturbance) distances, and avoid the response (detectable response) and flushing (bird leaves) distances. This is also beneficial for bird tourists, because they desire to observe the birds, and this option is lost if they reach the critical distance. In a case study specifically focusing on the effect of jet-skis and outboard-powered boats on waterbirds, conducted in Florida (Rodgers and Schwikert 2002), the results were:

- Flush distances varied between 8 and 156 m.
- Shorebirds had a flush distance of 11–82 m.
- Larger species were more disturbed by both jet-skis and motorboats than small species, requiring more time to take off.
- Birds reacted more to the visible size of the approaching object than to the noise it created.

Measured according to the research data, the authors suggested a minimum buffer zone of 180 m for larger wading birds (the size of pelicans, flamingos, herons, egrets), 140 m for gulls and terns and 100 m for shorebirds such as plovers and sandpipers. These zones may be narrower in places with infrequent traffic. A general recommendation of 100 m has been made for mixed-species situations, such as those at the wetlands of coastal Namibia. Response distances being species specific, stricter regulations may be required for endangered and vulnerable species, or for species of great economic importance for tourism. Aerial movement being the most disturbing form of human activity, kite-boarding, paragliding and aircraft should not be allowed close to wetlands with breeding or migratory birds.

Dolphin Cruises

At the beginning of this chapter, an administrator described the general view of tourism as a relatively insignificant activity in Walvis Bay. The reality is, however, quite different. One example speaks volumes about the unnoticed scale of wildlife tourism. The number one tourism activity in Walvis Bay, 'dolphin cruises' to the bay area, includes observation of Bottle-nosed and Heaviside's Dolphins, Cape Fur Seals and several bird species in a 3.5 hour cruise programme. White Pelicans are fed and played with initially (see Fig. 8.3), Kelp Gulls, skuas and occasionally storm petrels are met midway through the trip, and thousands of Cape Cormorants are seen at the Bird Rock guano platform, where an oyster and champagne snack is enjoyed at the end of the cruise. Otherwise, attention is paid to oyster farming, the lighthouse of Pelican Point, the Russian-operated fishing fleet and the port of Walvis Bay.

During the fieldwork it was discovered that there were at least 11 operators offering a package on a regular basis. The two main companies, Mola Mola and Levo Tours, together had over 50,000 paying passengers per year, the 10-year-old Mola Mola being most prominent. The other operators had another 50,000 customers, the total of the product reaching an impressive 100,000 tourists per year, in a town of 65,000 inhabitants. In addition to this,

Fig. 8.3. Meeting the White Pelicans on a 'dolphin cruise' off Walvis Bay.

there were thousands of other visitors using private boats to cruise the bay area for similar purposes. The number of customers is notable also on a global scale. As an example another well-established operation, at Shannon Estuary, UK, had 200 cruises with 12,000 customers annually (Garrod and Wilson 2004, 97, 110).

In 2007, each passenger paid on average NAD380 for the trip, creating a NAD3.8 (€0.3) million cash flow annually. According to Hoyt (2000), a multiplier effect of 3.5 may be adopted for whale-watching day trips in urban locations and 7.67 in remote ones. Conservatively adopting the lower multiplier figure, a total of NAD13.3 (€1.1) million is reached in a supposedly 'non-touristic' town with a NAD200 million annual budget and NAD14 million deficit (Office of the Auditor-General 2006). According to a municipality of Walvis Bay source, the current 'guesstimate' of tourists visiting Walvis Bay is 300,000 per year. One may assume that those who are keen on wildlife observation might be interested in staying longer if the sector were expanded by provision of guided birdwatching services.

Bird Tourism Guides

There are many job opportunities in a business based on skill and knowledge rather than on capital investment, such as bird tourism. The demand for wildlife guides, including bird guides, has increased dramatically during the last decade. Customers bring their own transportation and equipment, looking for local knowledge. In one example, according to Visit Scotland

(2003), there was a 70% increase in tourists using the services of wildlife guides between 1997 and 2002. On the coast of Namibia, however, not a single full-time bird guide is available for the visitors, despite frequent demand. Among the employed and well-educated whites, working as a bird guide is apparently not considered a desirable enough career, or they have other engagements, including more general nature guiding for tour groups. Among the unemployed blacks, other factors tend to deter participation. The following case, based on interviews and field observations, describes the situation.

Toivo (not his real name), a young man with an interest in birdwatching, lives in Kuisebmond close to Walvis Bay. He has recently completed his basic education. Even though Toivo got excellent grades at school and would have been keen to continue with studies, shortage of money prevented it. Consequently, he started to work as a part-time petrol station attendant two days a week, for a meagre €30 monthly salary. That is what his education qualifies him to do, the primary requirements being reliability, courteous servitude and willingness to work. For the majority of Namibians, education fails to provide any significant means to improve their social status. They are born in a certain position and tend to remain there, or go down on the ladder of the postcolonial society.

Living in a township, Toivo has limited chances of realising his personal dreams. There is hard competition for jobs in a community where more than half of the people are unemployed, petty crime and prostitution being some of the main alternatives. Every fourth person in Kuisebmond has HIV/AIDS and very few indeed have the skills required for a proper job. In the general atmosphere of low self-esteem and hopelessness, alcohol and drugs provide a temporary release, but not for Toivo. Determined not to join the ranks of 'deadbeats', he has been looking for a way out, just like thousands of others. Nevertheless, little seems to happen as the years pass by and school becomes an increasingly distant memory. In Walvis Bay, there are not many jobs available.

Toivo has made some attempts to cross the ethnic borderlines of his home town. Interested in birds, he decided to venture out with the predominantly white birdwatching community. He joined their bi-annual Walvis Bay Lagoon bird count and was impressed by the number and variety of birds available so close to his home, on the 'sunny side' of the town. Since then, he has continued to attend the censuses. Having heard about the shortage of bird guides, Toivo has considered becoming one. Today, he has got his own field guide to study the birds and is able to borrow binoculars from a nearby Walvis Bay Multipurpose Center, an USAID-financed organization. He also knows that the municipality will arrange guide training for him, if requested.

Somehow, something prevents him from taking the definite steps towards a process which is called black economic empowerment. Is he ready to cross even more borders, believing in himself and taking his future into his own hands? It is, after all, a risky investment. Is he committed enough to study the birds for years by himself, to become sufficiently qualified as a bird guide? In order to become a professional, one has to develop a high degree of expertise on Namibian birds, and there are hundreds of species with their variety of plumages, calls and behaviours to learn. It would be so much easier to just let it go, or choose a less demanding job in service of others. There would be demand for Toivo's services, but also a long way to go and little outside support. There are no role models, just a road wide open for pioneers.

In the end, Toivo preferred a more secure option by joining the ranks of youth to be trained as policemen. In this position, others tell him what to do and carry the burden of responsibility. There were other cases where similar decisions were made at an earlier stage. In this context, the restraints of black economic empowerment appear to be double-edged: the educational system does not provide the quality and length of studies required, and the culture of underachievement and risk avoidance limits the use of existing opportunities. Investment in knowledge-building in general is a major challenge in Africa, with its endemic shortage of skilled labour (Jenkins 2000; Mbaiwa 2004). A professional guide needs to be fully committed and responsible, and able to project abilities required in a demanding career. Such persons are not easy to find in Namibia.

Part of the problem lies in a 'colonized mindset', widespread across ethnic borderlines. The peripheral location and recent history of Namibia form a breeding ground for insularity and low self-esteem. Many prefer to be acted upon instead of acting themselves, perceiving the powers of decision and development to be located away from their living quarters, somewhere beyond their horizon. In the 'lager mentality', one lives on an island of his or her community, surrounded by Others with Namibian citizenship. For some, their primary reference group may be located abroad, for others in some other part of Namibia. According to the colonized world view, prosperity will one day be delivered to the people as a gift from the government or foreign donors. On the other hand, national cohesion and understanding will eventually develop, if one is patient and waits for a decade or two. These are not matters requiring personal attention, not to mention action.

Sectoring of Quiet and Noisy Recreation

One of the crucial points of strategic planning in tourism development is the identification of initiatives that would meet development goals while minimizing the risk of social and environmental damage (Fletcher and Cooper 1996, 198). The business of tourism should be economically profitable but also socially and ecologically sustainable (MET 2005a). For the responsible authorities, managing the resources of wildlife tourism is a complicated matter requiring constant attention. For example in Kenya, the flourishing ecotourism trade declined in the 1990s (Sindiga 1999). One reason for this was that the administration did not invest enough in the preservation of nature or in roads, sanitation and water, thereby degrading the quality of the product.

From an ecological point of view it is, in principle, relatively easy to manage destinations with small human population and low habitat diversity such as coastal Namibia, even though potable water is locally in short supply. The development of a coastal region for tourism may, however, become a complicated matter if contradictory activities are combined on a single site (e.g. Bacon 1987; Butler and Fennell 1994). On the Erongo coast, wildlife tourism, environmentally questionable forms of tourism and industrial activities are simultaneously introduced on sites occupied by sensitive fauna and flora, in a landscape with considerable aesthetic value (see Fig. 8.4).

This complicated situation has partly been solved by sectoring the conflicting forms of land use. Between the towns of Swakopmund and Walvis Bay, parcels of land have been allocated for birds and other wildlife, beach activities and off-road driving. The breeding grounds of the globally endangered Damara Tern have been secured by fencing, as a joint effort by the state and NGOs, with funding from Rössing Uranium. Additionally, the artificial guano platform of Bird Rock provides secure breeding and roosting for tens of thousands of birds. The coastal migratory birds have not, however, really benefited from the zoning as yet.

Activities such as birdwatching, angling, enjoying scenic views, hiking and walking, horse-riding and visiting historic sites have been termed as 'quiet recreation' (Miller *et al.* 2001). Both wildlife and beach tourism flourish in places where peaceful conditions dominate. Conversely, the thousands of quadbikers and other 4×4 enthusiasts who arrive at the Namibian coast constitute a form of 'noisy recreation', causing audible disturbance and environmental degradation. Off-road driving is banned in sensitive coastal habitats in the neighbouring nations, but not in the Central Coastal Region. Between Swakopmund and Walvis Bay there are three sectors reserved for quadbikes and other 4×4s: one south of the Swakop River, a 4 km stretch by Langstrand and the Dune 7 area (see Fig. 8.5).

Fig. 8.4. An assortment of investment opportunities for 'sustainable development', as marketed on the coast.

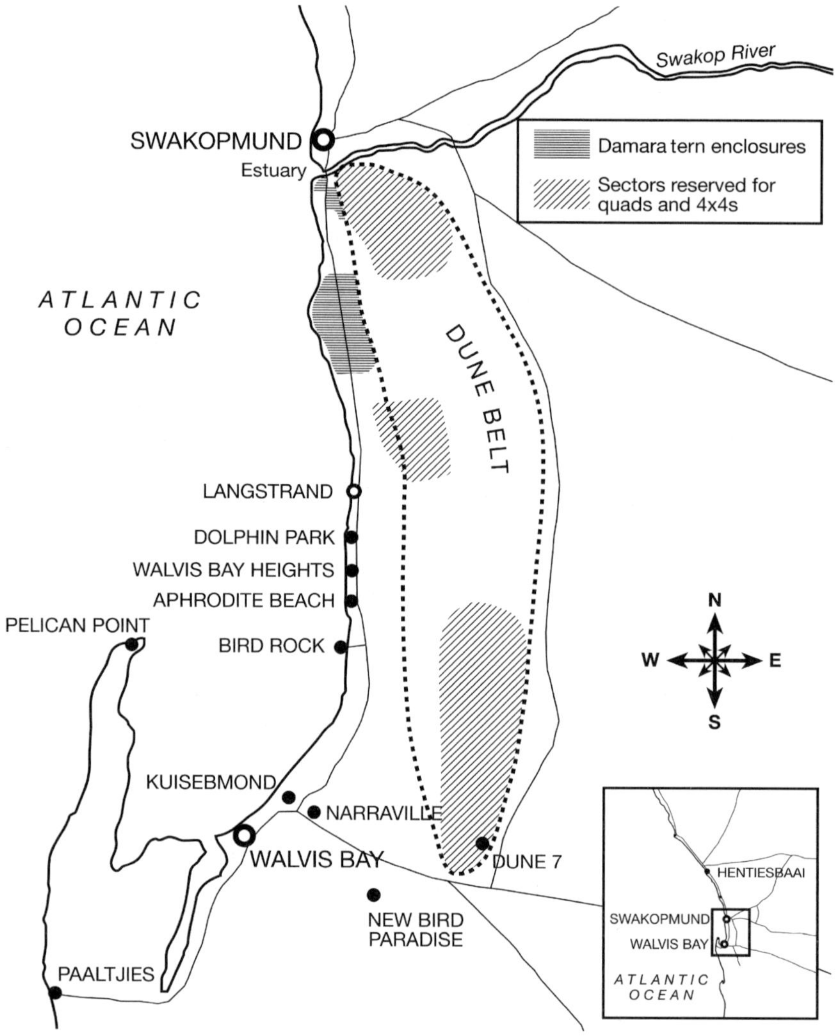

Fig. 8.5. The approximate location of protected and motor sports zones between Swakopmund and Walvis Bay in 2008.

Whenever local management fails, outsiders tend to be invited – or they arrive without invitation – to identify and exploit the lay resources and potential (Lepp 2002, 65). Similarly, on the coast of Namibia, much of the control of regional development has been given to foreign investors, with limited monitoring and considerable leakage effect (cf. Jauch 2001, 39; Tapscott 2001, 316). The incoming businesses naturally aim towards developing their own competitive edge, partly at the expense of locally initiated developments. Consequently, large sections of the formerly open coastal lands are in the process of being closed to tourism and leisure by new second home developments (Langstrand–Aphrodite Beach), geared for the anticipated arrival of members of the foreign jet set and others who could afford to live there. In the near future, industrial projects such as port expansion (Walvis Bay), a coal-fired or nuclear power plant, a water desalination plant and hydrofarming are planned to be introduced next to the coastal tourism locations (e.g. *Namibia Economist* 2008).

The sectoring plan is an admirable one, as it would create a relatively sustainable tourism environment if the established rules were followed and enforced and the concept expanded to cover all the wildlife tourism resources. This is unfortunately not the case, as quadbikes and 4 × 4s frequently encroach into sections more suitable for conservation and tourism. In fact, most of the coastal dunes have recently been occupied by motor sports, with tyre tracks criss-crossing the formerly pristine scenery. Important bird areas are trespassed on a daily basis. As a rule, the culprits do not face any consequences for their behaviour. According to field observations, they are rogue groups and individuals of white, middle-class Namibians and South Africans and not off-road tourism entrepreneurs and their customers, who act responsibly.

Cases such as that of Michaelmas Cay, Australia, prove that sectoring can be effective in places with breeding terns and frequent tourism, as long as the rules are followed to the letter (cf. Muir and Chester 1992; Muir 1993). During a field visit, I was personally able to observe that a simple rope on the sand was enough to separate the people on the beach and a breeding colony of 30,000 terns, the nearest nests being located 1 m beyond the borderline. No human footprints were seen on the other side of the rope. Such an approach does, however, not work on mainland sites with uncontrolled access. At Boulders, Cape Peninsula (South Africa), the breeding colony of African Penguins was eventually physically separated from visitors, even though the majority of the latter behaved responsibly and the birds were well habituated to people (see also Newsome *et al.* 2002).

Neglected Resources

The lack of integrated planning and management has already had its effect on some of the main bird tourism resources on the coast. The coastal strip between Bird Rock, Langstrand and beyond (see Fig. 8.5), also known as the 30-Kilometre Beach Important Bird Area (*BirdLife International* 2008), with its record densities of wintering birds (CETN 2007), has partly been run down by developers. There is a new, intensively used 4 × 4 track right on the tidal zone, a narrow space of crucial importance for tens of thousands of migratory birds and resident wildlife. The world-renowned Walvis Bay Lagoon, a Ramsar site for wetland protection but without management, monitoring or official conservation status, is silting up. Uncontrolled kite-boarding persistently disturbs the wetland and birders, even though the presence of shorebirds would require a ban on such activities. In Swakopmund, the Swakop River Estuary lacks a formal conservation status, being vandalized by off-road driving and a large binge-drinking camp in December–January, the high season for both tourism and migratory birds.

There are no observation towers or photography blinds at any of the 17 main bird tourism sites in the Central Coastal Region, even though several of them would benefit from such services (Hottola 2008). At Swakopmund Sewage Works, the future of 'bird pools' has become insecure as the plant develops its functions. The former Walvis Bay Bird Paradise, an artificial wetland, has become poisoned and barren after mosquitoes breeding in its reed beds became a nuisance in the town. A new wetland has been constructed by Walvis Bay Sewage Works a few kilometres farther away, where most of the treated sewage water outflow is channelled between dunes. Unfortunately, there is no proper access road to the site. Two 4×4 access tracks have, however, been created and the Coastal Environmental Trust of Namibia (CETN) is monitoring the development of bird populations on a regular basis.

With regard to the business side of coastal bird tourism, there is neither comprehensive marketing nor branding. The current marketing materials are based on outdated information and may guide people to already lost attractions. The branding concept of a coastal birding route with a common signage and guide materials has been proposed (Hottola 2008), but who would be the coordinator of the project? There is no regional tourism authority, and local stakeholders tend to distrust one another. In South Africa, birding routes have proved to be commercially viable, with positive results also in terms of conservation and birdwatching as an educational leisure activity.

At the moment the stakeholders on the coast, including the local birding community, communicate too little with tourism-originating areas, both regionally and internationally. In today's bird tourism, the Internet presence plays a key role in marketing, peer information updates and reviews forming the main basis for destination selection. This rapport among the international birdwatching community would be vital for Namibia, also because Africa has the worst regional image of all the continents on earth (Carter 1998). Any potential visitors need reassuring contacts to balance media information that tends to underline high levels of infection and disease (e.g. HIV/AIDS), unreliable infrastructures, political turmoil and general hazards. Namibia is, after all, a nation only relatively recently opened up for international tourism, after a long period of political and military conflict (Ankomah and Crompton 1990).

The coastal bird tourism scene would also benefit from new products. After visiting the hot and dry interior of Namibia, bird tourists are inclined to spend some time by the cool sea, preferably for observing seabirds. There are two coastal sites, Paaltjies–Pelican Point and Cape Cross, from where albatrosses, petrels and shearwaters may be seen, especially so if observation conditions were improved (more in Hottola 2008). Pelagic cruises are occasionally arranged, but the product has not really been established yet with regard to marketing and reporting. With its dramatic light conditions, sceneries and a multitude of desirable targets, the coast would also be an ideal location for field courses in nature photography. Photography being a common hobby, such courses would undoubtedly attract a variety of customers in the already existing wildlife tourism niche.

Last but not least, there is space for special occasions. The seasonal bird counts, arranged by CETN as a part of their monitoring effort, have already been a step in this direction. In the USA there are over 240 birdwatching festivals that generate millions of dollars for the rural communities (Newsome *et al.* 2002, 36). The sports-like aspects of birding agree particularly well with tourism development. There are thousands of bird races all over the world, some of them with decades of tradition, such as the Hong Kong Big Bird Race (China), the Fraser's Hill International Bird Race (Malaysia), the Kuusamo Bird Race (Finland), the Bangalore Bird Race (India), the Athens Bird Race (Greece) and the World Series of Birding (USA). In neighbouring South Africa such events have for long been a part of birdwatching culture. A 'Skeleton Coast Bird Race' would have the potential for another successful event.

Some Promising Developments

Fortunately, positive developments have recently been observed on the coast, in addition to the aforementioned 'New Bird Paradise' project. Questions on the direction of wildlife tourism development, or lack of it, have been publicly raised. Local NGOs such as the CETN of Walvis Bay, and a few individuals and administrative units, have adopted an increasingly cooperative role in sustainable tourism development, especially with regard to resource preservation. In practice, they fill up some of the vacuum left by the state and municipalities, apparently too busy with other matters to address tourism in a comprehensive way. The NGOs have built on their expertise, and have therefore gained power in the regional decision-making process (cf. Tosun and Timothy 2003; Tosun 2005).

Coastal tourism is often thought to require a stronger government involvement than other forms of tourism (OTA 1993, 310), for four primary reasons: (i) reliance on public common property resources such as the ocean and coastal environment; (ii) direct competition between tourists and local populations for use of the resources; (iii) a high degree of risk to people and property from natural hazards; and (iv) the complex and dynamic nature of coastal and ocean environments that make impacts difficult to predict. In a situation of congested coastal space, the necessity of professional management becomes especially significant. In the Central Coastal Region, the need for integrated planning and a comprehensive coastal policy with firm enforcement and monitoring has also been acknowledged, as an afterthought, and work for a draft Namibian Coastal Management White Paper has recently started as a part of the Namibia Coast Conservation and Management (NACOMA) project.

A massive new national park uniting the Namib–Naukluft and Skeleton Coast parks has been proposed, with the support of the Ministry of Environment and Tourism, Namibia Nature Foundation (NNF) and local stakeholders, and apparently accepted by the Cabinet in November 2008. The new park should include many of the bird tourism locations on the coast. The first draft of the proposed regulations (NACOMA 2008) for the coastal sections of the Namib–

Skeleton Coast National Park failed, however, to address several of the main problem issues between conflicting land uses, such as the future of the Swakop River Estuary, and even advocated limitless kite-boarding anywhere on the coast, also within the sensitive Ramsar shorebird wintering sites. The establishment of the new park may eventually address some of the restraints of bird tourism development, but only time will tell the actual nature of the changes, which could also remain superficial.

BirdLife Namibia, widely supported by Namibian birders (see also Shäffer 2005), appears to be on its way to becoming established, under the wing of NNF. This proposal has been accepted by BirdLife International and forwarded to its regional body, BirdLife Africa, for ratification. More steps have also been taken across the borders of ethnic segregation, with the emergence of a few young, black birdwatchers, one of whom may eventually follow the example of indigenous bird tourism in East Africa and initiate the much-needed guide services for the coast. Many learner guides of inland safari companies already take part in coastal bird censuses as a part of their training. The peer community support remains, however, strained, much like most of the interaction across ethnic borderlines. According to observations, activities are shared in an accommodating way, but apprenticeship-like attachments between people remain scarce, after a history of disappointments in regard to commitment among the learners.

Overall, there are many people on the coast who would welcome more bird tourists. All tourism businesses approached had a very positive view of tourism based on birds, and they expressed a readiness to become involved if the functional environment were improved. Businesses are looking for ways of supplementing their product range by bird tourism, also because birdwatching can be sold year round and could therefore balance the current seasonality (see also Garrod and Wilson 2004, 111). There are others who would see such developments as their chance of finding empowering employment, income and eventually entrepreneurship. Finally, there are many residents who would like to see the positive consequences of such a strategic move towards sustainability in their living environment, social and ecological, on the coast they love so much.

Conclusions

Properly managed, bird tourism could be instrumental in reaching the strategic goals of tourism development on the Erongo coast, as stated by the Government of Namibia (MET 2005a). The Central Coastal Region has several exceptional strengths for bird tourism. Many other international destinations struggle to establish themselves in the global consciousness of birdwatchers in the way, for example, that Walvis Bay managed to do several decades ago. They look for ways of constructing the basic infrastructure for tourism and providing gateway access for international visitors, both of which already exist in Namibia. They suffer from the non-availability of field identification guidebooks for their avifauna, whereas visitors to Namibia may choose from several excellent publications. They seldom have an extant core of wildlife tourism such as the 'dolphin cruises' from which to expand and diversify. Nevertheless, the coast of Namibia may not start benefiting from its strengths if the current inertia continues.

The exceptional success of the 'dolphin cruises' and their significant economic input in the region provide some idea of the potential of bird tourism in terms of economic growth and as an agent for the expansion of current wildlife activities. Birdwatching is, after all, the fastest-growing branch in the field. From the national point of view, there are good reasons for providing alternatives to the traditional 'Namibia tour' and attracting new international customers. Bird tourism may offer only a limited number of new jobs in high-skill field positions but its multiplier effects should not be underestimated. Each additional day the tourists stay on the coast creates employment in the general tourism and services sector, and also for those in need of low-skill jobs. Moreover, Namibia needs more high-skill service entrepreneurs as role models in the desired structural change of the economy, i.e. towards more productivity (e.g. Hansohm 2000). New second home developments, for example, are not likely to change the current status quo in this sense.

The bird tourism business not being capital-intensive, there are ways of enhancing economic empowerment for the 'previously disadvantaged classes', for releasing gifted youth from their current cycle of unemployment or poorly paid, part-time jobs. During the fieldwork, dozens of neglected opportunities for small-scale bird tourism business were identified. In terms of environmental and ecological sustainability, birding is not only sustainable but also beneficial in terms of nature conservation, education and monitoring. Among the strategic goals of tourism development, only the reduction of regional inequalities remains unrealistic in the present case. The expansion of wildlife tourism would strengthen the already vibrant province of Erongo. Nevertheless, tourism would have some potential for decreasing inequalities within the coastal communities.

In the present case, the restraints of bird tourism development have been produced both by societal and sociopolitical factors, delivered by individuals, communities and the state. Both the bottom-up and top-down avenues for development (Telfer and Sharpley 2008, 11–15) offer a rough ride for development optimists. In general, the transition from colonized dependency to independency in its full sense is not an easy one; it requires a major effort in knowledge building and a fundamental change in the mentality of the people to transform them from colonized objects into independent subjects. Having gained independence only in 1990, with the enclave of Walvis Bay annexed 4 years later, Namibia is a young nation with developing functions. The new administration is still learning to do its job, not to mention getting rid of corruption, and the educational system struggles to provide new cadres to lead the transition. The long duration of a one-party majority in Namibia, since independence, has had its benefits in terms of stability but the challenges are mounting and more diverse governance might be part of the solution.

Because of its subordinate role, a successful tourism development strategy needs the support of other national development policies (Kerr 2003). A shortage of skilled labour remains one of the key problems of tourism development in Namibia, and the situation has not really changed since the turn of the century (Jenkins 2000). From the strategic point of view, the Namibian educational system should perhaps start focusing on quality rather than quantity (the current priority), in order to train more people competitive enough to run a business, including tourism. The standards should be raised. With regard to administrative support and law enforcement, accountability and appointments based on professional qualifications would be a way forward. The plans and draft papers are largely meaningless unless they are realized within a reasonable time span.

One should also not disregard the effect of media information in support of formal education (e.g. Buckingham 2003; Raento and Hottola 2005). In today's world, most of our knowledge arrives through media channels. The current content of television in Namibia provides very little information on the ways people live their everyday lives in the tourism-originating regions, construct their values and struggle to find their place in society. Informative documentaries would improve the national understanding of tourism and the tourists, provide new models and innovations and open up the insularity of the Namibian society in a productive way. The international 'boom' of birdwatching itself has often been explained by the introduction of television programmes on birds and birdwatching (e.g. Sheard 1999).

All in all, the coast of Namibia has ample resources in terms of birds and their habitats, infrastructure and basic tourism services, but there is a shortage of human resources and proper administration. Unemployment is rife, but society struggles to produce people qualified to work in tourism, or to provide a secure enough environment for tourism development. It is therefore quite understandable that the desired progress and product diversification have not yet occurred or they may be proceeding at a rather slow pace, and that the strategic goals of tourism development remain more distant than they might be expected to. The positive developments which have recently occurred in East African bird tourism provide some hope, but do not necessarily predict similar changes in Namibia in the near future. Namibia has a shorter history of postcolonial existence and may therefore join the self-empowering movement later.

9 The Responses of the Southern African Tourism Sector in Combating HIV/AIDS

HARRI SIISKONEN

Introduction

The release of Nelson Mandela in 1990 and transition to democratic rule in South Africa meant a fundamental change in the country's tourism industry. From a small domestic market and less than one million annual foreign arrivals during the two decades before 1990, South Africa became a destination for more than nine million foreign visitors in 2007. South Africa's democratization and Namibia's independence in 1990 have promoted the attractiveness of the Southern African region as a travel destination. In Namibia, the number of foreign visitors increased from 255,000 in 1993 to 833,000 in 2006. In the global ranking of tourist destinations based on the number of visitors, South Africa was in 28th place and the only sub-Saharan country on the list of the top 30 tourist destinations worldwide. Another African destination that has been attractive for decades is Egypt, with 10.4 million visitors in 2007, and in the ranking it is just one place above South Africa (Government of Namibia 2008, 160; SATRU 2008b, 11–12).

In South Africa, as well as in other Southern African countries, tourism has become an important sector of the economy. In 2007, its direct and indirect contribution to South Africa's gross domestic product (GDP) was 8.1% and it employed, directly and indirectly, 940,000 people. Labour intensiveness, the young age-structure of employees and high job mobility are characteristic to the tourism industry. In South Africa, tourism has been prioritized as one of five economic growth sectors and it is also a strategic sector in other Southern African countries (SATRU 2008b, 1; see also Government of Namibia 2008).

One major threat to the development of the tourism industry in the Southern African countries is the widely spread Human Immunodeficiency Virus (HIV) epidemic. The impacts of HIV and Acquired Immune Deficiency Syndrome (AIDS) are affecting the operational preconditions and competitiveness of the tourism industry. In 2007, Southern Africa accounted for one-third of new infections and AIDS-related deaths globally. National HIV/AIDS prevalence rates within the adult population exceeded 15% in eight Southern African countries (Botswana, Lesotho, Mozambique, Namibia, South Africa, Swaziland, Zambia and Zimbabwe). Despite the fact that the pandemic appears to have reached its peak [in 2008] and seems to be stabilizing – and in some countries there is a slight decline in new HIV infections – it is not yet fully reflected in the labour force. The total number of HIV infected is still rising, and the great variation in the prevalence rates among countries is characteristic of this pandemic (UNAIDS 2008).

From the perspective of the tourism sector, it is a positive that the high HIV prevalence rates in the Southern African countries have not influenced the travelling decisions of Western tourists. The risk of exposure to an HIV infection is particularly related to sexual intercourse and the use of intravenous drugs, but there are numerous 'indirect' ways of being exposed to the infection, such as blood transfusion and unclean needles in the case of accident or sickness. However, in the African context, HIV has first and foremost been a sexually transmitted infection (see, e.g. Oppong and Kalipeni 2004).

The Southern African labour markets have created exceptional conditions for the spreading of HIV. The migrant labour system introduced by the mining industry at the end of the 19th and early 20th centuries is still widely in use in many countries. The recruitment of workforce from faraway regions and over national borders has been characteristic of regional labour markets (Campbell 2003). When analysing the spread of HIV in Southern Africa, several studies have confirmed that members of the mobile population, such as migrant workers and truck drivers, have usually been infected through commercial sex and have then spread the infection to their sex partners in their home districts (Williams *et al.* 2002). Webb and Simon's report (1995) on the HIV/AIDS situation in north–central Namibia pointed out the role of migrant workers, truck drivers and other smaller groups of mobile populations as carriers of HIV from the urban centres to the rural areas. The report illustrated how the prevalence of HIV decreased within north–central Namibia as the distance from main roads and local urban centres increased (Webb and Simon 1995, 11–12).

The spreading of HIV in Africa is characterized by its bimodal socio-economic nature. HIV affects not only the poor and poorly educated population, but the incidence is also high among the wealthiest and best-educated segment of the population, the white-collar elite. Even though this group constitutes only a small fraction of the population, it forms the backbone of Southern African societies (Simon *et al.* 2000; Siiskonen 2004).

Tourism belongs to those sectors of the economy characterized by a high degree of employee mobility, partly because of the seasonality of tourism work. In South Africa, the high season starts in October and ends in February. June, on the other hand, has traditionally been the month of least mobility. High job mobility concerns those working in managerial positions and those in customer services and other jobs linked to the tourism industry. The young age structure of employees also affects the mobility of the workforce in the tourism sector. Due to these factors, tourism is a risk industry in terms of exposure to HIV infection (see e.g. Rosen *et al.* 2006, 1; SATRU 2008b, 35–36).

The objective of this chapter is to explore the awareness and responses of the Southern African tourism sector in combating HIV and AIDS. Special reference is paid to the HIV/AIDS strategies adopted by the tourism organizations operating in Namibia, South Africa, Zambia and Botswana. The responses of the tourism sector to HIV/AIDS are compared with the national AIDS control programmes coordinated by the ministries of health and the programmes launched by other organizations operating in the private sector. The main emphasis is on investigating the responses of the various tourism organizations to HIV/AIDS and their own perceptions of the impacts of the epidemic on their operational environment at the grassroots level. The chapter also assesses the impacts of HIV/AIDS on the strategic development goals of the tourism sector in the Southern African countries.

One major problem related to the evaluation of the impacts of HIV/AIDS on the tourism sector is the lack of health care information, particularly concerning small and medium-sized organizations operating in the tourism business. Only large enterprises have provided occupational health care services for their employees. Due to the lack of quantitative data from the corporate level, it has been difficult to estimate the economic and other impacts of HIV/AIDS on tourism enterprises by direct methods. A similar situation also prevails among small and medium-sized enterprises (SMEs) operating in the other fields of the private sector. To overcome the lack of health information from the corporate level, researchers have collected data for their purposes by using survey methods and have also utilized general health statistics and findings of health surveys, such as Demographic and Health Survey (DHS) reports.

Furthermore, the heterogeneity of the organizations operating in the tourism business complicates the analysis of the impacts of HIV/AIDS. The gamut of tourism organizations varies from large international hotel chains and government agencies to small guide services. In a similar way, the workforce employed by tourism organizations varies from highly educated professionals to unskilled temporary labour. Due to the lack of data, there are only a few studies that focus on the impacts of HIV/AIDS on tourism organizations. This chapter is based on the comparative analysis of the available research reports and it focuses on tourism organizations, web sites of the central tourism organizations, private tourism companies and government agencies.

National AIDS Control Plans and Tourism

HIV/AIDS became regarded as a public health issue in the Western world in the 1980s. The focus was on risk groups such as homosexuals, intravenous drug users and sex workers. Schoepf (2004, 16) recalls that this risk-group paradigm also fostered belief in both biomedical and popular circles that AIDS was above all an urban disease. Instead of addressing community-based approaches, the early awareness campaigns concentrated on individual risk reduction, both in the industrialized world and in developing countries (Mann 1996, 2; see also Low-Beer and Stoneburner 2004).

Dr Jonathan Mann, the architect of the World Health Organization's Special Programme on AIDS, self-critically admitted the dominant role played by medical discourse in the implementation of the first HIV/AIDS prevention programmes:

> Some potential difficulties include: the inevitable accusation that public health is 'meddling' in societal issues which 'go far beyond' its scope of competence; the unfamiliarity of public health workers with right concepts and language; a desire by public health workers to 'own' the problem of HIV/AIDS, since by keeping the discourse at a medical and public health level the pre-eminent role of health workers is assured; and finally, that issues of human rights inherently and inevitably put the person concerned with rights potentially 'at odds' with governmental and other sources of power in the society.
>
> (Mann 1996, 16)

When trying to understand the responses of the tourism sector to HIV and AIDS, it is essential to be aware of the activities conducted by national governments to combat the pandemic. An evaluation report of 2004 focusing on the HIV/AIDS policies in the Southern African countries crystallizes the objectives of the first HIV/AIDS programmes (Nompumelelo *et al.* 2004). The Botswana example epitomises the general situation in Southern Africa in the early 1990s. In Botswana, the first short-term plan was launched in 1987 and it was followed in 1990 by the first Medium-term Plan covering the next 5 years: 'This emergency plan was followed by a 5-year Medium-term Plan (MTP I). This plan was health sector oriented and driven. It later became apparent that this approach was not adequate to address all issues relating to HIV/AIDS. A new multi-sectoral strategic plan, MTP II, was then developed' (Nompumelelo *et al.* 2004, 22).

The strategies adopted in combating HIV/AIDS in Southern Africa were not at all unique. The first AIDS control programmes were based on World Health Organization (WHO) recommendations and experiences gained from the implementation of corresponding programmes in North America, Europe and neighbouring African countries. The identification of risk groups and the classification of people into normal and others increased the stigmatization of those who were classified as abnormal, and prompted discrimination against them (cf. Schoepf 2004, 18). The straightforward Western-style campaigning for the use of condoms included in governments' AIDS prevention programmes was a controversial matter. It caused confusion among the general public because sexuality could not be a topic of open discussion between men and women, nor between certain categories of kin, especially between parents and children. Another major problem related to the first AIDS awareness campaigns was that they were implemented at a time when there were so few cases of AIDS that it was easy to doubt the whole existence of the disease. In Botswana, AIDS was referred to in the early 1990s as the 'radio disease', as most people at that time had only heard of it through radio programmes (Heald 2004, 221–227).

Even though the scope of the national HIV/AIDS strategic plans widened in the second half of the 1990s, the multi-sectoral approach meant that the involvement of other sectors should occur under the guidance of the health professionals. The private sector, non-governmental organizations (NGOs), community-based organizations (CBOs), faith-based organizations (FBOs), labour unions and others were expected to prepare their own programmes and follow the priorities outlined in the national AIDS control programmes. The problem with the first multi-sectoral programmes was that actors outside the health sector were not heard in the preparation of the new strategic plans. For example, tasks assigned to the Namibian churches in MTP II (1999–2004) were still in sharp contrast to the moral and theological principles respected by the churches. The dissemination of information designed to promote the use of condoms, particularly among unmarried young adults, could not be accepted within churches (Siiskonen 2007, 452–455).

Until the late 1990s, the national AIDS controlling strategies bypassed the multi-sectoral aspect. However, the rapidly growing number of HIV-infected and affected required the social mobilization of all stakeholders to combat the pandemic. In addition to the public sector activation for HIV/AIDS, work also occurred in the private sector and among NGOs and FBOs.

Activation of Central Tourism Organizations

In the late 1990s, one obstacle to the involvement of the private sector in HIV/AIDS work was the lack of realistic action plans and examples. The involvement of the African private sector and NGOs in the fight against HIV/AIDS often followed the model and instructions received from their international or regional central organizations. Combating HIV/AIDS was on the agenda of the International Labour Conference in 2000 and, a year later, the International Labour Office (ILO) published *An ILO Code of Practice on HIV/AIDS and the World of Work* (ILO 2001). This Code highlighted ILO's willingness to increase its support for international and national commitments to protect the rights and dignity of workers and all people living with HIV/AIDS. Director-General Juan Somavia declared that: 'In sub-Saharan Africa, where the pandemic has already had a devastating impact, the crisis has created a state of emergency' (ILO 2001, iii). ILO's reactions reveal that it was only the explosion of the HIV/AIDS epidemic in sub-Saharan Africa that had awakened the international organization.

In the tourism sector, the need for guidelines in building an industry-wide response to HIV/AIDS was first discussed in 1995 at the Think-Tank Human Resources Strategy of the International Hotel & Restaurant Association (IH&RA). In 1998, the IH&RA Think-Tank on Safety and Security made a decision to prepare, in collaboration with the Joint United Nations Programme on AIDS (UNAIDS), a guide for hotels and restaurants of all sizes to develop their own HIV/AIDS policies and educational awareness programmes. *The Challenge of HIV/AIDS in the Workplace: A Guide for the Hospitality Industry* (1999) was directed at the hospitality industry operating in the developing world (IH&RA and UNAIDS 1999).

At the regional level, the Council of the Southern African Development Community (SADC) approved a regional code on HIV/AIDS and employment in 1997. The objective of this code was to create a regional standard for the best practices for responding to HIV/AIDS in the employment setting. The aim of the SADC code was to encourage the enactment of national codes on HIV/AIDS in employment (UNAIDS 2000). In 2002, SADC (2002, 30–35, 46–47) returned to the subject by reviewing the national and sectoral HIV/AIDS policies within its member countries. The report introduced a multi-sectoral approach to the pandemic by developing sector-specific programmes that should be extended to the workplace level. The report also revealed that, at the ministry level, the initiatives to encourage tourism enterprises to launch corporate-level HIV/AIDS action plans had been modest. The SADC study recommended following the Uganda example, where interactive implementation systems between the national secretariat and ministries, districts and village councils had been developed in order to decentralize responsibility and resources to the community level in combating HIV/AIDS. This approach included the building of partnerships with all stakeholders such as the private sector, NGOs, FBOs, labour unions, the media and others (SADC 2002, 30–31).

Tourism Enterprises and HIV/AIDS

In the late 1990s, Namibian private sector enterprises still believed that HIV/AIDS was not their responsibility. However, Phororo's surveys confirmed that international and regional codes on combating HIV/AIDS at the workplace level and the multi-sectoral approach of the national AIDS controlling programmes encouraged companies to develop their own HIV/AIDS action plans. In Namibia, the major companies operating in the energy, water supply and transportation sectors were forerunners in this field (Phororo 2000, 2003).

The activation of tourism enterprises to fight against HIV/AIDS in Southern Africa began in 1999, when the Southern African Hospitality Association (SAHA) – representing national hospitality associations in Zimbabwe, Zambia, South Africa, Namibia, Lesotho and Botswana – highlighted the impacts of HIV/AIDS on the hospitality workforce. The Federated Hospitality Association of South Africa (FEDHASA) took the first concrete step by distributing the IH&RA and UNAIDS joint publication *The Challenge of HIV/AIDS in the Workplace: A Guide for the Hospitality Industry* (IH&RA and UNAIDS 1999) to its member companies. *An ILO Code of Practice on HIV/AIDS and the World of Work* (ILO 2001) became another widely used model in tackling HIV in the tourism companies. The general guidelines to combating the epidemic at the workplace level were defined in South Africa by the Department of Labour in the *Code of Good Practice on Key Aspects of HIV/AIDS and Employment* of 2000 (South African Department of Labour 2000).

At a practical level, the implementation of HIV/AIDS policies in the private sector began only in the early 21st century. A survey conducted in

South Africa by the Bureau for Economic Research (BER), among 1008 companies of various sizes operating in different sectors, revealed that HIV/AIDS policies among the private sector enterprises were the exception at the end of the last century. By 2004, the situation had improved so far that the majority of larger firms operating in mining, financial services and manufacturing were implementing HIV/AIDS policies, whereas only one-fifth of retailers, wholesalers, vehicle dealers and building and construction companies had activated HIV/AIDS policies (Ellis and Terwin 2004, 20–21; see Fig. 9.1).

The hospitality industry was not represented in Ellis and Terwin's sample, and most of the companies operating in the tourism business belong to the category SMEs (small and medium enterprises). It is assumed that the tourism sector enterprises were suggestive of other SMEs in their willingness and readiness to combat HIV/AIDS. Compared with many other sectors of the economy, such as mining or manufacturing, the tourism sector is more heterogeneous in its structure. The tourism industry is composed of large international hotel chains, a great number of small hotels and motels, guest farms, national parks and others. In order to understand how the tourism sector has reacted to the spreading of HIV, and how the virus has affected an individual organization, the question must be approached in the context of different organizations and their operational environments.

Awareness of HIV/AIDS in the Tourism Sector

Most of the studies investigating the impacts of HIV/AIDS have focused on the sectoral level, such as education or agriculture, whereas studies focusing on the problems caused by the pandemic to private enterprises or public sector organizations at grassroots level are rare. There are only a few studies

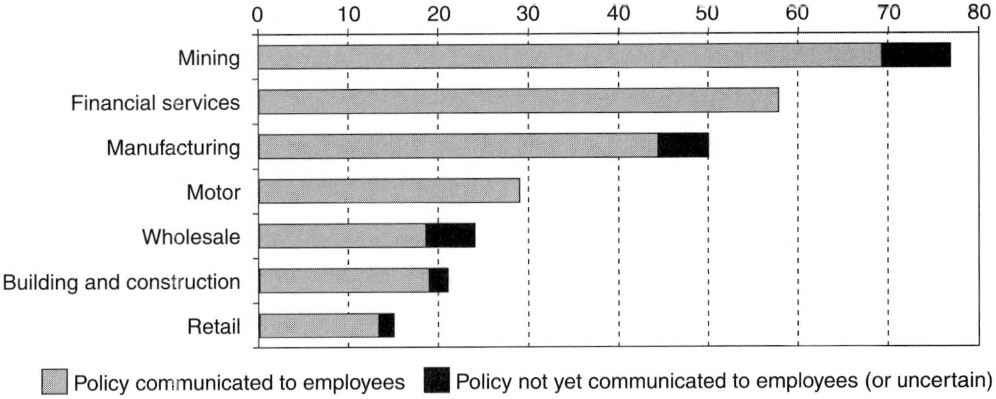

Fig. 9.1. Percentages of the companies surveyed in South Africa implementing HIV/AIDS policy (n = 1008) (from Ellis and Terwin 2004, 21).

available that concentrate purely on the impacts of HIV/AIDS on tourism enterprises. In this study, the awareness of tourism organizations of HIV/AIDS and their readiness to combat the disease are discussed in the context of large international hotel chains, SMEs operating in the tourism business and government agencies involved in tourism.

HIV/AIDS programmes launched by the international and national central organizations of the tourism industry encouraged the Tourism, Hospitality and Sport Education and Training Authority (THETA) (THETA 2003a) to implement in 2002/03 an HIV/AIDS knowledge, attitudes, practices and behaviour (KAPB) survey among employees working in the South African hospitality industry. This survey was conducted by Grant Thornton Strategic Solutions and included 5000 enterprises. The organizations surveyed were randomly selected, covering the entire sector, and no HIV testing was conducted during the survey. In late 2003, another survey was conducted in the South African hotel sector. Herholdt-Smith's survey (2003) focused on independent hotels and hotel chains and included 306 enterprises.

The latest studies investigating the impacts of HIV and AIDS on tourism enterprises were published by Sydney Rosen's research teams in 2006 and 2007. The studies were conducted among tourism organizations operating in Livingstone on the Zambian side of Victoria Falls. Livingstone is the major tourist destination in the country, and this has generated a wide range of recreational activities for tourists who come to see the falls. Increasing tourism has led to rapid population growth in Livingstone: in 2000 the population of Livingstone was 97,500 (Rosen *et al.* 2006).

The above-mentioned studies concentrated on three major problems. First, they explored the awareness of the tourism organizations of HIV/AIDS. Their second objective was to evaluate the economic impacts of the pandemic on different organizations. The third research problem focused on analysing existing opportunities for mitigating the impact of HIV/AIDS on the development of the tourism sector.

The findings concerning the awareness of the tourism organizations of HIV/AIDS indicate that there is no consensus on the responsibilities in the fight against the disease: Should the tourism organizations themselves act or leave the matter to national HIV/AIDS controlling programmes? The THETA (2003a) survey revealed that 93% of the organizations surveyed did not have an HIV/AIDS policy, and in 75% of the respondent hospitality organizations no one was responsible for managing HIV/AIDS in the workplace. More than 90% of the organizations surveyed did not provide any training or care services with respect to HIV/AIDS. Herholdt-Smith's (2004) findings are a little more encouraging compared with the THETA survey. Of the hotels surveyed, 75% were aware of the impacts of HIV/AIDS on their companies and 60% of these companies had an HIV/AIDS policy. According to Herholdt-Smith, about 60% of employers had an opinion as to the percentage of HIV positive employees, but only 15% actually knew the numbers of HIV infected employees in their establishments. Rosen *et al.* (2006, 48) also perceived that HIV/AIDS was not considered a serious concern among the small and medium-sized tourism companies.

This low level of awareness of HIV/AIDS at the corporate level is not surprising. International hotel chains operating in the Southern African countries began to launch their own HIV/AIDS action plans only in the early 21st century, and in smaller hotels the process is still unfinished. For example, the Holiday Inn hotels in Zimbabwe introduced their HIV/AIDS policy in 2003, and similar processes were proceeding in the Sun International and Cresta Hotels (Jauch 2007b, 28–30). Jauch's report on working conditions in the African hotel sector pays attention to the need for adopting common practices in relation to HIV/AIDS:

> Some hotels have established good practices regarding HIV/AIDS and thus it seems possible to establish a common set of standard policies at all hotel chains. Such policies should include non-discrimination based on HIV status; awareness campaigns; voluntary testing and counselling; and the provision of anti-retroviral drugs and food supplements.
>
> (Jauch 2007b, 30)

Economic Impacts of HIV/AIDS on Tourism Organizations

The lack of information about HIV infection rates among employees and lack of awareness of the economic effects of the pandemic at the corporate level emerge clearly from the surveys focusing on the hotel sector. The effects of HIV/AIDS are classified in the literature as either internal or external effects. The internal effects, such as increasing absenteeism, higher pension payouts and breakdowns in worker discipline and morale, require responses from companies. The external effects, such as decreases in demand for companies' products and rising costs associated with breakdowns in institutions, are hard for companies to manage or control. Studies focusing on the economic impacts of the pandemic on tourism organizations concentrate on discussing the direct internal costs, which can be measured by using human resources and financial data that large companies routinely collect, whereas indirect costs, as illustrated in Fig. 9.2, are difficult to measure (see Simon *et al.* 2000, 1, 6).

The THETA (2003a) survey revealed that 64% of the respondent companies believed that the pandemic would have negative impacts on their business operations. Of that 64%, 44% believed that the impacts would only be slight. Herholdt-Smith's (2004) survey confirms the THETA findings of the unawareness of the hotel sector about the real economic costs of the pandemic.

It was Rosen's research team that first tried empirically to measure the costs of HIV/AIDS to the tourism sector. To overcome the lack of occupational health care data, they had developed, in their previous studies dealing with the effects of HIV/AIDS on labour productivity in South Africa and Kenya, a model for analysing the costs caused by the disease for an individual enterprise. Information collected from the tourism organizations was compared with the Demographic and Health Survey (DHS) and Antenatal Clinic (ANC) survey data. The study focused on three different types of tourism organizations in Livingstone in Zambia:

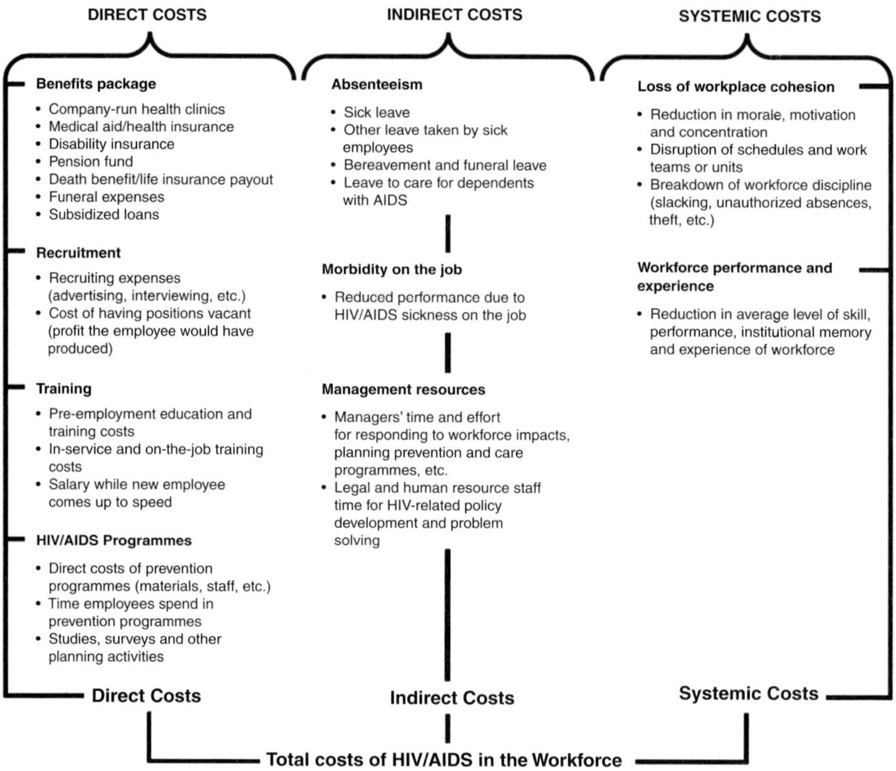

Fig. 9.2. Internal economic impact of HIV/AIDS on the workforce in the private sector (from Simon *et al.* 2000, 6).

1. The Royal Livingstone and Zambezi Sun hotels, which belong to the Sun International hotel chain and represent a large tourism company. In 2005, their workforce was composed of 357 permanent and about 500 non-permanent employees.
2. The Zambia Wildlife Authority (ZAWA), which is one of the most important government agencies involved in the tourism sector. In 2005, ZAWA had 1454 employees who consisted mainly of wildlife police officers based in the national parks and of whom 90% were male. Patrolling data were collected for 242 patrol officers, but the final dataset contained records for only 87 patrol officers.
3. SMEs represented the third type of tourism organization. This category included hotels, lodges, guesthouses, restaurants, tourist transport firms, gift and curio shops and companies providing all types of services for tourists. An SME was defined as having fewer than 200 employees. Of the 123 companies listed as fulfilling the requirements in Livingstone, 37 companies were selected for the final sample.

It was estimated that labour costs of the Sun International hotels in Livingstone would increase by nearly 11% if employees did not have access to effective HIV treatment (Rosen *et al.* 2006, 11–13). In the ZAWA case, measuring the costs of HIV/AIDS was more difficult because the failure to achieve its mission imposes social costs on Zambia as a whole and has an immediate effect on ZAWA's own budget. To increase the comparability of the ZAWA case with that of Sun International, the costs of HIV/AIDS for ZAWA were estimated in the context of its capability to produce patrol nights. The production costs per patrol night were estimated to rise by 10% if no treatment was available. In 2005, HIV/AIDS reduced ZAWA's service delivery capacity by 6.0% and increased labour costs by 9.3% (Rosen *et al.* 2006, 18–35; Rosen *et al.* 2007).

Accounting the costs of the pandemic for SMEs operating in the tourism business proved most difficult. Small companies do not usually keep records of absenteeism, which made it impossible to analyse absenteeism quantitatively, and this has also complicated managers' capability to estimate the economic impacts of absenteeism. It was found that the cost per employee loss due to HIV/AIDS was substantial, but there was great variation between companies. The pandemic seemed to increase labour costs roughly by 2.4%. The companies investing more in worker training were facing higher costs when they lost an employee to the disease. Managers' views of the current economic impact of HIV/AIDS on their companies indicate the difficulties in recognizing the problem in SMEs. One explanation why HIV did not appear as a big problem in SMEs was that job vacancies were reported to be brief, less than 3 months in most cases. Most companies reported little difficulty in finding new employees. The only exceptions were for tour guides and chefs, both positions that require training and experience (Rosen *et al.* 2006, 36–50).

The report of Rosen's research team indicates that Sun International and ZAWA had become aware of the high costs HIV/AIDS was causing for their organizations, but in the majority of the SMEs the rise in labour costs had been moderate. Compared with other enterprises operating in the private sector, it is predictable that HIV/AIDS will increase labour costs faster in the tourism sector due to the young age structure and mobility of the workforce. A survey carried out between 1999 and 2001 among large companies in South Africa and Botswana indicated that the rise of labour costs varied from 0.4 to 5.9% depending on the firm (Rosen *et al.* 2004, 323; see also Simon *et al.* 2000).

Adjustment of the Tourism Sector to HIV/AIDS

The rise in labour costs in Southern Africa due to HIV/AIDS is diminishing the competitiveness of African business in the global markets. Rosen and Simon (2003, 131–132) present four strategies for readjusting to the new situation at the level of an individual company. They point out that the options are not mutually exclusive, and many companies have adopted a mixture of all of them. The first strategic option is to invest in HIV prevention programmes designed to reduce the incidence of the infection among their employees. The second option is to provide treatment, care and social support to employees who are HIV-infected and those who have AIDS. The third option is to invest in training of new workers and broaden the skills of those already employed in order to maintain and replenish their human capital base. The fourth option is to alter the benefits policy, contract structure and hiring practice of the company in order to reduce its HIV/AIDS-related costs.

The last strategic option has been called in literature the 'burden shift'. This means reducing or avoiding the costs caused by HIV/AIDS for the company and shifting the burden to governments, NGOs and households. The instruments used have been classified in literature into three categories. First, the company can reduce the total number of permanent employees in the workforce by substituting them with new technology (mechanizing) or increasing the proportion of non-permanent workers. Secondly, the company can try to reduce the number of HIV-positive employees in the workforce, for example by pre-employment screening or altering the terms of employment contracts. Thirdly, the company can reduce the cost it bears per HIV-employee, by taking steps such as cutting the levels of retirement, death, health or sick leave benefits. Sometimes the cutting of benefits is not only dependent on actions taken by the company. In one example, a South African in-house health insurance provider reduced its ceiling for HIV-related claims by 85%, to the loss of the insured company (Simon *et al.* 2000, 8; Rosen and Simon 2003, 131–132).

Putting the claimed 'burden shift' into a historical context gives a slightly misleading interpretation of the situation. In Southern Africa, the great majority of SMEs have not provided occupational health care services but their employees have been using public health services. When approaching the issue from the perspective of an individual SME, avoidance of costs illustrates the attitude of an SME towards the implementation of HIV/AIDS prevention and treatment programmes better than does the 'burden shift'.

The rise in labour costs touches particularly the labour-intensive lines of business such as the tourism sector. The attractiveness of the Southern African tourist destinations is based not only on unique nature, political stability, working infrastructure and good-quality accommodation but also on a professional and skilled labour force. Large hotel chains have understood this by launching their own HIV/AIDS action plans. Since 2003, the Holiday Inn hotels in Zimbabwe have been implementing an HIV/AIDS programme that provides training on awareness of HIV/AIDS, voluntary counselling testing (VCT) services and treatment of HIV positives. The company also assists HIV positive staff with dietary supplements and antiretroviral therapy (ART) drugs. In Namibia, Sun International provides its staff with HIV/AIDS education and training based on a peer education model and has also arranged condom distribution. In addition to direct support to their permanent staff, hotel chains have launched social responsibility programmes for supporting the families of HIV-infected and AIDS orphans (Jauch 2007b, 28–29).

The cost accounting model of Rosen's research team predicts that the implementation of the HIV/AIDS prevention and treatment programme among the permanent staff of Sun International in Zambia is viable at all job levels. The savings per employee are the highest among managers and senior staff members. Furthermore, these savings will keep on occurring several years into the future. In a similar way, treatment of AIDS-related cases with ART drugs had positive results. Due to the HIV/AIDS policy implemented at Sun International, a majority of those sick with AIDS were already obtaining ART both through private and public health services (Rosen *et al.* 2006, 12–15).

According to Rosen *et al.* (2007), the implementation of an HIV/AIDS prevention and treatment programme would also be beneficial at the Zambian government agency ZAWA, at all job levels. Even though ZAWA did not have its own HIV/AIDS action plan, it was supporting sick employees and their families by paying their travelling expenses due to the sickness, life insurance benefits, funeral costs and costs of training new employees. The cost accounting model was based on the assumption that an HIV-positive employee would begin ART 2 years before he would otherwise have died of an AIDS-related cause and would remain on ART and fully productive in his job for 7 years, whereafter the treatment was assumed to cease to be effective and the employee would retire on medical grounds. The benefits of HIV/AIDS treatment would be even greater for ZAWA because it cannot easily dismiss or retrench sick workers, as is happening in the private sector.

The studies dealing with HIV/AIDS among the staff of the national parks and related institutions highlighted one factor in combating the disease. When patrolling in isolated areas, the staff members were separated for weeks from their families, which increased their risk of HIV infection through extra-marital sexual relations. This risk could be reduced by arranging a condom distribution system, but the arrangement of permanent housing to employees and their families close to the parks was considered the most effective means of avoiding HIV infection (Gelman *et al.* 2005; Lopez *et al.* 2005).

Willingness to systematically combat HIV/AIDS was lowest among SMEs operating in the tourism business. Rosen's research team noticed that direct costs caused by HIV/AIDS were modest among SMEs in Livingstone compared with those at Sun International or ZAWA. However, it was estimated that actual losses would have been bigger than reported because some HIV-positive workers had probably resigned before becoming disabled. Despite avoiding the expenses caused by HIV/AIDS, the SMEs surveyed in Livingstone were still more active in responding to HIV/AIDS than the same-sized private companies in South Africa (Rosen *et al.* 2006, 49–50).

In their study concentrating on HIV/AIDS prevention, treatment and care provided by SMEs in South Africa, Connelly and Rosen (2005, 623–625) found four main explanations for the low activity of SMEs in tackling HIV/AIDS:

1. SME managers are lacking information about HIV/AIDS and companies are not large enough to develop and implement programmes in-house, and so services must be bought from outside providers.

2. SMEs have a low willingness to pay additional costs caused by HIV/AIDS prevention and treatment programmes. This also concerns companies that are losing employees to AIDS because the cost of replacing unskilled workers, who make up the vast majority of AIDS-related terminations, is negligible.

3. Stigma is closely related to HIV infection. Some managers believed that many employees had resigned without claiming any benefits, to avoid exposure of their HIV status.

4. International firms have to adhere to international standards and face pressure from organized labour and shareholders, but SMEs do not have great external or internal pressures to implement HIV/AIDS programmes. This has led to the situation where SMEs are seldom able to cover the full cost of workplace HIV/AIDS programmes, but employees have to turn to the public health services for procuring ART or other medical treatment.

It is probable that the same problems also concern SMEs operating in the tourism sector. For increasing awareness of HIV/AIDS, particularly among SMEs, THETA (2003b) has published the *HIV/AIDS Handbook for South African Tourism and Hospitality Companies*, that includes information about the HIV/AIDS pandemic, with its background and detailed information for developing an HIV/AIDS workplace policy, tools for preventing the spreading of the epidemic, tools for HIV/AIDS treatment, care and support and tools for monitoring the implementation of the HIV/AIDS policy. The detailed instructions and the style of presentation suggest that the handbook is targeted at SMEs.

Herholdt-Smith (2004) insists that HIV/AIDS was considered among hotel managers as being only of interest and concern to the human resource specialists or health care professionals, instead of being the concern of every manager in the hotel business. From this aspect, it is easier to understand why it has been difficult to give up the paradigm that HIV/AIDS is only a public health issue. SMEs operating in the tourism business have not yet faced problems in recruiting new employees for replacing the HIV-infected and AIDS-affected staff members. It seems that avoidance of costs, instead of investing in HIV/AIDS prevention, care and treatment, will continue among SMEs until there arises a shortage of cheap labour (see also Stevens *et al.* 2004).

Jänis' (2008, 8–10) recent findings from the Caprivi region in northern Namibia suggest that lodges already have problems in replacing lost employees. However, the greatest problem encountered at the company level was the lack of clear instructions and action plans, and how HIV-positive employees should be treated and supported. The lodge managers felt hesitant about how to handle the issue and were waiting for clear guidelines for the implementation of an HIV/AIDS policy at the company level. Jänis' findings indicate that the socio-economic impacts of HIV/AIDS will soon touch SMEs on a larger scale, and they will be compelled to adjust to the new situation. Customers of the hospitality industry can accelerate the process by raising the implementation of the HIV/AIDS policy as a brand issue.

HIV/AIDS and the Strategic Tourism Policy Goals

Tourism has a very important role for all the Southern African economies and it has been prioritized as a growth sector. Namibia's latest development plan for 2007/2008–2011/2012 highlights the direct and indirect benefits of the development of the tourism sector:

> Tourism is regarded as the world's largest and fastest growing sub-sector. Namibia is strongly positioned to be a major long-term beneficiary of this growing trend. The rich and growing wildlife, diverse landscapes and cultures, and majestic wilderness settings provide internationally competitive tourist attractions for game viewing and hunting and nature viewing.
>
> As in other developing countries, tourism has been identified as an important sub-sector in Namibia not only for accelerating economic growth but also for poverty eradication and empowerment of vulnerable groups. Namibia's innovative approaches of linking conservation to poverty alleviation through its communal area conservancy programmes and pro-poor tourism initiatives have gained worldwide acclaim. The Government, together with its development partners in non-governmental organizations, the private sector and international community, has introduced several programmes and legislative framework to develop the tourism sub-sector overall and to bring previously disadvantaged communities into mainstream tourism. Thus, tourism is a conservation and socioeconomic development tool for rural development and national economic growth.
>
> (Government of Namibia 2008, 141–142)

In Namibia, as well as in South Africa and Botswana, the national aims of the tourism policy can be condensed into six overall objectives:

- poverty reduction;
- employment creation;
- economic growth;
- black economic empowerment;
- reduction of regional inequities; and
- ecological sustainability (MET 2007; see also Goodwin *et al.* 2002; Government of Namibia 2008, 141–143).

The strategic goals of the tourism sector reveal the problems related to narrow approaches in development planning. HIV/AIDS is widely discussed under population and health policy but has been totally bypassed when forecasting the development prospects of the tourism industry. The high HIV prevalence rates tell that the epidemic cannot be considered a minor problem, and should also be recognized in sectoral planning.

The fast spread of HIV is threatening the attainment of strategic goals in the tourism sector. The economic effects of the pandemic are not only restricted to an individual employee but also touch the family and relatives of the person who has AIDS, particularly among sections of the population in need of empowerment. The declining working ability of the AIDS-affected employees, sick leave, ART and other drugs, training of extra staff to replace the sick employees and other tasks and problems incur extra expenses that will decrease the profitability of the tourism business. The growing labour costs and shortage of skilled labour due to the spread of HIV/AIDS may reduce the competitiveness of the Southern African region as a tourist destination, but the tourism sector has been unwilling to assess this scenario. Not even the tourism marketing growth strategy of South Africa for 2008–2010 recognizes HIV/AIDS as a challenge for the hospitality industry (SATRU 2008a). The same conclusion can also be made with regard to similar scenarios that attempt to predict the future of the tourism sector in Southern Africa.

HIV/AIDS is threatening all the strategic goals of the tourism industry in both direct and indirect ways. The findings of Gelman's research team (Gelman *et al.* 2005, 16–17) indicate that HIV/AIDS is indirectly affecting, for example, ecological sustainability. Her research team paid attention to the use of the funds budgeted for conservation purposes in the Southern African national parks. They also noticed that the limited conservation funds were diverted to training of new staff members to replace the sick and dead, rising medical expenses, sick leave, insurance payments and funeral costs caused by HIV/AIDS. Some protected area authorities had hired additional personnel, such as occupational health nurses and social workers, to provide increased services to the staff members, or had contracted health clinics to provide services.

Gelman's example points out the need to take the real costs of HIV/AIDS into account in planning. This should be done at the national, sectoral and enterprise levels. It seems that some expenses caused by HIV/AIDS are hidden in the balance sheets of enterprises and organizations. However, the heaviest burden from HIV/AIDS has fallen on the infected and affected and their relatives. In the Caprivi Region of northern Namibia, the increasing incidence of bushfires since 2003 has been connected to HIV and AIDS, as AIDS orphans and remaining family members have used fire as a cheap, labour-saving method to clear agricultural land (Gelman *et al.* 2005, 17). It may be difficult to reduce regional inequalities within nations through tourism if special measures are not targeted on those regions with high HIV/AIDS prevalence. The most undesirable scenario is that HIV/AIDS would lead to a decline in the tourism business. This is possible if the tourism sector continues to be unwilling to invest in HIV/AIDS prevention, treatment and care. In the near future, the shortage of skilled labour will become evident if nothing is done to keep the infected and affected staff members for as long as they are capable of working.

Conclusions

Until the mid-1990s HIV/AIDS was considered a public health issue that, along with malaria or tuberculosis, was to be solved by the health authorities. In the second half of the 1990s national AIDS-controlling programmes began to emphasize a multi-sectoral approach to combat the disease, but it was expected that the commitment of the private sector, NGOs, FBOs and others should occur purely according to the guidelines provided by the health authorities. Unlike in the industrialized countries, in Africa HIV did not focus on risk groups – such as homosexuals or intravenous drug users – but touched all population groups, particularly the sexually active young and mobile population.

In the late 1990s, the explosive spreading of the HIV epidemic in sub-Saharan Africa awakened international organizations to tackle the problem. HIV/AIDS prevention and treatment programmes launched by international organizations, such as ILO and IH&RA, worked as examples and encouraged national central organizations, such as FEDHASA, to introduce HIV/AIDS action plans to be implemented in their member organizations.

The commitment of the tourism sector to HIV/AIDS work began first in the large hotel chains in the early 21st century. Due to the fact that HIV/AIDS has not been socially selective, effects of the pandemic have been felt by skilled employees working in key positions in tourism organizations, as well as by the unskilled workforce. Unlike large hotel chains, SMEs operating in the tourism business have slowly activated HIV/AIDS work. Until now, their investments in occupational health care services have been minimal and they have considered that an HIV/AIDS action plan would mean a new cost to them. One explanation for the indifferent attitude of SMEs towards investing in HIV/AIDS work is that they have not yet encountered a labour shortage because a large share of their workforce is composed of unskilled labour that has been easily available. However, there are signs that labour shortages will soon affect SMEs too.

Studies focusing on the economic impacts of HIV/AIDS on tourist organizations have indicated that investments in HIV/AIDS action plans are economically beneficial in the long term at all job levels and in different tourism organizations. Despite the fact that the number of new HIV infections has stabilized, the social and economic burdens of the pandemic will increase in the near future due to the high HIV prevalence rate among the young adult population. Therefore, the cost avoidance policy adopted by SMEs operating in the tourism business appears to be short-sighted. Based on the latest research findings, the best solution recommended is to invest in HIV/AIDS prevention and treatment programmes that would ensure the competitiveness of the Southern African tourism business in the future.

HIV/AIDS is threatening the attainment of the strategic tourism policy goals. Therefore, it is essential that the assessed impacts of the pandemic are also taken into account in sectoral development planning. Due to the important economic role of the tourism industry, a decline in tourism business would cause serious problems for all Southern African economies. To avoid the realization of this scenario, it is necessary to encourage and support enterprises to launch and implement HIV/AIDS programmes at the corporate level.

10 Interplay Between Local Service Suppliers and Incoming Tour Operators: the Case of Madagascar

Øystein Jensen

Introduction

Tour operators play an important role by the generation of organized tourism to many African countries. The problems in many countries and areas that have not been exposed to tourism include their difficult access to attractive areas, lack of facilities and other types of infrastructure and lack of information and organization. In this situation, tour operators can compensate for the dearth of services and information that international tourists need.

From the perspective of sustainable tourism, tourist visitations to a country or an area should contribute to positive local development (Milne 1998; Hall 2000; Richards and Hall 2000; Tosun and Timothy 2003). One of the questions is how to build a local tourism industry that can participate in the national and local development of a country. When it comes to tourism generated by international tour operators, an important question will thus be how to create a context in which tour operators are able or willing to cooperate with local service suppliers in the development and delivery of organized tourist products. How can such cooperation take place without jeopardizing service quality if there are no local service suppliers with the required competence and resources?

This situation raises additional questions: How willing are tour operators to cooperate with other local suppliers? When an actual business exchange takes place between such unequal parties, what are its characteristics? In a long-term perspective, how can sufficient competence and other capabilities be developed among local actors? What role could the tour operators themselves play in nurturing such competence among potential or actual local service suppliers? The purpose of this chapter is to find answers to these questions by presenting the results of an empirical study in Madagascar of incoming tour operators, regional tour operators, regional and local guides and villages. Hotels and restaurants are thus excluded from this study.

Methodological Approach, Theory and Research Material

The study adopted a qualitative approach (Miles and Huberman 1984; Strauss and Corbin 1990) based on personal interviews and field studies in Madagascar. The collection of research material was carried out by the author during 5 months over the course of four stays in 2005, 2006 and 2007. The interviewees were incoming tour operators (TOs) in the capital (Antananarivo), regional TOs in two central regions (Fianarantsoa and Vakinakaratra), regional guides and regional and national tourist organizations and authorities. The author made field trips to villages and interviewed guides, village chiefs and project leaders. The interviewees in companies, organizations and public agencies were the managers or owners. Incoming TOs represented the demand side – actual or potential buyers of local services; regional TOs and guides and villages represented the supply side. The organizations and public agencies performed a neutral or a facilitating role for business exchange between incoming TOs and local service suppliers.

Most of the interviews were conducted in French. Local guides served as translators for the interviewees who spoke Malagasy. The sources comprised a selection of 12 incoming TOs based on criteria of variations linked to range of experience, size and type of products; 20 regional TOs and regional/local guides; as well as 12 tourism business organizations, NGOs and national and regional public tourism agencies. Systematic observations and interviews were conducted during six field trips that also included five villages. Many people were interviewed several times during the different periods of stay.

The topics of the interviews were based on pre-categories from theoretical frameworks that had been established in the research on marketing channels in tourism, exchange relationship governance (concentrating on contracts) and competence sharing, business partner selection and local sustainable tourism development. The interview questions were adjusted during the interview process as relevant themes emerged (Miles and Huberman 1984; Strauss and Corbin 1990). The main targets of the inquiry included the wish to enter exchange relationships, exchange-specific behaviour, criteria for choice of exchange partners, the role played by the participants in exchange relationships, activities, strategic considerations, competence and considerations of the conducting of tourism in Madagascar. Gradually, the focus turned even more to the last aspect and to the role and situations of the different parties. The material analysed in this chapter is embedded in a wider project analysing organized tourism in Madagascar, and the text is based on selected parts of the complete research findings.

Some Conceptual and Structural Clarifications

There have been some limited empirically based studies on cooperative behaviour among TOs in international distribution channels (Bywater 1992, 2001; Buhalis 2000; Casarin 2001; Jensen 2001; Medina-Muñoz *et al.* 2003; Roper *et al.* 2005). However, empirical research on incoming TOs is rather scarce (Jensen 2000, 2002). National incoming TOs are the hubs in a network of exchange relationships in the international distribution system or value chain of organized tourism (Holloway 1989; Laws 1997; Middleton and Clarke 2001). Externally, the incoming TOs have their primary communication and exchange relationships with global TOs abroad. The incoming TOs design and distribute the tours and service packages through global TOs, who then market the products under their own brand name to tourist market segments and/or travel agents. Some incoming TOs can also produce their own packages and offer them directly to the consumer markets, mainly over the Internet. Internally, the incoming TOs can also have exchange relationships with smaller regional or local TOs and other local service producers: providers of food, accommodation, guiding, transport, activities and performances as elements of a tour package arranged by the operator. Regional TOs can also function as intermediaries for other local sub-suppliers of service.

In order to develop appealing tours and resort holidays for international tourist markets, the incoming TOs need access to local attraction resources of distinct natural, cultural or social characteristics. A major dilemma for incoming TOs is the degree to which they should lay the groundwork and carry out the activities themselves or rely on local service suppliers. Besides quality and cost, their own image and market profile will be important factors in their decisions (Jensen 2000). They also need to make judgements about their own competence and knowledge, their desire for control, their confidence in local exchange partners' abilities and willingness to supply reliable services and their ability to add perceived value to their products (Jensen 2002).

Contracts reflect the way in which economic exchange between buyers and sellers, or between incoming TOs and local service suppliers, is managed or arranged. Contracts of exchange could be categorized along the continuum of discreteness (with focus on the actual formal and legal conditions) on the one hand, and relational orientation (with focus on social norms or trust as governance mechanism) on the other (Heide and John 1992; Heide 1994; Jensen and Borch 1999). In the latter case, the exchange can be based on 'relational contracts', building on mutual social norms between the parties (Macneil 1980; Jensen and Borch 1999); these are characterized by open information, solidarity and flexible arrangements (Heide and John 1992). The exchange-specific behaviour among, for example, incoming TOs can differ considerably, such as from regarding the price of a service as just one single transaction to considering the other party as a partner with whom one wants to develop and maintain a close and long-term cooperative relationship. The latter case can produce favourable conditions for information sharing that can contribute to increased mutual learning and competence for both partners; such 'learning relationships' can, for example, also be found between small entrepreneurial firms and large companies (Johannisson 1990; Brown and Butler 1993; Borch and Arthur 1995; Tremblay 1998; Borch 1999; Borch and Brastad 2003).

The selection of business exchange partners will be influenced by the contractual orientation of the parties' search for new exchange partners. For example, in a study of exchange relationships between European TOs and

Norwegian service suppliers, where both categories of actors had preferences for long-term cooperative arrangements, the perceived abilities of interaction and performance by the other party were the most critical factors in the selection (Jensen 2002). Within this context, reliability, professionalism and interactional skills were considered particularly important. Some of the reasons for this priority among the TOs were linked to the desire to minimize the uncertainty for things going wrong in the 'moment of truth' (Normann 2000): when the tourists actually entered the field. The most serious issue was the potential damage to the reputation of the tour operator if something went wrong (Jensen 2000, 2002). These types of considerations would presumably have relevance for cooperation with service suppliers in most parts of the world.

Small firms within a local, fragmented tourism industry tend to struggle in competition with external TOs in the exploitation of local resources (Porter 1980; Borch 1992; Jensen 1993, 1996; Jensen and Borch 1999; Buhalis 2000; Wearing and McDonald 2002; Kirstges, 2003; Medina-Muñoz *et al.* 2003). In the literature on sustainable tourism, these problems have been discussed with emphasis on local participation and involvement (Milne 1998; Hall 2000; Richards and Hall 2000; Tosun 2000; Tosun and Timothy 2003; Jensen 2004; Hall 2005; Saarinen 2006). Within the context of developing countries, the critical problem of local participation and empowerment has been pointed out (Robinson 1999; Scheyvens 2002; Sofield 2003). Exchange conditions with asymmetric distribution of power contrast with the conditions in relational contracts (Macneil 1980), where the other party with whom one shares goals is considered a partner and not a counter-party. The uncovering of the contractual arrangements between incoming TOs and local service suppliers, in addition to the embedding contextual conditions, can yield greater insights into these critical issues.

The Situation in Madagascar

Organized tourism to Madagascar is relatively young compared with tourism in neighbouring countries on the Indian Ocean and the African mainland. The attractions of the Malagasy destination have so far been linked to its rich biodiversity (Ormsby and Mannle 2006), unique landscapes and exotic seaside resorts. TOs, organizations and guidebooks have often commented on the friendliness of the people, and on their life and traditions in remote villages. Most forms of organized tourism in Madagascar consist of all-inclusive round trip tours (for example along the national road, RN7), visits to the most exciting national parks, trekking and adventure, stays at 'eco-lodges' and resort holidays in exotic beach areas. It is assumed that the lack of service education and infrastructure for visitors in Madagascar poses serious barriers for the exploitation of the country's great potential as a tourism destination. There were almost 345,000 arrivals of foreigners in Madagascar in 2007 and The National Tourist Office estimated that about 275,000 (80%) of them were tourists. There has been a substantial increase in these numbers and in demand. The physical (infrastructure) and human and financial resources are still very scarce, leaving much of the field of tourism to the national and international private sector and dependent on support from external partners.

The incoming TOs included in this project, all located in Antananarivo, tend to perceive themselves as the main creators of the tourism growth in Madagascar. Some of them were formed in the mid-1990s and participated in the gradual increase of organized tourism. Despite the barriers to tourism, such as lack of local infrastructure, service facilities, education, service skills and mentality of giving 'professional' service, the TOs were able to use their own systems to compensate for the shortcomings. A few of them have also lobbied the political system. The majority of the incoming TOs are owned or run by foreigners, by 'native' foreigners (for example, people of French parents who grew up in Madagascar), by foreign nationals with Malagasy spouses or vice versa. The French represent the dominant foreign influence in this respect.

An examination of the sample of incoming TOs reveals several variations in service properties and profiles. One of the more important dimensions in terms of cooperative behaviour at the local level is the organizations' predilection to participate in nature- or culture-based visitor experiences. Some incoming TOs, especially the larger ones, are focused on standard programmes based on attractions that are already known or established. Many of them offer standard comprehensive tours with traditional hotel accommodation and tours to more 'luxurious' seaside resorts, but some additionally offer special tours for niche segments. The incoming TOs that are more involved with product development at the local level tend to specialize in trips with elements of adventure, trekking or discovery, primarily in dramatic or exotic natural environments. The extent to which local life and culture are explored, however, varies considerably between the programmes.

At the local level, the single most important service supply needed in the tour packages of incoming TOs is accommodation and catering: hotels, other accommodation alternatives and restaurants whose standards and service capacity are acceptable to foreign tourists. In addition, the supply and production of service at the regional level from *prestataires specialicés* include regional TOs, transportation suppliers, guiding, food, entertainment and translation. Most of the service suppliers are found in bigger towns and regional centres and they will frequently be members of regional tourism organizations. At the village level, basic hospitality and services can be required, such as building a campfire, navigating a pirogue (canoe) and ensuring safety. The national park system and its guides constitute a comprehensive national system under the authority of the National Association for the Management of Protected Areas (ANGAP).

The national guide authorization system is an important development, instigated by the creation of the qualification of tourist guides in Madagascar. The levels of authorization reflect the guides' range, qualifications, skills and areas of legal operation. The education and training system of authorized guides still has many shortcomings and the scarcity of professional guide education and training, in addition to much-needed financial support arrangements for candidates, varies considerably. In most of the regional centres exposed to tourism, a great number of the active guides do not have formal authorization and/or operate independently of the public guide registers and organizations. Many of these guides prefer to operate more independently, without paying taxes; others do not have the resources, time or qualifications needed (such as a high school diploma) to obtain an authorization. Any local or regional guide can be a service supplier to incoming TOs. Some of them are also employed or engaged directly by the TO companies.

Empirical Findings

Based on the interviews and observations, the main findings are organized into seven topical areas.

Differences in attitudes and policies among the incoming TOs (users and developers)

Based on the interviews with the incoming TOs, one main distinction in local commitment can be drawn between developers and users. The users took advantage of already existing or recognized attractions and facilities in their programme; the developers were active in local product development. Most of the developers could be characterized as specialists; users tended to offer traditional, relatively safe 'classical' tours or stays at resorts, though some members of both categories offered a more diverse selection of tours. The specialists were more involved with local product development and were responsible for creating experiences linked to adventure, trekking or discovery of the exotic natural environment. The orientation of the programmes towards the exploration of local life and culture varied.

The developers expressed enthusiasm for the work of uncovering different parts of the country for tourists. An ethically based engagement could be registered, for example, through a strong commitment to ecotourism, to sustainable tourism development in Madagascar, and to a wish to highlight its cultural uniqueness. Only one of the 12 incoming TOs, however, cited local culture as a main component of the product. The main ideas of ecotourism were officially recognized by all incoming TOs, and these ideas became key principles for the TOs who affiliated with the trade organization GoToMadagascar, and with the national TO organization Tour Operators Professionnels de Madagascar (TOP).

The disposition to use regional TOs and local/regional guides

A great majority of regional/local guides (authorized and not) were relatively young (many of them between 20 and 30 years of age). The authorized guides had at least a high school diploma, and some had attended university.

All shared an entrepreneurial spirit, great enthusiasm for their work and the desire to assist in the development of their communities. This idealism seemed to be a driving force in their work. Some of them had formed their own small regional tour operation, in which they were active guides.

The willingness to participate in cooperative relationships with local TOs varied between users and developers. The latter could initiate local cooperation linked to tours and regions where there was a need for specific local knowledge, fluency in the Malagasy dialect and other special skills. Among the users there was a focus on 'buying' the service items needed and adding them to their programme rather than on entering into long-term cooperation.

One interesting discovery was that, when compared with round trips, the demand for the local supply of services tended to be greater by permanent installations owned by the TOs, such as eco-lodges, or by other types of seasonal permanent campsites where local residents could be employed on a permanent basis.

Utilization of existing local knowledge and links

Among the local guides/regional TOs, the strongest assets for developing local tour products were the possession of detailed local knowledge of cultural norms and traditions and Malagasy dialects, as well as an understanding of the local mentality, due to their close linkage to the region where they operated. These qualifications were offered to individual travellers as well as to TOs, and it was these qualifications that brought them into the business. It was, however, claimed that just a small proportion of the incoming TOs were interested in making use of these qualities, and there was a dominant perception that incoming TOs in the capital were ignorant of the capacities of regional and local guides. Still, most regional TOs did not put much effort into marketing their services to the incoming TOs. According to the owner of a regional TO, 'Sometimes the tour operators in Tana [the capital, Antananarivo] are too far away'.

The incoming TO interviews revealed that all TOs in the capital brought their own guides who looked after the clients of the organized tours from the start to the end. These guides possessed a good general knowledge but could not be expected to know everything about specific local traditions and culture. However, the disposition to rely exclusively on the overall knowledge of accompanying guides for the tours also varied to some degree among the different types of TOs. The developers, with a more active orientation towards local experiences of culture or nature, tended to be more disposed towards engaging local guides compared with the users, with their more traditional all-round orientation.

Though not explicitly expressed, the interviews with many of the incoming TOs in Antananarivo left an impression of a centralized orientation (specifically among the users) that could create a contact barrier between the actors at the central and local levels. Part of the explanation for this could, on the one hand, be the lack of wide, external contact among people in rural areas (where the great majority of the population lives) and, on the other, by an urban attitude among the incoming TOs in Antananarivo and by the concentration on foreign markets and their requirements. A potential danger of such an attitude could be the maintenance of more shallow tourism products (Newsome *et al.* 2002) if the unique local culture and lifestyles are not sufficiently appreciated in product development.

Local coordination and initiatives

One of the most serious shortcomings of the two main provincial/regional centres included in this project, according to incoming TOs, was the organization of the tourism industry and the attitudes towards joint efforts (as compared with other more active regional centres). Better coordination among actors in the tourism industry in the cities and in cooperation with regional and provincial actors was absent. The incoming TOs also opined that the tourism industry should be considerably more active in order to persuade them to include these destinations. There was a great need for more information to be made available to incoming TOs in presenting destinations to their customers, especially to foreign TOs in other markets. As expressed by one of the incoming TOs, 'One has to demonstrate more concretely what one has ... [there are] ... possibilities if better organized'.

The interviews with the regional authorities, organizations and tourism business actors within the two main regions of this project also revealed major shortcomings of cooperation and coordination of activities and planning. This was due not only to the scarcity of resources but also to opportunistic behaviour among individual business actors and tourist organizations – their failure to establish uniting strategic initiatives. The individual tourism business actors' trust in public offices and organizations dealing with tourism was quite low; business actors preferred to work for themselves, and therefore the marketing of the regions clearly suffered from this mentality.

Selection and training of local partners

During the search for regional TOs and local guides, reliable information about potential candidates was important. Besides the confidence in actual or potential partners, their abilities to work efficiently were highly valued by the incoming TOs. In addition, the need to set standards of service delivery and good mutual interaction were perceived as important in the selection of potential local partners. In the words of one incoming TO, 'It is not [a] place for amateurs, one has to be professional'. The costs of relationship building and training seemed to be more important than the exact price or salary paid for the services.

With regard to the need for local guides, incoming TOs preferred to select and train young, promising candidates. However, the need to demonstrate a serious attitude and goodwill or intentions was of basic concern to one incoming TO: 'If they don't respect the rules, we don't work with them [anyone]'.

A trend in the interview material was that the training of local people was limited to the performance of functional tasks, such as navigating a canoe (pirogue), cooking, building a campfire, conducting local tours or possibly explaining some local traditions. The management tasks were, however, conducted by the incoming TO. Compared with accompanying guides, the education of local informal guides was less complicated and they needed approximately 3 months of training. A culturally oriented incoming TO explained that they educated their accompanying guides themselves and recruited them from different backgrounds; however, most held university degrees. Additionally, promising youngsters were locally trained to become informal guides, for example in connection with tourist visits to remote villages.

Time investment in working with locals

A manager of one of the incoming TO companies stressed that cooperation with the locals was fine as long as the company invested in giving good information and explaining its expectations to the participants. Building local commitment was also considered important, as one incoming TO stated: 'When they see that this is in their own interest, they will work better for this'. The time investment among TOs who were and were not devoted to this work varied considerably. With seasonal programmes, time constraints were a critical factor for incoming TOs.

Local suppliers emphasized that the development of a village product took a considerable amount of time and there was a strong need for patience. Such a process consists of selecting a village, getting the population interested in receiving tourists, screening host families and training them to welcome foreign tourists. This entailed several trips to the village and collaboration with chiefs and other people who were involved. Establishing the village visitation product often took at least 3 years. Many local guides claimed that most incoming TOs lacked the patience to see the process through. They implied that impatience among incoming TOs limited their involvement in these products.

Working with local villages and community-based projects

The interviews with TOs revealed that the lack of local structures posed a problem. This encompassed lack of physical and institutional infrastructure (unsanitary conditions, lack of potable water, the weakness of educational and public institutions and the poor organization of the local tourism industry). Some incoming TOs were already incorporating visits and stays in villages into their programme and many others were also interested in doing so. However, in addition to the lack of infrastructure, the low level of education and experience with tourism were significant barriers to this. For those TOs who were interested, the main task was to ensure that the host villages understood the requirements of tourism and the practical functions they had to perform. The TOs insisted on the need to 'sensitize' and to educate the villagers to do good work, meaning to perform basic tasks such as entertaining or preparing good meals. The search for suitable candidates was, therefore, crucial for successful cooperation with the villages.

As part of the trust-building process, regional guides/TOs frequently offered some social benefit to the village, such as school supplies or medical and other services. The role of the guide in the host society was thus of great significance. The incoming TOs who had experience in developing products at the local level seemed to appreciate the significance of social commitment in order to create confidence to forge strong long-term relationships with their local partners. Normally, the approach to the villages had to go through the traditional leadership – first of all the chief, who finally had to agree to receive foreign visitors.

In many communities in Madagascar, foreign NGOs were involved with community-based development projects in which ecotourism and local cultural tourism were central elements. This research project includes pilot studies of five such projects. Some of the challenges identified were linked to human resources, skill building, organization, infrastructure and marketing. In most of the cases studied in this project, the NGOs (primarily French) hired external tourism experts. Some regional TOs were invited to participate in training local guides and in marketing the visitation products. However, one of the limitations of these projects was the reluctance to involve incoming TOs in the development and marketing of the local products and in linking those offerings to the tourism business sector. There were some indications that this could delay the progress of such projects in terms of a 'take-off' in customer numbers and in terms of their economic sustainability.

Many incoming TOs were quite critical of the failure of such projects to enlist the experience of incoming TOs in developing and marketing the village visitation products. One of the leading incoming TOs in Madagascar (a user) claimed that they had realized the significance of 'solidarity tourism' both as a future tourism trend and as a way of reaching the goal of sustainable tourism development. The projects in which this user was involved offered socially oriented products in which the tourist would confront the challenges facing ordinary Madagascans in the villages and in the cities.

Discussion

An overall consideration of exchange-specific behaviour among the incoming TOs reveals distinct limitations in the range and the depth of cooperation with local service suppliers if making a comparison with long-term relational arrangements, for example by relational contracts (Macneil 1980). First of all, the arrangements are characterized by an almost exclusively functional focus.

The emphasis was mostly on simple, discrete tasks that needed to be performed locally, such as cooking, piloting a canoe and demonstrating traditional crafts (see Fig. 10.1). Based on the knowledge of mutual learning relationships identified in innovative industries within dynamic markets (Hitt *et al.* 2000; Kale *et al.* 2000) in a Western business context, it can be claimed that the types of exchange relationships demonstrated in Madagascar, dominated by a low level of 'intelligent' learning domains, will make only a small contribution to long-term local competence building.

Fig. 10.1. Wooden funerary sculptures, the characteristic locally produced souvenirs of Madagascar.

This leads to the question of the degree to which current competence-building activities really improve the value-adding capacities of local service providers, and thus to a more symmetrical distribution of power (Cadotte and Stern 1979) between the central and local levels. It can be argued that the form of cooperation that limits the educational focus to basic functional tasks would not significantly change the dependency of the local service suppliers (whether local TOs or individuals) on the incoming TOs or lead to cooperation on equal terms (Sofield 2003). This argument should still be contrasted with the question of what possibilities and incentives incoming TOs actually have to develop deeper learning-based exchange relationships with local service suppliers. Another consideration that could affect conservative local cooperation involvement among the incoming TOs is the perceived risk of image damage (Jensen 2002) in international markets in cases of failure in the service delivery from local service suppliers.

In comparison with findings from European TOs (Jensen 2002), requirements such as an acceptable professional attitude, good intentions (benevolence) (Ganesan 1994) and the willingness to work seriously are central to both contexts; however, the challenges of ensuring that local service providers meet these requirements are considerably higher in Madagascar. This is primarily due to shortcomings in education levels, management traditions, experiences and infrastructure development.

The initial interest of the incoming TOs in Madagascar is the access to local attraction-specific resources in the destinations. These are attractive features or settings that are believed to appeal to tourists in a processed or unprocessed form (Jensen 1996). Examples include 'original products factors' (Geigant 1962; Krippendorf 1980) such as exotic and interesting features of nature, climate, culture (including traditional festivals and markets), lifestyle and people, as well as managed or 'marked' (MacCannell 1976) tourist attractions. However, incoming TOs in Madagascar will continuously be exposed to existing context-specific factors: conditions at the destination (for example politics or general regulations) that facilitate or restrict the access to the local attractions or activities. Among the context-specific factors are physical or institutional infrastructure, coordination and marketing of the local tourist organization and the level of service skills and facilities.

Many of the barriers to developing competence-building exchange relationships between incoming TOs and local service suppliers are context-specific. Among the incoming TOs there was, for example, a frequent complaint that 'local structures' were absent. Many of the context-specific factors influenced the capacities of local service suppliers to become exchange partners with incoming TOs: education, cultural and social norms and values, rules and regulations and former exposure to tourism at the destination. It is noticeable that incoming TOs would demand a minimum level of education and capacity to understand the requirements for service production before considering a long-term arrangement with a local service supplier. The interplay between incoming TOs in Madagascar and local service providers is thus assumed to be strongly influenced by several current context-specific factors.

With reference to the role of the guides in local activity products (Pond 1993; Weiler and Ham 2002; Christie and Mason 2003), in particular in trekking products, the training of local guides is an important tool in the development of local products, participation and competence building. However, the preferences among incoming TOs to use their own guides as opposed to local guides can be seen as a demonstration of both a centralized mode of thinking and risk-averse behaviour that demonstrate a short-term competence-building perspective. The training of local guides above the level of just being path-finders (Cohen 1985) could, in fact, be an important step in raising the level of the critical abilities needed, adding to human resource development at the local level.

As the incoming TOs represent value chain actors with the most extensive experience in tour production and marketing through international distribution channels, cooperative links between them and regional TOs could be appropriate channels for knowledge transfer. Further back in the value chain, the links between regional TOs and local sub-suppliers of service could provide adequate channels for nurturing local knowledge that are driven by regional TOs as 'locomotives' (Axelsson and Elbe 2000).

The efforts to develop organized tourism to Madagascar from Western countries have created an arena where Western culture meets (and possibly collides with) Malagasy culture (Robinson 1999; Scheyvens 2002; Duffy 2006). The cultural and communicative platforms (Borch 1992, 1999) should thus be given attention when examining the cooperation between incoming TOs that are linked to Western attitudes and standards and local actors rooted in Malagasy traditions (Bloch 1971, 1989; Astuti 1995). Traditional norms of kinship can influence the commitments of people in different communities to contracts with and trust in external partners (Bloch 1971). The insight into such social structures can lead to an understanding of the attitudes demonstrated by local service suppliers in Madagascar with regard to local actors as individual business partners for external incoming TOs.

Finally, incoming TOs have the potential to maintain or increase the number of tourists coming to the island without developing close exchange relationships with local service suppliers. The basic question within a long-term perspective is still the extent to which an expansion with very limited involvement of local service entrepreneurs will contribute to the development of a sustainable tourism industry in Madagascar and what is lost in the potential richness of the tourist experiences if local and regional actors remain passive and continue to perform just simple functional tasks.

Tentative Conclusions and Recommendations

Based on empirical findings and the discussion above, some conclusions related to the Madagascar case can be suggested. First, the current practice associated with very limited long-term exchange relationship involvement between incoming TOs and local service suppliers at different levels offers only slight competence development at the local level. There seems to be a need for stronger incentives for incoming TOs to invest in long-term exchange relationships with local service suppliers. This can probably not be achieved without a national policy that favours incoming TOs who like to form long-term commitments with local service suppliers and with local product development projects. The encouragement of international NGOs to work more closely with incoming or international TOs in community-based tourism projects could be an additional direction. One such direction is the Malagasy NGO Fanamby, that combines local community and professional tourism company involvement through training programmes in their community development projects.

Secondly, there is a need for specific strategies and resources for improvement of contextual conditions that could strengthen the capacities of local service suppliers to enter into 'intelligent' learning relationships with incoming TOs. The improvement of the communication between tourism business/organizational actors in regional centres and at the central level in the capital should also be stressed. These objectives would also require a considerable enforcement of local coordination, cooperation and networking. In order to achieve this, however, there is obviously a need for substantial and coordinated support for institutional infrastructure improvements, planning capabilities and education with assistance from the government, international NGOs, organizations and other agencies. One example of measures for basic education in the tourism businesses is the cooperative programmes initiated by the Malagasy tourism business organization, GoToMadagascar, which also actively supports the standards for socially responsible tourism.

Thirdly, a more comprehensive system for the education/training of authorized guides with updated professional skills and for the support of regional entrepreneurial TOs is emphasized as a specific means of embarking on more effective local initiatives. This demands a more conscious and active involvement of central and regional authorities, the National Park system (ANGAP) included, and a better dialogue between them and the tourism industry and NGOs, with the willingness to invest in such systems.

Finally, incoming TOs and other international actors should demonstrate increased recognition of local cultural norms and traditions, both as attraction resources and as barriers to cooperative activities. For example, the initial differences between Malagasy social norms and Western ways of 'doing business' should be appreciated and incorporated into the goals linked to education, professionalism and mutual learning by international cooperation. A more extensive use of local TOs and guides as intermediaries between the two 'worlds' would be one means of facilitating the processes of mutual understanding.

In conclusion, the findings of this study are assumed to have value beyond Madagascar and could thus be applicable to several other 'developing destinations'. However, increased research efforts are needed to address these critical issues more thoroughly.

11 Tourism Development and the Polemic of ICT Advocacy in Namibian Schools

Kenneth Matengu

Introduction

Worldwide, the demonstrated ability of tourism to create jobs makes it an important economic growth driver and a valuable tool for achieving the Millennium Development Goals (MDGs), which seek to reduce the number of people living in abject poverty by 50% over a 25-year period from 1990 to 2015 (Nadkarni 2008, 1). In Namibia, since the turn of the century, tourism has been consistently rated as the third largest foreign currency contributor to the gross domestic product (GDP), after mining and fisheries. Although there has been tremendous growth, it has tended to be largely urban-based and has not impacted on the livelihoods of the entire population, particularly those living in rural areas (Kazenambo 2003). The problem is not representative of Namibia alone, as it is also evident in other developing, or least developed, countries (Boniface and Cooper 1996, 18–27). Part of the reason is the economic limitedness of the peripheral areas of Namibia that are typically characterized by low levels of productivity, poverty, lack of information and training opportunities, and outdated know-how.

Realizing these challenges, and in order to drive the development of tourism to be inclusive, the Government of Namibia has set the following goals in its public policy (draft National Tourism Policy for Namibia) (MET 2005a):

- poverty reduction;
- employment creation;
- economic growth;
- black economic empowerment;
- reduction of regional inequalities; and
- ecological sustainability.

Furthermore, the Policy states that the government plans to 'develop the tourism industry in a sustainable and responsible manner that would significantly contribute to the economic development of Namibia, improve the quality of life of all her people; and the plan is that a broader section of the population should be involved in the ownership and management of the tourism sector' (MET 2005a). Availability of information, be it symmetrical or asymmetrical, plays a very important role in the broadening of the economic base of people at the grassroots level. Furthermore, it has been argued that lack of information is the key element that perpetuates the vicious circle of sluggish economic growth and poverty, and that information and communication technology (ICT) offers realistic opportunities to redress this problem (Castells 1999). In Namibia and elsewhere, civil society groups and many of the non-governmental organizations (NGOs) that work in both conservation and development have gained cognizance of the potential role ICT has in alleviating obstacles to tourism development, resulting in the concept of ICT for Development, often labelled ICT4D (Nadkarni 2008, 5).

In addition, although tourism enterprises are generally in the form of lodges, up-market safari campsites and associated services, there has been growing interest in local tourism development, particularly in campsites and craft centres in communal areas of Namibia (Ashley 2000, 8). A strong, but not exclusive, focus has been directed at community-based tourism, which involves collective actions and the establishment of an institutional base for managing tourism at the grassroots level (Long 2004, xiii–xxviii). Most people, however, would agree that in Namibia's peripheral areas a sizeable number of communities as implementing units do not possess the capacity and the resources to take advantage of the potential of ICT in tourism development. In fact, rural tourism in its broad terms is a new activity adopted by only a minority of rural households (Ashley 2000, 9). That is why schools as rural-based institutions are now being considered as vital in the development of tourism through ICT as a form of diversified livelihood strategies.

ICTs in Schools for Marketing Tourism

Why should schools be used as hubs for marketing tourism? There are many possible answers to this question. The simplest rationale for using schools as information hubs for tourism marketing is that schools are often public goods and they are more connected to the communities they serve than are tourism marketing companies. Students, teachers and other staff, the 'social capital' of schools, are members of the community that forms a part of the resource that tourism consumers are seeking. In addition, income can be generated not only for the schools themselves, but also for the communities around such centres. From the implementation perspective, e-tourism through the use of the Internet can help communities build networks that can encourage the communities to market their destinations and to organize the local tourism industry better, while reducing the leakage 'repatriation of tourism' earnings to upmarket firms.

Another reason is related to the implications of tourism on society and on local development. Tourism has important developmental, as well as social, implications on a community where it is operated. Developmental implications, in the sense that one rationale for establishing tourism is that such an economic leisure activity considers the needs of the poor in developing countries to help them leapfrog into 'decent' human existence, and social implications in the sense that it is often marketed not by the communities but by the industry, are among the essential elements of achieving a dignified rural life. There is documented evidence (Chafy 1997, 634–636; Premkumar and Roberts 1999, 469; Lam *et al.* 2004, 41) in support of both 'developmental' and 'social' arguments – some weak and others strong. The social aspect is more related to moral obligations, while the developmental is attached to creation of employment, diversification of economic opportunities as well as reduction of over-dependence on subsistence farming in most rural areas of the developing world. The latter is more in line with the argumentations put forth by the 2005 *National Tourism Policy* for Namibia. The infusion of ICTs in schools is also advocated for on the same basis. Of course, one needs to have the right tourism skills and a developed technological and business capacity in order to turn the potential of ICTs into tangible benefits.

At the World Summit on Information Society (in Geneva, 2003), organized by the United Nations, the executive director (Joris Komen) of one of Namibia's most successful non-governmental organizations, SchoolNet, which assists schools with access to computers and Internet connection, said the following: 'The need for computers is overwhelming, enthusiasm to use them is great and the potential that ICT has in a country's education system is enormous. There are so many unused and/or under-utilized computers here in developed countries; they have got to give them to us where they are needed most – the developmental impact [of] that will be enormous.'

He was responding to my question: What is the rationale for donating ICT to Namibia when there are many other pressing needs in the country, and could the money spent on this perhaps be used for something else? He was probably right, and this view is not held by him alone. In fact, the summit was called for the purpose of finding a sustainable mechanism for providing the people of the developing world with access to ICT.

The disparity in access to information is one of the reasons why the gap between the rich and the poor has continued to widen. Is this the reason why communities are not marketing tourism themselves? Perhaps it is. Sceptical about the veracity of the 'need is overwhelming' hypothesis, I asked: Have you done research on this issue? What are the teachers and learners generally saying about ICT? What would you say has been the impact of ICT on education and on development in these schools? 'We do not do research, other people can do that. Our main task is to provide schools with access to computers and Internet connection in most disadvantaged communities in the country,' Mr Komen responded. It does not seem to matter what the schools do with the computers so long as they have them: it is alright, teachers and administrators will see to it that they are put to good use. Whose responsibility is it? Somehow, with the use of these devices, will an information society spring up and development then surface?

Prior to the interview, a previous study on The Diffusion of Modern Technologies in Namibia (Matengu 2003, 85) had shown that, across many sectors, 'an Information Society does not come about merely because of the technological market feasibility ICTs have, but comes primarily out of an assemblage of non-technological forces and considerations' and 'that to reject/ adopt a certain technology, the adopter did have or lacked appropriate skills, institutional technological capabilities, outside-network, coupled with internal and external demand conditions'. Technology use in everyday life has much to do with the social aspect – people adopt devices if they have meaning for them, that is, if they are in conformity with their values, beliefs and convictions.

What meaning do rural communities attach to ICT? The meaning communities ascribe to technologies is dependent on their awareness of the existing and potential capacity of the technological tool in question to positively change their life. The question then is: How does awareness emerge? In principle, the answer given by ICT advocates is that 'awareness' should be conducted and achieved in a generational sense; in other words, through the schooling period. In the case of a pupil exposed to Internet use at the primary school, advocates argue that such a learner might one day, perhaps after high school graduation, consider this tool as a development option. The trouble is that one does not adopt technological innovations just because they have the potential for positively changing one's life circumstance.

The Social Side of Technological Innovation Adoption

Since the introduction of ICT carries with it elements of joy and annoyance, challenging the learnt way of doing things, some sort of *reflectivity* has to take place, in the affirmative or in the negative, and it is uncertain how long it takes before an innovation is adopted or rejected by a society. In order for technologies to be widely used, some form of social acceptance is necessary. Reflectivity refers to the process through which people and institutions question their basis of being, that is, the deeply rooted analysis of why they exist (*culture–context strata*), how (*lucidity strata*) and why they do things the way they do (*motive–complex strata*), and why change is necessary over time (*need satisfaction strata*). There is no space to discuss these strata here, except to mention that achieving an understanding of them will eventually reveal a strategy for ICT community-based development. The concept of reflectivity entails a set of sequential socio-organizational steps, until the stage where a particular technology is culturally understood as a device that was created out of a particular context and that context is central to the use and modification in application of such an innovation. Thus, the word reflectivity refers to a perceived function of a thing or process that may affect technology adoption or affect the use of it, or the operational context in which a larger meaning exists and is sought after to meet a need or a want.

From this perspective, the adoption of technological innovations, such as computers, is therefore fundamentally a matter that concerns social relationships and economic networks (Rogers 2003, 341), and is not merely based on the availability and potential benefits of the innovations. Yet, they are created by these relationships and networks. In societies such as Namibia, the geopolitics of computer adoption is not simply about access to technology, motivation to use it and competence to surpass others, but also about the social meaning of technology that is constructed at the various levels of cultural interactions. In other words, the cultural construction of knowledge creates one's understanding of available innovations and the subsequent adoption is subject to the cultural meaning of it.

Generally speaking, we know that the main drivers of the 'information age' are computers and the Internet. Both have a colossal need for resources that are insignificantly available for the majority of Namibians. They hunger for electricity and fibre-optical networks. They yearn to replace the poor man's intensive hard labour. They require a different type of literacy with which to make things work and sell. They demand and produce political power. It is doubtful that the society under investigation understands and thinks about information society in the same way the West does. It is probably true that the concept itself, however it may be defined, is a product of geopolitics of a type different from geopolitics in African countries. My point here is not to argue that Western technologies are of lesser value to Namibia or that these innovations have been tremendously useful. Rather, I argue that the context in deploying communication technologies is one of many critical success factors in community-based tourism development. Furthermore, the aim is to suggest that indigenous knowledge contains innovations that are relevant to the Namibian situation. When technological innovations are set out, it may be meaningful to reflect on how indigenous knowledge can best be utilized in schools for tourism development rather than on transferred technologies as such.

The Change Factor

Technological and managerial innovations bring about change in individuals and organizations. Change, as has been observed, not just in organizations and institutions but also in schools, is 'riddled with paradox' (Evans 2001, 4). It is paradoxical because, although change as innovation has been studied in great depth, and in as much as change can be planned for, it is also full of unpredictable barriers. To actually try to get a school to 'do something new, the result is often painful and futile' (Evans 2001) and may give birth to institutional instability through staff anxiety. Defined as 'the devices and techniques employed by society to sustain its existence and improve its quality of life' (Wilbanks 2004, 3), technologies are products of social processes. Since they are outputs of social processes of Western culture, they are bound to seed some discomfort. They were created either to respond to a potential or existing problem or to advance certain things that aim to keep societies satisfied in the particular context and environment for which they were originally made.

By 'originally', I refer to the 'thing that provoked the invention of a product' – intent of invention, not the end application of the innovation. In this sense, when ICT is juxtaposed as the critical condition for leapfrogging into a new rural development stage, the actual impetus for tourism development may be missed through strong emphasis on ICT capacity and potential rather than on the cultural attributes that would attract tourists in the first place. In fact, it has been cautioned that the successful harnessing of ICT in rural (grassroots) tourism, particularly the Internet, as a business tool has proved elusive, especially when the operations are modest in scale (Nadkarni 2008, 3).

Too often, in Africa and most of the developing world, innovation adoption and eventual implementation are approached with a definite non-reflection. We see the value of technology and innovation, and the case for innovation adoption is readily made in the positive – seeing that it is associated with benefits such as efficiency, cost savings, employment creation and economic growth – without really reflecting on its deeper ramifications. That is the reason why the use of ICT by communities for marketing their heritage for tourism is so weak (almost non-existent). Evidence has shown that in seeking innovations from others, even when we have no experience of the technology in question, we almost always tend to see them in the positive (Chafy 1997, 637; Rayman-Bacchus and Molina 2001, 597–599). Why is it that people who are unfamiliar with ICTs trust the innovations that they have never used themselves? Further research is warranted to answer this question. However, it is probable that the answer lies in the exaggeration of the power of the Internet and computers.

Rationale and Implemental Challenges: Gaps Exposed

We are familiar with the apparently extraordinary power of ICTs. Voluminous work has been written about the potential of these devices to help teachers and administrators to accommodate the diversity of the needs of their learners and to provide them with up-to-date educational information and other resources (e.g. Zorfass *et al.* 1991; Kulik 1994; Cuban and Kirkpatrick 1998; Kähkönen and Sutinen 2003). Literature on ICT and tourism remains minimal, largely focusing on provision of services, education and agronomic activities (Nadkarni 2008, 2). None the less, those who link ICTs firmly to development have even suggested that ICTs 'enhance the quality of life [and] stimulate political participation and promote social cohesion and equality' (van Audenhove *et al.* 2001, 18). As other researchers such as Katz *et al.* (2001, 408) have shown, it is difficult to measure the improvements in the quality of life among the citizenry that can be or have been brought about by ICTs. Nevertheless, much of the recorded success shows a consideration of certain elements of societal context. In Finland, for example, studies have concluded that most people adopt innovations based on three factors, namely access, competence and motivation (Viherä 2000), and that for technologies to make a meaningful contribution, a society needs to be exposed to new technologies in a way that makes local cultural sense (Sutinen 2003, 19). These factors are united in their influence on an adoption decision (Rogers 2003).

In recent decades, the knowledge base about innovations and their subsequent diffusions has accumulated to a level where it has been described by some researchers as a new discipline (Tuomi 2002; Rogers 2003). Some scholars feel that we know more about innovations that have educational and developmental ramifications than we have ever known (Miles and Thomas 1996, 29–30). Yet, there remain several knowledge gaps about the implementation of technological innovations in places where they were not originally planned to be used, e.g. rural areas in developing countries such as Namibia. One gap involves the end-users in the place where the innovations are to be used – the adopting place. Many of the technological innovations today have financial tags in economic systems that are of little relevance to poor Africans in the periphery (Wade 2002). Information is abundant about who the end-users are in most developed countries, particularly in the USA and Europe. Information societies, as we know them nowadays, emerge because of interaction between scientific, economic and sociopolitical systems (Pyka and Küppers 2002, 7). The form of interaction may be loosely systematic – largely without any form of policy guidelines or rule-fixed process with a clear vision of how and what type of information society to build. In terms of Namibian tourism, national policies do recognize the importance of ICT in marketing tourism, but they do not firmly link it to actual grassroots activities and do not outline how, and with which type of assistance, communities can be helped.

Another gap involves the context of technology transfer, which usually happens on sound moral intentions but is of a somewhat pre-assumptive and misleading nature. This problem is even larger. Many rural communities and schools have no capacity to manage and utilize ICTs effectively (Matengu 2006). This is partly because of the perceived irrelevance of the new technology. Despite the fact that technology and culture have a long partnership (Komers 2003), the appropriate contextual implementation of transferred technologies remains a challenge. I refer to transfer because the 'thing that provoked' the invention in question is out of the cultural context of those who are to adopt it. The innovation – a computer for instance – is not only a culturally unfamiliar device but also something that is significantly meaningless in the value system of that society. Meaning and usefulness only begin to emerge when purpose is reflected into the context of the culture. Without it, a computer is as is: the meaning and value remain as intended by the inventor but the application remains irrelevant. A great deal is known about deployment of technology but less is comprehended about the social side of implementing technological innovations.

We human beings tend to embrace technologies that make everyday life easier and are beneficial, but we are cautious of those technologies that tend to substitute the joy of working in our mastered formula (Wilbanks 2004, 8). Yes, we are dealing with schools and teachers. Schools are institutions with visions, goals, cultures and organizational structures that form part of the context of the system that guides rural communities. In most societies, teachers are bound by these attributes. The implementation and subsequent success or failure of the innovation in question remain with the individual teachers and their students. Individuals are, as Jussila (1987) observed among Finnish farmers, the people 'who ultimately decide to adopt or reject an innovation'. However, in order to decide, one must have a capacity to perform a diagnosis of the phenomenon and control it. Schools do not have the capacity to function as a tourism development hub for their communities. Even if schools had such a capacity, there are negative implications on the schools themselves, on their capital and on society in general (Pelgrum 2001). Education administrators, school boards, teachers and their students are part of the society in which individual decisions are either constrained or motivated by the existing values, norms and beliefs. They adopt technology if beneficial or reject it if assumed detrimental.

Conclusions

While calling for the importance of further empirical and theoretical scrutiny of the value of ICT deployment in schools and how these tools can be used for tourism development at the grassroots, one must acknowledge that ICTs are just tools – and they will remain just that if rural communities are not empowered. Clearly, it is wrong to draw definitive conclusions about the problematic nature of ICT for development advocacy and the subsequent rationale behind the integration programmes that Namibia set in place. Consequently, the assumption of schools operating as information hubs particularly for grassroots tourism also remains questionable. However, bearing in mind the rich cultural heritage of rural Namibia and the diversity of its tourism opportunities, a feasibility study on the elusive nature of ICT and tourism that aims to investigate the possible role schools can play in using ICT tools for marketing local products for tourists' consumption should be made. Moreover, in order to strengthen synergies that permit community competence, more collaboration and partnership with local tourism entrepreneurs are necessary.

The questions still to be answered are: How does one develop tourism marketing competency in a community where the only viable institution to build such capacity is the school? For whom is the infusion of ICT for tourism in schools beneficial and to what extent does it really impact on grassroots development? What criteria should be followed for a technology to be considered beneficial? Who makes the decisions about the benefits: school board, regional management, headmaster, teachers, the community or perhaps the learners? With these questions in mind, we can easily see that the infusion of 'ICT for tourism' would appear not only as a policy-needing system but also one that involves politics and ultimately produces, or is produced by, power; that is, if we agree with the classical Weberian definition of power as the ability to get things done through a process of regulating and controlling who gets what, when and why (Haralambos and Holborn 1995). Overall, it should be noted that the actual implementation of ICT for grassroots tourism may entail redressing policies and redefining the roles of different stakeholders, their interests and responsibilities. For instance, employment creation is not something that happens only through policy coercive instruments, but it is also dependent on individuals' own initiatives. Only then will communities really claim ownership and interest in tourism, which in fact may provide an important alternative source of livelihood.

Acknowledgement

The author is grateful to the Academy of Finland for funding the work that led to this work through the project Tourism and the Regional Modernization of Namibia.

12 Transfrontier Tourism and Relations Between Local Communities and the Private Sector in the Great Limpopo Transfrontier Park

MARJA SPIERENBURG, HARRY WELS, KEES VAN DER WAAL AND STEVEN ROBINS

Introduction

The Great Limpopo Transfrontier Park (TP) is one of the largest Transfrontier Conservation Areas (TFCAs) in the world, encompassing the Kruger National Park in South Africa, the Limpopo National Park in Mozambique and the Gonarezhou National Park in Zimbabwe (see Fig. 12.1). TFCAs are promoted by most international conservation organizations (Aberly 1999; Wolmer 2003), following the rationale that ecosystems generally do not coincide with national political boundaries. In addition, significant global threats to interconnected ecosystems and migrating species allegedly require large-scale conservation efforts.

Chapin (2004) and Ramutsindela (2004b, 62) point out that growing commercial interest in biodiversity is also driving TFCAs. Especially in the South, they are hailed as opportunities for economic growth through tourism (Wolmer 2003). TFCA proponents stress that local people living in or close to TFCAs will benefit from the economic opportunities that TFCAs generate, especially through the development of tourism. This provides the large-scale transfrontier conservation efforts with social legitimacy and follows, in principle, the global conservation priority of 'people and parks', set out in the wake of the 1982 Bali Declaration and the 1987 report by the Brundtland Commission. Public–private partnerships are seen as the main vehicle for this type of economic development (Ramutsindela 2004a,b).

Some authors, including Hutton *et al.* (2005, 345), argue that the call to allow local communities to benefit from conservation through the promotion of public–private partnerships conforms with the neo-liberal 'new public management' and 'new policy agenda' that stress the need for a reduction in the role of the central state and assign an important role to the private sector

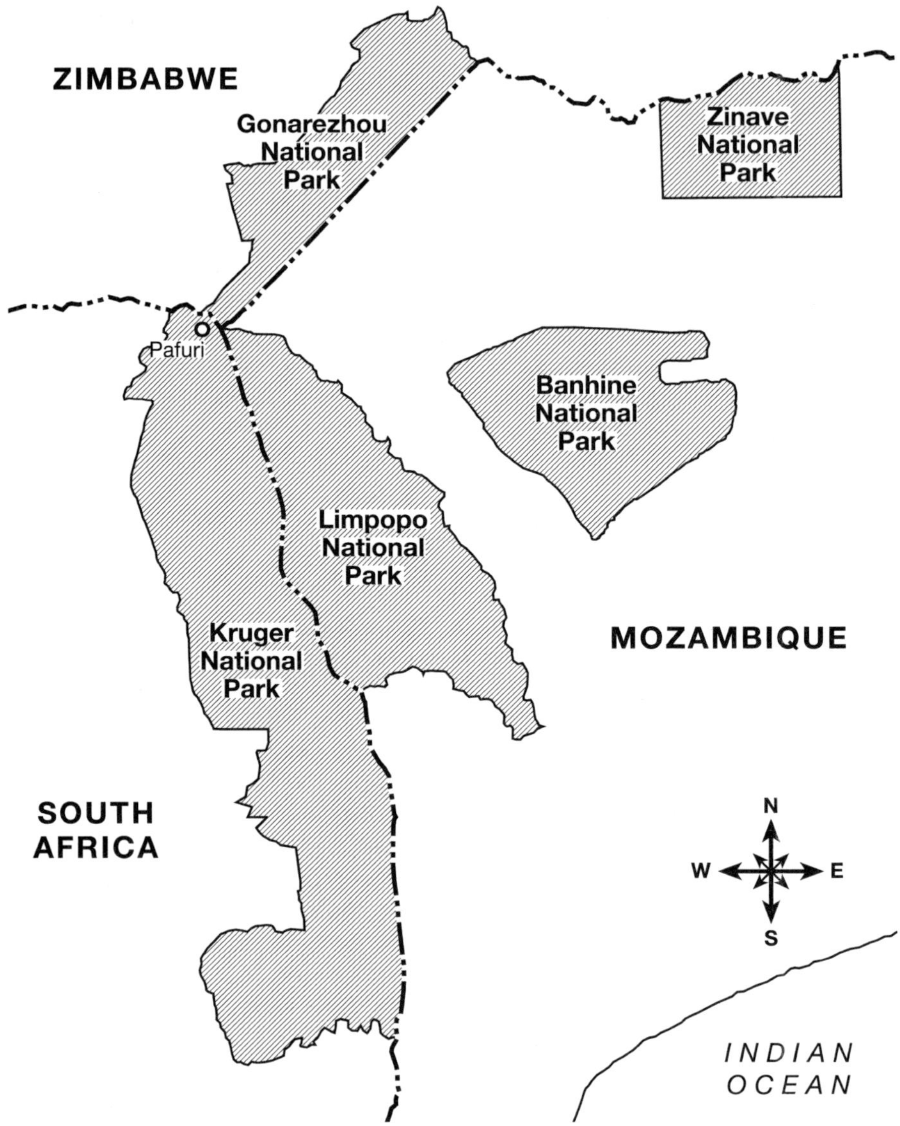

Fig. 12.1. The Great Limpopo Transfrontier Park.

– for profit and non-profit alike – in service delivery. The idea is to foster an entrepreneurial spirit among communities, individuals and households to exploit the economic values of conservation resources to ensure both sustainable livelihoods and conservation. Faikir (2001) – the former Director of IUCN South Africa – initially suggested that a community approach to conservation could very well be combined with public–private partnerships. He believed the private sector to be more efficient in exploring and developing local possibilities for economic development and service delivery to local communities. However, 3 years later, Faikir (2004) warned that powerful (transnational) companies were using the partnerships to appropriate natural resources on a large scale, especially in developing countries (see also Hughes 2001; Dzingirai 2003; Chapin 2004).

Looking at the specific case of the Great Limpopo TP, Ramutsindela (2004a,b) argues that a number of factors facilitated the establishment of this TP: (i) the abolition of apartheid in South Africa, which opened up possibilities for regional cooperation; (ii) the end of the civil war in Mozambique in 1992; and (iii) the fact that both countries have adopted a free-market approach (see also Carmody 2002; Castel-Branco 2002). He furthermore maintains that conservationists promoting the establishment of the Great Limpopo and other TFCAs in the region took advantage of the financial demands being placed at that time on the new democracies of South Africa and Mozambique. Given the pressure put on these governments to redress the historically skewed distribution of resources and services and to address economic growth and poverty alleviation as top priorities, nature would be conserved only if it could pay for itself. This condition encouraged the privatization of conservation and allowed the private sector to step in (Ramutsindela 2004b, 69).

The South African Government has proposed a strategic framework for sustainable tourism development that aims to integrate the interests of the private sector and communities in and adjacent to conservation areas. This framework, developed by the Department of Environmental Affairs and Tourism (DEAT 2005), stresses the need to 'develop tourism with dignity' and active attempts – through, for instance, training – to involve local communities and ensure that they will benefit from tourism development.

In this chapter, we discuss the possibilities for communities in and close to the Great Limpopo TP to benefit from tourism development. The main focus is on the South African side of the Great Limpopo, in particular on the Makuleke community; contrasting experiences on the Mozambican side of the TP are addressed only briefly. The Makuleke community has received quite some attention, achieving an almost iconic status (Robins and van der Waal 2008). This partly resulted from the fact that they won a claim they lodged for the restitution of the land they lost when they were evicted in 1969 from the Kruger National Park – now part of the Great Limpopo TP. Rather than opting to move back to the land, they chose instead to enter into a partnership with the park's management and tourist operators. The Makuleke case came to represent 'the solution' to the dilemmas of how to manage relationships between communities and conservationists, between 'people and parks' (Robins and van der Waal 2008, 54).

We also critically analyse the partnerships between the Makuleke community, the park's management and the private sector. We argue that one of the issues often ignored in literature on tourism and community development – but also in literature on public–private partnerships in general – is the issue of power relations. Differences in capacities and access to information influence these relations (Spierenburg *et al.* 2008), and hence the impacts of private sector operations.

The Promise of Development through Transfrontier Conservation

The main lobbying organization for transfrontier conservation in Southern Africa, the Peace Parks Foundation (PPF), has enthusiastically worked through the media to disseminate the message that transfrontier conservation can offer exciting prospects for economic growth. It was highly successful in lobbying for the establishment of TFCAs and in fundraising (Speets 2001). PPF managed to mobilize funding for the Great Limpopo TP from a variety of parties, including the World Bank, the United States Agency for International Development (USAID), the German Development Bank Kreditanstalt für Wiederaufbau, the World Wildlife Fund (WWF) Netherlands, Novamedia, the Rufford Maurice Laing Foundation, the Dutch National Postcode Lottery, the Deutsche Bank, Südliches Afrika Initiative der Deutschen Wirtschaft (SAFRI)/DaimlerChrysler and the African Wildlife Foundation.

Since its inception in February 1997, PPF has stressed the importance of community development. John Hanks, its former executive director, repeatedly stated that: 'We feel very strongly about making the communities *our partners* in the growth of tourism' (Spierenburg *et al.* 2006, 21–22). Its current CEO, Professor Willem van Riet, and the PPF founder, the late Dr Anton Rupert, never tired of stressing the importance of community development and participation in TFCAs.

The high hopes for community benefits are sustained by a few high-profile cases of communities that have been portrayed as being successful in economically valorizing natural resources that are included – or to be included – in TFCAs. The Makuleke case is one of these cases. Another example is the Richtersveld community in the north-west corner of South Africa. This community has also successfully reclaimed land – which happened to be very rich in diamonds – from which it was removed in the 1920s. Not only did the community win its land back but it also, quite exceptionally, succeeded in claiming back the mineral rights (Business Report 2003). This community has also established the Richtersveld Community Conservancy, hoping to become part of the envisioned Greater !Gariep TFCA (Richtersveld 2008). This (transfrontier) initiative is being presented as promoting conservation, while at the same time 'boosting local livelihoods' and striving towards 'sustainable development' through tourism development (Thornton 2006), while one might question whether the tourism option is more profitable than the exploitation of the community's mineral rights.

These 'success stories' have fuelled the belief that transfrontier initiatives do not only foster nature conservation but also contribute to the economic development of the local population. For this to happen, partnering with the private sector is considered crucial in order to operationalize the assumed tourism potential of TFCAs. This partnership idea can be traced back to the early days of the Communal Areas Management Programme for Indigenous Resources (CAMPFIRE) programme in Zimbabwe, where local communities were stimulated to partner with hunting operators in some of the country's more marginal communal areas. The WWF supported CAMPFIRE wholeheartedly, and produced two papers explaining how rural district councils with the appropriate authority to manage the wildlife on their communal land could form partnerships with the private sector through joint ventures (Jansen undated). Dzingirai (2003, 243) heavily criticizes this partnering trend in conservation, as it could marginalize communities even further and argues:

> ... the new environmental management partnerships emerging in Southern Africa's countryside ... not only fail to deliver benefits to villagers, more importantly, they curtail the long-established rights to land and other natural resources of indigenous communities. While villagers may engage in a battle to recover these rights, it is a struggle in which the odds are stacked against them, and which the private sector and its partners are set to win.

Hughes (2001, 593) concurs: 'Ultimately, CAMPFIRE has come to denote an expensive public-private partnership for latter-day colonization'. Aided by state and donor funding, conservationists and private-sector partners have managed to obtain access to land that hitherto had been exclusively reserved for small-scale farmers, the latter running severe risks of having to give up farming for a relatively small share of the benefits from ecotourism that often does not compensate for the loss of income from farming.

While Hughes (2001) and Dzingirai (2003) discuss the fate of communities losing land to conservation, South African communities are trying to do the opposite and reclaim land in conservation areas. After the transition in 1994 to a democratic government, communities that had been displaced under discriminating legislation, such as the Group Areas Act of 1950, could file a land claim for the restitution of the land they had lost. Such claims are believed to greatly strengthen the bargaining power of local people relative to that of the conservation authorities, increasing their chances of extracting benefits from the parks – including those that are or will become part of TFCAs. Some of these were established by way of forced removals. In 1996, the South African Minister for Land Affairs announced that land claims were among the strongest mechanisms for correcting the balance of power between communities and conservation authorities (Reid 2001, 138). Such claims were facilitated by the Communal Property Association Act of 1996, which allows communities to set up a Communal Property Association (CPA) through which they can acquire, hold and manage property communally (Reid 2001).

The Makuleke Land Claim

One of the most widely publicized claims – and one that is often cited by both South African National Parks (SANParks) and PPF as proof that communities are benefiting from the Great Limpopo (see Peace Parks Foundation 2004; Koro 2005) – is the one lodged by the Makuleke community. In May 1998, the Makuleke and SANParks announced that they had reached a negotiated settlement of the Makuleke's claim for the restitution of what was then known as the Pafuri Triangle, the northernmost section of the Kruger National Park.

This area is quite central to the Great Limpopo, bordering on all three of the countries involved in the TP. The community was able to prove that it had occupied the area until August 1969, when it was removed by the then Department of Native Affairs to an area 60 km to the south and only 6000 ha in size (Harries 1987). After 18 months of tough bargaining, the Makuleke were successful. At the official signing ceremony in Makuleke village, the new CEO of SANParks announced that the settlement was a 'breakthrough for South African conservation' and promised that something like the Makuleke removal would '*never again* take place' (Spierenburg *et al.* 2006, 23). A new paradigm, he said, had been established within SANParks that aimed at transforming its relationship with its neighbours.

This celebrated statement, however, obscured the conflictual process that had preceded the settlement. It started with the introduction of the Transform (Training and Support for Resource Management) Project, a joint venture between the Department of Land Affairs and the Deutsche Gesellschaft für Technische Zuzammenarbeit (GTZ), a German development agency (Steenkamp 2000; Spierenburg *et al.* 2006). The project was introduced in 1995 to challenge the control that the National Party still held over the Environment Affairs and Tourism portfolio, and hence SANParks. As such, it provided the Makuleke with possible allies in their struggle with SANParks to regain control over the land they claimed in the Kruger National Park (Steenkamp 2000). Transform supported the Makuleke Ecotourism Project, a proposal whereby the community would establish a game lodge on the disputed land in partnership with the private sector. At that time, the Makuleke land claim had not been settled and the land was still under the stewardship of SANParks.

In 1996, the nature of Transform's support for the Makuleke project changed dramatically when SANParks became part of the Transform steering committee (Steenkamp 2000). Within the multi-stakeholder format used by Transform, which did not make a distinction between primary and secondary interest groups, it was possible for SANParks to participate directly in the planning of the projects affecting them. The result was a reorientation of GTZ funding away from the Ecotourism Project and towards a range of alternative community development projects. Notable emphasis was placed on the development of a buffer zone along the western periphery of the Kruger National Park, using Makuleke land. This would restrict the community's possibilities of using part of the limited land that had been allocated to them after their eviction from the Kruger National Park.

Unlike GTZ–Transform, which sought to reduce tensions between the Makuleke and SANParks through the multi-stakeholder platform, the Land Claims Commission recognized and exposed the conflict of interest between the Makuleke and SANParks and structured the decision-making process accordingly. A rigorous distinction was made between Makuleke and SANParks interests, a step that clearly undermined existing power relations between the two and strengthened the community's overall bargaining position. A particularly energetic land claims commissioner further ensured that the Makuleke claim was taken to its logical conclusion. The Commission intervened directly at the community level by putting the Makuleke Communal Property Association (CPA) in place as the vehicle for community ownership of the land claimed (Steenkamp 2000; Spierenburg *et al.* 2006).

The CPAs were originally designed to replace the politically discredited 'tribal authority' system from the apartheid era and to democratize land ownership and community development. The objective was to set in place accountable, transparent and representative institutions and thereby 'transform' community-level power relations. In Makuleke, there was a good deal of overlap and cooperation between the CPA and the traditional authority, though there was also conflict. The traditional leader (chief) of the Makuleke people was also elected as the chair of the CPA, thereby combining the two functions of traditional, ascribed leadership and democratic, achieved leadership. The leaders of the CPA were mostly from the elite that also controlled the tribal authority. In recent years, there have been attempts to separate the two bodies in order to find complementary foci and functions for them. Three women and a few teachers were recently elected onto the CPA in order to give it a stronger popular representation and to get younger and more skilled people on to a body that was seen as primarily concerned with development issues.

Although the Makuleke land claim was successful (see Steenkamp 2000, 2001), a number of conditions were attached to the restoration of land ownership. The land had to be used for conservation purposes for the next 99 years; no mining, prospecting, housing or agriculture would be permitted and no development was allowed without an environmental impact assessment. SANParks retained the right of first refusal should the land ever come on the market. Importantly, the Makuleke entered into a 25-year contractual national park agreement with SANParks. To manage the contractual park a Joint Management Board was established, consisting of three SANParks and three community representatives. SANParks is responsible for all of the management costs of the Makuleke part of the park for an initial period of 5 years and, after that, the Makuleke community's CPA will be liable for 50% of the costs (Steenkamp 2000, 143; Steenkamp 2001). The conditions amount to a compromise between the Makuleke and the state, encouraged by a statement made by the then Minister of Land Affairs that he was willing to support the Makuleke claim as long as they were willing to compromise and not be 'greedy'.

The Makuleke's quid pro quo for accepting the restrictions was that the CPA was given the right to make sustainable use of the land's natural resources, including hunting. They also gained exclusive commercial rights to the land, a right that they are able to exercise independently of SANParks. This is expressed by a clause in the agreement that specifies that a commercial decision by the Makuleke CPA is considered a decision by the Joint Management Board. SANParks is able to object only to the environmental dimensions of any proposed activities and may engage in the process through an environmental impact assessment. This places the Makuleke, in effect, on the same footing as the private game reserves adjacent to the park (Steenkamp 2000, 2001).

Hunting and Tourist Concessions

One of the first steps taken by the Makuleke was to establish a highly profitable hunting camp on the land, which they used for a limited number of high-profile hunts per year. This was a logical step in the commercialization of their land claim: hunting concessions are the biggest moneymaker in the wildlife tourism industry (Roth and Merz 1997). It was an unusual step in the sense that, in terms of the IUCN category of a national park, of which the Makuleke claim is a part, hunting is strictly prohibited (UNEP 2008). This has remained an issue with which SANParks is not happy. The first hunt, organized in 2001, boasted two elephants and two buffalo. The hunting offer doubled each year from 2001 to 2003.

The CPA planned the development of two lodges for tourists, and a training camp for students from the community. As the CPA lacked the funds needed for the investment, it sought partners in the private sector through a public tender procedure – a local non-governmental organization (NGO) called 'Friends of the Makuleke' assisted the CPA with training and support to enhance its capacity to negotiate with the investors and park management. The aim was for the community to receive a percentage of the revenues of the lodges and benefit from the jobs created at the lodges. The revenues would be distributed among the community by the CPA. Furthermore, after a period of about 15 years (depending on contract specifics), the ownership of the lodges would revert to the community.

The first lodge, or commercial development, was called Outpost. Commercial rights were signed over to a local tour operator; this decision was taken hastily and resulted in very few benefits for the community itself. CPA members ascribe this to an effort to 'get the ball rolling' – the CPA was eager to see productivity in whichever form. The commercial advantages for the Makuleke themselves constituted 10% of gross lodge revenue and a 2% signing fee (which amounted to about ZAR500,000 (€38,000)).

In the period that followed, the tour operator business was sold and taken over by new owners, Wilderness Safaris. They proposed to develop three lodges, totalling 88 beds. Each lodge was granted a concession of either 30 or 45 years of operation, and thereafter ownership would be transferred to the Makuleke under the Build–Operate–Transfer contractual arrangement. This change in tour operator led to a dramatic improvement in commercial gain: only members of the Makuleke community are now employed at Outpost and a 22% ownership interest was given to the CPA in addition to the 12% revenue.

The benefits from the hunting and tourist concessions were channelled into the Makuleke Community Development Trust, an entity created to administer the revenues, grants and other income for the CPA. It was decided to invest the income in projects that would benefit the community as a whole rather than to allocate the income to individuals. The community was paid about 10% of the turnover of the lodges, amounting to about ZAR500,000 (€38,000) per year, whereas the hunting concessions had brought in several million rand. This sudden financial windfall was used to bring electricity to two of the villages in the tribal area and to build another school. The population benefited from these infrastructural developments and the employment opportunities created thereby. A total of 66 employment opportunities were created in the lodges and their wildlife industry, whereas the total of new jobs created through development projects in the tribal area amounted to about 200.

However, the money that flowed into the Makuleke community was also used to pay for the running costs of the tribal authority. This was necessitated due to the hostility between the Makuleke and the Mhinga tribal authorities, arising from the claim of chief Mhinga that the Makuleke tribal authority actually constituted a headmanship under him, as had been the official situation during the time of the Gazankulu Bantustan (homeland). Chief Mhinga had stopped the money that was coming through his office for the tribal administration at Makuleke. Other large expenses that had been made from the Development Trust funds in recent years included the building of the Tribal Authority offices, including the offices of the CPA and the modern double-storey home of the Makuleke chief. While these were expensive items, the justification for these expenses in the eyes of some of the members of the community was that an independent chieftaincy needed to have these conspicuous symbols of administration. Furthermore, the recent preparation of the Communal Land Rights Act led to strong resistance from the Makuleke Traditional Authority, since it threatened to vest land rights in traditional leaders, which could strengthen the claim of chief Mhinga on the land administered by the CPA.

Apart from income from tourism and nature conservation, the Makuleke people benefited from the land restitution process in other ways. The involvement of government departments, NGOs and other interested parties over a number of years led to a considerable flow of expertise, skills training and development projects to this area. Pro bono legal, business and organizational advice was received and relatively large government and donor funded agricultural projects were initiated – for instance, the irrigated potato project that benefited several small farmers and agricultural workers in the area.

Though in many ways the contract with Wilderness Safaris results in significant gains, there is also a drawback: the contract contains a clause that effectively prevents the Makuleke from hunting on the land (Spierenburg *et al.* 2006). Opinions concerning this clause vary within the community. One of the Makuleke representatives on the Joint Management Board had the following to say about this clause:

> We have 24,000 hectares, we had all the rights, including the right to hunt. I am not afraid to say that the contract stopped the Makuleke from hunting. It is not SANParks that stopped us, but it is the way they develop the contract with the private sector. We were making a lot of money with hunting … There are many mistakes in the contract … [These companies have] been in business for a long time, they are negotiating with communities who have very little experience. You need very good advisors to compete with these big guys. Somewhere, somehow the community overlooked a few things in the contract.

The community did, however, have access to competent legal advisors. Responses from former Friends of Makuleke members were mixed. One felt that this was the best deal that the Makuleke were likely to get; another advised them not to sign the agreement as it stood, but this was just one day before the signing ceremony and the advice was not followed.

Opinions about the relative economic gain of the lodge versus the hunting also vary. Some argue that the game lodge currently generates less than was formerly brought in by the hunting operation and that it remains to be seen whether the higher projected income figures will eventually be achieved by Wilderness Safaris. Others, however, maintain that the revenues from hunting were less than expected, and believe that the lodges will provide the community with a more secure and stable source of income. It is hard to judge whether the decision made by the Makuleke CPA was the right one. In the interim, however, it is difficult to avoid the impression that the private sector had more experience with the negotiation of contracts in this sector than did the Makuleke legal advisor, and that the private tour operator and SANParks had similar (conservation) priorities in preventing hunting operations within the boundaries of the national park. The advantageous conditions applied to Wilderness Safaris with regard to the length of lease and conditions on their level of performance could be interpreted from this angle as leverage granted for cooperating with SANParks.

Dealing with national conservation agencies and policies is not easy for communities, as this case shows. The state is inconsistent in its approach to the communities, and some forces within the state were strongly opposed to the Makuleke claim. Furthermore, the alliances the communities concluded with development agencies and the private sector have generated mixed results. They variously helped the Makuleke secure their land and resource-use rights, such as hunting, but also oversaw the signing of an agreement with the private sector that reduced these rights. In the course of negotiations, the planned transfrontier park was repeatedly used by SANParks as a reason for the state to retain control over the land. Despite land ownership by the Makuleke, the community is not participating in the management structure of the overall TFCA (Spierenburg *et al.* 2006, 2008). At a workshop on tourism in the Great Limpopo TFCA at Wits Rural Facility in South Africa in April 2005, a representative from Makuleke addressed the audience, which included the TFCA's international coordinator and a SANParks representative: 'The way you present the plans, it appears that the communities are only subjects. But Makuleke have land, we have a contractual park, so we are part of the … [Great Limpopo TFCA]. But we are not part of the management board.'

The creation of a joint management structure for the TFCA would, he claimed, further dilute community representation:

> If there is a representative of the joint management board of our land in the [TFCA] board, that does not mean that the community is represented, it is the management structure of our conservation area that is represented. There are lessons to be learned. We must ensure that communities are represented, and that this area is not dominated by the elite. Who benefits who[m] between the communities and the Great Limpopo?

Mozambique: Freeing up Space for Investors

The situation of the people living in the Mozambican part of the TFCA looks much grimmer. According to the initial Mozambican conception, the Great Limpopo TP was meant to become a multiple-use area, to assist residents of the communal areas in Mozambique that would be included in the park (Milgroom and Spierenburg 2008; Spierenburg *et al.* 2008). However, the main focus became the joining of Coutada Sixteen with the Kruger National Park. Coutada Sixteen was a Wildlife Utilization Area and has about 27,000 people living within its borders. Soon after the signing of the agreement on the TFCA, Coutada Sixteen was declared a national park, and renamed the Limpopo National Park, but this was done without much thought as to what it would mean for the communities living on that land (Spierenburg *et al.* 2006, 2008). The PPF brochure celebrating the establishment of the Great Limpopo reflects the change in policy:

> ... all a Transfrontier Park means is that the authorities responsible for the areas in which the primary focus is wildlife conservation, and which border each other across international boundaries, formally agree to manage those areas as one integrated unit according to a streamlined management plan. These authorities also undertake to remove all human barriers within the Transfrontier Park so that animals can roam freely.

A member of the Mozambican National Steering Committee and the Technical Committee for the Great Limpopo concurred that what they had agreed upon was something 'completely different' from what they had worked so hard to establish for 5 years (interview, February 2001). Representatives of various organizations directly and indirectly involved in the implementation of the Great Limpopo TP felt that the Great Limpopo had also become a matter of prestige for PPF and the South African Government: it would be the largest TFCA on the continent and become a world-famous park. A great deal of pressure was therefore put on the various partners to make it happen and, in the process, the communities lost out. 'Community issues kept falling by the wayside due to the massive political pressure for tangible progress to be seen', said a senior conservation official in July 2005 (Spierenburg *et al.* 2006).

The majority of the people in the park live along its eastern and southern boundaries. Seven villages with a total of about 7000 inhabitants are located along the River Shingwedzi, which transects the southern part of the park. A study commissioned by the PPF concluded that the banks of the River Shingwedzi also hold the greatest tourism potential. On the map accompanying the plan (see Fig. 12.2), the villages along the river have been replaced by luxury lodges, and only one community lodge has been foreseen along the park's eastern border. A tender was put out on the Limpopo National Park's web site (Ministerio de Turismo de Moçambique 2006), inviting tourism investors to bid for concessions on parts of the area along the river. The closing date for bids was August 2006.

Both the government officials in the Ministry of Tourism who are responsible for the TFCA and the representatives of the major donor financing

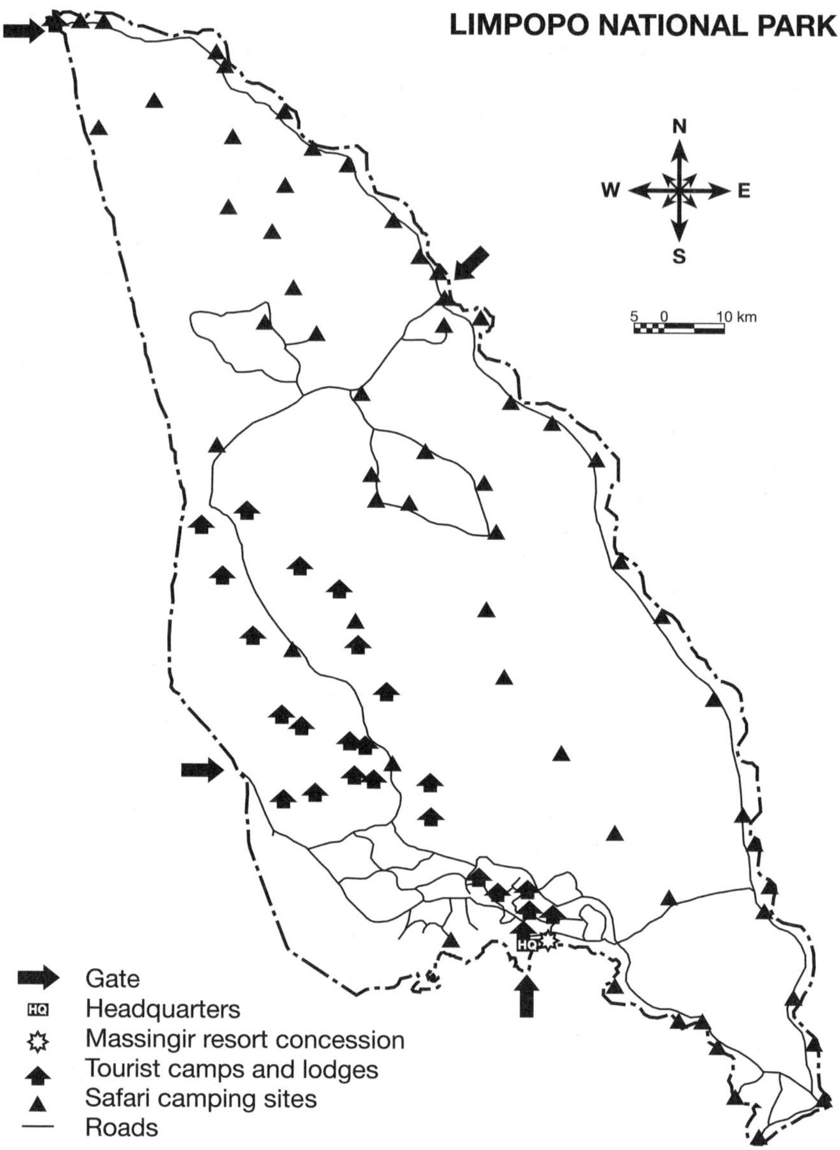

Fig. 12.2. The Limpopo National Park plan, with roads and accommodation services.

the park, Kreditanstalt für Wiederaufbau, insisted that no forced relocations would take place (interviews at the Ministry of Tourism and German Embassy, Maputo, June 2002, May 2005). At a press conference on 23 May 2005, the head of the TFCA's Project Implementation Unit in Mozambique claimed that resettlement would not only benefit the park but also the communities. He announced that the first 100 families would be resettled in October 2005 and remarked: 'It is hoped that this will lead the remaining families to understand that the park will not damage their interests but will actually improve their lives. Families in this area can never rely on farming to escape from poverty: the soils are poor and the semi-arid climate guarantees that yields from agriculture will always be low' (Smart News 2005).

This was not, however, how most community members judged their situation. When asked whether she would leave the area voluntarily to move to somewhere along the River Elephants south of the park as proposed by park management, a woman responded: 'We do not want to die from hunger over there, we do not want to leave the good soils here'. Similar sentiments were expressed by many of the people interviewed. A report by a consultant on possible resettlement areas concurs: 'They utilize alluvial soils in the Shingwedzi valley which have higher agricultural potential than generally occurs in the region. They have access to vast areas of grazing for livestock and to other forest resources ... The villages have access to reasonable supplies of water in nearby rivers' (Impacto 2005, 1).

Despite their objections, many people fear that they will be indirectly forced to move because of restrictions imposed by the park (see also Milgroom and Spierenburg 2008). They can move to the resettlement areas where access to fertile soils and water are quite problematic – even more so now that the land reserved for new grazing areas has been given out as a concession to a sugar cane company (interview with Park Director, 26 April 2007) – or they can 'stay and starve', as a consultant put it.

According to national parks legislation in Mozambique, cultivation inside national parks is forbidden. The communities along the Shingwedzi are allowed to continue farming the fields they had cleared before the declaration of the park but they are not allowed to clear new ones. Most farmers rotate their fields every few years and are worried what will happen when their current fields lose their fertility. Furthermore, accessing the emergency pastures used in times of drought has become illegal. Fishing is restricted and subsistence hunting forbidden. The park is also impinging on another livelihood strategy, namely illegal migration to South Africa to look for (temporary) work on commercial farms and as servants in communities living near the Kruger National Park. According to police officers in the Guarda Fronteira (interview, 12 May 2005), the increased presence of wildlife and the fact that people will now have to cross two wildlife areas (including the Kruger NP) with predator populations will deter possible migrants, as will the increased anti-poaching patrols.

Wildlife populations have significantly increased. More than 3000 animals, including 115 elephants and some lions, were translocated from the Kruger National Park and released in the area. The increased number of anti-poaching patrols has also resulted in an increase in the numbers of smaller ungulates. As a result, the communities are increasingly suffering from damage to their crops by wildlife and some have lost cattle to reintroduced predators. A village headman complained that: 'Whenever we report damage to our crops and the loss of our cattle to the people from the park, nothing is done, but whenever we try to defend ourselves against the wild animals they are there within a minute to arrest us'. The communities receive no compensation for wildlife damage, as one of the park's employees remarked: 'This is now a national park, agriculture and cattle-keeping are officially forbidden in the park, so how can we compensate for damage to things that are not allowed?'

By contrast, the Limpopo National Park's official web site states that: 'Fundamental to the concept of the Limpopo National Park is the requirement that it contributes to the welfare of the people of Mozambique through sustainable eco- [and] cultural tourism development'. Nevertheless, it is not clear how the communities will benefit from tourism development on the Mozambican side of the Great Limpopo TP. Arrangements have been made to set up community funds into which 20% of the entrance fees to the park will be paid (interview with staff member of the NGO responsible for administering the funds, 27 April 2007), yet the entrance fees paid by park visitors are not substantial. It is not clear whether and how benefits from the tourist operators will be shared with the communities. In other words, a whole area has been freed up for private-sector investments, while those who were made to sacrifice their homes for the investors are facing an insecure future in a resettlement area that appears less suitable for livestock husbandry and agriculture, without clarity about possible shares in the tourism ventures.

Concluding Remarks

In this chapter, we analysed the sometimes contradictory consequences of tourism development in transfrontier conservation for local communities. The processes of establishing the Great Limpopo TP and developing tourism within the park involved negotiations between the governments of three countries, and a wider network of national and international NGOs, private companies and development agencies. Such transnational negotiations are highly complex, and it appears that communities' interests, while emphasized in the promotion of the initiative, were not always accorded a high priority.

While the TP is opening up the borders to wildlife, tourists and investors, communities are becoming increasingly geographically bounded, even though their livelihood strategies often include border crossings (see also Hughes 2001). Yet in South Africa, the ideological binding of communities to certain territories has also facilitated the land claim process of the Makuleke. Nevertheless, the Makuleke negotiated the claim with state agencies that were not unanimous in their response, trying to reconcile – or perhaps to compromise – promises to redress past injustices (by the Land Claims Commission) with current conservation goals (by SANParks). The alliances the Makuleke have chosen, with NGOs and development agencies, to further their case are likely to have had varying effects on their empowerment. The Makuleke managed to secure rights of access to land within the TP through their alliances, but did not obtain (complete) control over the way they can use the land commercially. Apart from being a paradox in terms of the spirit of neoliberalism that seems to drive (part of the efforts towards) transfrontier conservation, it is also a form of disempowerment. Though their links with

NGOs strengthened their negotiating capacities, they struggled to define a favourable relationship with the private sector and ended up signing a contract that significantly reduced their control over their part of the TP. It seemed that the agendas of the public sector, i.e. SANParks, and the private sector, i.e. a tour operator, strengthened each other in enforcing the strict and categorical conditions towards conservation in a national park on the Makuleke community.

The communities on the Mozambican side of the TP are clearly in a much worse position. They have little to no bargaining power and, though the official policy is not to relocate them forcibly, the restrictions on land-use options and the increased presence of wild animals in the area are threatening their livelihoods. The change of status of the area they live in, from a Wildlife Utilization Area to a National Park, has undermined their right to the land. Since most development and land rights organizations find it difficult to challenge the state or the PPF on this issue, the communities' alliances with NGOs could serve only to improve their compensation once they have been resettled.

Partnerships between the state, communities, NGOs and the private sector in development in general, but also in tourism and community-based natural resource management (CBNRM), are advocated as important strategies towards development. However, in tourism and CBNRM, as we have shown in this chapter, large tracts of land that are – or are expected to come – under conservation, like the Great Limpopo TP, are effectively being brought under the control of such partnerships, which in some cases are dominated by non-state organizations and institutions. Despite the claims of conservation bodies and the private-sector parties involved that this leads to economic development, results vary, as we have shown, and some communities are in fact further marginalized and denied full development potential.

The Makuleke, compared with the Mozambican communities, have been relatively fortunate in that they had access to a range of well-established NGOs and other organizations shortly after the South African political transformation, when their restitution case was symbolic of the restoration of dignity to dispossessed African communities in South Africa. Through their alliances with these organizations, they managed to secure considerable benefits from tourism development, yet the possibilities of optimizing their benefits are threatened by their limited power and capacities in negotiating with private-sector companies. The Mozambican communities, on the other hand, are under-respected, under-skilled and under-resourced actors in this power game. Most likely, the benefits from tourism development on the Mozambican side of the TP that are to flow towards the communities will be few, and will not offset the tremendous costs in terms of losses of livelihood strategies resulting from their relocation.

What in both cases appears to be a persistent and also powerful tool in enforcing decisions and choices from almost all the parties involved is the categorization of land under conservation as 'national park'. In the case of the Makuleke, it has meant that the commercially lucrative business of trophy hunting has been contractually eliminated. In Mozambique, the concept of a national park has meant that, although people will not be forcefully removed from the park, they are left with no other option – in terms of livelihood opportunities – than to leave. The park concept has proved its resilience over time (Jones and Wills 2005), with its aim of preserving wildlife and its habitat, and of excluding humans. This idea still resonates today, also among tourism companies, and it often does not match – either in spirit or in practical execution – the rhetoric within transfrontier conservation circles of catalysing economic development to the benefit of those living in or close to the parks.

Acknowledgements

The authors would like to acknowledge the support of the South Africa–Netherlands Research Programme on Alternatives in Development (SANPAD) for its financial support of part of the research conducted for this chapter. Further support was received by the Transboundary Protected Areas Research Initiative, a programme running under the auspices of the IUCN South Africa, and funded through the Center for Integrated Study of the Human Dimensions of Global Change, by way of a cooperative agreement with the National Science Foundation (SBR-9521914). The authors acknowledge their gratitude to two students of Stellenbosch University, Izak van Zyl and François Louw, for their assistance in gathering some of the data.

13 Tourism Development Strategies: Lessons from the Southern African Experiences

Petri Hottola

Introduction

Tourism is not only about business and economic performance. In the developing world, it can be managed in a manner that delivers the strategic goals of development through tourism policies: economic and social empowerment, ecological sustainability and reduction in inequalities. This is the 'development first' perspective, embedded in the Southern African tourism strategies (Government of Botswana 1990; DEAT 1996, 2005; MET 2005a). The inclusion of development on the tourism agenda cannot, on the other hand, exclude the search for competitiveness and monetary profits. Together, these two dimensions have a potential to deliver genuine improvements in a society. Tourism development does not, however, happen in a vacuum. As Kerr (2003, 31) correctly points out, tourism policies are often subordinate to other policies, both national and supranational. Not infrequently in Africa, delays in related fields or policy-based introduction of conflicting activities prevent the progress in tourism. It is a complicated, interwoven process, with a number of challenges for states, communities and individuals (Dredge and Jenkins 2008).

The continent of Africa has, since the times of colonial conquest, been seen as a region of neglected resources, waiting to be mobilized – a fertile garden without a gardener. Despite well-argued criticism, also in this volume, the ideology of modernization remains strong in development agendas. Modernization has, at least for the time being, 'worked' on all continents of the Earth. Yes, it has been a monologue, and yes, the people have been forced to adjust, but not all of them have been able to do that. At this point in history, Asia is taking the lead in economic development. Asian nations formerly colonized by Europe have developed an economy capable of challenging their former masters and invest in global markets, the way for example the Tata Group of India has done. Recently, the Chinese have made their move to 'help' the African nations benefit from selected lay resources. To them, the region appears not only 'waiting' but 'empty', if compared with the congested East Asia. A new era of economic colonization and modernization has started, with invitation from local governments. The postcolonial states have not been fully able to govern their territories by themselves, and there is a risk of growing dependency, also in the field of tourism.

The outcomes of tourism development policies in Southern Africa are multifarious, as witnessed by the case studies in this volume. There are some outstanding victories, fair results, but also disappointments and failures. Are the positive developments occurring fast enough to be effective? At the moment, Africa in general lags several steps behind other continents, as measured by the relatively unbiased human development index of the United Nations Development Programme (2007). There is some progress, but at a moderate pace. Meanwhile, most nations at the top of the scale do their best to accelerate the speed of change, to keep up with the developments in global markets. There is always the next period of prosperity to benefit from, or a recession to overcome, with novel innovations to be tested. Only time will tell where the 'fast' and 'slow lanes' will finally lead. Meanwhile, the authors of the Southern African tourism development studies have good reason to keep their eyes open and to critically evaluate the current situation. There are lessons to be learned from the Southern African experiences.

Public–Private Partnerships in Tourism Development

The one theme above all the rest in this book is the applicability of public–private partnerships in tourism development, and the consequences of various approaches in terms of strategic tourism development, particularly in regard to the so-called disadvantaged people and communities. It is an interesting and important discussion which illuminates one of the main issues of everyday debates in the field, wherever tourism is developed and managed in Southern Africa. Working models are proposed, based on experiences in South Africa, Botswana and Madagascar. Conversely, some of their potential shortcomings are exposed, to be considered for implementation. Each time an already tested practice is adopted in a tourism development project, it needs to be modified according to the situational context. Even then, the end results cannot entirely be predicted. There are many operational, structural and cultural restraints involved, and their combined effects are difficult to estimate (cf. Tosun 2000).

Looking from the 'development first' viewpoint, the future of community-based tourism (CBT) becomes a particularly relevant topic in Southern Africa. Towards the end of this decade, conclusions and decisions are made in regard to the continuation of CBT enterprises (CBTEs). The idealistic, and perhaps to some degree unrealistic, expectations of CBT in the Namibian tourism policies are well described by Saarinen and Niskala (Chapter 5). Should autonomous community-based tourism projects continue to be seen as a strategic resource for the developing nations, or could their future be based mainly on partnerships under state and private sectors? Jänis (Chapter 2) concludes that the private sector puts more weight on profit and competitiveness than poverty reduction and empowerment, whereas the CBT sector is more concerned about ensuring the daily income than about the economic success of the enterprise. Nevertheless, it is the private sector that delivers most of the poverty reduction and empowerment through foreign exchange, jobs, social security, education, resource preservation and the multiplier effect.

From the regional point of view, in most of the strategic core areas, there is a considerable difference between private and CBT businesses in terms of delivering tourism development. This difference should initiate a number of serious questions. In private discussions with governmental and commercial stakeholders, CBT is often seen as an inefficient playground for people trying to learn the business but not capable of managing it in a sustainable way, not to mention creating significantly high foreign exchange income, the preferred source of capital. There are signs that the patience of governments is running out and more decisive policies may be adopted for the 'marginalized community-based tourism enterprises' (MCBTEs; see Rogerson, Chapter 3). A tourism development resource reserved by an aimless CBTE becomes a lay resource, or worse, and could possibly be better managed for the common good by another stakeholder. A tourism enterprise is expected to become self-sufficient after a short trial period. Otherwise, the rationality of conducting the business becomes questionable. MCBTEs may, however, continue to exist for decades.

At its best, CBT can be a productive tool for rural development on communal lands. Some partnerships between private companies, governments and communities, such as the cases of the Midlands Meander and the Okavango Delta, appear to be close to what can realistically be called ideal. Moreover, there are a few CBTEs doing reasonably well by themselves and contributing to the economy at the local level. There is good reason to suspect, however, that a number of cases in the latter category would deliver in a more substantial way if they were professionally run in a partnership environment. Occasionally, one cannot help feeling pity for the people who have been 'thrown into' the business of tourism with inadequate knowledge and skills. The locals may be enthusiastic about the visions of consulting development organizations but struggle in realizing them, often being restrained by a variety of issues born from their history in a marginalized position. Consequently, tourism development requires time, more than is actually available in an environment of increasing rather than decreasing challenges.

To overcome this situation, a more direct government intervention might be needed in the CBT sector, with more substantial incentive in vocational training and monitoring of the CBTEs, in terms of investment, marketing and resource management. The experiences of South Africa, highlighted by Rogerson (Chapter 3), place local governments in a central role in the partnerships between the private sector, non-governmental organizations (NGOs) and CBT groups in location-based tourism development (see also Goodwin 2006; Lourens 2007a, in Rogerson). 'Local economic development', an instrument for economic regeneration and diversification in the field of tourism (e.g. Rogerson and Visser 2007), appears to be a promising best practice for tourism development. In situations where shortage of human resources tends to limit business ventures, it is naturally advisable to let the contributions of all potential stakeholders complement one another in order to bring their strengths together. Partnerships may cause problems for CBTEs, for example in regard to their autonomy, but the incoming partners are also taking risks. Tour operators may have limited tolerance for experimenting with their customers in order to help their partners learn their business. For them, the most serious issue is the potential damage to their reputation, if something were to go wrong (see Jensen, Chapter 10).

In the Okavango Delta, government authorities, private tourism enterprises and local communities formed a partnership, much like the people of the Midlands Meander realized a route tourism project in KwaZulu-Natal. At least as important as combining forces for the partnership was the establishment of committed leadership with a clear vision, before the lengthy processes of market research, product development, strategy creation and operational and financial management plans were finished (cf. Lourens 2007b, in Rogerson, and the parameters of participatory development by Dyll (Chapter 4)). In Madagascar, the incoming tour operators acted as the professional hubs between the international markets and local service providers (Jensen, Chapter 10). They lead the operations, looking after the needs of both foreign companies and domestic stakeholders, in addition to their own businesses. By preferring long-term partnerships rather than single transactions, some of them established learning relationships with local service providers, empowering one another and enabling the providers to utilize and develop their strongest asset, local knowledge of nature and culture. From the strategic point of view, there is a clear difference between 'developers' and 'users', the latter buying services here and there without establishing lasting relationships.

On the Erongo coast of Namibia, a region with vast potential for bird and other wildlife tourism, the lack of momentum in tourism was also linked with the lack of partnership and leadership (Hottola, Chapter 8). The 'user' attitude to tourism was widespread. There was neither understanding of the local resources nor a clear vision of the future. The local governments had been passive, sending signals of indecisiveness and lack of commitment. The NGO sector had knowledge and ideas, but lacked strength. In this climate of distrust communities were understandably not very open to cooperative initiatives, and the private tourism sector was left somewhere in between, their hands full with work but with no partners or employees for the desired diversification of their products. The voluntary giving away of key resources to foreign developers was a resounding signal of defeat under the pressures of mounting problems and limited time. Ideally, a nation should control its main economic assets, and develop them by locally delivered projects.

In Chapter 12, Spierenburg, Wels, van der Waal and Robins provide a critique of the public–private partnership approach in the case of the Great Limpopo Transfrontier Park. As they describe, the partnerships between the

Makuleke community, state authorities and the private sector first empowered the Makuleke by returning them their land rights, with certain limitations, but eventually it led to a situation where these rights were once again limited as a consequence of a contract with a wildlife tourism operator. On the Mozambican side, community issues were also gradually overshadowed by the needs of more powerful stakeholders in tourism and conservation. Despite their advantages, the new South African tourism routes may also be criticized for their limited linkages with disadvantaged black communities, and the lack of pro-poor focus (Rogerson, Chapter 3). The Midlands Meander has been a success for the white rural communities, but it has also missed one of the main strategic development goals by maintaining the marginalization of black South Africans from the tourism economy.

Similarly, in his analysis of cooperation between incoming tour operators and local service suppliers in Madagascar, Jensen (Chapter 10) notes shortcomings in the interaction and coordination of activities between the regional authorities, NGOs and tourism enterprises. Much as on the coast of Namibia, local authorities had failed to establish trust among individual operators in the private sector, thereby weakening their strategic position in tourism development and the chances of development-oriented tourism policies being realized. If the tourism stakeholders do not trust one another, it is difficult to project a convincing regional image to the tourism markets. Assumingly, if trust could be re-established, a partnership approach along the lines presented by Rogerson and Mbaiwa (Chapters 3 and 7) could guide the process to a more productive course.

Minority Issues

Ethnic and cultural minorities – as highlighted by Dyll (Chapter 4) and Saarinen and Niskala (Chapter 5) – form a particular challenge in the context of development through tourism (see also Saugestad 2001). The practice of regional tourism development in Southern Africa does not place much emphasis on minorities but, as Dyll indicates, tends to reserve the participatory communication features for groups with real voting power in national elections. As unfair as it may be for the minorities, the dual drives of modernization and globalization, and regional politics, leave them with few choices. Minorities such as the ≠Khomani of South Africa, the !Xoo of Botswana and the Ovahimba of Namibia are more or less forced to adopt some type of role in tourism. In order to have their say in the developments, the minorities can either withdraw and protest or take an active role in tourism by accepting most of the rules of the game. In the first option, somebody else would take their identity and exploit it, and their marginalization would only increase. The second option, on the other hand, would inevitably lead to changes in their lives and customs, both positive and negative.

The situation of the Ovahimba, a relatively powerful minority with ample communal lands, evident high self-esteem and relatively secured cultural subsistence, is somewhat different from that of the more marginalized minorities. The Ovahimba have strong regional identity and they (mainly women) are idealized as the primary symbol of Namibian cultural heritage in tourism. From an aesthetic point of view, they have earned a global status of style and beauty: Ovahimba, the beautiful people, as many Internet travel or art photography blogs declare. Unlike some other Southern African minority women, Ovahimba women pose as famed objects of erotic–aesthetic gaze, not only heterosexual male gaze as Saarinen and Niskala claim, but across the borders of gender and sexual preference, in the manner of glamour or fashion models. There are the rare cases of disrespectful portrayals, but the problems in regard to the mainstream of Ovahimba photography are more subtle. The women of the Internet travel images do not pose provocatively, being sexualized only by their feminine bodies and normal everyday dress, as seen and conceptualized by some Western observers. The role of the Ovahimba women and men in tourism can also be seen as a predominantly empowering one, from the postfeminist point of view (e.g. Bordo 1997; Davis 1997).

The situations of the Ovahimba and other Southern African minorities have their counterparts in Europe. In the Nordic region, the estimated 75,000 Sámi people (Ministry of Social Affairs and Health 2008), originally nomadic reindeer herders and fishermen, form a colourful contrast to the majority Scandinavian population and have been exploited in travel and tourism for centuries (see Fig. 13.1). Their role in the branding of Nordic tourism has been so extensive that many ethnic majority entrepreneurs have adopted a Sámi role by wearing their traditional clothes, at times constructing rather degrading fantasy representations of the 'northern wild men' (e.g. Saarinen 1999, 2001). Consequently, a debate on cultural rights has been going on between the Sámi, who demand more respect for Sámi traditions and identity, and the Finns, Swedes and Norwegians who take part in Sámi region (Lapland) tourism.

The regional position of the Sámi is not without strength for a minority, as a consequence of specific state policies created in a dialogue with their representatives. For example in Finland, the 7000 Finnish Sámi, split into three main language groups, have an indigenous people status, with a degree of autonomy (e.g. Lehtola 1997). The Sámi have their own Sámi Parliament, *Sámediggi*, with an official status, and a cross-border Nordic Sámi Convention with participants from Norway, Sweden, Finland and Russia. They have representatives in state and local administration, the right to use their own language in schools and when dealing with administration, and Sámi language newspapers, magazines and radio and television broadcasts. The language has not become a restraint in integration. All Finnish learners, including the Sámi, learn a minimum of three languages at school: their first language (as a rule, Finnish, Swedish or Sámi), another official language (mostly Finnish or Swedish) and the first foreign language (in most cases, English).

Problems continue to exist, especially in land-use and ownership issues, many Sámi being dependent on public (formerly communal) lands in reindeer herding, hunting and gathering, with other stakeholders using the same

Fig. 13.1. Sámi culture for sale in northern Finland, including Sámi Barbies and Kens.

resources for commercial forestry and tourism, to name two significant examples (e.g. Lehtola 1997). The land-use policy has, however, not been thoroughbred dog-eat-dog laissez-faire but market capitalism with government control and intervention. All Nordic nations have a strong nation-state tradition but nevertheless accommodate the minorities in a relatively supporting way, with simultaneous integration into the wider society. A forced assimilation agenda was adopted early on, but abandoned after negative results, the scars of the 'cultural rehabilitation schools' still being visible today among the Sámi 'assimilation generation' (cf. Minde 2005).

In terms of development, the relationship between the postcolonial state and its minorities is an interesting one. Is it possible to build nation-state identity and at the same time preserve the diversity of ethnicities, the rich cultural variety of Southern Africa? For the sake of national cohesion, stability and efficiency, governments have tried to construct a common identity, suppressing 'tribalism' (e.g. Saugestad 2001). The many ethnic enclaves within Southern African nations create a degree of unique metaspatiality in the region (cf. Hottola 2005, 2006b). In this particular context, metaspatiality refers to 'nations' within nations, with a number of separating and also separationist features such as different cultures, values and even legal structures. In the background of many present-day problems in Southern

Africa looms the colonial heritage of arbitrary boundaries that have later made the construction of solid nations an arduous process. The nations of the region are also hampered by inter-ethnic mistrust, misconceptions and prejudices, created by communication problems, power struggles and the common human features of Othering and territorialism (e.g. Sack 1986; Duncan 1993).

Education and Tourism Development

The tourism development strategies of Southern African nations have been, and remain, subordinate to educational policies in the sense that the education system has not been able to deliver competent labour for the tourism sector (e.g. Jenkins 2000; Mbaiwa 2004). No solutions in this respect can be expected in the near future without significant changes in educational policies, from the primacy of quantity to the preference of quality. The Southern African nations have made advances in terms of the availability of education since their independence, but not yet to the level where the dividends really begin to accumulate and tourism and other socio-economic sectors are released from the impasse. There could be more information, both formal and informal through the media and, above all, higher-quality education with firm standards, continuity, accountability and competitive edge to meet any challenges that the future may bring.

In the CBT sector, there is a widespread lack of entrepreneurial skills. As Jänis points out in Chapter 2, quite often the most basic concepts of business – such as profit making and marketing – remain unfamiliar, thereby undermining the economic performance of CBTEs. This lack of knowledge is hardly surprising, as the operators of CBT normally have no formal training for their business, and may learn only through everyday activities. As several authors indicate, low capability to invest in tourism development is a significant problem, especially in more peripheral, low-income locations. Low investments are, however, not only about financial capital. CBTEs may periodically reap considerable income from trophy hunting, for example. In that situation there is, however, a temptation to distribute most of the money for the pressing daily needs of the people instead of developing the enterprise, if the importance of the investments remains unclear.

More often than not, the concepts of tourist and tourism too do not belong in the community lifeworlds the way they do in the tourism-originating regions. Indicatively, for example in North Sotho, the primary language of Hananwa at Blouberg, there were no words for tourist or tourism (Boonzaaier, Chapter 6). According to one perception encountered in the field in South Africa, a tourist is a person who has graduated to become a tourist, and is also paid for travelling. Not surprisingly, limits in intercultural understanding hinder tourism developments, or their sustainability, in a number of Southern African locations. How can one successfully conduct the business of tourism if the phenomenon itself remains unclear, not to mention the culture and needs of the customers who are supposed to use the services?

The fact that the majority of the Namibians involved with CBT, even though belonging to the prime target group, were not aware of the existence of black economic empowerment (see Jänis, Chapter 2) or seriously doubted it, speaks volumes of the gaps that exist in top-down communication in development policies. At the same time, the white private entrepreneurs understood their role in the national economy, their multiplier effect and had also adopted the strategic goals of tourism development with pride, to some degree including black economic empowerment, even though they might not support the SWAPO (South-West African People's Organization) policies in some other contexts and complained that the government gave them insufficient support.

They had to, for example, train their own personnel, as the staff's primary education, if it existed, did not provide enough skills for service careers, and there was seldom any public vocational education available. As the case studies in this book have shown, private hunting farms, game lodges, community-based tourism enterprises and tour operators have been able to alleviate the situation by their own educational activities. The task of vocational training should nevertheless not be entirely the responsibility of tourism operators, because they need to be able to focus on the core aspects of their operations. Providing adequate education is the responsibility of governments, and in fact one of their primary responsibilities. Internationally, a working model has been a combination of good basic education, preferably to secondary or tertiary level in a university or a polytechnic, and task-specific training by the receiving company.

There is a plenitude of unrealized human resource potential in the peripheries of Africa. Examples such as the perceptive young man of Blouberg (Boonzaaier, Chapter 6) prove that the concepts of development through tourism can be well understood also in rural communities with limited access to information if somebody actually takes on the task of explaining their content. With education, communication and information, fundamental societal changes can be made, but there is also the need for commitment. As soon as the skills, knowledge and awareness are established, commitment becomes a realistic option. It may be born out of revelation, an understanding of the interdependency of a number of factors in one's life which lead either to progress or stagnation, or something in between. More mundanely, it may grow out of practical results, the improvements in a person's living conditions as a result of investment in his or her future.

Insularity, Information and the Fear of Change

Helping the people in need is a noble idea, but one important question when considering all development projects is how to avoid the assistance becoming an instrument of dependency. In theory, aid is only supposed to help people up before they start to walk on their own and, possibly, run. In practice, people may become seduced by their own subordination, preferring to stay dependent as long as a reasonable living standard can be maintained, the obstacles of change, both intrinsic and extrinsic, appearing too large to be challenged. Therefore, it is important for state development policies to promote strategic changes of fundamental effect, by enabling, attracting and, if necessary, forcing people to move on to the next level, to become independent subjects of their lives instead of colonized objects. Breaking the circle of postcolonial dependency is, however, a complicated matter. The donors may also have fallen into the same trap. At both ends, there are people and organizations benefiting from the current situation, resisting the necessary changes and acting with a self-serving 'double vision'.

Readiness for societal changes characterizes much of the modern/postmodern world. Traditional societies, on the other hand, have a tendency towards risk avoidance and conservatism, resisting rapid and profound transitions. In cultural regions defined by a degree of insularity rather than by interaction across cultural borders, old traditions and values, both locally produced and imported, tend to persist and may occasionally create situations where rationality is replaced by the fear of change. A good example is the HIV/AIDS pandemic, as elaborated by Siiskonen (Chapter 9). In Namibia, the churches could not in the beginning accept the promotion of condoms, or other sexual health measures, even though the deadly seriousness of the rapidly growing epidemic was known. Similarly, the traditional leaders of rural communities could not allow open discussion on sex by men and women, parents and children, even though the silence meant suffering and death for many who did not know how to protect themselves.

Traditions may be worth our support, but not in every situation. As the example of the Midlands Meander shows, opportunism and readiness to change one's way of life are positive attributes in a transition between old and new economies. Sometimes, the need for change is difficult to detect locally, because people have no references to the benefits of change. For example, the CBT people of Jänis (Chapter 2) did not perceive themselves as being poor or as having a specific need for poverty eradication, probably because they had no measure for their living standards. What appeared to be poor to an outside observer were familiar and acceptable living conditions to the locals, who therefore saw no urgent need to improve their situation. One may wonder how these people would react if television provided them with material on everyday life in Europe or East Asia, with detailed explanations on how the wealth was accumulated by society and its citizens? Would they eventually start to make changes in their lives, decline the work-centred lifestyle or prefer a short cut by migrating to the north, holding on to the common assumption that the 'good life' is a 'present' given to the First World people? At the moment, many choose the latter option, even though they might have had an overall better life by making some changes back home.

In the Namibian birdwatching community, and in society in general, the consequences of insularity, created by a peripheral position and the prevalent ethnic borderlines, have limited the adoption of new ideas and cultures that would be useful in building competitiveness in the international business of bird tourism and could be complemented by local knowledge and innovations.

Moreover, the locals might later discover the positive effect of the changes in their domestic activities. In tourism, intercultural understanding is necessary for both hosts and guests, but especially for the hosts, who should attract and satisfy foreign customers with modes of communication understood by them. The birds and the coast of Namibia are attractive by themselves, but to maximize their potential and make the local strengths really stand out one would need to create products with an international edge.

Globalization was originally thought to more or less automatically bring the nations together in a shared cultural realm where intercultural understanding had increased (e.g. Featherstone 1995). Much of this cultural hybridization was expected to occur via the media. In the First World, technological innovations, together with content production, are often seen as the driving force of development in postmodern societies. The business of tourism also occurs increasingly on the platform of the Internet, other channels of communication drifting to the margins. In the tourism-originating regions, people are reluctant to return to the old-fashioned methods of communication – (mobile) telephone, facsimile or 'snail mail'. Without a personal e-mail, a service provider becomes excluded from the mainstream of international markets.

At the same time, in the African developing nations the accessibility of ICT is becoming a bottleneck for tourism development, particularly in the sector of small and medium-sized enterprises (SME). The regional markets have been too small for diverse media services, and national broadcasting and telecommunications companies have not yet reached maturity. In the young postcolonial states, the Internet and television networks are in general limited to larger settlements along the main national highways (e.g. Matengu 2006). Unlike, for example, in tightly populated South and East Asia, where technical accessibility was quickly created for all, including the poor, because the sheer number of customers allowed a construction of extensive networks, the long distances and low populations of Southern Africa have not yet allowed a similar coverage. Consequently, one key agent of societal change in the region has not realized its full potential.

As Matengu explains in Chapter 11, many CBTEs in Namibia and other Southern African locations would not possess the capacity to use the new technology, even if it were available. In the future, the learners may be taught to master new communicative tools, but the process of implementation in the everyday will remain more complicated than is seen from the nations donating the computers – and ideologies within. Locally, indigenous applications of information technology solutions may well be the most productive. Internationally, one has to understand and follow the evolution of the global Internet culture, based on mainly Western societal processes, in order to be present here and now. The relations of power are clear: those who master the new media also define the direction of its future, together with service providers. This development is almost organic, and is produced by cross-cultural cyber-communities, and therefore perhaps somewhat frightening to the elites of many developing nations, with their authoritarian power structures.

To return to the issue of the HIV/AIDS pandemic, the disease must not be regarded as an unstoppable force of nature. The epidemic can be stopped if people are ready to change their behaviour. Given the amount of information available in most urban and rural communities, even though possibly not adequate, and the fact that the number of HIV infections continues to rise (UNAIDS 2008), there must be societal factors supporting the epidemic. Alcoholism, also widespread in the Southern African region, creates an environment particularly vulnerable to sexually transmitted diseases. Apathy and carelessness commonly occur, both in socially marginalized and privileged situations. The societal root causes of these interlinked problems should continue to be critically assessed and attended, as a part of national health policies, to facilitate changes both in attitudes and behaviour. The tourism sector has begun proactive measures to control the consequences of HIV/AIDS, but it is not able to stop the pandemic (more in Siiskonen, Chapter 9).

Tourism and Nature Conservation

In most of Southern Africa, tourism is predominantly wildlife tourism. Several nations of the region have succeeded in creating environmentally sustainable tourism in national parks and other reserves, Botswana being one of the leading examples. One indicator species, the African elephant, tells a great deal about the quality of the nation's national parks, the primary tourist attractions. Chobe National Park in the north of Botswana has 120,000 elephants, one-fifth of the world population (WWF 2008a), being the core reserve for the species. The parks in northern Botswana also supply wildlife to neighbouring nations, including the Namibian Caprivi Strip, where large mammal species have been dwindling under human pressure and experiencing difficulty in reproducing successfully. Botswana is the least corrupt nation in Africa (Transparency International 2008) and is therefore more able to realize its policies than its neighbours, providing a reliable environment for tourism investment. Illegal hunting also occurs there but, judging by its animal populations, it is effectively controlled.

Commercial nature reserves and hunting farms have had a major positive effect on nature conservation in Southern Africa. Trophy hunting, at first sight in contradiction with conservation, has also become a success in ecological terms, more than fulfilling the environmental aspect of strategic tourism development. In Namibia, South Africa and Botswana hunting is carried out in a sustainable manner, allowing the population expansion of several game species (e.g. Mendelsohn *et al.* 2003; Lindsey 2008). Many other positive effects on fauna and flora have followed as the environmentally damaging and economically inferior cattle have been replaced by indigenous herbivores. Biodiversity is improved and invaluable resources such as water are saved in this mostly arid region. The game meat itself is an important by-product. The farms could have used their animal resources more intensively without endangering sustainability, but have preferred otherwise for ideological reasons, to 'let the real Africa' come back. They have this option, living on private land in a region of low population.

In the overpopulated communal lands, on the other hand, the situation has become characterized by widespread over-harvesting of natural resources, such as overgrazing by cattle, over-utilization of water sources, unsus- tainable collection of firewood and consequent extinction and erosion – the ingredients of an eco-catastrophe. The expansion of agriculture, particularly cattle grazing, has reached a stage where a dead end is visible and the environment will be unable to sustain the next generations. From the strategic point of view it is time for a structural change, and the future of communal land ownership could perhaps also be reconsidered. The pressure of a growing population is simply too strong to be managed if the traditional ways of land use are continued. In the light of what I have personally witnessed in the field, the criticism against CBT in not being able to look after nature conservation, listed by Mbaiwa (Brandon 1998; Oates 1999; Terborgh 1999; Duffy 2000; Diamond 2003), is well deserved in a number of cases. Many communal lands suffer from habitat eradication, logging and poaching, and inhabitants find it difficult to maintain the resources, not to mention improve them for tourism. The traditional ways of management, once effective, have lost their charm as the ecological limits have been over-reached.

The case of the Okavango Delta, presented by Mbaiwa (Chapter 7), is an interesting one for the conservation, development and tourism debate, because nature conservation has also made sense to the local communities of the area. The monitoring and control of the hunting areas have been meticulously enforced by both governmental and community bodies. This is an important policy instrument in securing the most vulnerable of strategic resources, the natural environment. There is a certain ranking order among the strategic goals of tourism development, and the preservation of nature is the first issue to be attended. In fact, there is no rational alternative to environmental conservation in situations where the finiteness of resources would otherwise soon be reached and a lose–lose scenario realized. By joining the conservation effort, the people of the delta have gradually earned a more empowered position and reaped the benefits of wildlife through tourism activities. By this strategy, they have been able to duplicate the success of private hunting farms in the CBT context, while simultaneously increasing biodiversity and economic profits. Tourism development has worked for wildlife conservation with a win–win result, creating an important model for others to follow.

In a number of situations complete success is impossible to attain. In the everyday of human societies, compromises and less than ideal but satisfactory solutions carry us on, being followed by other decisions that are hoped will produce improved results. In wildlife reserves, the outcomes of tourism development may be evaluated from anthropocentric and biocentric positions. In a national park, the logical preference is the latter, the primary purpose of the parks being the preservation of biodiversity and the secondary one its exploitation. In nature reserves the requirements of natural ecosystems and their inhabitants, in most cases far less capable of adapting to change than human beings, do not always allow compromises. In sustainable wildlife management it is not possible to fundamentally change the ecological niche of species as part of a compromise to please the interests of less profound nature, thereby exterminating those species. At the grassroots level, when the survival of, for example, Black Rhinos and humans has become mutually exclusive, the wisdom of the human being allows his relocation for a new start, leaving both parties alive.

According to Spierenburg and her colleagues (Chapter 12), the Great Limpopo Transfrontier Park has had mixed results. From the conservational and commercial point of view the transfrontier park appears to have been a step forward, but the success would have been more complete if the relocation of the communities within had received more attention. In the developed world, most people are not that strongly attached to land or a certain location, and may move without much hesitation. In rural Southern Africa the attachment to one's birthplace remains strong, and people are often literally dependent on their land. On the other hand, it is next to impossible for farming to coexist with large herbivorous mammals in a national park. The farmers who need to move deserve proper compensation and support in their new location. At the Coutada Sixteen section of the transfrontier park, this has not, apparently, occurred.

In the case of the South African Makuleke communal property association and their lost hunting activities in the park, one may argue that hunting is not, after all, that exceptional in nature reserves. For example, elephants are periodically culled to protect the habitats from erosion, the animals not being allowed to find other pastures beyond the park boundaries. Moreover, aggressive animals are occasionally shot if close to tourist accommodations (see Fig. 13.2). In this specific case, the logic of tourism operators is, however, to avoid hunting in order to minimize the risk of damaging the image of the national park and its wildlife product, the controversy between hunting and nature conservation being a particularly sensitive topic in the tourism-originating nations. A controversy such as this also has potential to damage the image of South Africa in general.

Five Nations Safari

Tourism promotion projects often focus on geographically limited situations, enterprises run by one community or developments within a single nature reserve. Route tourism development – clustering and packaging things into themed routes – has been a success in South Africa but it would be a relatively new innovation in the rest of the region. Functional tourism routes are also able to spread the benefits of tourism along roads between its main service nodes, creating small-scale business opportunities in rural areas. On the other hand, governments have also been ready to 'think big'. Transfrontier wildlife tourism is expected to be another successful formula. In this volume, the transfrontier situations have included the Kgalagadi (Kalahari) Transfrontier Park and the Great Limpopo Transfrontier Park. Strategic tourism

Fig. 13.2. A 'problem animal', a young bull hippo, shot at Namushasha Lodge, Caprivi, Namibia, in 2007.

development should indeed not only be about local and national tourism resources, even though current policies seem to imply this. There are occasions where tourism attractions extend across borderlines or congest around them. From the viewpoint of tourism-originating regions, Southern Africa is often seen as a single market with a variety of destinations.

In Southern African tourism there are untapped transfrontier opportunities of a global scale, with the potential to be realized as a common effort in the current, politically favourable climate – with the exception of Zimbabwe, until its national reconstruction. One such opportunity is located in the north–central part of the region. Along the great Zambezi, five nations with significant wildlife tourism resources meet in a relatively small area, with mostly fine, recently upgraded road connections. In that area, an establishment of a 'Five Nations Safari' could potentially create a major tourism product, capable of challenging East Africa as the leader of the safari field. It would not be just about cross-border tourism in the proposed Kavango–Zambezi Transfrontier Conservation Area, as suggested by Viljoen (2007, in Rogerson, Chapter 3), but a full-scale industry encompassing all the tourist attractions within the five-nation border region.

A visitor could take an intercontinental flight to Livingstone, Zambia, the gateway to the region, and start at Victoria Falls, one of the iconic tourism sights in Africa. Crossing to Zimbabwe, the National Parks of Victoria Falls and Hwange would be two interesting options close by. The next stop would be right across the border in Kasane, Botswana, the gateway to Chobe National

Park, with its elephants and the rest of the 'big five'. At Ngoma, 65 km west, the River Chobe may be crossed to eastern Caprivi, Namibia. This area's wildlife tourism attractions and services are scarce, at the moment, but could conveniently be improved by the previously planned conservation zone between the River Kwando (Mudumu National Park), Linyanti Swamp and the northern shores of the Chobe to Impalila Island. Given the opportunity, large mammals would cross the Chobe from Botswana by themselves. Along this route it would be possible to create cruises to the Zambezi with its rich birdlife, hippos and other wildlife. At Katima Mulilo, the regional centre of Caprivi, another crossing to Zambia across the Zambezi has recently been enabled by a new bridge and road connection.

The national park of Sioma Ngwezi (Zambia) and upper Zambezi lodges could be accessed next, as well as Mucusso National Park at the south-eastern corner of Angola, for a more rugged safari experience in places currently seldom visited. At Sioma Ngwezi and Mucusso, infrastructural development would be needed to allow tourism operations. The new Katima Mulilo–Livingstone highway would guarantee a fast final leg to Livingstone, completing the loop with more exploration of the 'Big Falls' region. The visitors could choose between a wide range of programmes along the route, the shortest round trip being 350 km on tarmac, game drives excluded. The tour could be completed in a week or two, depending on one's programme. All in all, the 'Five Nations Safari' would provide a comprehensive African safari experience, with impressive sceneries and charismatic mammals, including some restricted-range species such as Lechwe and Puku, and a smattering of cultural aspects to spice up the safari. The chance to visit four or five African nations in a single trip, including the 'new' destinations of Angola and Zimbabwe, would provide the additional status attractive to many customers.

The main requirement for the 'Five Nations Safari' product development would be a specific visa that would allow visitors and their vehicles to cross the borders on a fast-track basis, instead of the otherwise time-consuming, holiday-spoiling procedures. All the above-mentioned states being members of SADEC (Southern African Development Community), such a regional arrangement could be possible, if the political will were there. Considering the potential scale of tourism and profits created once the product has established itself, the effort would certainly be worthwhile. From the viewpoint of development strategies, the benefits of regional cooperation across the borders would exceed any locally run tourism developments. At the moment, Zambia (Livingstone) and Botswana (Kasane) are doing quite well, but they would profit, too, from an increase in the volume of tourism. Instead of competing with one another, the above-mentioned locations would form a common tourism destination, with mutual benefits and shared regional image.

The development of the new transfrontier tourism route and the new nature reserves would probably be vulnerable to some problems similar to those of the Great Limpopo Transfrontier Park (Spierenburg *et al.*, Chapter 12), the establishment of the tourism product requiring the replacement of cattle and herders by game and tourists in parts of Caprivi. In the light of the Okavango Delta experience, a working compromise might, however, be feasible. On the other hand, there is CBT on the Namibian side that has not shown much progress, mainly as a consequence of low visitor numbers in eastern Caprivi (see Fig. 13.3). There are no game lodges on the northern shore of the Chobe. At the same time, in Kasane and Livingstone, accommodations tend to be well booked, year round. The transfrontier park and route also could bring the tourists to Caprivi and the currently peripheral regions of Zambia and Angola, changing their status and revitalizing the border area. The current restraint would be transformed into an asset.

Final Conclusions

In order to succeed, the current tourism policies and strategies of the Southern African nations need the support of other interconnected policies, primarily in education, nature conservation, health and information and communication technology. Three best practices for tourism development – in route tourism, hunting and wildlife tourism and cooperation between incoming tour operators and local service providers – are introduced by Rogerson, Mbaiwa and Jensen (Chapters 3, 7 and 10, respectively). A critique to complement the public–private partnership approach is provided by Dyll, Saarinen and Niskala, Boonzaaier and Spierenburg *et al.* (Chapters 4, 5, 6 and

Fig. 13.3. The community crafts centre at Bukalo, Caprivi, Namibia, by the highway between Botswana and Zambia; closed for most of the time due to lack of customers.

12, respectively) in regard to minorities and other communities within tourism destinations. A comprehensive view on national development through tourism strategies, as perceived by tourism operators, is presented by Jänis (Chapter 2), with the issue of subordination between policies being discussed by Hottola, Siiskonen and Matengu (Chapters 8, 9 and 11, respectively), in connection with neglected tourism resources and the HIV/AIDS pandemic.

The commercial success stories portrayed in the book, the Midlands Meander, the Okavango Delta and, with reservations, the Great Limpopo Transfrontier Park, can also be categorized as high-profile cases with exceptional qualities. The main factor that sets them apart from others is their resource base. The Midlands Meander is favoured by its close proximity to Durban and Pietermaritzburg, which provide the route with an extensive customer pool. The delta and the transfrontier park contain wildlife resources on a global scale, being therefore in a more favourable situation than the majority of their competitors. The results have been impressive, and lessons can be learned from the strategies which have lead to the positive outcomes, but one should not automatically expect similar results if these practices are applied in other places. Each situational context requires its own modifications. On the other hand, resource base is not everything. The Erongo coast of Namibia has not been able to fully profit from its wildlife resources, due to sociopolitical and cultural restraints.

The need for leadership has been well attended in the tourism development case studies. There certainly is space for many small-scale tourism enterprises in Southern Africa (Dahles 1997, 23–24), but they need to be professionally managed. Given the shortage of skilled people, partnerships may provide transitional solutions until educational systems begin to deliver. In South Africa, regionally led tourism development appears to have made good results. From a strategic point of view, the dualism of national and regional tourism policies may provide the sensitivity and productivity people are expecting at the local level. The Southern African nations that do not yet have regional governance in tourism could consider establishing it. Tourism is, after all, a major source of income in each nation of the region (WTO 2006). In the developed world, national governments have a major role in some aspects of the tourism industry, such as resource preservation, infrastructure construction, monitoring and control, but they need the local governments for the effective mediation of their policies at the local level.

It is clear that tourism is not the vehicle for development for all, at least not directly. One may prefer to call minor positive dividends development, but subsistence-level gains do not really indicate development in a strategic sense. There needs to be a substantial increase in knowledge and wealth, from dependency to independency, from marginal to centre, from aimless existence to a new reality with direction and future. Not everybody is ready to lead in transition. Some may discover other professions after experimenting in tourism. Others may find subservient but nevertheless satisfactory roles in cooperatives run by more capable stakeholders. Too often in Southern Africa it is thought that any person or any community may prosper in tourism. At the same time, only a few succeed in the core areas of world tourism, with their hundreds of millions of customers and highly educated entrepreneurs. Jensen makes an important point by revealing how much effort incoming operators invest in identifying the suitable candidates for local partners in Madagascar. Locating persons and communities with the professional attitude, benevolence and the willingness to work seriously, in addition to skill and knowledge requirements, remains a challenge in Africa.

A number of research agendas arise from the current issues of strategic tourism development in Southern Africa. First of all, the long-term sustainability of the route tourism and community-based natural resource management (CBNRM) models should be evaluated in the future. For example, how do the successful tourism routes revitalize themselves in order to maintain their competence in the long run? According to the tourism life cycle theory, tourism destinations are established, become popular, gain a prominent status, degrade and lose their fame in the end (Butler 1980). On the other hand, how does the CBNRM approach of the Okavango Delta deal with the pressures of population growth? The wealth created by CBNRM is helping families to grow, but the delta has its limits in accommodating people and wildlife.

Secondly, the issue of tourism policies and strategies would need further empirical research. To what degree do governments actually follow their own guidelines by administrative measures in tourism, or in tourism locations fully controlled by them, such as many national parks and reserves? Will the communicational gaps between the state policies and tourism entrepreneurs diminish or widen as evolution of the sector proceeds? What about the relations between the parallel development policies? Which specific features could first be addressed to release the subordinated fields of development out of their restraints? On the other hand, during the transition from old economies to new ones, characteristic of many research situations in Southern Africa, the developments at the local level may produce surprising outcomes for analysis. The evolving role of minorities such as the Ovahimba is one question, but the changes will affect each community in a specific way. As Dyll concludes, different paradigms of development are often simultaneously adopted in communities involved with tourism, making the processes and outcomes more difficult to forecast than the theories may have led one to assume. There are many research questions waiting to be solved, even though the political sensitiveness of policy analysis may present certain limits to the enquiry, particularly at the administrative level.

There are also gaps in our knowledge on the prevalence of HIV/AIDS and its impacts on the tourism sector, particularly in regard to small and medium-sized enterprises, the backbone of tourism in peripheral areas. As Siiskonen found out, the situation with regard to tourism HIV/AIDS policies is improving, at least among the larger tourism companies of South Africa, Namibia, Zimbabwe and Zambia, but more research will be needed on this topic to activate the SMEs. Beyond the discourse of tourism: What are the root causes of the widespread demoralization in Southern Africa, with the exceptional prevalence of alcoholism and sexually transmitted diseases? In the context of incoming tour operators and local service providers, Jensen suggests more research on intercultural issues. In Madagascar, local guides accused the French tourism operators of being impatient when they pressed the village visitation project to be finished in under 3 years. In Europe, anything more than a few months would probably be considered extraordinary. Similar situations are commonly found in other spheres of Southern African tourism.

The 'Five Nations Safari' may be an attractive idea, but preliminary surveys and studies would need to be conducted before any action could be taken. The region of Erongo will be one of the growth poles of Namibia in the foreseeable future, despite the simultaneous occurrence of serious social and environmental problems. The coast, in particular, has already undergone a series of changes and would require several interdisciplinary studies, not only in regard to tourism but also other aspects of regional development. The Hananwa of Blouberg have demonstrated a good start for CBT, and the monitoring of local developments will provide the full picture in the future. Similarly, the issue of ICT and peripheral tourism could be followed as an interesting interface of developing regions and the so-called information society. The new transfrontier parks have created a plethora of research questions in tourism, and practical problems to be solved by applied research. As could be expected, the investigation of tourism development strategies in Southern Africa has raised even more questions than it has been able to answer. The discourse of tourism development is a young one, with a rich and interesting field of phenomena to be followed and studied as tourism continues its expansion in Africa.

References

Aberly, D. 1999. *Interpreting Bioregionalism: A Story from Many Voices.* In McGinni, M.V. (ed.), *Bioregionalism,* pp. 13–42. Routledge, London.

Abrahams, D. 2007. The Military as an Economic Agent in Local Economic Development: The Case of South Africa. *Urban Forum* 18(2): 13–30.

!Ae!Hai Kalahari Heritage Park Agreement 2002. !Ae!Hai Kalahari Heritage Park Agreement. Document, whereby the land restitution claims of the ≠Khomani San Community and the Mier Community are finalised, 29 May.

Agar, M. and MacDonald, J. 1995. Focus Groups and Ethnography. *Human Organization* 54(1): 78–86.

Andriotis, K. 2002. Scale of Hospitality Firms and Local Economic Development – Evidence from Crete. *Tourism Management* 23(4): 331–341.

Ankomah, P.K. and Crompton, J.L. 1990. Unrealized Tourism Potential: The Case of Sub-Saharan Africa. *Tourism Management* 11(1): 11–28.

Applegate, J.E. and Clark, K.E. 1987. Satisfaction Levels of Birdwatchers: An Observation of the Consumptive–Nonconsumptive Continuum. *Leisure Sciences* 9(2): 129–134.

Archer, B.H. 1982. The Value of Multipliers and Their Policy Implications. *Tourism Management* 3(2): 236–241.

Arntzen, J.W. 2006. *Case Studies on Successful Southern Africa NRM Initiative and Their Impacts on Poverty and Governance: Country Case Study Botswana.* International Resources Group (IRG), United States Development Agency (USAID). Washington, DC.

Arntzen, J.W., Molokomme, K., Tshosa, O., Moleele, N., Mazambani, D. and Terry, B. 2003. *Review of CBNRM in Botswana.* Applied Research Unit. Gaborone, Botswana.

Arntzen, J.W., Buzwani, B., Setlhogile, T., Kgathi, D.L. and Motsolapheko, M.K. 2007. *Community-Based Resource Management, Rural Livelihoods and Environmental Sustainability.* Centre for Applied Research. Gaborone, Botswana.

Asheeke, J. and Katjiuongua, O. 2007. *Development of Sustainable Tourism Country Report: Namibia.* Federation of Namibian Tourism Associations and Namibia Community Based Tourism Assistance Trust (NACOBTA). Windhoek, Namibia.

Ashley, C. 2000. The Impacts of Tourism on Rural Livelihoods: Namibia's Experience. Working Paper No. 128. Overseas Development Institute. London.

Ashley, C. 2006. *How Can Governments Boost The Local Economic Impacts of Tourism?: Options and Tools*. Overseas Development Institute and Stichting Nederlandse Vriwilligers (SNV). London.

Ashley, C., Goodwin, H. and McNab, D. 2005. *Making Tourism Count for the Local Economy in Dominican Republic: Ideas for Good Practice*. Pro-Poor Tourism Partnership. London.

Ashley, C., Goodwin, H., McNab, D., Scott, M. and Chaves, L. 2006. *Making Tourism Count for the Local Economy in the Caribbean: Guidelines for Good Practice*. Pro-Poor Tourism Partnership. London.

Astuti, R. 1995. *People of the Sea. Identity and Descent among the Vezo of Madagascar*. Cambridge University Press. Cambridge, UK.

AWU 2008. Avian Watch Uganda (AWU) (http://www.avianwatchuganda.co.ug/, accessed 28 November 2008).

Axelsson, B. and Elbe, J. 2000. Improved Resource Utilisation through Entrepreneurial Activities: The Role of the Tourist Organisation Interpreted by Using a Network Perspective. Paper presented at the 3rd International Forum on the Sciences, Techniques and Art Applied to Marketing. Madrid, Spain.

Babbie, E. and Mouton, J. 2001. *The Practice of Social Research*. South African Edition. Oxford University Press. Cape Town, Republic of South Africa.

Bacon, P.R. 1987. Use of Wetlands for Tourism in the Insular Caribbean. *Annals of Tourism Research* 14(1): 104–117.

Bandyopadhyay, S., Shyamsundar, P., Wang, L. and Humavindu, M. 2004. Do Households Gain from Community-Based Natural Resource Management? An Evaluation of Community Conservancies in Namibia. DEA Discussion Paper No. 68. Ministry of Environment and Tourism. Windhoek, Namibia.

Bank of Namibia 2004. Annual Report 2004. Bank of Namibia. Windhoek, Namibia.

Baran, P. 1957. *The Political Economy of Growth*. The Monthly Press. New York.

Barkin, D. and Bouchez, C.P. 2002. NGO–Community Collaboration for Ecotourism: A Strategy for Sustainable Regional Development. *Current Issues in Tourism* 5(3/4): 245– 253.

Barnes, J.I. and Novelli, M. 2008. Trophy Hunting and Recreational Angling in Namibia – An Economic, Social and Environmental Comparison. In Lovelock, B. (ed.), *Tourism and the Consumption of Wildlife – Hunting, Shooting and Sport Fishing*, pp. 155–168. Routledge. London.

Bartik, T.J. 2003. Local Economic Development Policies. Staff Working Paper No. 03-91. Upjohn Institute. Kalamazoo, Michigan.

Beeton, S. 2006. *Community Development through Tourism*. Landlinks. Collingwood, Victoria, Australia.

Berlo, D. 1960. *The Process of Communication: An Introduction to Theory and Practice*. Rinehart. San Francisco, California.

Berno, T. 1999. Cross-cultural Research Methods: Content or Context? A Cook Islands Example. *Annals of Tourism Research* 26(3): 656–675.

Bester, R. and Buntman, B. 1999. Bushman(ia) and Photographic Intervention. *African Arts* (Winter): 50–59, 93–94.

Beyer, A., Peterson, C. and Sharma, A. 2003. The Role of Participation and Partnerships in Local Economic Development in Africa. Working Paper, New York University's Robert Wagner Graduate School of Public Service. New York.

Biesele, M. 1995. Representation and Communication. Social Challenges in Ju'/hoan Community Education. Anthropological consultancy report, Nyae Nyae village schools project. Windhoek, Namibia.

Biesele, M. 2000. To Whom It May Concern: Or, Is Anyone Concerned? The Nyae Nyae Ju/'hoan Tape Archive, 1987–1993. *Critical Arts* 14(2): 145–174.

Binns, T. and Nel, E. 2002. Tourism as a Local Development Strategy in South Africa. *The Geographical Journal* 168(3): 235–247.

Binns, T. and Nel, E. 2003. The Village in a Game Park: Local Response to the Demise of Coal Mining in KwaZulu-Natal, South Africa. *Economic Geography* 79: 41–66.

BirdLife International 2008. IBAs in Namibia (http://www.birdlife.org/datazone/sites, accessed 24 November 2008).

Blankenberg, N. 1999. In Search of a Real Freedom: Ubuntu and the Media. *Critical Arts* 13(2): 42–65.

Bloch, M. 1971. *Placing the Dead: Tombs, Ancestral Villages, and Kinship Organization in Madagascar.* Seminar. London.

Bloch, M. 1989. *Ritual, History and Power.* Selected Papers in Anthropology, Athlone. London.

Bolaane, M. 2004. The Impact of Game Reserve Policy on the River BaSarwa/Bushmen of Botswana. *Social Policy and Administration* 38(4): 399–417.

Bollig, M. and Heinemann, H. 2002. Nomadic Savages, Ochre People and Heroic Herders: Visual Presentation of the Himba of Namibia´s Kaokoland. *Visual Anthropology* 15(3): 267–312.

Bond, P. 2004. *Talk Left, Walk Right: South Africa's Frustrated Global Reforms.* University of KwaZulu-Natal Press. Durban, Republic of South Africa.

Boniface, B.G. and Cooper, C. 1996. *The Geography of Travel and Tourism.* Second Edition. Butterworth-Heinemann. Oxford, UK.

Boonzaaier, C.C. 1990. *Die familie-, erf-, en opvolgingsreg van die Nkuna van Ritavi, met verwysing na ander aspekte van die privaatreg.* PhD Thesis, University of Pretoria. Pretoria, Republic of South Africa.

Boonzaaier, C.C. and Philip, L. 2007. Community-Based Tourism and Its Potential to Improve Living Conditions among the Hananwa of Blouberg (Limpopo Province), with Particular Reference to Catering Services during Winter. *Journal of Family Ecology and Consumer Sciences* 35 (1): 26–38.

Borch, O.J. 1992. Small Firms and the Governance of Inter-Organizational Exchange. *Scandinavian Journal of Management* 8(4): 321–334.

Borch, O.J. 1999. Business Strategy in Transitional Industries. Entrepreneurial Response to the Globalization of a Fragmented Industry. In Wright, R. (ed.), *International Entrepreneurship: Globalization of Emerging Businesses.* Research in Global Strategic Management, Vol. 7, 101–130. JAI. Stamford, Connecticut.

Borch, O.J. and Arthur, M.B. 1995. Strategic Networks among Small Firms: Implications for Strategy Research Methodology. *Journal of Management Studies* 32(4): 419–441.

Borch, O.J. and Brastad, B. 2003. Strategic Turnaround in a Fragmented Industry. *Journal of Small Business and Enterprise Development* 10(4): 393–407.

Bordo, S. 1997. *Twilight Zones: The Hidden Life of Cultural Images from Plato to O.J.* University of California Press. Berkeley, California.

Botha, C. 2005. People and the Environment in Colonial Namibia. *South African Historical Journal* 52(1): 170–190.

Boxall, P.C. and McFarlane, B.L. 1993. Human Dimension of Christmas Bird Counts: Implications for Nonconsumptive Wildlife Recreation Programs. *Wildlife Society Bulletin* 21(4): 390–396.

Brandon, K. 1998. Perils to Parks: The Social Context of Threats. In Redford, K., Brandon, K. and Sanderson, S. (eds), *Parks in Peril: People, Politics, and Protected Areas,* 415–439. Island Press. Washington, DC.

Bregin, E. and Kruiper, B. 2004. *Kalahari Rainsong.* University of KwaZulu-Natal Press. Durban, Republic of South Africa.

Breutz, P.L. 1953. *The Tribes of Marico District.* Department of Native Affairs Ethnological Publications No. 30. Government Printer. Pretoria, Republic of South Africa.

Briedenhann, J. 2007. The Role of the Public Sector in Rural Tourism: Respondents' Views. *Current Issues in Tourism* 10(6): 584–607.

Briedenhann, J. and Wickens, E. 2004a. Tourism Routes as a Tool for the Economic Development of Rural Areas – Vibrant Hope or Impossible Dream? *Tourism Management* 25(1): 71–79.

Briedenhann, J. and Wickens, E. 2004b. Rural Tourism – Meeting the Challenges of the New South Africa. *International Journal of Tourism Research* 6(3): 189–203.

Brown, B. and Butler, J.E. 1993. Networks and Entrepreneurial Development: The Shadow of Borders. *Entrepreneurship and Regional Development* 5(2): 101–116.

Brown, C. 2007. Interview of Chris Brown, Director of Namibia Nature Foundation (NNF), Windhoek, Namibia, February.

Bruner, E.M. 2002. The Representation of African Pastoralists: A Commentary. *Visual Anthropology* 15(3): 387–392.

Bruwer, J. 2003. South African Wine Routes: Some Perspectives on the Wine Tourism Industry's Structural Dimensions and Wine Tourism Product. *Tourism Management* 24(4): 423–435.

Buckingham, D. 2003. *Media Education: Literacy, Learning and Contemporary Culture.* Polity. Cambridge, UK.

Buhalis, D. 2000. Relationships in the Distribution Channel of Tourism: Conflicts between Hoteliers and Tour Operators in the Mediterranean Region. In Crotts, J.C., Buhalis, D. and March, R. (eds), *Global Alliances in Tourism and Hospitality Management,* 113–139. The Haworth Hospitality Press. London.

Burger, J. 1981. The Effect of Human Activity on Birds at a Coastal Bay. *Biological Conservation* 21(1): 231–241.

Burger, J. 1986. The Effect of Human Activity on Shorebirds in Two Coastal Bays in Northeastern United States. *Environmental Conservation* 13(2): 123–130.

Burns, P. 1999. Paradoxes in Planning: Tourism Elitism or Brutalism? *Annals of Tourism Research* 26(2): 329–348.

Business Report 2003. http://www.Busrep.Co.Za/Index.Php?Farticleid=260221, accessed 10 December 2006.

Butler, J.R., Hvenegaard, G.T. and Krystofiak, D.K. 1994. Economic Values of Birdwatching at Point Pelee National Park, Canada. In Munasinghe, M. and McNeely, J. (eds), *Protected Area Economics and Policy. Linking Conservation and Sustainable Development,* 253–262. International Union for Conservation of Nature (IUCN), World Bank. New York.

Butler, R.W. 1980. The Concept of a Tourist Area Cycle of Evolution: Implications for Management of Resources. *Canadian Geographer* 24(1): 5–12.

Butler, R.W. 1999. Sustainable Tourism: A State-of-the-Art Review. *Tourism Geographies* 1(1): 7–25.

Butler, R.W. and Fennel, D.A. 1994. The Effects of North Sea Oil Development on the Development of Tourism: The Case of the Shetland Isles. *Tourism Management* 15(5): 347–357.

Bywater, M. 1992. The European Tour Operator Industry. Special report, *The Economist* Intelligence Unit. London.

Bywater, M. 2001. Who Owns Whom in the Travel Distribution Industry? In Buhalis, D.L. and Laws, E. (eds), *Tourism Distribution Channels: Practices, Issues and Transformations,* 151–171. Continuum. London.

Cadotte, E.R. and Stern, L.W. 1979. A Process Model of Interorganizational Relations in Marketing Channels. In Sheth, J.N. (ed.), *Research in Marketing,* 127–158. JAI. Greenwich, Connecticut.

Campbell, C. 2003. *'Letting Them Die': Why HIV/AIDS Prevention Programmes Fail.* James Currey. Oxford, UK.

Campbell, L.M. 1999. Ecotourism in Rural Developing Communities. *Annals of Tourism Research* 26(3): 534–553.

Carmody, P. 2002. Between Globalisation and (Post)Apartheid: The Political Economy of Restructuring in South Africa. *Journal of Southern African Studies* 28(2): 255–275.

Carter, R. 2001. Interview, Northern Cape, Republic of South Africa, July.

Carter, S. 1998. Tourists' and Travellers' Social Construction of Africa and Asia as Risky Locations. *Tourism Management* 19(4): 349–358.

Casarin, F. 2001. Tourism Distribution Channels in Europe: A Comparative Study. In Buhalis, D. and Laws, E. (eds), *Tourism Distribution Channels: Practices, Issues and Transformations*, 137–150. Continuum. London.

Castel-Branco, C.N. 2002. Economic Linkages between South Africa and Mozambique. Report, Southern Africa Office of the UK Department for International Development (DFID). Pretoria, Republic of South Africa.

Castells, M. 1999. Information Technology, Globalisation and Social Development. United Nations Research Institute for Social Development (UNRISD) Discussion Paper No. 114. Geneva.

Cater, E. and Lowman, G. (eds) 1994. *Ecotourism: A Sustainable Option?* John Wiley and Sons. Chichester, UK.

CETN 2007. Coastal Bird Count September 2007 – Bird Island to Dolphin Park. Survey report, Coastal Environmental Trust of Namibia (CETN). Walvis Bay, Namibia.

Chafy, R. 1997. Confronting the Culture of Progress in the 21st Century. *Futures* 29(7): 633–648.

Chapin, M. 2004. A Challenge to Conservationists. *World Watch Magazine* (November/December): 17–31.

Chennells, R. 2005. The Role and Efficacy of Contracts in the Promotion of Access and Benefit Sharing. Paper presented at the *Third Round on ABS Governance under CBD*, Paris, France (http://www.wimsanet.org/inpub_library.asp, accessed 7 March 2008).

Cheong, S.-M. and Miller, M.L. 2000. Power and Tourism: A Foucaultian Observation. *Annals of Tourism Research* 27(2): 371–390.

Chien, S.-S. 2007. Institutional Innovations, Asymmetric Decentralization, and Local Economic Development: A Case Study of Kunshan in Post-Mao China. *Environment and Planning C: Government and Policy* 25(2): 269–290.

Christie, M. and Mason, P. 2003. Tour Guides as Critically Reflective Practitioners: A Proposed Training Model. *Tourism Recreation Research* 28(1): 23–33.

Clarke, J. 2005. Effective Marketing for Rural Tourism. In Hall, D., Kirkpatrick, I. and Mitchell, M. (eds), *Rural Tourism and Sustainable Business*, 87–102. Channel View. Clevedon, UK.

Clarke, S. and Gaile, G. 1998. *The Work of Cities*. University of Minnesota Press. Minneapolis, Minnesota.

Coetzee J.K., Graaff, J., Hendricks, F. and Wood, G. 2001. *Development Theory, Policy, and Practice*. Oxford University Press. Oxford, UK.

Coetzee, R. 1982. *Funa Food from Africa: Roots of Traditional African Food Culture*. Butterworths. Durban, Republic of South Africa.

Cohen, E. 1985. The Tourist Guide. The Origins, Structure and Dynamics of a Role. *Annals of Tourism Research* 12(1): 5–29.

Collins, K. 1999. *Participatory Research. A Primer*. Prentice Hall. Johannesburg, Republic of South Africa.

Connelly, G. 2007. Testing Governance – A Research Agenda for Exploring Urban Tourism Competitiveness Policy: The Case of Liverpool 1980–2000. *Tourism Geographies* 9(1): 84–114.

Connelly, P. and Rosen, S. 2005. Will Small and Medium Enterprises Provide HIV/AIDS Services to Employees? An Analysis of Market Demand. *South African Journal of Economics* 73(1): 613–626.

Cornelissen, S. 2005. *The Global Tourism System. Governance, Development and Lessons from South Africa*. Ashgate. Aldershot, UK.

Cornelius, C., Navarrette, S.A. and Marquet, P.A. 2001. Effects of Human Activity on the Structure of Coastal Marine Bird Assemblages in Central Chile. *Conservation Biology* 15(5): 1396–1404.

Correia, L., Passos Ascencao, M.J. and Charters, S. 2004. Wine Routes in Portugal: A Case Study of the Bairrada Wine Route. *Journal of Wine Research* 15(1): 15–25.

Crandall, D.P. 2000. *The Place of Stunted Ironwood Trees: A Year in the Lives of the Cattle-Herding Himba of Namibia*. Continuum. London.

Crang, M. 1997. Picturing Practice: Research Through the Tourist Gaze. *Progress in Human Geography* 21(3): 359–373.

Crawhall, N. 2001. Written in the Sand: Auditing and Managing Cultural Resources with Displaced Indigenous Peoples – A South African Case Study. Unpublished report, South African San Institute (SASI) & United Nations Educational, Scientific and Cultural Organization (UNESCO). Cape Town, Republic of South Africa.

CSO 2005. *Wildlife Statistics 2004*. Ministry of Finance and Development Planning, Central Statistic Office (CSO). Gaborone, Botswana.

Cuban, L. and Kirkpatrick, H. 1998. Computers Make Kids Smarter—Right? *Technos* 7(2): 26–31.

Curtin, S. and Wilkes, K. 2005. British Wildlife Tourism Operators: Current Issues and Typologies. *Current Issues in Tourism* 8(6): 455–478.

Dahles, H. 1997. *Tourism, Small Entrepreneurs, and Sustainable Development*. Association for Tourism and Leisure Education (ATLAS), Tilburg University. Tilburg, The Netherlands.

Dann, G. 1996. The People of Tourist Brochures. In Selwyn, T. (ed.), *The Tourist Image. Myths and Myth Making in Tourism*, 61–82. John Wiley and Sons. Chichester, UK.

Darkoh, M.B.K. and Mbaiwa, J.E. 2005. *Natural Resource Utilization and Land Use Conflicts in the Okavango Delta, Botswana*. Department of Environmental Science and Harry Oppenheimer Okavango Research Centre, University of Botswana. Gaborone, Botswana.

Davis, K. 1997. Embody-ing Theory: Beyond Modernist and Postmodernist Readings of the Body. In Davis, K. (ed.), *Embodied Practices*, 1–26. Sage. Thousand Oaks, California.

DEAT 1996. *People – Planet – Prosperity: A Strategic Framework for Sustainable Tourism Development in South Africa*. Draft September 1996. Department of Environmental Affairs and Tourism (DEAT). Pretoria, Republic of South Africa.

DEAT 2005. *Tourism 10 Year Review*. Department of Environmental Affairs and Tourism (DEAT). Pretoria, Republic of South Africa.

de Villiers, B. 2008. *People and Parks: Sharing the Benefits*. Konrad-Adenauer-Stiftung. Wesseling, Germany.

Diamond, J. 2003. *Collapse: How Societies Choose to Succeed or Fail*. Viking. New York.

Diener, I. 2001. Ethnicity and Nation-building: Towards Unity Respectful of Heterogeneity? In Diener, I. and Graefe, O. (eds), *Contemporary Namibia – The First Landmarks of a Post-Apartheid Society*, 231–257. Gamsberg Macmillan. Windhoek, Namibia.

Directorate Tourism 2002. *African Ivory Route Ecotourism Operational Project*. Directorate Tourism, Department of Finance, Economic Affairs and Tourism and the SMME. Polokwane, Limpopo Province, Republic of South Africa.

Donaldson, R. 2007. Tourism in Small Town South Africa. In Rogerson, C.M. and Visser, G. (eds), *Urban Tourism in the Developing World: The South African Experience*, 307–325. Transaction. New Brunswick, Canada.

DoT 2000. *Botswana's Tourism Master Plan*. Government of Botswana, Department of Tourism (DoT). Gaborone, Botswana.

Dredge, D. and Jenkins, J. 2008. *Tourism Planning and Policy*. John Wiley and Sons. Milton, Queensland, Australia.

Drumm, A. 1998. New Approaches to Community-Based Ecotourism Management: Learning from Ecuador. In Lindberg, K., Wood, M. and Engeldrum, D. (eds), *Ecotourism, A Guide for Planners and Managers*, Vol. 2, 197–213. International Ecotourism Society (TIES). North Bennington, Vermont.

Dubresson, A. and Graefe, O. 2001. The State, Accumulation and Regulation: For a Political Economy of Namibia. In Diener, I. and Graefe, O. (eds), *Contemporary Namibia – The First Landmarks of a Post-Apartheid Society*, 53–74. Gamsberg Macmillan. Windhoek, Namibia.

Duffy, R. 2000. Shadow Players: Ecotourism Development, Corruption and State Politics in Belize. *Third World Quarterly* 21(3): 549–565.

Duffy, R. 2006. Global Environmental Governance and the Politics of Ecotourism in Madagascar. *Journal of Ecotourism* 5(1/2): 128–144.

Duncan, J. 1993. Sites of Representation: Place, Time and the Discourse of the Other. In Duncan, J. and Ley, D. (eds), *Place/Culture/Representation*, 39–47. Routledge. London.

du Pisani, A. 2000. State and Society under South African Rule. In Keulder, C. (ed.), *State, Society and Democracy. A Reader in Namibian Politics*, 49–76. Namibia Institute for Democracy. Windhoek, Namibia.

DWNP 1995–2007. *Visitor Statistics – Revenue by Type of Fee*, January–December. Department of Wildlife and National Parks (DWNP). Gaborone, Botswana.

DWNP 2006. *Annual Reports 1998–2006*. Department of Wildlife and National Parks (DWNP). Gaborone, Botswana.

Dyll, L. 2004. Close Encounters with the First Kind: What Does Development Mean in the Context of Two Bushmen Communities in Ngwatle and the Northern Cape? MA Dissertation, Culture, Communication and Media Studies, University of KwaZulu-Natal. Durban, Republic of South Africa.

Dyll, L. 2007. In the Sun with Silikat. In Tomaselli, K.G. (ed.), *Writing in the San/d: Autoethnography among Indigenous Southern Africans*, 117–130. Altamira Press. Walnut Creek, California.

Dzingirai, V. 2003. The New Scramble for the African Countryside. *Development and Change* 34(2): 243–264.

Echtner, C.M. and Prasad, P. 2003. The Context of Third World Tourism Marketing. *Annals of Tourism Research* 30(3): 660–682.

ECIAfrica 2006a. Community/routes Tourism Sector Study: Growth Strategy. Unpublished report, Fund for Research into Industrial Development Growth and Equity (FRIDGE) Trade and Industry Chamber. ECIAfrica Consulting (ECI). Johannesburg, Republic of South Africa.

ECIAfrica 2006b. Community/routes Tourism Sector Study: Task 2 – Desk Review. Unpublished report, Fund for Research into Industrial Development Growth and Equity (FRIDGE) Trade and Industry Chamber ECIAfrica Consulting (ECI). Johannesburg, Republic of South Africa.

ECIAfrica 2006c. Community/routes Tourism Sector Study: Executive Summary. Unpublished report, Fund for Research into Industrial Development Growth and Equity (FRIDGE) Trade and Industry Chamber. ECIAfrica Consulting. Johannesburg, Republic of South Africa.

Edensor, T. 1998. *Tourists at the Taj: Performance and Meaning at a Symbolic Site*. Routledge. London.

Edwards, E. 1996. Postcards: Greetings from Another World. In Selwyn, T. (ed.), *The Tourist Image. Myths and Myth Making in Tourism*, 197–222. John Wiley and Sons. Chichester, UK.

Edwards, V.M. 2004. The Commons in an Age of Global Transition: Challenges, Risks and Opportunities. Paper presented at the *10th Biennial Meeting of the IASCP*, Oaxaca, Mexico.

Egziabher, T.G. and Helmsing, A.H.J. (eds) 2005. *Local Economic Development in Africa: Enterprises, Communities and Local Development*. Shaker. Maastricht, The Netherlands.

Ellis, C. and Bochner, A.P. 2000. Autoethnography, Personal Narrative, Reflexivity: Researcher as Subject. In. Denzin, N.K. and Lincoln, Y.S. (eds), *The Handbook of Qualitative Research*, 733–762. Sage. London.

Ellis, L. and Terwin, J. 2004. *The Impact of HIV/AIDS on Selected Business Sectors in South Africa, 2004*. Bureau for Economic Research (BER). Stellenbosch, Republic of South Africa.

Ellis, W. 2001. *Domains of Trust in the Southern Kalahari: Production of Knowledge, Authenticity and Community Heterogeneity. Programme for Land and Agrarian Studies.* School of Government, University of Western Cape. Bellville, Republic of South Africa.

Evans, R. 2001. *The Human Side of School Change: Reform, Resistance, and the Real-life Problems of Innovation.* Jossey-Bass. San Francisco, California.

Fabricius, C. 2004. The Fundamentals of Community-Based Natural Resource Management. In Fabricius, C., Koch, E., Turner, S. and Magome, H. (eds), *Rights, Resources and Rural Development. Community-Based Natural Resource Management in Southern Africa*, 3–43. Earthscan. London.

Faikir, S. 2001. CPPPs, a Way Forward in CBNRM. IUCN Policy Think Tank No. 5. International Union for Conservation of Nature (IUCN). Gland, Switzerland.

Faikir, S. 2004. Globalisation and its Influence on Poverty and Environment. IUCN Policy Think Tank No. 17. International Union for Conservation of Nature (IUCN). Gland, Switzerland.

Favero, P. 2007. 'What a Wonderful World!' *Tourist Studies* 7(1): 51–81.

Featherstone, M. 1995. *Undoing Culture: Globalization, Postmodernism and Identity.* Sage. London.

Ferreira, S. 2007. Role of Tourism and Place Identity in the Development of Small Towns in the Western Cape, South Africa. *Urban Forum* 18(3): 191–209.

Ferreira, S. and Visser, G. 2007. Creating an African Riviera: Revisiting the Impact of the Victoria and Alfred Waterfront. *Urban Forum* 18(3): 227–246.

Fidzani, B., Mlenga, W.S., Atlhopheng, M. and Shatera, M.M. 1999. *Socio-economic Effects of CBPP in Ngamiland.* Division of Agricultural Planning and Statistics, Ministry of Agriculture. Gaborone, Botswana.

Finch, B. 2007. Interview of Brian Finch, bird guide and tour operator, Antananarivo, Madagascar, January.

Finlay, K. In press. The Un/changing Face of the ≠Khomani: Representation through Promotional Media. *Visual Anthropology* in press.

Finney, S.K., Pearce-Higgins, J.W. and Yalden, D.W. 2005. The Effect of Recreational Disturbance on an Upland Breeding Bird, the Golden Plover *Pluvialis apricaria. Biological Conservation* 121(1): 53–63.

Fletcher, J. and Cooper, C. 1996. Tourism Strategy Planning – Szolnok County, Hungary. *Annals of Tourism Research* 23(1): 181–200.

Flyman, M. 2000. Community Mobilisation: Living for Tomorrow in the Southern Kalahari (http://www.cbnrm.bw/pagessubdir/CommunityMobilisation.htm, accessed 8 June 2002).

Fourie, M. 2006. *Ethnotourism at Blouberg in the Limpopo Province, South Africa: A Quest for Sustainability.* MPhil Thesis, University of Johannesburg. Johannesburg, Republic of South Africa.

Gadi 2003. Interview, Ngwatle, Botswana, July.

Ganesan, S. 1994. Determinants of Long-Term Orientation in Buyer–Seller Relationships. *Journal of Marketing* 58(April): 1–19.

Gaomab, M. 2005. Black Economic Empowerment in Namibia and Its Relation to the National Economy. Speech presented at the *SME BBEE Launch of Publication* organized by the Joint Consultative Group of Namibia, Windhoek, Namibia, 15 September.

Garrod, B. and Wilson, J.C. 2004. Nature on the Edge? Marine Ecotourism in Peripheral Coastal Areas. *Journal of Sustainable Tourism* 12(2): 95–120.

Geigant, F. 1962. Die Standorte des Fremdenverkehrs. Eine Sozialökonomische Studie über die Bedingungen und Formen der Räumlichen Entfaltung des Fremdenverkehrs. Volkswirtschaftliche Abteilung, Deutches Wirtschaftswissenschaftliches Institut für Fremdenverkehr (DWIF), University of Munich. Munich, Germany.

Gelman, N.B., Oglethorpe, J. and Mauambeta, D. 2005. The Impact of HIV/AIDS: How Can It Be Anticipated and Managed? *Parks* 15(1): 13–24.

Giampiccoli, A. 2006. Hegemony, Globalisation and Tourism Policies in Developing Countries. In Burns, P. and Novelli, M. (eds), *Tourism and Politics: Global Frameworks and Local Realities,* 175–191. Elsevier. Amsterdam.

Glasmeier, A.K. 2000. Economic Geography in Practice: Local Economic Development Policy. In Clark, G.L., Feldman, M.P. and Gertler, M.S. (eds), *The Oxford Handbook of Economic Geography,* 559–579. Oxford University Press. Oxford, UK.

Glasson, J., Godfrey, K. and Goodey, B. 1995. *Towards Visitor Impact Management: Visitor Impacts, Carrying Capacity and Management Responses in Europe's Historic Towns and Cities.* Avebury. Aldershot, UK.

Gonzalez, L.R.C. and Medina, J.S. 2003. Cultural Tourism and Urban Management in Northwestern Spain: The Pilgrimage to Santiago de Compostela. *Tourism Geographies* 5(4): 446–460.

Good, K. 2003. *Bushmen and Diamonds (Un)Civil Society in Botswana.* Nordic Africa Institute. Uppsala, Sweden.

Goodey, B. 1997. *Heritage Trails: Rural Regeneration through Tourism.* University of Gloucestershire. Gloucester, UK.

Goodwin, H. 1998. Sustainable Tourism and Poverty Alleviation. Paper presented at the *DFID/DETR Workshop on Sustainable Tourism and Poverty,* London.

Goodwin, H. 2006. The Poverty Angle of Sun, Sea and Sand – Maximising Tourism's Contribution. Unpublished paper, Leeds Metropolitan University. Leeds, UK.

Goodwin, H. 2007. Measuring and Reporting the Impact of Tourism on Poverty. In Tribe, J. and Airey, D. (eds), *Developments in Tourism Research,* 63–75. Elsevier. Oxford, UK.

Goodwin, H., Spenceley, A. and Maynard, B. 2002. Development of Responsible Tourism Guidelines for South Africa (http://www.nri.org/NRET/nret.htm, accessed 23 August 2008).

Government of Botswana 1990. The Tourism Policy. Government Paper No. 2 of 1990. Government Printer. Gaborone, Botswana.

Government of Namibia 1994. White Paper on Tourism. Approved by the Cabinet 29 March. Government of Namibia. Windhoek, Namibia.

Government of Namibia 2006. Namibia Household and Income Expenditure Survey 2003/04. Preliminary Report. Central Bureau of Statistics and National Planning Commission. Windhoek, Namibia.

Government of Namibia 2007. First Draft of the Third National Development Plan (NDP3): 2007/08–2011/12. Office of the President and National Planning Commission. Windhoek, Namibia.

Government of Namibia 2008. Third National Development Plan (NDP III) 2007/2008–2011/12, Volume 1. National Planning Commission. Windhoek, Namibia (http://www.npc.gov.na/docs/NDP3_Vol.1_Revised_Draft_05.06.2008.pdf, accessed 26 August 2008).

Greeff, M. 2005. Participatory Action Research. In de Vos, A.S., Strydom, H., Fouche, C.B. and Delport, C.S.L. (eds), *Research at Grass Roots,* 286–313. Van Schaik. Pretoria, Republic of South Africa.

Greffe, X. 1994. Is Rural Tourism a Lever for Economic and Social Development? *Journal of Sustainable Tourism* 2(1): 23–40.

Grémillet, D., Tuschky, I. and Kierspel, M. 1998. Body Temperature and Insulation in Diving Great Cormorants and European Shags. *Functional Ecology* 12(3): 386–394.

Grobler, J.H.F. 2005. Community Perceptions of Tourism in the Tshivhase Area, Limpopo Province. MHCS Mini-Dissertation, University of Pretoria. Pretoria, Republic of South Africa.

Grossman, D. 2007. Interview, Molopo Lodge, Northern Cape, Republic of South Africa, 24 January.

Grossman, D. and Holden, P. 2002. Kalahari Land Claims: Towards Settlement. Unpublished report, ≠Khomani San Project. Kgalagadi, Botswana.

Gunder Frank, A. (1967). *Capitalism and Underdevelopment in Latin America*. Monthly Press. New York.

Gunn, C. 1994. *Tourism Planning*. Third Edition. Taylor and Francis. New York.

Hall, C.M. 1995. *Introduction to Tourism in Australia: Impacts, Planning and Development*. Longman. London.

Hall, C.M. 2000. *Tourism Planning. Policies, Planning and Relationships*. Prentice Hall. London.

Hall, C.M. 2005. *Tourism. Rethinking the Social Science Mobility*. Pearson. Harlow, UK.

Hall, C.M. (ed.) 2007. *Pro-poor Tourism: Who Benefits? Perspectives on Tourism and Poverty Reduction*. Channel View. Clevedon, UK.

Hall, C.M. 2008. *Tourism Planning. Policies, Processes and Relationships*. Second Edition. Pearson Prentice Hall. Harlow, UK.

Hall, C.M. and Page, S.J. 1999. *The Geography of Tourism: Environment, Place and Space*. Routledge. London.

Hall, C.M., Mitchell, R. and Sharples, L. 2003. Consuming Places: The Role of Food, Wine and Tourism in Regional Development. In Hall, C.M., Sharples, L., Mitchell, R., Macionis, N. and Camborne, B. (eds), *Food Tourism around the World: Development, Management, and Markets*, 25–59. Butterworth-Heinemann. London.

Hall, S. 1992. The West and the Rest. In Hall, S. and Gieber, B. (eds), *Formations of Modernity*, 275–332. Polity. London.

Hall, S. 1997. The Work of Representation. In Hall, S. (ed.), *Representation: Cultural Representations and Signifying Practices*, 13–64. Sage. London.

Halstead, L. 2003. Making Community-based Tourism Work: An Assessment of Factors Contributing to Successful Community-owned Tourism Development in Caprivi, Namibia. DEA Research Discussion Papers, No. 60. Directorate of Environmental Affairs. Ministry of Environment and Tourism (MET). Windhoek, Namibia.

Hansohm, D. 2000. Macro-economic Framework. In Melber, H. (ed.), *Namibia – a Decade of Independence 1990–2000*, 19–27. Namibian Economic Policy Research Unit (NEPRU). Windhoek, Namibia.

Haralambos, M. and Holborn, M. 1995. *Sociology: Themes and Perspectives*. Fourth Edition. Collins. London.

Harries, P. 1987. A Forgotten Corner of the Transvaal: Reconstructing the History of a Re-located Community through Oral Testimony and Song. In Bozzoli, B. (ed.), *Class, Community and Conflict*, 93–134. Ravan. Johannesburg, Republic of South Africa.

Harrison, D. 2008. Pro-poor Tourism: a Critique. *Third World Quarterly* 29(5): 851–868.

Harvey, D. 1989. From Managerialism to Entrepreneurialism: the Transformation in Urban Governance in Late Capitalism. *Geografiska Annaler* 71B(1): 3–17.

Heald, S. 2004. An Absence of Anthropology: Critical Reflections on Anthropology and AIDS Policy and Practice in Africa. In Ellison, G., Parker, M. and Campbell, C. (eds), *Learning from HIV and AIDS*, 210–237. Cambridge University Press. Cambridge, UK.

Heide, J.B. 1994. Interorganizational Governance in Marketing Channels. *Journal of Marketing* 58(January): 71–85.

Heide, J.B. and John, G. 1992. Do Norms Matter in Marketing Relationships? *Journal of Marketing* 56(April): 32–44.

Helmsing, A.H.J. 2001a. Partnerships, Meso-institutions, and Learning: New Local and Regional Economic Development Initiatives in Latin America. Unpublished paper, Institute of Social Studies. The Hague.

Helmsing, A.H.J. 2001b. Local Economic Development in Africa: New Generations of Actors, Policies and Instruments. Working Paper No. 12, Regional and Local Development Studies, Addis Ababa University. Addis Ababa, Ethiopia.

Helmsing, A.H.J. 2001c. Externalities, Learning and Governance: New Perspectives on Local Economic Development. *Development and Change* 32(2): 277–308.

Helmsing, A.H.J. and Egziabher, T.G. 2005. Local Economic Development in Africa: Introducing the Issues. In Egziabher, T.G. and Helmsing, A.H.J. (eds), *Local Economic Development in Africa: Enterprises, Communities and Local Development*, 1–17. Shaker. Maastricht, The Netherlands.

Henrichsen, D. 2000. Pilgrimages into Kaoko. Herrensafaris, 4x4s and Settler Illusion. In Miescher, G. and Henrichsen, D. (eds), *New Notes on Kaoko*, 159–185. Basler. Basel, Switzerland.

Herholdt-Smith, J. 2003. A Research Study on the Impact of HIV/AIDS in the Hospitality Industry in Africa (http://www.africacncl.org/HIV_AIDS/about_aai/sectors/hospitality.asp, accessed 8 June 2008).

Herholdt-Smith, J. 2004. HIV: The Culture of Silence Must be Overcome (http://www.hotelandrestaurant.co.za/news/2004/07/hiv.asp, accessed 8 June 2008).

Hill, T.R., Nel, E.L. and Illgner, P. 2007. Partnership for Success – Community-Based Economic Development: A Case Study of Ngolowindo Co-operative, Malawi. *Environment and Planning C: Government and Policy* 25(4): 573–590.

Hintch, T. and Butler, R. 1996. Indigenous Tourism: a Common Ground for Discussion. In Butler, R. and Hintch, T. (eds), *Tourism and Indigenous People*, 3–21. Thomson. London.

Hirsch, A. 2005. *Season of Hope: Economic Reform under Mandela and Mbeki*. University of KwaZulu-Natal Press. Durban, Republic of South Africa.

Hitchcock, R.K. 1998. The Politics and Economics of Bureaucratic and Ethnic Identity among Remote Area Populations in Botswana. In Bank, A. (ed.), *The Khoisan Identities and Cultural Heritage Conference*, 303–313. University of the Western Cape, Institute for Historical Research. Bellville, Republic of South Africa.

Hitchcock, R.K. 2002. We are the First People: Land, Natural Resources and Identity in the Central Kalahari, Botswana. *Journal of South African Studies* 29(4): 797–824.

Hitt, M.A., Dacin M.T., Levitas, E., Arregle, J.L. and Borza, A. 2000. Partner Selection in Emerging and Developed Market Contexts: Resource-based and Organizational Learning Perspectives. *Academy of Management Journal*, 43(4): 449–467.

Holden, A. 1996. A Profile of UK Outbound 'Environmentally Friendly' Tour Operators. *Tourism Management* 17(1): 60–64.

Holloway, J.C. 1989. *The Business of Tourism*. Pitman. London.

Holman Jones, S. 2005. Autoethnography: Making the Personal Political. In Denzin, N.K. and Lincoln, Y.S. (eds), *Handbook of Qualitative Research*, Third Edition, 763–791. Sage. London.

Hottola, P. 1999. *The Intercultural Body – Western Woman, Culture Confusion and Control of Space in the South Asian Travel Scene*. Publications of the Department of Geography No. 7, University of Joensuu. Joensuu, Finland.

Hottola, P. 2005. The Metaspatialities of Control Management in Tourism: Backpacking in India. *Tourism Geographies* 7(1): 1–22.

Hottola, P. 2006a. Paradise Confused? – Marketing South Africa and KwaZulu-Natal for Tourism in 1985 and 2002. *Aurora* 0(1): 93–111.

Hottola, P. 2006b. *The Social Psychological Interface of Tourism and Independent Travel*. In Hannam, K., Jarvis, J. and Ateljevic, I. (eds), *Global Nomad II – Backpacker Travel in Theory and Practice*, 26–37. Channel View. Clevedon, UK.

Hottola, P. 2008. *Coastal Bird Tourism in Namibia – An Evaluation Report with Suggestions for Action*. Finnish University Network for Tourism Studies (FUNTS), Centre for Tourism Studies, University of Joensuu. Savonlinna, Finland.

Howlett, M. and Ramesh, M. 1995. *Studying Public Policy: Policy Cycles and Policy Subsystems*. Oxford University Press. Toronto, Canada.

Hoyt, E. 2000. *Whale Watching 2000: Worldwide Tourism Numbers, Expenditures and Expanding Socioeconomic Benefits*. Whale and Dolphin Conservation Society. Bath, UK.

HSRC 2006. Success and Challenges in Pro-poor Tourism. Unpublished report, Human Sciences Research Council (HSRC). Pretoria, Republic of South Africa.

Hughes, D.M. 2001. Rezoned for Business: How Eco-Tourism Unlocked Black Farmland in Eastern Zimbabwe. *Journal of Agrarian Change* 1(4): 575–599.

Hutton, J., Adams. W.M. and Murombedzi, J. 2005. Back to the Barriers? Changing Narratives in Biodiversity Conservation. *Forum for Development Studies* 10(2): 341–370.

Hvenegaard, G.T. 1994. Ecotourism: a Status Report and Conceptual Framework. The *Journal of Tourism Studies* 5(2): 24–35.

IH&RA and UNAIDS 1999. *The Challenge of HIV/AIDS in the Workplace: a Guide for the Hospitality Industry.* International Hotel and Restaurant Association (IH&RA) and United Nations Joint Programme on HIV/AIDS (UNAIDS). Geneva.

ILO 2001. *An ILO Code of Practice on HIV/AIDS and the World of Work.* International Labour Organization (ILO). Geneva.

Impacto 2005. Possible Voluntary Resettlement of Communities Living along the Shingwedzi River: Preliminary Identification of Areas with Potential for Resettlement. Interim Report for Limpopo National Park, Impacto Consulting. Maputo, Mozambique.

Institute for Public Policy Research 2007. 2 BBEE or Not 2 BBEE? An Eclectic Review of Namibia's Black Economic Empowerment Landscape. Institute for Public Policy Research (IPPR) Research Report No. 10. Windhoek, Namibia.

International Tourism Partnership 2004. *Tourism and Local Economic Development: How Can Businesses in Travel and Tourism Increase the Contribution of the Industry to Local Economic Development and Pro-Poor Growth.* International Tourism Partnership. London.

Jänis, J. 2008. *Current Challenges in Promoting Tourism through Development in Namibia. Experiences of Private and Community-Based Tourism Enterprises and Practical Recommendations.* Finnish University Network for Tourism Studies (FUNTS), Centre for Tourism Studies, University of Joensuu. Savonlinna, Finland.

Jansen, D.J. Undated. What is a Joint Venture? Guidelines for District Councils with Appropriate Authority. WWF Project No. 3749, Project Paper No. 16. World Wildlife Fund (WWF). Gland, Switzerland.

Jauch, H. (ed.) 2001. *Playing for Globalisation Game: The Implications of Economic Liberalisation for Namibia.* Labour Resource and Research Institute (LaRRI). Windhoek, Namibia.

Jauch, H. 2007a. A Labour Perspective on Black Economic Empowerment. In 2 BEE or Not 2 BEE? An Eclectic Review of Namibia's Black Economic Empowerment Landscape, 9–10. Institute for Public Policy Research (IPPR) Report No. 10. Windhoek, Namibia.

Jauch, H. 2007b. *Hotel Workers in Africa.* Labour Resource and Research Institute (LaRRI). Windhoek, Namibia.

Jenkins, C.L. 2000. The Development of Tourism in Namibia. In Dieke, P.U.C. (ed.) *The Political Economy of Tourism Development in Africa,* 113–128. Cognizant. New York.

Jenkins, O.H. 2003. Photography and Travel Brochures: The Circle of Representations. *Tourism Geographies* 5(3): 305–328.

Jensen, Ø. 1993. The Relationships between Local Suppliers and Tour Operators with Regard to the Development of Inclusive Tour Products for the International Tourist Markets. Paper presented at the *FIBE Conference,* Norges Handelshøyskole, Bergen, Norway.

Jensen, Ø. 1996. Competence Development by Small Firms in a Vertically Constrained Industry Structure. In Sanchez, R., Heene, A. and Thomas, H. (eds), *Dynamics of Competence-Based Competition: Theory and Practice in the New Strategic Management,* 165–181. Elsevier. Oxford, UK.

Jensen, Ø. 2000. Critical Factors by the Choice of Cooperative Partners: A Study of Norwegian Tourist Firms and European Tour Operators. Paper presented at the *10th Conference on Nordic Interorganisational Research,* Norwegian University of Science and Technology, Trondheim, Norway.

Jensen, Ø. 2001. Service Quality and the Distribution Chain of Inclusive Tours. In Laws, E. and Buhalis, D. (eds), *Tourism Distribution Channels: Practices, Issues and Transformations*, 119–134. Continuum. London.

Jensen, Ø. 2002. Criteria in the Selection of Exchange Partners – Significance of a Dynamic Relational Perspective. Paper presented at the *Inaugural Conference of the IMP Group in Asia*, Perth, Australia.

Jensen, Ø. 2004. Sustainable Tourism Planning in Destinations and the Role of Social and Institutional Trust Relationships. Paper presented at the *13th Nordic Symposium in Tourism and Hospitality Research*, Aalborg, Denmark.

Jensen, Ø. and Borch, O.J. 1999. Effective Governance within Inter-Firm Relationships – The Role of Individual Social Norms. Paper presented at *the 1999 Strategic Management Society International Conference*, Berlin, Germany.

Jianyang, L. 2006. Getting Serious about Birding in China. *Birding* 38(2): 54–59.

Johannisson, B. 1990. Economies of Overview – Guiding the External Growth of Small Firms. *International Small Business Journal* 9(1): 32–44.

Jones, B.T.B. and Murphree, M.W. 2004. Community-Based Natural Resource Management as a Conservation Mechanism: Lessons and Directions. In Child, B. (ed.), *Parks in Transition*, 63–103. Earthscan. London.

Jones, C. and Munday, M. 2001. Tourism and Local Economic Development: Three Case Studies. Paper presented at the *European Regional Science Association 41st Annual Meeting*, Zagreb, Croatia.

Jones, K.R. and Wills, J. 2005. *The Invention of the Park. From the Garden of Eden to Disney's Magic Kingdom.* Polity. Cambridge, UK.

Jon Jon 2002. Interview, Ngwatle, Botswana, July.

Joubert, A. and van Schalkwyk, J.A. 1999. War and Remembrance: the Power of Oral Poetry and the Politics of Hananwa Identity. *Journal of Southern African Studies* 25(1): 27–45.

Jussila, H. 1987. Spatial Diffusion of Modernisation: a Study of Farm Mechanisation in Finland at Regional and Local Levels. PhD Thesis, Department of Geography, University of Oulu. Oulu, Finland.

Kähkönen, E. and Sutinen, E. (eds) 2003. *Proceedings of the First International Conference on Educational Technology in Cultural Context.* Proceedings Series No. 3, Virtual University of Eastern Finland. Joensuu, Finland.

Kale, P., Singh, H. and Perlmutter, H. 2000. Learning and Protection of Proprietary Assets in Strategic Alliances: Building Relational Capital. *Strategic Management Journal* 21(3): 217–237.

Kanguma, B. 2000. Constructing Himba: the Tourist Gaze. In Miescher, G. and Henrichsen, D. (eds), *New Notes on Kaoko*, 129–132. Basler. Basel, Switzerland.

Karamata, C. and Gwari, C. 2007. Economic Empowerment in the Tourism Sector: Showing Signs of Being Broad Based. *In 2 BEE or Not 2 BEE? An Eclectic Review of Namibia's Black Economic Empowerment Landscape*, 45–62. Institute for Public Policy Research (IPPR) Report No. 10. Windhoek, Namibia.

Kariel, H.G. 1989. Socio-cultural Impacts of Tourism in the Austrian Alps. *Mountain Research and Development* 9(1): 59–70.

Karski, A. 1990. Urban Tourism – A Key to Urban Regeneration. *The Planner* 76(13): 15–17.

Katjiuongua, O. 2008. Personal communication with Olga Katjiuongua, Executive Director of Namibia Community-Based Tourism Assistance Trust (NACOBTA), Windhoek, Namibia, 25 July.

Katz, E. and Lazarsfeld, P.F. 1955. *Personal Influence: the Part Played by People in the Flow of Mass Communication.* Free Press. Glencoe, Illinois.

Katz, J.E., Rice, R.E. and Aspden, P. 2001. The Interest 1995–2000: Access, Civic Involvement, and Social Interaction. *American Behavioral Scientist* 45(3): 405–419.

Kazenambo, K. 2003. Sustainable Community Development and Local Community Participation: the Case of the Ovahimba Community in Northwest Namibia. In Miettinen, S. (ed.), *Helsinki-Opuwo-Helsinki: Encounters with Crafts, Tourists and Women in the Local Communities of Namibia*, 33–55. Like. Helsinki.

Keim, K.S., Swanson, M.A., Cann, S.E. and Salinas, A. 1999. Focus Group Methodology: Adapting the Process for Low-income Adults and Children of Hispanic and Caucasian Ethnicity. *Family and Consumer Sciences Research Journal* 27(4): 451–465.

Kelly, K. and van der Riet, M. 2001. Participatory Research in Community Settings: Process, Methods and Challenges. In Seedat, M., Duncan, N. and Lazarus, S. (eds), *Community Psychology: Theory, Method and Practice. South African and Other Perspectives*, 159–187. Oxford University Press. Cape Town, Republic of South Africa.

Kerr, W. 2003. *Tourism Public Policy and the Strategic Management of Failure*. Pergamon. Oxford, UK.

Kgathi, D.L., Bendson, H., Blaikie, P., Mbaiwa, J.E., Ngwenya, B.N. and Wilk, J. 2004. *Rural Livelihoods, Indigenous Knowledge Systems, and Political Economy of Access to Natural Resources in the Okavango Delta, Botswana.* Harry Oppenheimer Okavango Research Centre, University of Botswana. Maun, Botswana.

Kiambo, W. 2005. The Emerging Role of Tourism in Mozambique's Post-war Reconstruction. *Africa Insight* 35(4): 142–148.

Kirstges, T. 2003. Basic Questions of 'Sustainable Tourism': Does Ecological and Socially Acceptable Tourism Have a Chance? In Lück, M. and Kirstges, T. (eds), *Global Ecotourism Policies and Case Studies. Perspectives and Constraints*, 1–20. Channel View. Clevedon, UK.

Komers, P. 2003. Visual Representations for Conceptual Awareness in Learning Cultures. In Kähkönen, E. and Sutinen, E. (eds), *Proceedings of the First International Conference on Educational Technology in Cultural Context*, 27–44. Proceedings Series No. 3, Virtual University of Eastern Finland. Joensuu, Finland.

Koro, E. 2005. New Development Model Spurs Growth in South African Rural Community (http://Newsroom.Wri.Org/Wrifeatures_Text.Cfm?Contentid=3323andNewsletterid=83, accessed 15 September 2008).

Kort Jan 2002. Interview, Ngwatle, Botswana, July.

Kotler, P., Haider, D. and Rein, I. 1993. *Marketing Places*. Macmillan. New York.

Krige, J.D. 1937. Traditional Origins and Tribal Relationships of the Sotho of the Northern Transvaal. *Bantu Studies* 11(4): 321–356.

Krippendorf, J. 1980. *Marketing im Fremdenverkehr*. Peter Lang. Bern, Switzerland.

Krippendorf, J. 1982. Towards New Tourism Policies. *Tourism Management* 3(1): 135–148.

Kruiper, B. 2000. Interview, Northern Cape, Republic of South Africa, March.

Kruiper, B. 2001a. Interview, Northern Cape, Republic of South Africa, 24 July.

Kruiper, B. 2001b. Interview, University of Natal, Durban, Republic of South Africa,18 October.

Kruiper, B. 2002. Interview, Blinkwater, Northern Cape, Republic of South Africa, 19 July.

Kruiper, L. 2007. Interview, !Xaus Lodge, Kgalagadi Transfrontier Park, Republic of South Africa, 25 November.

Kruiper, T. 2002. Interview, Witdraai, Northern Cape, Republic of South Africa, 16 July.

Kulik, J. 1994. Meta-analytic Studies of Findings on Computer-based Instruction. In Baker, E.L. and O'Neil, H.F. (eds), *Technology Assessment in Education and Training*, 9–34. Lawrence Erlbaum. Hillsdale, New Jersey.

Lam, D., Boymal, J. and Martin, B. 2004. Internet Diffusion in Vietnam. *Technology in Society* 26(1): 39–50.

Lange, K. 2004. Himba. Consulting the Past, Divining the Future. *National Geographic* (January): 32–47.

Lange, K. 2008. Himba. Consulting the Past, Divining the Future (http://ngm.national geographic.com/ngm/0401/feature2/, accessed 21 February 2008).

Lasswell, H.D. 1948. The Structure and Function of Communication in Society. In Bryson, I. (ed.), *The Communication of Ideas*, 37–51. Harper and Brothers. New York.

Law, C.M. 1992. Urban Tourism and Its Contribution to Economic Regeneration. *Urban Studies* 29(3–4): 599–618.

Law, C.M. 1993. *Urban Tourism: Attracting Visitors to Large Cities.* Mansell. London.

Law, C.M. 1996. Introduction. In Law, C.M. (ed.), *Tourism in Major Cities,* 1–22. Thomson. London.

Laws, E. 1997. *Managing Package Tourism: Relationships, Responsibilities and Service Quality in the Inclusive Holiday Industry.* Thomson. London.

Leach, M., Mearns, R. and Scoones, I. 1999. Environmental Entitlements: Dynamics and Institutions in Community-Based Natural Resources Management. *Wildlife Development* 27(2): 225–247.

Leechor, C. and Fabricius, M. 2005. Developing Tourism in Botswana: Progress and Challenges. Discussion Draft. A commissioned background study to the World Bank-BIDPA Botswana Export Diversification Study, Botswana Institute for Development Policy Analysis (BIDPA). Gaborone, Botswana.

Lehtola, V.-P. 1997. *Saamelaiset: Historia, Yhteiskunta ja Taide* [The Sámi: History, Society and Art]. Kustannus-Puntsi. Inari, Finland.

Lepp, A. 2002. Globalization, Ecotourism and the Promise of Development in Sub-Saharan Africa. *Tourism Recreation Research* 27(1): 61–68.

Lerner, D. 1958. *The Passing of Traditional Society.* Free Press. New York.

Lestrade, G.P. 1928. Some Notes on the Political Organization of the Bechwana. *South African Journal of Science* 25: 427–432.

Lindsey, P.A. 2008. Trophy Hunting in Sub-Saharan Africa: Economic Scale and Conservation Significance. In CIC Technical Series Publication No. 1, Best Practices in Sustainable Hunting, 41–48. International Council for Game and Wildlife Conservation (CIC). Budakeszi, Hungary.

Linehan, D. 2008. Re-ordering the Urban Archipelago: Kenya Vision 2030, Street Trade and the Battle for Nairobi City Centre. *Aurora* 1(1): 21–42.

Long, S.A. 2004. *Livelihoods and CBRNM in Namibia. The Findings of the WILD Project.* Ministry of Environment and Tourism (MET). Solitaire. Windhoek, Namibia.

Lopez, P., Bergmann, U., Dresrüsse, P., Fröde, A., Hoppe, M. and Rotzinger, S. 2005. Linking Protected Area Management and HIV/AIDS Prevention – Experiences from Ankarafantsika National Park, Madagascar. *Parks* 15(1): 25–36.

Lourens, M. 2007a. Route Tourism: a Roadmap for Successful Destinations and Local Economic Development. *Development Southern Africa* 24(3): 475–489.

Lourens, M. 2007b. The Underpinnings of Successful Route Tourism Development in South Africa. Unpublished MA Dissertation, University of the Witwatersrand. Johannesburg, Republic of South Africa.

Low-Beer, D. and Stoneburner, R.L. 2004. AIDS Communications through Social Networks: Catalyst for Behaviour Change. *African Journal of AIDS Research* 3(1): 1–13.

Ma, L.J.C. 2005. Urban Administrative Restructuring, Changing Scale Relations and Local Economic Development in China. *Political Geography* 24(4): 477–497.

MacCannell, D. 1976. *The Tourist: a New Theory of the Leisure Class.* Schocken. New York.

Mackoy, R.D. and Osland, G.E. 2004. Lodge Selection and Satisfaction: Attributes Valued by Ecotourists. *Journal of Tourism Studies* 15(2): 13–25.

Macneil, I.R. 1980. *The New Social Contract: an Inquiry into Modern Contractual Relations.* Yale University Press. New Haven, Connecticut.

Magole, L.I. and Gojamang, O. 2005. The Dynamics of Tourist Visitation to National Parks and Game Reserves in Botswana. *Botswana Notes and Records* 37(1): 80–96.

Maloti Route 2007. Welcome to the Maloti Route (http://www.malotiroute.co.za, accessed 20 July 2007).

Mann, J.M. 1996. Human Rights and AIDS: the Future of the Pandemic. In Schenker, I.I., Sabar-Friedman, G. and Sy, F.S. (eds), *AIDS Education: Interventions in Multi-cultural Societies*, 1–7. Plenum. New York.

Manyara, G., Jones, E. and Botterill, D. 2006. Tourism and Poverty Alleviation: the Case for Indigenous Enterprise Development in Kenya. *Tourism, Culture and Communication* 7(1): 19–37.

Manyara, K. 2007. Community-Based Tourism Enterprises Development in Kenya: an Exploration of Their Potential as Avenues of Poverty Reduction. *Journal of Sustainable Tourism* 15(6): 628–644.

Mashinini, V. 2003. Tourism Policies and Strategies in Lesotho: a Critical Appraisal. *Africa Insight* 33(1–2): 87–93.

Massyn, P.J. 2007. Communal Land Reform and Tourism Investment in Namibia's Communal Areas: a Question of Unfinished Business. *Development Southern Africa* 24(3): 381–392.

Matenga, C. 2005. Pro-poor Tourism in Zambia – Concept and Reality. In Eberlei, W., Meyens, P. and Mutesa, F. (eds), *Poverty Reduction in a Political Trap? The PRS Process and Neopatrimonialism in Zambia*, 189–211. University of Zambia Press. Lusaka, Zambia.

Matengu, K.K. 2003. *The Diffusion of Modern Technology in Namibia*. Unpublished Licentiate Degree Thesis, Department of Geography, University of Joensuu. Joensuu, Finland.

Matengu, K.K. 2006. *The Adoption of ICT at Schools in Core and Periphery Settings of Namibia. Exploring Innovation, Technology Policy and Development Issues*. Shaker. Aachen, Germany.

Mathfield, D. 2000. Impacts of Accommodation and Craft-based Tourism on Local Economic Development: The Case of the Midlands Meander. Unpublished Master's Research Report, University of Natal. Durban, Republic of South Africa.

Mbai, J. and Sherbourne, R. 2004. Have Priorities Changed? Budget Trends since Independence. Briefing Paper No. 32. Institute for Public Policy Research (IPPR). Windhoek, Namibia.

Mbaiwa, J.E. 2003. Community-Based Tourism in Ngamiland District, Botswana: Development Impacts and Challenges. In Darkoh, M. and Rwomine, A. (eds), *Human Impact on Environment and Sustainable Development in Africa*, 279–401. Ashgate. Aldershot, UK.

Mbaiwa, J.E. 2004. The Socio-economic Benefits and Challenges of a Community-Based Safari Hunting Tourism in the Okavango Delta, Botswana. *The Journal of Tourism Studies* 15(2): 37–50.

Mbaiwa, J.E. 2005a. Community-Based Tourism and the Marginalised Communities in Botswana: the Case of the Basarwa in the Okavango Delta. In Ryan, C. and Aichelle, M. (eds), *Indigenous Tourism: the Commodification and Management of Culture*, 87–110. Elsevier. Amsterdam.

Mbaiwa, J.E. 2005b. Wildlife Resource Utilization at Moremi Game Reserve and Khwai Community Area in the Okavango Delta, Botswana. *Journal of Environmental Management* 77(2): 144–156.

Mbaiwa, J.E. 2008. Tourism Development, Rural Livelihoods and Conservation in the Okavango Delta, Botswana. PhD Dissertation, Department of Recreation, Park and Tourism Sciences, Texas A&M University. College Station, Texas.

McCormick, D. 2001. Enterprise Clusters in Kenya: Urban Production, Upgrading Strategies and Joint Action. *Africa Insight* 31(1): 3–11.

McLennan-Dodd, V. 2002. Why is Our Voice Not Being Heard by 'Developers'? Development as Empowerment. Paper presented at the *South African Communication Association Conference*, University of Potchefstroom, Republic of South Africa.

McLennan-Dodd, V. 2003. Hotel Kalahari: You Can Check Out Any Time You Like, But You Can Never Leave. *Cultural Studies – Critical Methodologies* 3(4): 448–469.

Medina-Muñoz, R.D., Medina-Muñoz, D.R. and Garcia-Falcon, J.M. 2003. Understanding European Tour Operators' Control on Accommodation Companies: an Empirical Evidence. *Tourism Management* 24(2): 135–147.

Meethan, K. 2001. *Tourism in Global Society: Place, Culture, Consumption.* Palgrave. Basingstoke, UK.

Meintjies, A. 2002. Interview, Erin, Northern Cape, Republic of South Africa,17 July.

Melber, H. 2003. Limits to Liberation. An Introduction to Namibia's Postcolonial Political Culture. In Melber, H. (ed.), Re-*examining Liberation in Namibia. Political Culture since Independence,* 9–24. Nordic Africa Institute. Uppsala, Sweden.

Melkote, S.R. and Steeves, H.L. 2001. *Communication for Development in the Third World: Theory and Practice for Empowerment.* Second Edition. Sage. London.

Mendelsohn, J., Jarvis, A., Roberts, C. and Robertson, T. 2003. *Atlas of Namibia: a Portrait of the Land and Its People.* David Philip. Cape Town, Republic of South Africa.

MET 1995a. *Namibia Tourism Development Programme. Phase I – Foundation.* Ministry of Environment and Tourism (MET). Windhoek, Namibia.

MET 1995b. The Promotion of Community-Based Tourism. Policy Document. Ministry of Environment and Tourism (MET). Windhoek, Namibia.

MET 2005a. *A National Tourism Policy for Namibia.* Draft February 2005. Ministry of Environment and Tourism (MET). Windhoek, Namibia.

MET 2005b. Programmes: Community-Based Natural Resource Management (CBNRM) (http://www.met.gov.na/programmes/cbnrm/cbtourism_guide.htm, accessed 21 January 2008). Ministry of Environment and Tourism (MET). Windhoek, Namibia.

MET 2007. *National Tourism Policy for Namibia.* Draft September 2007. Ministry of Environment and Tourism (MET). Windhoek, Namibia.

Metzger, D. 2008. Introduction to Trophy Hunting as a Lucrative Form of Land Utilization. A public speech presented at *Upcoming Farmers Workshop,* Nampower Convention Centre, Windhoek, Namibia, 28 July.

Meyer, D. 2004. *Tourism Routes and Gateways: Key Issues for the Development of Tourism Routes and Gateways and Their Potential for Pro-poor Tourism.* Overseas Development Institute (ODI). London.

Meyer, D. 2006. Caribbean Tourism, Local Sourcing and Enterprise Development: Review of the Literature. Working Paper No. 18, Pro-Poor Tourism Partnership. London.

Meyer, D. 2007. Pro-Poor Tourism: From Leakages to Linkages. A Conceptual Framework for Creating Linkages between the Accommodation Sector and 'Poor' Neighbouring Communities. *Current Issues in Tourism* 10(6): 558–583.

Meyer, D., Ashley, C. and Poultney, C. 2004. Developing Local Excursions for Tourists. Case Study Brief No. 5, Pro-poor Tourism Pilots (Southern Africa) Programme (http://www.ppt pilot.org.za, accessed 15 May 2008).

Meyer-Cech, K. 2003. Food Trails in Austria. In Hall, C.M., Sharples, L., Mitchell, R., Macionis, N. and Camborne, B. (eds), *Food Tourism around the World: Development, Management, and Markets,* 149–157. Butterworth-Heinemann. London.

Meyer-Cech, K. 2005. Regional Cooperation in Rural Theme Trails. In Hall, D., Kirkpatrick, I. and Mitchell, M. (eds), *Rural Tourism and Sustainable Business,* 137–148. Channel View. Clevedon, UK.

Michael, E.J. 2003. Tourism Micro-clusters. *Tourism Economics* 9(2): 133–145.

Michael, E.J. 2007. *Micro-clusters and Networks: The Growth of Tourism.* Elsevier. Amsterdam.

Middleton, V.T.C. and Clarke, J. 2001. *Marketing in Travel and Tourism.* Butterworth-Heinemann. Amsterdam.

Mikalsen, O. In press. Development Communication and the Paradox of Choice: Imposition and Dictatorship in Comparing Sámi and the San Bushmen Experiences of Cultural Autonomy. *Critical Arts* in press.

Miles, I. and Thomas, G. 1996. User Resistance to New Interactive Media: Participants, Processes and Paradigms. In Bauer, M. (ed.), *Resistance to New Technology,* 255–276. Cambridge University Press. Cambridge, UK.

Miles, M.B. and Huberman, A.M. 1984. *Qualitative Data Analysis. A Sourcebook of New Methods.* Sage. Thousand Oaks, California.

Milgroom, J. and Spierenburg, M. 2008. Induced Volition: Resettlement from the Limpopo National Park, Mozambique. *Journal of Contemporary African Studies* 26(4): 435–448.

Miller, L., Dickinson, J.E. and Pearlman-Houghie, D.J. 2001. Quiet Enjoyment in the National Parks of England and Wales: Public Understanding of the Term and Its Influence on Attitudes towards Recreational Activities. *Leisure Studies* 20(1): 19–40.

Milne, S.M. 1998. Tourism and Sustainable Development: Exploring the Global–Local Nexus. In Hall, C.M. and Lew, A.A. (eds), *Sustainable Tourism*, 35–48. Pearson. Harlow, UK.

Milne, S.M. and Ateljevic, I. 2001. Tourism, Economic Development and the Global–Local Nexus: Theory Embracing Complexity. *Tourism Geographies* 3(4): 369–393.

Minde, H. 2005. Assimilation of the Sami – Implementation and Consequences. *Gáldu Ĉála – Journal of Indigenous Peoples Rights* No. 3: 1–33.

Ministerio de Turismo de Moçambique 2006. Parque Nacional do Limpopo , Estretura do processo da concessão (http://www.limpopopn.gov.mz/, accessed 6 September 2008).

Ministry of Social Affairs and Health 2008. *Saamelaiset* [The Sámi People]. Ministry of Social Affairs and Health, Finland (http://pre20031103.stm.fi/suomi/tao/julkaisut/omakieli/saamelaiset.htm, accessed 24 December 2008).

Miriam 2003. Interview, Monong, Botswana, 19 July.

Mitchell, R.E. and Reid, D.G. 2001. Community Integration: Island Tourism in Peru. *Annals of Tourism Research* 28(1): 113–139.

Molina, A. and Esteban, Á. 2006. Tourism Brochures: Usefulness and Image. *Annals of Tourism Research* 33(4): 1036–1056.

Moulin, C. and Boniface, P. 2001. Routing Heritage for Tourism: Making Heritage and Cultural Tourism Networks for Socio-economic Development. *International Journal of Heritage Studies* 7(3): 237–248.

Mowforth, M. and Munt, I. 1998. *Tourism and Sustainability: a New Tourism in the Third World.* Routledge. London.

Muir, F. 1993. Managing Tourism to a Seabird Nesting Island. *Tourism Management* 14(2): 99–105.

Muir, F. and Chester, G. 1992. Managing Tourism to a Seabird Nesting Island in the Great Barrier Reef Marine Park: Management of Michaelmas Cay and Reef. In Weiler, B. (ed.), *Ecotourism Incorporating the Global Classroom, 1991 International Conference Papers*, 184–191. Bureau of Tourism Research. Canberra, Australia.

Murphy, C. and Roe, D. 2004. Livelihoods and Tourism in Communal Area Conservancies. In Long, A. (ed.), *Livelihoods and CBNRM in Namibia: The Findings of the WILD Project*, 119–138. Ministry of Environment and Tourism (MET). Windhoek, Namibia.

Murphy, P. 1985. *Tourism: a Community Approach.* Methuen. New York.

Murray, M. and Graham, B. 1997. Exploring the Dialectics of Route-based Tourism: the Camino de Santiago. *Tourism Management* 18(8): 513–524.

Mwenya, A.N., Lewis, D.M. and Kaweche, G.B. 1991. *Policy, Background and Future: National Parks and Wildlife Services, New Administrative Management Design for Game Management Areas.* United States Agency for International Development (USAID). Lusaka, Zambia.

NACOMA 2008. Regulations for the Central Area of the Namib–Skeleton Coast National Park, First Draft. Namibia Coast Conservation and Management Project (NACOMA). Swakopmund, Namibia.

NACSO 2007. Namibia's Communal Conservancies: a Review of Progress 2006. Namibian Association of CBNRM Support Organisations (NACSO). Windhoek, Namibia.

Nadkarni, S. 2008. Defining the ICT4D Plus Pro-Poor Tourism Convergence Space: Synergies for Natural Allies in the Global War on Poverty. *The Electronic Journal on Information Systems in Developing Countries* 33(5): 1–17.

Namibia Economist 2004. Tourism Sector Adopts a BBBEE Charter. 26 November.

Namibia Economist 2008. NamPower Plans Additional Power Plant in Walvis Bay. 16 May.

Namibia Tourism Board 2008. *Namibia Tourism Satellite Account.* Second Edition. Namibia Tourism Board (NTB). Windhoek, Namibia.

NAPHA 2008. Introduction to Trophy Hunting as a Lucrative Form of Land Utilization. Namibia Professional Hunting Association (NAPHA), *Proceedings of Upcoming Farmers Workshop,* Windhoek, Namibia.

Nasha, M. 2002. Interview with *Carte Blanche,* South Africa (http://www.mnet.co.za/carteblanche/display/display.asp?id=1893, accessed 26 February 2008.

Naudé, W.A. and Saayman, A. 2005. Determinants of Tourist Arrivals in Africa: a Panel Data Regression Analysis. *Tourism Economics* 11(3): 365–391.

Ndlovu, N. and Rogerson, C.M. 2003. Rural Local Economic Development through Community-Based Tourism: the Mehloding Hiking and Horse Trail, Eastern Cape, South Africa. *Africa Insight* 33(1–2): 124–129.

Nel, E. 2001. Local Economic Development: a Review and Assessment of its Current Status in South Africa. *Urban Studies* 38(7): 1003–1024.

Nel, E. 2007. Critical Reflections on Urban and Local Development in Africa. *Environment and Planning C; Government and Policy* 25(4): 459–465.

Nel, E. and Binns, T. 2002. Place Marketing, Tourism Promotion and Community-Based Local Economic Development in Post-apartheid South Africa: the Case of Still Bay – The 'Bay of Sleeping Beauty'. *Urban Affairs Review* 38(2): 184–208.

Nel, E. and Rogerson, C.M. (eds) 2005a. *Local Economic Development in the Developing World: The Experience of Southern Africa.* Transaction. New Brunswick, Canada.

Nel, E. and Rogerson, C.M. 2005b. Pro-poor Local Economic Development in South Africa's Cities: Policy and Practice. *Africa Insight* 35(4): 15–20.

Nel, E. and Rogerson, C.M. 2007. Evolving Local Economic Development Policy and Practice in South Africa with Special Reference to Smaller Urban Centres. *Urban Forum* 18(2): 1–11.

Neumann, R.P. 1998. *Imposing Wilderness: Struggles over Livelihood and Nature Preservation in Africa.* University of California Press. Berkeley, California.

Neumann, R.P. 2000. Primitive Ideas: Protected Area Buffer Zones and the Politics of Land in Africa. In Broch-Due, V. and Schroeder, R.A. (eds), Producing Nature and Poverty in Africa, 220–242. Nordic Africa Institute. Uppsala, Sweden.

New Era 2008a. Riverfront to Assume New Look. 5 March.

New Era 2008b. Trophy Hunters Bring in Millions. 10 March.

New Era 2008c. Influx of International Trophy Hunters Expected. 16 April.

Newsome, D., Moore, S.A. and Dowling, R.K. 2002. *Natural Area Tourism. Ecology, Impacts and Management.* Channel View. Clevedon, UK.

Njagi, N.G. 2005. The Sustainable Livelihood Approach: a Vulnerability Context Analysis of Ngwatle's !Kung Group Basarwa Botswana. MA Dissertation, Social Science of Development Studies, University of KwaZulu-Natal. Durban, Republic of South Africa.

Nompumelelo, Z-D., Shissana, O., Udjo, E., Mosala, T. and Seager, J. (eds) 2004. *An Audit of HIV/AIDS Policies in Botswana, Lesotho, Mozambique, South Africa, Swaziland and Zimbabwe.* Kellogg Foundation. Cape Town, Republic of South Africa.

Normann, R. 2000. *Service Management.* Cappelen. Oslo.

Novelli, M. and Gebhardt, K. 2007. Community-based Tourism in Namibia: 'Reality Show' or 'Window Dressing'? *Current Issues in Tourism* 10(5): 443–479.

Novelli, M. and Humavindu, M. 2005. Wildlife Tourism – Wildlife Use vs Local Gain: Trophy Hunting in Namibia. In Novelli, M. (ed.), *Niche Tourism: Contemporary Issues, Trends and Cases,* 171–182. Elsevier. Oxford, UK.

Nowers, R., de Villiers E. and Myburgh, A. 2002. Agricultural Theme Routes as a Diversification Strategy: the Western Cape Wine Routes Case Study. *Agrekon* 41(2): 195–209.

NWDC 2003. District Development Plan Six 2003/4-2008/9. North West District Council (NWDC). Maun, Botswana.

Oates, J.F. 1999. *Myth and Reality in the Rainforest: How Conservation Strategies are Failing in West Africa.* University of California Press. Berkeley, California.

Office of the Auditor-General 2006. *Audit Report on the Accounts of the Municipality of Walvis Bay for the Financial Year Ended 30 June 2006.* Office of the Auditor-General Report No. 472. Windhoek, Namibia.

Okello, M.M., Wishitemi, B.E.L. and Lagat, B. 2005. Tourism Potential and Achievement of Protected Areas in Kenya: Criteria and Prioritization. *Tourism Analysis* 10(2): 151–164.

Olsen, M. 2003. Tourism Themed Routes: a Queensland Perspective. *Journal of Vacation Marketing* 9(4): 331–341.

Open Africa. 2006. *The Story So Far.* South Africa Tourism Services Association (SATSA). Randburg, Republic of South Africa.

Oppong, J.R. and Kalipeni, E. 2004. Perceptions and Misperceptions of AIDS in Africa. In Kalipeni, E., Craddock, S., Oppong, J.R. and Ghosh, J. (eds), *HIV and AIDS in Africa: Beyond Epidemiology*, 47–57. Blackwell. Oxford, UK.

Ormsby, A. and Mannle, K. 2006. Ecotourism Benefits and the Role of Local Guides at Masoala National Park, Madagascar. *Journal of Sustainable Tourism* 14(3): 271–287.

OTA 1993. Science and Technology Issues in Coastal Ecotourism. Edited Version of a Background Paper by the US Office of Technology Assessment (OTA). *Tourism Management* 14(4): 307–316.

Owen, C. 1990. Tourism and Urban Regeneration. *Cities* 7(3): 194–201.

Palm, P. and Pye, O. 2001. *The Potential of Community-Based Tourism and the Role of Development Cooperation in Namibia.* Deutsche Gesellscaft für Technische Zusammaenarbeit (GTZ). Eschborn, Germany.

Park, B.-G. 2005. The Territorial Politics of Regulation under State Capitalism: Regional Parties and the Politics of Local Economic Development in South Korea. *Space and Polity* 9(3): 237–259.

Patton, M. 2002. *Qualitative Research and Evaluation Methods.* Third Edition. Sage. Thousand Oaks, California.

Peace Parks Foundation 2004. New Makuleke Tourism Development (http://www.richtersveld.net/index.php/site/town/richtersveld_community_conservancy/, accessed 28 November 2008).

Pelgrum, W.J. 2001. Obstacles to the Integration of ICT in Education: Results from a Worldwide Educational Assessment. *Computers and Education* 37(2): 163–178.

Pelto, P.J. and Pelto, G.H. 1993. *Anthropological Research.* Second Edition. Cambridge University Press. Cambridge, UK.

Peterson, R.T. 1991. Ecotourism – The New Buzzword. *Bird Watcher's Digest* (July/August): 12–22.

Phororo, H. 2000. Why the Private Sector Should Be Concerned about HIV/AIDS. Hanns Seidel Foundation Namibia Occasional Paper No. 1. Windhoek, Namibia.

Phororo, H. 2003. HIV/AIDS and the Private Sector in Namibia: Getting the Small Business on Board. Hanns Seidel Foundation Namibia Occasional Paper No. 3. Windhoek, Namibia.

Pike, A., Rodriguez-Pose, A. and Tomaney, J. 2006. *Local and Regional Development.* Routledge. London.

Plummer, R., Telfer, D., Hashimoto, A. and Summers, R. 2005. Beer Tourism in Canada along the Waterloo–Wellington Ale Trail. *Tourism Management* 26(3): 447–458.

Plummer, R., Telfer, D. and Hashimoto, A. 2006. The Rise and Fall of the Waterloo–Wellington Ale Trail: a Study of Collaboration within the Tourism Industry. *Current Issues in Tourism* 9(3): 191–205.

Pond, K.L. 1993. *The Professional Guide: Dynamics of Tour Guiding.* Van Nostrand Reinhold. New York.

Porter, M.E. 1980. *Competitive Strategy.* Free Press. New York.

Premkumar, G. and Roberts, M. 1999. Adoption of New Technology in Rural Small Businesses. *Omega – The International Journal of Management Science* 27(4): 467–484.

Pritchard, A. and Morgan, N. 2003. Mythic Geographies of Representation and Identity: Contemporary Postcards of Wales. *Tourism and Cultural Change* 1(2): 111–130.

Prosser, R. 1994. Societal Change and the Growth in Alternative Tourism. In Cater, E. and Lowman, G. (eds), *Ecotourism – A Sustainable Option?,* 19–38. John Wiley and Sons. Chichester, UK.

Pyka, A. and Küppers, G. 2002. The Self-organisation of Innovation Networks: Introductory Remarks. In Pyka, A. and Küppers, G. (eds), *Innovation Networks: Theory and Practice,* 5–21. Edward Elgar. Cheltenham, UK.

Quin, P.J. 1959. *Foods and Feeding Habits of the Pedi.* Witwatersrand University Press. Johannesburg, Republic of South Africa.

Raento, P. and Hottola, P. 2005. Where on Earth is New York? Pedagogical Lessons from Finnish Geography Students' Knowledge of the United States. *International Research in Geographical and Environmental Education* 14(1): 5–27.

Ramutsindela, M. 2004a. *Parks and People in Postcolonial Societies: Experiences in Southern Africa.* Kluwer. Dordrecht, The Netherlands.

Ramutsindela, M. 2004b. Glocalisation and Nature Conservation Strategies in 21st-Century Southern Africa. *Tijdschrift voor Economische en Sociale Geografie* 95(1): 61–72.

Ranta, T. 2004. Sata vuotta luonnonsuojelua [One Hundred Years of Nature Conservation]. In Pikkarainen, M., Ranta, T., Sitari, T. and Vasanen, A. (eds), *Namibia – Elämää Kuivuuden Keskellä* [Namibia – Life in an Arid Region], 39–59. Turun maantieteellinen seura. Turku, Finland.

Rayman-Bacchus, L. and Molina, A. 2001. Internet-Based Tourism Services: Business Issues and Trends. *Futures* 33(7): 589–605.

Reid, H. 2001. Contractual National Parks and the Makuleke Community. *Human Ecology* 29(2): 135–155.

Richards, G. and Hall, D. 2000. The Community: a Sustainable Concept in Tourism Development? In Hall, D. and Richards, G. (eds), *Tourism and Sustainable Community Development,* 1–14. Routledge. London.

Richtersveld 2008. Richtersveld Community Conservancy (http://www.richtersveld.net/index.php/site/town/richtersveld_community_conservancy, accessed 28 November 2008).

Ritchie, J. and Lewis, J. 2003. *Qualitative Research Practice. A Guide for Social Science Students and Researchers.* Sage. London.

Roberts, N. 1916. The Bagananoa or Ma-Laboch: Notes on Their Early History, Customs and Creed. *South African Journal of Science* 12: 241–256.

Robins, S. 2001. NGOs, Bushmen and Double Vision: The ≠Khomani San Land Claim and the Cultural Politics of 'Community' and 'Development' in the Kalahari. *Journal of Southern African Studies* 27(4): 833–853.

Robins, S. and van der Waal, K. 2008. Model Tribes and Iconic Conservationists? The Makuleke Restitution Case in Kruger National Park. *Development and Change* 39(1): 53–72.

Robinson, M. 1999. Cultural Conflicts in Tourism: Inevitability and Inequality. In Robinson, M. and Boniface, P. (eds), *Tourism and Cultural Conflicts,* 1–32. CAB International. Wallingford, UK.

Rodgers, J.A. Jr and Schwikert, S.T. 2002. Buffer-zone Distances to Protect Foraging and Loafing Waterbirds from Disturbance by Personal Watercraft and Outboard-powered Boats. *Conservation Biology* 16(1): 216–224.

Rodriguez-Pose, A. and Arbix, G. 2001. Strategies of Waste: Bidding Wars in the Brazilian Automobile Sector. *International Journal of Urban and Regional Research* 25(1): 134–154.

Rodriguez-Pose, A. and Gill, N. 2003. The Global Trend towards Devolution and Its Implications. *Environment and Planning C: Government and Policy* 21(3): 331–351.

Rodriguez-Pose, A. and Tijmstra, A.R. 2007. Local Economic Development in Sub-Saharan Africa. *Environment and Planning C: Government and Policy* 25(7): 516–536.

Roe, D., Grieg-Gran, M. and Schalken, W. 2001. *Getting the Lion's Share from Tourism: Private Sector–Community Partnerships in Namibia.* The International Institute for Environment and Development (IIED) and Namibia Community-Based Tourism Association (NACOBTA). Windhoek, Namibia.

Roe, D., Goodwin, H. and Ashley, C. 2004. Pro-poor Tourism: Benefiting the Poor. In Singh, T.V. (ed.), *New Horizons in Tourism: Strange Experiences and Stranger Practices*, 147–161. CAB International. Wallingford, UK.

Roehl, W. 1998. The Tourism Production System: the Logic of Industrial Classification. In Ioannides, D. and Debbage, K.G. (eds), *The Economic Geography of the Tourism Industry*, 53–76. Routledge. London.

Rogers, E.M. 1962. *Diffusion of Innovations.* Free Press. New York.

Rogers. E.M. 2003. *Diffusion of Innovations.* Fifth Edition. Free Press. New York.

Rogerson, C.M. 1995. Local Economic Development Planning in the Developing World. *Regional Development Dialogue* 16(2): v–xv.

Rogerson, C.M. 1997. Local Economic Development and Post-Apartheid Reconstruction: the Case of South African Cities. *Singapore Journal of Tropical Geography* 18(2): 175–195.

Rogerson, C.M. 2000. Local Economic Development in an Era of Globalisation: the Case of South African Cities. *Tijdschrift voor Economische en Sociale Geografie* 91(4): 397–411.

Rogerson, C.M. 2002a. Tourism and Local Economic Development: the Case of the Highlands Meander. *Development Southern Africa* 19(1): 143–167.

Rogerson, C.M. 2002b. Urban Tourism in the Developing World: the Case of Johannesburg. *Development Southern Africa* 19(1): 169–190.

Rogerson, C.M. 2002c. Tourism-led Local Economic Development: the South African Experience. *Urban Forum* 13(1): 95–119.

Rogerson, C.M. 2004a. Black Economic Empowerment in South African Tourism. In Rogerson, C.M. and Visser, G. (eds), *Tourism and Development Issues in Contemporary South Africa*, 321–334. Africa Institute of South Africa. Pretoria, Republic of South Africa.

Rogerson, C.M. 2004b. Tourism and Uneven Local Economic Development: the Experience of Route Tourism in South Africa. In Rogerson, C.M. and Visser, G. (eds), *Tourism and Development Issues in Contemporary South Africa*, 399–419. Africa Institute of South Africa. Pretoria, Republic of South Africa.

Rogerson, C.M. 2004c. Urban Tourism and Economic Regeneration: the Example of Johannesburg. In Rogerson, C.M. and Visser, G. (eds), *Tourism and Development Issues in Contemporary South Africa*, 466–487. Africa Institute of South Africa. Pretoria, Republic of South Africa.

Rogerson, C.M. 2006a. Tourism Policy, Local Economic Development and South African Cities. In Tomlinson, R., Pillay, U. and du Toit, J. (eds), *Democracy and Delivery: Urban Policy in South Africa*, 230–250. Human Sciences Research Council (HSRC). Pretoria, Republic of South Africa.

Rogerson, C.M. 2006b. Pro-poor Local Economic Development in South Africa: the Role of Pro-poor Tourism. *Local Environment* 11(1): 37–60.

Rogerson, C.M. 2006c. Local Economic Development in Post-apartheid South Africa: a Ten-year Research Review. In Padayachee, V. (ed.), *The Development Decade?: Economic and Social Change in South Africa, 1994–2004*, 227–253. Human Sciences Research Council (HSRC). Cape Town, Republic of South Africa.

Rogerson, C.M. 2006d. Creative Industries and Urban Tourism: South African Perspectives. *Urban Forum* 17(2): 149–166.

Rogerson, C.M. 2007a. Tourism Routes as Vehicles for Local Economic Development in South Africa: the Example of the Magaliesberg Meander. *Urban Forum* 18(2): 49–68.

Rogerson, C.M. 2007b. Reviewing Africa in the Global Tourism Economy. *Development Southern Africa* 24(2): 361–379.

Rogerson, C.M. 2008a. Consolidating Local Economic Development in Post-apartheid South Africa. *Urban Forum* 19(3): 307–328.

Rogerson, C.M. 2008b. Shared Growth and Tourism Small Enterprise Development in South Africa. *Tourism Recreation Research* 33(3): in press.

Rogerson, C.M. and Visser, G. (eds) 2004a. *Tourism and Development Issues in Contemporary South Africa.* Africa Institute of South Africa. Pretoria, Republic of South Africa.

Rogerson, C.M. and Visser, G. 2004b. Tourism and Development in Post-Apartheid South Africa: a Ten-Year Review. In Rogerson, C.M. and Visser, G. (eds), *Tourism and Development Issues in Contemporary South Africa,* 2–25. Africa Institute of South Africa Pretoria, Republic of South Africa.

Rogerson, C.M. and Visser, G. (eds) 2007. *Urban Tourism in the Developing World: the South African Experience.* Transaction. London.

Roper, A., Jensen, Ø. and Jegervatn, R-H. 2005. The Dynamics of the Norwegian Package Tour Industry. *Scandinavian Journal of Hospitality and Tourism* 5(3): 193–211.

Rose, G. 2001. *Visual Methodologies: an Introduction to the Interpretation of Visual Materials.* Sage. London.

Rosen, S. and Simon, J.L. 2003. Shifting the Burden: the Private Sector's Response to the AIDS Epidemic in Africa. *Bulletin of the World Health Organization* 81(2): 131–137.

Rosen, S., Vincent, J.R., MacLeod, W., Fox, M., Thea, D.M. and Simon, J.L. 2004. The Cost of HIV/AIDS to Business in Southern Africa. *AIDS* 18(2): 317–324.

Rosen, S., Hamazakaza, P. and Long, L. 2006. *The Impact of HIV/AIDS on the Tourism Sector in Zambia.* Center for International Health and Development, Boston University, and Farming Systems Association of Zambia (FASAZ). Boston, Massachusetts.

Rosen, S., Hamazakaza, P., Feeley, P. and Fox, M. 2007. The Impact of AIDS on Government Service Delivery: the Case of the Zambia Wildlife Authority. *AIDS* 21 (suppl. 3): S53–S59.

Rostow, W. 1960. *The Stages of Economic Growth: a Non-Communist Manifesto.* Cambridge University Press. Cambridge, UK.

Roth, H.H. and Merz, G. (eds) 1997. *Wildlife Resources: a Global Account of Economic Use.* Springer. Berlin.

Rothfuss, E. 2000. Ethnic Tourism in Kaoko: Expectations, Frustrations and Trend in a Post-Colonial Business. In Miescher, G. and Henrichsen, D. (eds), *New Notes on Kaoko,* 133–158. Basler. Basel, Switzerland.

Rylance, A. 2008. Local Economic Development in Mozambique: an Assessment of the Implementation of Tourism Policy as a Means to Promote Local Economies. In Spenceley, A. (ed.), *Responsible Tourism: Critical Issues for Conservation and Development,* 27–39. Earthscan. London.

Saarinen, J. 1999. Representations of Indigeneity: Sami Culture in the Discourses of Tourism. In Sant, P.M. and Brown, J.N. (eds), *Indigeneity: Constructions and Re/Presentations,* 231–249. Nova Science. New York.

Saarinen, J. 2001. The Transformation of a Tourist Destination – Theory and Case Studies on the Production of Local Geographies in Tourism in Finnish Lapland. Nordia 30(1): 1–105.

Saarinen, J. 2006. Traditions of Sustainability in Tourism Studies. *Annals of Tourism Research* 33(4): 1121–1140.

Saarinen, J. 2007a. Cultural Tourism, Local Communities and Representations of Authenticity: the Case of Lesedi and Swazi Cultural Villages in Southern Africa. In Wishitemi, B., Spenceley, A. and Wels, H. (eds), *Culture and Community: Tourism Studies in Eastern and Southern Africa,* 140–154. Rozenberg. Amsterdam.

Saarinen, J. 2007b. Tourism in Peripheries: the Role of Tourism in Regional Development in Northern Finland. In Jansson, B. and Müller, D. (eds), *Tourism in High Latitude Peripheries: Space, Place, and Environment,* 41–52. CAB International. Wallingford, UK.

Sack, R.D. 1986. *Human Territoriality – Its Theory and History.* Cambridge Studies in Historical Geography, Cambridge University Press. Cambridge, UK.

SADC 2002. *National and Sectoral HIV/AIDS Policies in the Member States of the Southern African Development Community.* Southern African Development Community (SADC).

SAHRC 2004. *Report on the Inquiry into Human Rights Violations in the ≠Khomani San Community.* South African Human Rights Commission (SAHRC). Andriesvale, Republic of South Africa.

SATRU 2008a. *The Marketing Tourism Growth Strategy for South Africa 2008–2010.* South African Tourism Research Unit (SATRU). Pretoria, Republic of South Africa (http://www.southafrica.net/satourism/research/viewResearchDocument.cfm?ResearchDocumentID=478, accessed 26 August 2008).

SATRU 2008b. *Annual Report 2007.* South African Tourism Research Unit (SATRU). Pretoria, Republic of South Africa (http://www.southafrica.net/satourism/research/viewResearchDetail.cfm?ReportTypeCategoryID=66, accessed 26 August 2008).

Saugestad, S. 2001. *The Inconvenient Indigenous: Remote Area Development in Botswana, Donor Assistance, and the First People of the Kalahari.* Nordic Africa Institute. Uppsala, Sweden.

Schade, K. 2000. Poverty. In Melber, H. (ed.), *Namibia – a Decade of Independence 1990–2000,* 111–124. Namibian Economic Policy Research Unit (NEPRU). Windhoek, Namibia.

Schapera, I. 1959. *The Bantu-speaking Tribes of South Africa.* Maskew Miller. Cape Town, Republic of South Africa.

Scheyvens, R. 2002. *Tourism for Development: Empowering Communities.* Prentice Hall. Harlow, UK.

Schilcher, D. 2008. Growth versus Equity: the Continuum of Pro-Poor Tourism and Neoliberal Governance. In Hall, M. (ed.), *Pro-poor Tourism: Who Benefits? Perspectives on Tourism and Poverty Reduction,* 56–83. Channel View. Clevedon, UK.

Schoepf, B.G. 2004. AIDS, History, and Struggles over Meaning. In Kalipeni, E., Craddock, S., Oppong, J.R. and Ghosh, J. (eds), *HIV and AIDS in Africa: Beyond Epidemiology,* 15–28. Blackwell. Oxford, UK.

Schramm, W. 1964. *Mass Media and National Development.* Stanford University Press. California.

Schurink, W.J., Schurink, E.M. and Poggenpoel, M. 1998. Focus Group Interviewing and Audio-visual Methodology in Qualitative Research. In de Vos, A.S. (ed.), *Research at Grass Roots. A Primer for the Caring Professions,* 313–333. Van Schaik. Pretoria, Republic of South Africa.

Schuster, B. 2007. *Proceedings of the 4th National CBNRM Conference in Botswana and the CBNRM Status Report,* 20–23 November 2006. International Union for the Conservation of Nature (IUCN) Botswana. Gaborone, Botswana.

Scott, D. and Thigpen, J. 2003. Understanding the Birder as a Tourist: Segmenting Visitors to the Texas Hummer/Bird Celebration. *Human Dimensions of Wildlife* 4(1): 50–67.

Seely, M. 2001. Environment: Harsh Constraints, Political Flexibility. In Diener, I. and Graefe, O. (eds), *Contemporary Namibia – the First Landmarks of a Post-Apartheid Society,* 35–51. Gamsberg Macmillan. Windhoek, Namibia.

Sekercioglu, C.H. 2002. Impacts of Birdwatching on Human and Avian Communities. *Environmental Conservation* 29(3): 282–289.

Selin, S. 1999. Developing a Typology of Sustainable Tourism Partnerships. *Journal of Sustainable Tourism* 7(3): 260–273.

Servaes, J. 1995. Development Communication – For Whom and for What? *Communication* 21(1): 39–49.

Shäffer, N. 2005. Namibia and *BirdLife International*. Evaluation report, *BirdLife International*. Girton, UK.

Shaw, G. 2004. Entrepreneurial Cultures and Small Business Enterprises in Tourism. In Lew, A.A., Hall C.M. and Williams A.M. (eds), *A Companion to Tourism*, 122–134. Blackwell. Oxford, UK.

Shaw G. and Williams A.M. 1990. Tourism, Economic Development and the Role of Entrepreneurial Activity. In Cooper, C.P. (ed.), *Progress in Tourism: Recreation and Hospitality Management Vol. 2*, 67–81. Belhaven. London.

Shaw, W.W. and Mangun, W.R. 1984. Nonconsumptive Use of Wildlife in the United States. Research Publications No. 154. US Fish and Wildlife Service. Washington, DC.

Sheard, K. 1999. A Twitch in Time Saves Nine: Birdwatching, Sport, and Civilizing Processes. *Sociology of Sport Journal* 16(2): 181–205.

Shepperson, A. and Tomaselli, K.G. 2002. Development and the Supermarket of Ideas: Pragmatism and Development Communication Theory. Paper presented at the *South African Communication Association Conference*, University of Potchefstroom, Republic of South Africa.

Shih, H.-Y. 2006. Network Characteristics of Drive Tourism Destinations: an Application of Network Analysis in Tourism. *Tourism Management* 27(5): 1029–1039.

Siiskonen, H. 2004. The Spread of Disease. Sex, City and AIDS in Namibia. In Niemi, M. and Vuolanto, V. (eds), *Reclaiming the City: Innovation, Culture, Experience*, 148–161. Studia Fennica Historica 6, Finnish Literature Society. Helsinki.

Siiskonen, H. 2007. The Namibian Mainline Churches and HIV/AIDS. In Bollig, M., Bubenzer, O., Vogelsang, R. and Wotzka, H-P. (eds), *Aridity, Change and Conflict in Africa*, 441– 469. Colloquium Africanum 2, Heinrich-Barth-Institut. Cologne, Germany.

Simões, A. 2001. Issues of Identity in Relation to the Kalahari Bushmen of Southern Africa: a Comparative Analysis of Two Different Bushmen Groups during the Late 1990s and into 2001. MA Thesis in Culture, Communication and Media Studies, University of Natal. Durban, Republic of South Africa.

Simon, J., Rosen, S., Whiteside, A., Vincent, J.R. and Thea, D.M. 2000. The responses of African Businesses to HIV/AIDS. In *HIV/AIDS in the Commonwealth 2000/01*. Kensington. London.

Sinclair, I., Hockey, P. and Tarboton, W. 2002. *Sasol Birds of Southern Africa*. Third Edition. Struik. Cape Town, Republic of South Africa.

Sindiga, I. 1999. Alternative Tourism and Sustainable Development in Kenya. *Journal of Sustainable Tourism* 7(2): 108–127.

Singh, R. 2008. Urban Tourism – The Development of Dinokeng as a City Game Reserve Destination. Unpublished BA (Hons) Report, University of the Witwatersrand. Johannesburg, Republic of South Africa.

Smart News 2005. Press Statement (http://www.bernama.com/cgi-bin/ssn2/list_item.cgi?peserta/mozambique/mo2505_2.txt, accessed 27 May 2005).

Sofield, T.H.B. 2003. *Empowerment for Sustainable Tourism Development*. Pergamon. Oxford, UK.

Sonntag, C. Undated. *My Friend Maleboch, Chief of the Blue Mountains*. Sigma. Pretoria, Republic of South Africa.

Speets, S. 2001. The Muddy Road to Transfrontier Conservation: a Study on Community Development within the Largest Transfrontier Conservation Area in Southern Africa. MA Thesis, Vrije Universiteit. Amsterdam.

Spierenburg, M., Steenkamp, C. and Wels, H. 2006. Resistance against the Marginalization of Communities in the Great Limpopo Transfrontier Conservation Area. *Focaal, European Journal of Anthropology* 47(1): 18–31.

Spierenburg, M., Steenkamp, C. and Wels, H. 2008. Enclosing the Local for the Global Commons: Community Land Rights in the Great Limpopo Transfrontier Conservation Area. *Conservation and Society* 6(1): 87–97.

Squire, S.J. 1994. Accounting for Cultural Meanings: the Interface between Geography and Tourism Studies Re-examined. *Progress in Human Geography* 18(1): 1–16.

Steenkamp, C. 2000. *The Makuleke Land Claim: Power Relations and CBNRM.* International Institute for Environment and Development (IIED), Evaluating Eden Series. London.

Steenkamp, C. 2001. *The Makuleke Land Claim: an Environmental Conflict.* PhD Thesis, University of Witwatersrand. Johannesburg, Republic of South Africa.

Steenkamp, E. and Schönfeldt, H.C. 2005. Nutrient Content of Five Traditional Green Leafy Vegetables of South Africa. Poster presented at the *6th International Food Data Conference, Food Composition and the Nutrition Dilemma South Africa,* Pretoria, Republic of South Africa.

Stevens, M., Blaauw, D. and Mapolisa, S. 2004. Comparisons over Time: Managing HIV/AIDS in the Workplace. In *HIV/AIDS in the Workplace: Symposium Proceedings,* 296–304. University of the Witwatersrand. Johannesburg, Republic of South Africa.

Stobart, J. and Ball, R. 1998. Tourism and Local Economic Development: Beyond the Conventional View. *Local Economy* 13(3): 228–238.

Stoddart, H. 2008. Route Tourism and Local Economic Development in South Africa: The Magalies Meander and the Crocodile Ramble, Gauteng and North-West Provinces, South Africa. Unpublished MA Dissertation, University of the Witwatersrand. Johannesburg, Republic of South Africa.

Stoddart, H. and Rogerson, C.M. 2009. Tourism Routes, Local Economic Promotion and Pro-poor Development: the Crocodile Ramble in South Africa. *Africa Insight* 38(4): 10–26.

Strauss, A. and Corbin, J. 1990. *Basics of Qualitative Research.* First Edition. Sage. Thousand Oaks, California.

Strauss, A. and Corbin, J. 1998. *Basics of Qualitative Research.* Second Edition. Sage. Thousand Oaks, California.

Stronza, A. 2007. The Economic Promise of Ecotourism for Conservation. *Journal of Ecotourism* 6(3): 210–230.

Strydom, H. 2005a. Information Collection: Participant Observation. In De Vos, A.S., Strydom, H., Fouché, C.B. and Delport, C.S.L. (eds), *Research at Grass Roots,* 274–285. Van Schaik. Pretoria, Republic of South Africa.

Strydom, H. 2005b. Participatory Action Research. In De Vos, A.S., Strydom, H., Fouché, C.B. and Delport, C.S.L. (eds), *Research at Grass Roots,* 408–423. Van Schaik. Pretoria, Republic of South Africa.

Sutinen, E. 2003. Challenges of Cultural Adaptation in Computer Science. In Kähkönen, E. and Sutinen, E. (eds), *Proceedings of the First International Conference on Educational Technology in Cultural Context,* 19–23. University of Joensuu Press. Joensuu, Finland.

Swarbrooke, J. 1995. *The Development and Management of Visitor Attractions.* Butterworth and Heinemann. Oxford, UK.

Swarbrooke, J. 1999. *Sustainable Tourism Management.* CAB International. Wallingford, UK.

Swarbrooke, J. 2000. Tourism, Economic Development and Urban Regeneration: a Critical Evaluation. In Robinson, M., Sharpley, R., Evans, N., Long, P. and Swarbrooke, J. (eds), *Developments in Urban and Rural Tourism,* 269–285. Centre for Travel and Tourism, Sheffield Hallam University. Sheffield, UK.

Swaziland National Trust Commission. 2007. Ministers Launch New Lubombo Tourism Route at Indaba 2006 (http://www.sntc.org.sz/tourism/lubomboroute, accessed 20 July 2008).

Symonds, A. 2008. Personal communication with Annie Symonds, freelance consultant in Community-Based Craft Centres, Windhoek, Namibia, 27 July.

Tao, C.-H., Eagles, P.F.J. and Smith, S.L.J. 2004. Implications of Alternative Definitions of Ecotourists. *Tourism Analysis* 9(1): 1–13.

Tapscott, C. 2001. Class Formation and Civil Society in Namibia. In Diener, I. and Graefe, O. (eds), *Contemporary Namibia – The First Landmarks of a Post-Apartheid Society,* 307–325. Gamsberg Macmillan. Windhoek, Namibia.

Telfer, D.J. 2001a. Strategic Alliances Along the Niagara Wine Route. *Tourism Management* 22(1): 21–30.

Telfer, D.J. 2001b. From a Wine Tourism Village to a Regional Wine Route: an Investigation of the Competitive Advantages of Embedded Clusters in Niagara, Canada. *Tourism Recreation Research* 26(2): 23–33.

Telfer, D.J. 2002. Tourism and Regional Development Issues. In Sharpley, R. and Telfer, D.J. (eds), *Tourism and Development: Concepts and Issues,* 112–148. Channel View. Toronto, Canada.

Telfer, D.J. and Hashimoto, A. 2003. Food Tourism in the Niagara Region: the Development of Nouvelle Cuisine. In Hall, C.M., Sharples, L., Mitchell, R., Macionis, N. and Camborne, B. (eds), *Food Tourism Around the World: Development, Management, and Markets,* 158–177. Butterworth-Heinemann. London.

Telfer, D. and Sharpley, R. 2008. *Tourism and Development in the Developing World.* Routledge. London.

Teo, P. 2002. Striking a Balance for Sustainable Tourism: Implications of the Discourse on Globalisation. *Journal of Sustainable Tourism* 10(6): 459–474.

Terborgh, J. 1999. *Requiem for Nature.* Island/Shearwater. Washington, DC.

Thakadu, O.T. 2005. Success Factors in Community-Based Natural Resource Management Projects' Mobilisation in Northern Botswana: Lessons from Practice. *Natural Resource Forum* 29(3): 199–212.

THETA 2003a. National Study on HIV in the Hospitality Sector 2002/3. Tourism, Hospitality and Sport Education and Training Authority (THETA). Rivonia (http://www.theta.org.za/downloads/HIV_National_Study2002_3.ppt, accessed 13 July 2008).

THETA 2003b. HIV/AIDS Handbook for South African Tourism and Hospitality Companies. Tourism, Hospitality and Sport Education and Training Authority (THETA). Rivonia (http://www.theta.org.za/downloads/HIV_AIDS_HANDBOOK.pdf, accessed 13 July 2008).

Thomas, R. and Thomas, H. 2006. Micro Politics and Micro Firms: a Case Study of Tourism Policy Formation and Change. *Journal of Small Business and Enterprise Development* 13(1): 100–114.

Thornton, M. 2006. Taking Charge. *Africa Geographic* (February): 61–69.

Timothy, D. 2002. Tourism and Community Development Issues. In Sharpley, R. and Tefler, D. (eds), *Tourism and Development. Concepts and Issues,* 149–164. Channel View. Clevedon, UK.

Tomaselli, K.G. 1999. Encounters in the Kalahari: Some Points of Departure. *Visual Anthropology* 12(2–3): 131–136.

Tomaselli, K.G. 2005. *Where Global Contradictions are Sharpest: Research Stories from the Kalahari.* Rozenberg, Vrije Universiteit. Amsterdam.

Tomaselli, K.G. 2007. *'Op die Grond'*: Writing in the San/d, Surviving Crime. In Tomaselli, K.G. (ed.), *Writing in the Sand: Autoethnography among Indigenous Southern Africans,* 117–130. Altamira. Walnut Creek, Republic of South Africa.

Tomaselli, K.G. and Dunn, H. 2001. *Media, Democracy and Renewal in Southern Africa: Critical Studies on African Media and Culture.* International Academic Publishers. Colorado Springs, Colorado.

Tomaselli, K.G. and Shepperson, A. 2005. Negotiating Research with First Peoples. In Tomaselli, K.G. (ed.), *Where Global Contradictions are Sharpest: Research Stories from the Kalahari,* 9–20. Rozenberg, Vrije Universiteit. Amsterdam.

Tomaselli, K.G., McLennan-Dodd, V. and Shepperson, A. 2005. Research to Do, Results to Sell: Enabling Subjects and Researchers. *Society in Transition* 36(1): 24–37.

Tomaselli, K.G., Dyll, L. and Francis, M. 2008. 'Self' and 'Other': Auto-Reflexive and Indigenous Ethnography. In Denzin, N., Lincoln, Y. and Tuhiwai Smith, L. (eds), *Handbook of Critical and Indigenous Methodologies,* 347–372. Sage. London.

Tosun, C. 2000. Limits to Community Participation in the Tourism Development Process in Developing Countries. *Tourism Management* 21(6): 613–633.

Tosun, C. 2005. Expected Nature of Community Participation in Tourism Development. *Tourism Management* 27(3): 493–504.

Tosun, C. and Timothy, D. 2003. Arguments for Community Participation in the Tourism Development Process. *Journal of Tourism Studies* 14(2): 2–15.

Transparency International 2008. Corruption Perceptions Index (http://www.transparency.org/news_room/in_focus/2008/cpi2008/cpi_2008_table, accessed 16 December 2008).

Tremblay, P. 1998. The Economic Organization of Tourism. *Annals of Tourism Research* 25(4): 837–859.

Trollip, A.M. 1991. Die betekenis van geakkultureerde kledingpraktyke vir geselekteerde Ndzundza-Ndebele-vroue. PhD Thesis, University of Pretoria. Pretoria, Republic of South Africa.

Truman, H.S. 1949. Inaugural speech, Truman Library (http://wwwtrumanlibrary.org, accessed 3 March 2008).

Tsing, A.L., Brosius, J.P. and Zerner, C. 1999. Assessing Community-Based Natural Resource Management. *Ambio* 28(2): 197–198.

Tuomi, I. 2002. *Networks of Innovation. Change and Meaning in the Age of the Internet.* Oxford University Press. New York.

Turok, I. 2005. Promoting Economic Development through Policy Decentralisation in Japan. *Town and Country Planning* 74(12): 348–350.

Twyman, C. 2000. Participatory Conservation? Community-Based Natural Resource Management in Botswana. *The Geographical Journal* 166(4): 323–335.

UNAIDS 2000. *A Human Rights Approach to AIDS Prevention at Work. The Southern African Development Community's Code on HIV/AIDS and Employment.* The United Nations Joint Programme on HIV/AIDS (UNAIDS). Geneva.

UNAIDS 2006. Epidemiological Fact Sheets on HIV/AIDS and Sexually Transmitted Infections: Namibia. United Nations Joint Programme on HIV/AIDS (UNAIDS). Geneva.

UNAIDS 2008. 2007 AIDS Epidemic Update. Sub-Saharan Africa. United Nations Joint Programme on HIV/AIDS (UNAIDS). Geneva.

UNEP 2008. United Nations List of Protected Areas. United Nations Environment Programme (UNEP) (http://www.unep-wcmc.org/protected_areas/UN_list/index.htm, accessed 28 November 2008).

van Audenhove, L., Burgelman, J.C., Nulens, G. and Cammaerts, B. 2001. Telecommunication and Information Society Policy in Africa. The Dominant Scenario Reassessed. In Nulens, G., Hafkin, N., van Audenhove, L. and Cammaerts, B. (eds), *The Digital Divide in Developing Countries: Towards an Information Society in Africa*, 17–53. Brussels University Press. Brussels.

van Eeden, J. 2006. Land Rover and Colonial-Style Adventure. *International Feminist Journal of Politics* 8(3): 343–369.

van Schalkwyk, J.A. 1995. Ideologie en die konstruksie van 'n landelike samelewing: 'n antropologiese studie van die Hananwa van Blouberg. PhD Thesis, University of South Africa. Pretoria, Republic of South Africa.

van Schalkwyk, J.A. and Moifatswane, S.M. 1991. The Siege of Leboho: South African Republic Fortifications in the Blouberg, Northern Transvaal. *Krygshistoriese Tydskrif* 8(5): 175–183.

van Wyk, B.-E. and Gericke, N. 2000. *People's Plants: a Guide to Useful Plants of Southern Africa.* BRIZA. Pretoria, Republic of South Africa.

van Wyk, E.B. 1966. *Die Bantoetale.* Van Schaik. Pretoria, Republic of South Africa.

van Wyk, S. and Kruiper, V. 2001. Interview, Northern Cape, Republic of South Africa, 20 July.

Viherä, M.-L. 2000. Citizen's Communication Capabilities in Civil Society. *Foresight* 2(2): 189–197.

Viljoen, A.T., Botha, P. and Boonzaaier, C.C. 2005. Factors Contributing to Changes in Food Practices of a Black South African Community. *Journal of Family Ecology and Consumer Sciences* 33(1): 46–62.

Viljoen, F. 2007. Sustainability Indicators for Monitoring Tourism Route Development in Africa. Unpublished MA Thesis, University of Stellenbosch. Stellenbosch, Republic of South Africa.

Visit Scotland 2003. *Marketing Boost for Wildlife Tourism* (http://www.TravelMole.com), Responsible Tourism News homepage, accessed 1 August 2007.

Visser, G. 2004a. Reflections on Student Research into the South African Tourism System. In Rogerson, M. and Visser, G. (eds), *Tourism and Development Issues in Contemporary South* Africa, 26–77. Africa Institute of South Africa. Pretoria, Republic of South Africa.

Visser, G. 2004b. The World Wide Web and Tourism in South Africa: the Case of Open Africa. In Rogerson, C.M. and Visser, G. (eds), *Tourism and Development Issues in Contemporary South Africa*, 335–354. Africa Institute of South Africa. Pretoria, Republic of South Africa.

Visser, G. and Rogerson, C. 2004. Researching the South African Tourism and Development Nexus. *GeoJournal* 60(4): 201–215.

Vorflauer, K. 2007. Kommunale Conservancies in Namibia: Ansätze der Biodiversitätssicherung und Armutsbekämpfung? *Erdkunde* 61(1): 26–53.

Wade, R.H. 2002. Bridging the Digital Divide: New Route to Development or New Form of Dependence? *Global Governance* 8(4): 443–466.

Waitt, G. 1999. Naturalising the 'Primitive': a Critique of Marketing Australia's Indigenous Peoples as 'Hunter-Gatherers'. *Tourism Geographies* 1(2): 142–163.

Walpole, M.J. and Goodwin, H. 2000. Local Economic Impacts of Dragon Tourism in Indonesia. *Annals of Tourism Research* 27(3): 559–576.

Wandschneider, T. 2004. *Small Rural Towns and Local Economic Development: Evidence from Two Poor States in India.* Natural Resources Institute (NRI). Chatham, UK.

Wang, N. 1999. Rethinking Authenticity in Tourism Experience. *Annals of Tourism Research* 26(2): 349–370.

Wargenau, A. and Che, D. 2006. Wine Tourism Development and Marketing Strategies in Southwest Michigan. *International Journal of Wine Marketing* 18(1): 45–60.

Warmelo, N.J. 1951. *Notes on the Kaokoveld (South West Africa) and Its People.* Ethnological Publications 26, Department of Bantu Administration. Pretoria, Republic of South Africa.

Wassermann, I. and Kriel, J.D. 1997. *Facts and Fallacies: Perspectives on Development.* The Authors. Pretoria, Republic of South Africa.

Wearing, S. and McDonald, M. 2002. The Development of Community-Based Tourism: Re-thinking the Relationship between Tour Operators and Development Agents as Intermediaries in Rural and Isolated Area Communities. *Journal of Sustainable Tourism* 10(3): 191–206.

Weaver, D. and Elliott, K. 1996. Spatial Patterns and Problems in Contemporary Namibian Tourism. *The Geographical Journal* 162(2): 205–217.

Weaver, J. and Jameson, K. 1978. *Economic Development: Competing Paradigms – Competing Parables.* Development Studies Program, Agency for International Development (AID). Washington, DC.

Webb, D. and Simon, D. 1995. Migrants, Money and the Military: the Social Epidemiology of HIV/AIDS in Owambo, Northern Namibia. Namibian Economic Policy Research Unit (NEPRU) Occasional Paper No. 4. Windhoek, Namibia.

Weibing, Z. and Xingqun, L. 2006. Globalization of Tourism and Third World Tourism Development: a Political Economy Perspective. *Chinese Geographical Science* 16(3): 203–210.

Weiler, B. and Ham, S.H. 2002. Tour Guide Training: a Model for Sustainable Capacity-Building in Developing Countries. *Journal of Sustainable Tourism* 10(1): 52–69.

Wels, H. 2004. About Romance and Reality: Popular European Imagery in Postcolonial Tourism in Southern Africa. In Hall, C.M. and Tucker, H. (eds), *Tourism and Postcolonialism: Contested Discourses, Identities and Representation*, 76–94. Routledge. London.

Werner, W. 2002. Promoting Development among Farm Workers: Some Options for Namibia. Namibian Economic Policy Research Unit (NEPRU) Research Report No. 24. Windhoek, Namibia.

White, H. 1995. *In the Tradition of the Forefathers: Bushmen Traditionality at Kagga Kamma.* University of Cape Town Press. Cape Town, Republic of South Africa.

Wilbanks, T.J. 2004. Geography and Technology. In Brunn, S.D., Cutter, S.L. and Harrington, J.W. Jr (eds), *Geography and Technology*, 3–16. Kluwer. Boston, Massachusetts.

Williams, B., Grouws, E., Lurie, M. and Crush, J. 2002. *Spaces of Vulnerability: Migration and HIV/AIDS in South Africa.* Southern African Migration Project, Migration Policy Series No. 24. Cape Town, Republic of South Africa.

Wilshusen, P.R., Brechin, S.R. and West, P.C. 2002. Reinventing a Square Wheel: Critique of a Resurgent 'Protection Paradigm' in International Biodiversity Conservation. *Society and Natural Resources* 15(1): 17–40.

Witbooi, B. 2007. Interview, Witdraai, Northern Cape, Republic of South Africa, 11 July.

Wolmer, W. 2003. Transboundary Conservation: the Politics of Ecological Integrity in the Great Limpopo Transfrontier Park. *Journal of Southern African Studies* 29(1): 261–278.

WTO 2003. *Tourism Market Trends – Africa.* World Tourism Organization (WTO). Madrid.

WTO 2006. *Africa: Tourism Market Trends.* World Tourism Organization (WTO). Madrid.

WTTC 2006. *Namibia. The Impact of Travel and Tourism on Jobs and the Economy.* World Travel and Tourism Council (WTTC). London.

WTTC 2007. *Botswana: the Impact of Travel and Tourism on Jobs and the Economy.* World Travel and Tourism Council (WTTC). London.

WWF 2008a. *African Elephants* (http://www.panda.org/about_wwf/what_we_do/species/about_species/species_factsheets/elephants/african_elephants, World Wildlife Fund (WWF), accessed 8 November 2008).

WWF 2008b. *Common Ground: Solutions for Reducing the Human, Economic and Conservation Costs of Human Wildlife Conflict.* World Wildlife Fund (WWF). Gland, Switzerland.

!Xaus Lodge 2008. Transfrontier Trails Kgalagadi – a Sharing Community Spirit (http://www.xauslodge.co.za/, accessed 8 November 2008).

Xuza, P. 2007. Ten Years and Ten Trends of Local Economic Development Practice in South Africa. *Urban Forum* 18(2): 117–123.

Yanow, D. 2000. *Conducting Interpretive Policy Analysis.* Qualitative Research Methods Series 47, Sage. Thousand Oaks, California.

Yanow, D. 2003. Accessing Local Knowledge. In Hajer, M. and Wagenaar, H. (eds), *Deliberative Policy Analysis. Understanding Governance in the Network Society*, 228–246. Cambridge University Press. Cambridge, UK.

Yanow, D. 2006. Thinking Interpretively: Philosophical Presuppositions and the Human Sciences. In Yanow, D. and Schwartz-Shea, P. (eds), *Interpretation and Method. Empirical Research Methods and the Interpretive Turn*, 5–26. M.E. Sharpe. Armonk, New York.

Zondi, S. 2003. Land Reform in Namibia in the Context of the Zimbabwean Crisis: a Regional Perspective. In Lee, M. and Colvard, K. (eds), *Unfinished Business: the Land Crisis in Southern Africa*, 317–349. Africa Institute of South Africa. Pretoria, Republic of South Africa.

Zorfass, J., Morocco, C. and Lory, N. 1991. *A School-based Approach to Technology Integration: ASCD Curriculum Handbook.* Association for Supervision and Curriculum Development (ASCD). Alexandria, Virginia.

Index